*Emerging
Issues in
Demographic
Research*

Emerging Issues in Demographic Research

Edited by

Cornelius A. HAZEU
Netherlands Organization for
Scientific Research (NWO)
The Hague, The Netherlands

Gerard A.B. FRINKING
Faculty of Social Sciences
Catholic University of Brabant
Tilburg, The Netherlands

ELSEVIER
Amsterdam • Oxford • New York • Tokyo

ELSEVIER SCIENCE PUBLISHERS B.V.
Sara Burgerhartstraat 25
P.O. Box 211, 1000 AE Amsterdam, The Netherlands

Distributiors for the United States and Canada:

ELSEVIER SCIENCE PUBLISHING COMPANY INC.
655 Avenue of the Americas
New York, N.Y. 10010, U.S.A.

ISBN: 0 444 88763 6

Printed in The Netherlands

The publication of this book has been made possible by the financial support of the Netherlands Organization for Scientific Research (NWO), The Hague, the Netherlands. NWO is the national research council in the Netherlands.

CONTENTS

Emerging Issues in Demographic Research
C.A. Hazeu and G.A.B. Frinking (Editors)
© Elsevier Science Publishers B.V., 1990

Chapter 1

EMERGING ISSUES IN DEMOGRAPHIC RESEARCH; AN INTRODUCTION

Gerard A.B. Frinking and Cornelius A. Hazeu

1   Towards a programme for demographic research

Far-reaching changes are emerging in the industrialized world: changes which include an ageing population and a decrease in the number of young people and changes in the composition of households. Such changes are expected to have a major impact on various sections of society. Our understanding of the background and social consequences of these changes in both size and composition of the population demands interdisciplinary population studies. The Netherlands Organization for Scientific Research (NWO) will therefore launch an extensive research programme on population studies in 1990. Preparatory to this research programme NWO organised an international workshop in September 1989 to which demographic researchers from various disciplines were invited to put forward their views on the most significant topics in demographic research for the next ten years. The papers presented at this workshop were commented upon by referees. This book presents the reader with both the papers and the referees' comments. Together they provide a broad overview of the most topical issues which are emerging in demographic research.

2   Population in transition

The present size, composition and growth of the population reflects the course of demographic processes in the past. We can expect that future population developments are already embedded in the present population structure. The course of demographic changes is generally referred to as 'demographic transition', implying a transition from a situation characterized by a high birth rate and high mortality rate to one in which both figures become less. In Europe this transition took place during the nineteenth and twentieth century, obviously with some regional and temporal variations.

Demographic transition was influenced by social changes such as industrialisation, urbanisation and secularisation and proceeded parallel to the process of modernization. The situation in the thirties caused the demographic transition to come to a temporary standstill but the decline in the birth rate set in again after World War II. By the mid-sixties the birth rate in most of the industrialized countries was below the mortality rate and consequently we saw a thinning out of the population. Changes in value and norm patterns especially seem to play a major role in this second demographic transition; the emphasis being on individualization, self-improvement and emancipation.

The transitions outlined above have resulted in the present demographic situation in industrialized countries being characterized by a progressively lower population growth with a perspective of negative growth and a decreasing population. As well as a rather drastic change in the age structure of the population (an ageing population and a decrease in the number of births) and equally radical changes in the composition of households, plus a growing diversity in life styles, are characteristic of the present situation in the more industrialized countries. Before going into further details of the coherence of processes of demographic and social change, let us first take a brief look at the framework within which research is carried out into population studies.

3   The framework of research into population studies

Within the demographic framework the national population can be regarded as a system of interrelated population groups such as regional populations (provincial, urban populations) and categorical populations (households, working population, school-going children, ethnic groups, etc.). In these population groups, which all have a common demographic characteristic, a role is also set aside for processes other than the demographic processes of change (birth rate, household composition, migration and mortality rate) such as entering the labour force, reaching school age, etc. In order to study the changes that occur in a population (or a section of the population), and especially when analysing the backgrounds leading up to developments within a population, it is essential that in addition to demographic assessments, one also has access to the knowledge and experience available in other branches of science. This is the reason why population studies are to a great extent characterized by their high level of interdisciplinarity and also explains why research into population studies is of importance to a wide range of disciplines.

The analysis of the backgrounds, dynamics and consequences of population processes forms the essence of research into population developments. Such analysis can be placed in the past (historic research), the present (present trends) and in the future (demographic forecasting), as well as in geographical settings (e.g. non-Western societies). The themes dealt with in this book relate for the greater part to those population processes observed in industrialized societies and special attention has been devoted to long-term demographic processes.

4   Demographic trends in a social perspective

From the above it is apparent that demographic trends are closely related to demographic processes of change: there is continuous interaction between the two. On the one hand this interaction is to be seen in the influence of social developments on demographic behaviour and on the other hand in the social consequences of demographic trends. The main point in analysing the interaction between social and demographic developments lies in studying how social and demographic changes (which influence – and maybe even strengthen – each other) relate to the way in which both present and future society is organised. In those cases where demographic developments indicate a greater freedom of choice for the individual and a stronger emphasis on emancipation the result is a higher level of social heterogeneity. This development can be regarded as a challenge to society. To what extent can individual decisions have undesirable effects from a societal point of view? How does the diversity of the population relate to the origin or to the continuation of (new) forms of inequality, for instance between the young and the elderly, men and women, family units and other lifestyles, inequality between different regions, etc? What are the consequences of a higher level of heterogeneity in society for social solidarity? What social limitations face the individual choice of freedom? Especially within the context of the Western welfare state, where the government is assigned with the important task of guaranteeing a certain level of well-being to all the members of its society, implicating that attention will also be given to the government's role in relevant social welfare and problems concerned with the distribution of income.

In summary: from a demographic point of view the main theme of a research programme is the study of the relationship between the individual and the collective, or in other words between developments at micro- and macro-level: between individual development and social solidarity.

In the following these general points of view will be translated into areas of priority and subjects of research.

5   Research priorities

As mentioned in the first section a number of experts in the field of population studies were invited to present their views. The central theme of the workshop was formulated as follows:

"The study of the growing tension between the individual and the collectivity from a demographic point of view, i.e. the developments at micro- and macro-level, between individual growth and social solidarity".

The topics selected were:

– decision-making processes of demographic behaviour at micro-level;
– development of (forecasting) models for primary relationships and household formation;
– the social impact of demographic trends in a number of important areas.

In treating the first topic particular attention was devoted to the economic determinants of household formation. In this case the choice is based on maximizing the utility

defined by economic factors. Given that up to now empirical research into the influence of socio-economic factors on household formation (birth rate, divorce, relationships) has been somewhat limited and the approach chosen corresponded perfectly with the main topic of the programme, the choice of this subject was obvious. The fact that the author available for this topic, the economist Nelissen (Chapter 7), also had experience in micro-simulation was an additional advantage. Micro-simulation is a method that offers the interesting possibility of researching, in terms of demography, the chosen behaviour of individual: vis-à-vis alternative forms of behaviour.

Even as early as the fifties had Vance (1952) reproached demographers for their weakness in producing theories. Taking into consideration the interdisciplinary character of demography it is essential that the formulation of theories on demographic phenomena be placed on the research agenda. Siegers, the author of Chapter 10, would be the last person to deny his economic background but he has also shown himself to be a researcher with an open mind for other disciplinary approaches. Siegers is a man who can be said to advocate interdisciplinarity.

The subject of demographic forecasting is virtually intrinsic to a demographic workshop. The social significance of demographic research is perhaps all too often, and sometimes without justification, mainly attributed to the results of demographic forecasts. We have progressed a great deal since the time when these prognoses were made by means of a simple components-model. The need for more detailed information about the demographic future went hand in hand with the increasing multiformity of demographic behaviour and has furthered the development of more refined forecasting and analyzing techniques. The origin of multidimensional population analysis has been of particular importance in the forecasting of categorical populations. Another important aspect is the construction of scenarios. The main advantage of scenarios is that potential demographic implications of policy plans can be recalculated and thus made more understandable. Willekens, the author of Chapter 2, is known as an international expert in this field.

The fourth topic that was placed on the agenda is a more general one:

"To what extent will demographic change influence the content and impact of those social 'contracts' that shape, both explicitly and implicitly, processes of (re)distribution in society and could lead to the emergence or continuation of (new types of) social inequality?"

This question needs to be explained. Demographic change in the decades to come will bring about considerable changes in the numerical relationships between the different generations and age groups concerned, between the employed and the unemployed, between those living alone and those living with a partner - either married or not, and between adults with and without children, etc. Individuals, who at the same time often form a part of these categories, are able to derive certain rights to benefits, grants, services, etc., from this fact. Should the numerical relationships between the various groups change then as a rule the existing contracts will also have to be adjusted. Given that the government is often a significant contract partner, in many cases political decision-making will also have to be incorporated in the analysis.

Dealing with such problems is a demanding task. Additionally, the problems can be approached from different angles: a disciplinary approach, which is characterized by the way in which the contents of contracts are looked at, and a sectoral approach, in which the nature of goods and services established by contract are focused upon. Both approaches were taken during the workshop.

Changes in demographic behaviour will gain in significance during the lifespan of individuals in successive generations. Belonging to a particular generation can be a decisive factor as to whether or not one is able to demand the provision of certain goods and services. The ways societal contracts function can therefore be explained for a greater part by the succession of generations. The sociologist Becker (Chapter 5) has further elaborated on Mannheim's (1928) ideas on generations. In this context, the consequences of both present and anticipated demographic trends have been explored in a number of fields.

Van Imhoff devoted particular attention in his paper (Chapter 13) to the effects on the distribution of economic resources and welfare across economic agents. The field is far too extensive to be dealt with in one paper and has therefore been limited to several aspects only.

Finally, the consequences of changes in the pattern of mortality have also been investigated. The reduction in the mortality rate, notably at higher ages, has far-reaching consequences , particularly in the public health service. It goes without saying that while life expectancy has been increased other problems have arisen. Contradictory to the efforts to increase life expectancy, we are still faced with the fact that these efforts have done little to diminish inequality in the face of death. The extent to which this applies in the Netherlands is, as yet, unknown.

Both sides of this problem are dealt with by Van Poppel in Chapter 15. During a period in which the financing of the health service has become more problematic, demographic research can help to find additional arguments for an efficient allocation of financial resources to the various sectors of the health service. Again, the main point of the programme is evident on this subject.

In another paper (Chapter 17), Hooimeijer scrutinized the consequences of demographic trends in housing. In this case he devoted attention to residential mobility, household relocation and spatial redistribution. In addition to a profound treatment of these topics, the relevant methodological innovation in these sectors has also been taken into account.

The paper of the historian Engelen (Chapter 19), the final contribution to the workshop, makes very clear that demographers often underestimate the historical dimension of this object of study. A recent and well chosen example of this view is the debate about the so-called 'secondary demographic transition'. His plea has led ultimately to the inclusion of historical demographic research in the adapted version of the research programme.

The various contributions of the Dutch authors have been commented on by an international team of referees. Their comments on the proposed research priorities had a major impact on the formulation of the emerging issues of population research as adopted in the definitive version of the research programme.

References

Mannheim, K. (1928), Das Problem der Generationen, *Kölner Vierteljahres hefte für Soziologie*, Vol. 7.

Vance, R.B. (1952), Is theory for demographers?, *Social Forces*, Vol. XXXI.

Emerging Issues in Demographic Research
C.A. Hazeu and G.A.B. Frinking (Editors)
© Elsevier Science Publishers B.V. , 1990

Chapter 2

DEMOGRAPHIC FORECASTING; STATE-OF-THE-ART AND RESEARCH
NEEDS

Frans J. Willekens[*]

1 Introduction

"Forecasting the future has long been a challenge for mankind. Fortune tellers, astrolo-
gers and prophets have sought to fulfill man's need to predict the future and reduce its
uncertainties." This statement by Makridakis and Wheelwright (1979, p. 1), two of the
most vocal advocates of a forecasting profession and a forecasting industry, illustrates
both the prospects of an ability to forecast and the impossibility of perfection. In today's
society, the fortune teller has been replaced by the scenario-writer and instead of looking
at the stars to decipher the processes that may result in future events, we look at output
of sophisticated computer models. The quest for knowledge of the future has moved from
the supernatural towards the scientific. But the frustration generally remains. As is
demonstrated every day by the weather forecasts, the reliability of weather predictions
is dependent on the understanding of the causal processes that produce the actual weather
and the ability to foresee the directions in which these processes move. Today, no weather
forecaster would keep his job for long if his forecast would be "The weather has been
nice for ten days, hence it is very likely that it will be nice again tomorrow." In other
words, prediction on the basis of past overt behaviour is bad practice in weather
forecasting, although the extrapolation of observed regularities produce accurate forecasts as long as they continue to hold.

In 1984, the Social Science Research Council sponsored a conference on Forecasting
in the Social and Natural Sciences, held at the National Center for Atmospheric Research
in Boulder, Colorado. At that meeting, Somerville illustrated that weather forecasting
has come a long way:

"The last thirty years have seen the development of comprehensive numerical models
of the large-scale circulation of the atmosphere. These models are computer programs,
based on physical principles which govern changes of wind, pressure, temperature,

[*] I like to thank Nathan Keyfitz and Nico Keilman for comments on an earlier draft.

and humidity. In the computer, the entire global atmosphere is represented by a threedimensional array of tens of thousands of points. At each point, the model continually predicts the weather, starting from observations of present weather conditions.
We know that present-day forecasts are quite skillful at describing the weather up to a few days ahead, despite the dual handicaps of both imperfect models and inadequate observational data. Yet even a perfect model, which exactly represented the dynamics of the real atmosphere, and which used data from the best conceivable observing system, could not produce an accurate forecast of indefinitely long range. Any forecast must eventually go bad because of the intrinsic instability of the atmosphere itself. Small errors in the initial conditions will inevitably amplify as the forecast evolves" (1984, p. 1).

What applies to weather forecasting increasingly applies to economic forecasting. In 1984, Harvard Business Review evaluated the forecasting performance of leading economists and forecasting organizations and published the results under the title "Are economic forecasters worth listening to?" (Bernstein and Silbert, 1984). Although some economists argue that the best forecast may simply be that tomorrow will look like today or like today's trends extrapolated to tomorrow, their view meets a growing controversy unless they are forecasting the financial markets. "The swings in real GNP, inflation, unemployment, industrial production, and earnings are part of a process, a process in which one stage leads inexorably to the next and in which decisions once made are difficult to reverse. Only the timing of the process is hard to predict; its fundamental character is by no means obscure. Hence the expectation that tomorrow's figures will be the same as today's, or an extrapolation of today's trend, is certain to be wrong. In fact, it is likely to be more wrong than a careful prediction based on some *understanding* of the process that leads the business cycle to evolve from today to tomorrow" (Bernstein and Silbert, 1984, p. 33; emphasis added, FW).

The state-of-the-art of weather forecasting and the comments on economic forecasting may provide an indication of the direction in which demographic forecasting needs to develop in order to produce forecasts that are reliable at all times, even at times of major changes in the demographic parameters and structure. The direction is toward the understanding of the underlying biological and behavioural mechanisms operating rather than the improved extrapolation of trends. In fact, the art and science of forecasting exhibits a development path of its own. In the early stages, the focus is on the identification and extrapolation of stable (regular) patterns (inertia). As the art and science develop, the focus shifts to an understanding of the observed patterns in terms of the underlying causal mechanisms. In 1972, Keyfitz wrote: "Demographic forecasting is seen as the search for functions of population that are constant through time, or about which fluctuations are random and small" (Keyfitz, 1972, p. 347). The search for regularity is transitionary. Understanding is the precondition for effective forecasting. Keyfitz concludes the article by pointing out that "The weakness of population forecasts is due to our ignorance of the mechanisms by which populations grow and decline. We know much about birth rates and their differentials among statistically recognizable population subgroups, as well as about changes over time as shown in past records, but this great volume of statistical information has contributed disappointingly little to the discernment of the comprehensive causal system underlying the differentials and changes" (Keyfitz, 1972, p. 361). I firmly believe that a breakthrough in our ability to foresee the future can only be expected if we come to grasp with the causal factors *and processes* that determine the level, sequence and timing of demographic events as we observe them. It requires not only to *identify* the factors and processes as well as their interrelatedness, but also to *understand* the mechanisms by which they produce the picture of demographic change that we are able to witness.

The transition of forecasting from pattern-oriented to process-oriented will have important implications for research, since much of the current knowledge in the field of population is not directly usable in forecasting (Keyfitz, 1982a, p. 747). At the end of a lengthy search for demographic knowledge that can improve population forecasts, Keyfitz concludes that population research tends to center on inferring *conditional* causal relations (if .. then .., everything else remaining equal) that are useful for understanding the past and for impact assessment but are inadequate for forecasting. Conditional relations are associated with partial theories, i.e. theories that address only one relation in the complex system of relations that determine population change. Other theories, such as the theory of demographic transition, are too general to provide the specific knowledge that is needed in forecasting. Furthermore, most knowledge is cast in statics (cross-sectional studies) and comparative statics, instead of in dynamics. The transition will therefore not be an easy one. It requires a major shift in the design of population research. Along the way, some scholars will become discouraged and conclude that "... Theory-based models...will probably move asymptotically to a level of predictive performance not much better than can be achieved by theoryless black-box methods of today" (Openshaw, 1986, p. 145; quoted by Keilman and Keyfitz, 1988, p. 266). Others will probably point not to the complexity of the real world but to the simplicity and the inertia that characterize the mental frames with which we try to perceive and interpret the world around us. In an earlier paper, I expressed the opinion that "The difficulty which the social sciences encounter in trying to understand the true processes may in part be due to the fact that these processes change faster than our patterns of thinking. Established patterns of thinking act as a filter, causing selectivity in scientific interest and in the organization and use of information... In order to reveal the true processes at work, we may have to adapt our patterns of thinking" (Willekens, 1984c, p. 365). Instead of focusing on the quantitative relations between variables, we should focus on the underlying causal mechanisms that produce the relations between variables. "Without a knowledge of these mechanisms, we cannot predict how variables will co-vary when the structure of the system under study is altered, either experimentally or by changes in the world around us" (Simon, 1979, p. 79). *The ultimate goal of forecasting-oriented demographic research should be a demographic forecasting rooted in an understanding of the causal processes at work.* It is unlikely that the goal will be achieved in the near future. In the meantime, "pending the discovery of a truly behavioural way of estimating the future, we cannot afford to be ashamed of extrapolating the observed regularities of the past" (Keyfitz, 1982a, p. 747).

Forecasting-oriented population research should emphasize the dynamics of demographic phenomena and their interdependence with the changing social, economic and cultural contexts. A conceptual framework which encompasses this requirement and which may guide future research is suggested in section 2 of the paper. The framework is not a theory nor a methodology, but a way of thinking about complex structures that are changing over time. Section 3 reviews the steps involved in any population forecast. The steps that compose the projection process are well-documented in the Dutch literature by several authors. An important step in the projection process is the design or selection of the projection model. If population is to be forecasted, the cohort-component model is generally used. The diversity of models used is much greater in the forecasting of the components of population change. The components that are traditionally distinguished are fertility, mortality and migration. Other components are considered in functional or categorical population projections, such as labour force projections, educational projections, regional projections and household projections. Most models that are currently in use build on empirical regularities in composition and pattern of change. Sections 4 to 11 present several approaches to modeling the trajectories of demographic variables. Section 12 returns to an essential feature of the future; namely, the uncertainty. It reviews the causes of uncertainty, presents measures to quantify uncertainty and strategies to deal with uncertainty. Two strategies are treated in detail: monitoring and scenario analysis. Monitoring is the periodic updating of forecasts to account for unforeseen changes in demographic behaviour of the population and in the context in which demographic behaviour takes place. The scenario approach is a method for dealing with uncertainty. Its goal is not to predict the future, but to provide the user with alternative, internally consistent futures against which decisions can be tested and actions planned. Both scenarios and forecasts may include judgmental factors. Expert opinions and the individual's expectations may be considered in the exploration or prediction of the future. Section 13 concludes the paper.

2 Conceptual framework

The state of the world at a given point in time is the consequence of events that have occurred in the past. For instance, the age structure of a population is a result of past regimes of fertility, mortality and migration. Similarly, the number of married people is a result of marriages, divorces and deaths during the past several years. When an initial population and the numbers and types of vital events during a period are known, then the size and composition of the population at the end of the period is known with certainty.

Events are themselves outcomes of ongoing processes, most of which remain latent until their existence is discovered in a diagnosis or manifested in the event occurring. Having identified the existence of a process does not mean that it is understood. The understanding implies knowledge of (i) the factors that determine the onset of the process and (ii) the factors determining its dynamics, i.e. the rate at which it generates events. One process, which is relatively well understood is the development of the foetus during pregnancy. Once the existence of the process is diagnosed and its characteristics established, a prediction of its outcome (birth; foetal loss) and the timing of the birth can be made quite accurately. A survey of pregnant women is therefore the best method for short-term forecasting of births. The factors that determine the onset of the process (conception) are very different from those affecting the advancement and hence the occurrence of the event. The substantive factors are biological and behavioural in nature. In addition, there are random factors that affect the process. Important behavioural factors relate to the decision to stimulate, inhibit or prevent the onset of the process or to interrupt the process (induced abortion). When the decision processes and the factors affecting the decision are not well understood, they are approximated by attributes of persons who experienced given outcomes of the process. For instance, we do not fully know the decision process that a women experiences who is confronted with an unwanted pregnancy and hence the decision whether of not to interrupt the pregnancy. But we know that women with some attributes are more likely to abort than women with other attributes, although we may not fully know the causal (behavioural) mechanisms that produce the differentials. The attributes, which are used to approximate the knowledge we have about the causal process, are referred to as risk factors or covariates. A risk factor or covariate is an attribute of an individual that affects the onset and/or the advancement of a process. The term 'risk factor' originated in the epidemiological literature and is generally also used in the insurance literature. The term 'covariate' is common in event history analysis. The rates at which the process starts and events occur in a population depend on the distribution of the risk factors.

The likelihood that a process generates an event during a given period is determined by the length of time the process is active and the rate at which the event occurs provided the process is active. Formulated alternatively, the likelihood that an individual experiences an event during a given period depends on the duration of exposure to the risk of experiencing the event and the rate at which the event occurs provided the individual is exposed. An individual is at risk during the period in which the process is active. In other words, the exposure starts at the onset of the process. Any model that tries to predict the occurrence of an event or, in case of a repeatable event, the number of occurrences should distinguish between rate of occurrence and duration of exposure. If the rate is given, the expected total number of times an event occurs in a population is determined by the total duration of exposure. The need to distinguish between the duration of exposure and the rate of occurrence has implications beyond the design of forecasting models. In many explanatory studies of demographic events, the propensity to experience an event (have a child, migrate, die from cancer) is calculated for the whole population or for a population that include people who are not at risk of experiencing the event. For instance, the number of events at a given duration are often reduced to (divided by) the population of the cohort having or having not experienced the event being studied ('reduced events'). Another example; the women who are using effective anticonceptives are generally not excluded from the calculation of the fertility rate. Consequently, the fertility rate confounds the effects of very different processes. To improve the ability to predict the occurrence of an event, more attention should be given to the factors that affect the onset of the process and hence the exposure. The rate at which an event occurs to a person at risk depends on several factors. Three types of factors are distinguished. The first set of factors consists of personal attributes (covariates, risk factors); they express the heterogeneity of the population at risk. For instance, married women are more likely to give birth than unmarried women. Most covariates change with age because they are related either to the processes of biological and psychological development or to norms influencing the scheduling of life events over the live-span. The second set of factors relate to the level of the risk factor. They are behavioural or biological in nature. For instance, the smoking behaviour (number of cigarettes per day) of a person who smokes affects the rate of dying from lung cancer. The third set of factors relate to the social, economic and cultural contexts in which demographic events occur to a person (in short, the historical context). A fourth factor which may affect the rate at which an event occurs is the duration of the process, i.e. the duration during which the person has been exposed. For a number of diseases (cancer, AIDS), the instantaneous rate of dying increases with the duration of the disease (infection). In case of unemployment, the probability of finding a job within a month decreases with the duration of unemployment. If the event under study can occur more than once during a person's lifetime (repeatable event), a fifth type of factor may be distinguished; namely, the number of times the event has already occurred. A process the rate of which depends on the number of occurrences is said to exhibit an occurrence dependence. This type of dependence is considered in fertility analysis, when the rate of fertility is dependent on parity. Duration dependence and occurrence dependence are difficult to measure. Duration dependence is partly a consequence of the unobserved heterogeneity of the population. Occurrence dependence is partly explained by withdrawal. For instance, the parity-specificity of women is more an indication that women with a desired number of children withdraw from the population at risk by using effective anticonceptives than that they are less fecund.

Sometimes an event needs at least two persons (processes) to occur. Marriage is an example. The event involves the *relationship* among people. The forecasting of such events raises additional problems; namely, the participants in the event must be present. These problems are referred to as problems of internal consistency. They are particularly relevant in the forecasting of families, households and social networks (e.g. kinships).

The dependence of the rates on several factors has its effect on the design of forecasting models. Population heterogeneity is a common design factor. The population is stratified on the basis of one or several personal attributes in addition to age. In nearly all applications, the attributes affecting the rate are discrete variables, consisting of a finite number of values (categories) and category-specific rates are distinguished. For instance, a separate rate may apply to each category of gender, age, parity, marital status, region of residence, etc. Most of these personal attributes change over the life-span. To be realistic, the forecasting model should allow for the passage from one value of a personal attribute to another value as life progresses and should adjust the rate upon each transfer. Most forecasting models today which consider category-specific rates do not relate the duration of exposure in each category to the time between passages but to some exogenously imposed distribution of the population among the categories. This class of models include models that allocate the members of a population to households on the basis of headship rates, to labour force categories on the basis of labour force participation rates and to other categories on the basis of a distribution function or a more advanced allocation procedure. Recently developed multistate models focus on the *transfers*.

Few forecasting models include risk levels explicitly. An exception is the OPCS model for the projection of mortality rates for the elderly (Alderson and Ashwood, 1985, p. 25) and Bongaarts'(1988) model for AIDS forecasting.

The effects of contextual variables are considered in two classes of models. The first class consists of explanatory models; the demographic rates during a given unit time interval are directly related to variables that describe the historical context during the period in which the rates are measured and/or during earlier periods. The historical context during periods prior to the period in which the rates are measured may have a significant explanatory power since a particular historical context (e.g. change in legislation, invention of new anticonceptive) may affect the demographic rates for years to come. A forecasting model, the parameters of which are related to contextual variables by an auxiliary model, is referred to as an open model, as opposed to a closed model (Vossen, 1988, p. 43). In the second class of models, the rates are indirectly related to contextual variables. Suppose the forecaster lacks information on the values of the explanatory variables, but has at his disposal a time series of demographic (age-specific) rates. The effects of (i) the historical context during the period of measurement and (ii) the historical context during earlier periods may be inferred from the time series. The analysis which decomposes the demographic rate, measured for a given age group during a given period, into an effect of age grouping (age effect), an effect of current context (period effect) and the lasting effect of previous contexts experienced by the group of people to which the rate applies (cohort effect) is known as age-period-cohort (APC) analysis. A (birth) cohort is generally defined as a group of people born during a given period; in APC analysis, it is interpreted as a group of people who lived through comparable historical contexts (e.g depression, war period, period of rapid technological change). Although the impact of past common experiences remaining at the time of observation is likely to differ for each member of the group, there is probably some effect that is still felt by all members of the group. That effect is the cohort effect. The APC model is not an explanatory model but a statistical accounting scheme. To interpret the period and cohort effects, one must look for attributes of the historical contexts that brought the effects about, analogous to the interpretation of age effects based on attributes of human development over the life-span. For a comprehensive treatment of APC analysis in demographic and social research, see Mason and Fienberg (1985).

The APC analysis combines the two viewpoints traditionally distinguished by a demographer when analyzing demographic data. One approach examines changes from year to year. Period analysis, as this approach is known, is particularly useful when rapid changes occur in the context, such as technological or legal changes that directly affect the controllability of demographic processes or a war resulting in transitory behavioural changes such as the postponement of births. The other approach, cohort analysis, is better suited for the study of fundamental changes in behaviour such as the decline in lifetime fertility and in the proportion married.

Duration dependence is included in only a few demographic forecasting models. Some models for forecasting fertility use duration-of-marriage specific fertility rates (e.g. the

CBS – Netherlands Central Bureau of Statistics – model used for the projections of 1970, 1972 and 1975).

Some forecasting models are built on the occurrence dependence. Since 1975, the Netherlands Central Bureau of Statistics uses parity-specific fertility rates to project the national population. Feeney's (1985) population projection model is in terms of parity progression.

The conceptual framework may be used to differentiate among forecasting methods. At the first level are the methods that predict the number of occurrences of an event from number of past occurrences, without recourse to the process generating the event. Trend extrapolations and stochastic time series methods (Box-Jenkins) belong to this class. At the second level are the methods that distinguish between exposure and rate of occurrence. Most demographic models belong to this class. At the third level are methods that relate exposure time to the onset of the process. Recently developed models for AIDS forecasting belong to this class. They differentiate between factors that affect the onset of the process (infection) and factors affecting the advancement (development of the disease and symptoms) (see e.g. Bongaarts, 1988). Models within each level may be age-specific and may provide for the effects of the historical contexts either directly or indirectly.

The conceptual framework and the distinction of levels of forecasting methods may be of relevance in evaluating the performance of different forecasting methods. Methods may perform differently depending on the forecasting horizon and the presence or absence of structural change in demographic processes and/or the historical context. If the population or the number of demographic events are forecasted for one or a few years ahead and no major structural changes occur, the extrapolation of past trends probably performs remarkably well. The reason is inertia. Demographic behaviour is closely linked to attitudes and values that most people do not change easily unless they are constrained by events or circumstances beyond their control or they are confronted with new opportunities that conflict with old values. As a consequence, most of the time, the parameters of the demographic processes (rates) do not change rapidly. The structure of the population (and the exposure) does not change much over a short period of time, since the structure is an outcome of demographic processes. To extrapolate the inertia, simple models are adequate and a linear extrapolation of the population and the number of events may outperform all other methods. Complex methods that categorize the population may perform worse than simple methods if different population categories are changing their demographic behaviour in opposite directions. For instance, if married women are reducing their fertility while the fertility of unmarried women is increasing and more women remain unmarried, a model with marital-status specific fertility is likely to perform worse in the short run than a simple births extrapolation method. The observed inertia may cover up important changes within different categories of the population, hence short term forecasts produced by simple methods should be approached with caution.

The forecasting performance of extrapolation methods and simple models is fully dependent on the prevailing inertia. In weather forecasting, extrapolation of the current weather may be successful if the weather is stable. But it is not considered a reliable and useful method by a professional forecaster since it cannot accurately forecast the weather when a forecast is most needed; namely, when a change in weather is on its way. Analogously, extrapolation methods may accurately forecast the population and numbers of demographic events in the short run. But they cannot produce accurate forecasts, when forecasts are needed most; namely, when trends and behavioural patterns are changing. These changes can only be predicted if the forecasting model encompasses the processes that produce the changes. Although the forecasting models that represent the best of our knowledge about the causal processes at work may perform worse than simple methods most of the time, they are the only models that perform at all when forecasts are needed most. Consequently, the issue of short-term versus long-term forecasting methods is a false issue in professional forecasting. The real issue is when we need professional forecasts to be accurate: when the population system is stable (most of the time) or when it is changing.

3   The forecasting process

Population forecasting involves a series of activities. Each activity is affected by the completion of previous activities and affects subsequent activities. In addition, it may be required to repeat a previous activity if it does not provide an adequate basis for any of the later activities. The CBS distinguishes seven steps in the forecasting process (Cruijsen and Keilman, 1984, p.22):

1. Systems identification
2. Systems description
3. Model design
4. Hypothesis formulation (selection of parameter values)
5. Sensitivity analysis
6. Implementation
7. Monitoring.

Other authors adopt a similar process perspective on forecasting (Willekens and Baydar, 1983, p. 3; Vossen, 1988, p. 25; Cruijsen and Keilman, 1988, p. 3).

In step 1, the various population categories to be projected are identified and their relations established. The categorization should meet the user requirements. Subpopulations, the size of which must be forecasted, should be identified during this stage. The categories should also be homogeneous with respect ot the demographic behaviour.

In step 2, a trend report is prepared on the evolution of the population and its categories. The model is developed is the next step. In step 4, the trajectory of the parameters of the model is predicted either by separate (secondary) models, expert opinions or ad hoc procedures. Sensitivity analysis aims at a better a better knowledge of the properties of the model. When the model is complex, e.g. a system of simultaneous equations, then a variation in the value of one parameter may cause changes throughout the population system. Sensitivity analysis is regularly carried out by the CBS (see e.g. Cruijsen and Van Hoorn, 1983). Implementation involves the presentation of projection results and the training of the user in utilizing the forecasts. The final step is the ex-post evaluation of the short-term forecasts by comparing the predicted figures with observations. Differences that are identified provide an important information for improving the subsequent forecasts.

4 The population projection model

In section 2, a hierarchy of models was distinguished. At the top of the hierarchy is the population projection model. Auxiliary models are used to predict the parameters of the projection model. Much of the research in population forecasting is devoted to or directly related to modeling. Introductory review papers with some technical detail include Keyfitz (1979), Murphy (1980), Willekens (1984b), Land (1985), Ahlburg (1987) and the book by Rogers (1985).

The population projection model is a structural model representing some underlying mechanism. It describes the mechanism by which the population size and structure is shaped by fertility, mortality and migration. To this end, a model is specified relating the population at any point in time to the population at a preceding point in time and to the components of change. The model takes the form of an integral equation, a matrix multiplication, a difference equation, and a partial differential equation. Although these mathematical forms look very different from one another, they are equivalent. In this section, three different model specifications are reviewed. They are attributed to Lotka, Leslie and Von Foerster, respectively. Once the model is specified, its parameters need to be estimated from the data. A few issues of parameter estimation are discussed for the Leslie model and its generalization to the multistate projection model.

a Model specification

An early formulation of a projection model is due to Sharpe and Lotka (1911). The authors were interested in the trajectory of births. The births B(t) at time (period) t are the outcomes of the births a years earlier, where a ranges from about 15 to 50, say from α to β in general. The newborns of a years earlier, B(t − a), have a probability l(a) of surviving to time t; those who survive have a probability m(a) da of themselves giving birth in the time interval a to a + da. The number of births B(t) must ultimately be equal to

$$B(t) = \int_{\alpha}^{\beta} B(t - a)\ l(a)\ m(a)\ da$$

The term l(a)m(a) is generally referred to as the net maternity function. It is the probability that a newly born child gives birth to a child of her own between the ages a and a + da. The birth process may be left censored, i.e. some women may already be born at the start of the process. The complication is not considered in this paper (see e.g. Keyfitz, 1985a, pp. 134ff).

The projection method which is commonly used today, is due to Leslie (1945,1948). Before him, Cannan (1895), Whelpton (1936) and others derived an analogous method, although with less mathematical rigour (see Keyfitz, 1985a, p. 136). The method has become known as the component method of population projection, a term coined by Whelpton. Leslie noted that the projection model can be written as a system of simultaneous linear equations, which can be presented compactly as a matrix multiplication. In this model, the population is survived along cohort lines. An additional advantage of the matrix representation of population growth is that several characteristics of the growth path can be inferred from the properties of the projection matrix (growth operator, Leslie matrix; see e.g. Keyfitz, 1968, Chapter 3). For instance, the analysis of the projection matrix provides information on the long-term implications of the current demographic rates. Many of the questions with respect to the feasibility and the characteristics of a stationary population can also be given answers by analyzing the projection matrix. The projection matrix has been studied extensively in demography, although it received relatively little attention in the Netherlands.

Lotka and Leslie developed their models for a population consisting of one sex (female) only and disaggregated by age. It is common in mathematical demography to consider males irrelevant unless they are in short supply. The reason is simple: males do not affect the growth path of a population. For projection purposes, the Leslie model has been extended to include the male population. In nearly all these extensions, fertility remains a matter of women only (the 'female-dominant' model).

Rogers (1975) generalized the Lotka and Leslie models by introducing personal attributes other than sex and age. Rogers added the attribute 'place of residence' since his main interest was in the mathematical description of the evolution of human populations over time *and space*. In doing this, he demonstrated the strength of matrix notation and the rich information on population growth that is contained in the projection matrix. The Rogers model, also known as the multistate projection model, provides an instrument for projecting a population that is composed of several interacting subpopulations defined on the basis of the attributes of their members. The growth operator of the multistate population contains substantial information on (i) the population structure (age composition and the distribution among the various states) implied in the current regimes of fertility, mortality and interstate transfers and (ii) the trajectory the population would follow to reach the implied structure. Few scholars succeeded in extracting the interesting information from the growth operator since the mathematical apparatus that is required is beyond reach for most social scientists. Liaw (1986) provides an excellent summary of the techniques involved and presents empirical applications.

A third type of projection model was first developed by Mekendrick (1928) but is generally attributed to Von Foerster (1959). The model describes the dynamics of a population in which the birth and death rates are not only age-dependent but also time-dependent. The Lotka, Leslie and Rogers models include the variation of the demographic rates along the age dimension only. The Von Foerster model takes the form of a linear first-order partial differential equation. Although the model appeared in several publications in biology (for a review, see Huddleston, 1983), it remained largely unknown in demography until Preston and Coale (1982) published their new synthesis of population dynamics. In exploring the dynamics of change in population size, Preston and Coale focus on the rates of change in three directions – as age increases, as time increases, and as age and time increase in tandem. The authors prove that the instantaneous rate of change in the cohort direction is the sum of the instantaneous rate of change in the age direction and the instantaneous rate of change in the direction of time. Arthur and Vaupel (1984) give an alternative proof which is more intuitive. The model, which became known as the 'generalized stable population method' and the 'variable r method', has shown to be extremely useful in attacking a wide range of problems in demographic analysis. Applications include the indirect estimation of parameters of demographic behaviour and the evaluation of the impact of international migration on population change. The model stimulated much innovative demographic research in the United States.

The model is potentially also of great value for population forecasting. By integrating the age, period and cohort perspectives, the model provides a proper link between the population projection model and models describing the changes in demographic parameters. No research has been done applying the Preston-Coale approach to projections. Much of the controversy related to period approach versus cohort approach and to short-term versus long-term projection models may be resolved by the development of a projection model that integrates the age, period and cohort dimension along which a population and its demographic parameters evolve.

b   *Parameter estimation*

The Leslie model and Rogers' generalization are sometimes referred to as belonging to the demographic accounting tradition (see e.g. Long, 1984). The reason is the demographic accounting technique that is used for estimating the parameters of the model, as opposed to statistical techniques. The accounting method is sometimes referred to as the actuarial method due to its popularity in actuarial science. To illustrate the technique, a projection model is derived for a population which is not disaggregated by sex, age or any other personal attribute. The steps involved in the derivation are taken in the derivation of any projection model of the accounting tradition, including the multistate projection model. The derivation is illustrative.

Let $K(t)$ denote the size of the population at time t and let $D(t, t + 1)$, $B(t, t + 1)$, $E(t, t + 1)$ and $I(t, t + 1)$ represent the numbers of deaths, births, emigrations and immigrations during the period from t to $t + 1$. If the population and the numbers of events are correctly measured, then the following accounting equation holds:

$$K(t + 1) = K(t) - D(t, t + 1) + B(t, t + 1) - E(t, t + 1) + I(t, t + 1) \tag{1}$$

The rate at which an event occurs during the $(t, t + 1)$-interval is the ratio between the number of occurrences and the total duration of exposure. Let $L(t, t + 1)$ denote the duration of exposure by the total population at risk. In case of the event of death, the rate at which the event occurs is

$$d(t, t + 1) = D(t, t + 1) / L(t, t + 1) \tag{2}$$

Unless the demographic behaviour of all individuals are recorded continuously, the exact duration for which an individual is exposed to an event is not known. In the accounting tradition, the duration of exposure is estimated from the accounting equation. Assume that the occurrences are *uniformly distributed* over the $(t, t + 1)$-interval. The total exposure time may be approximated by the mid-period population multiplied by the length of the interval, i.e.

$$L(t, t + 1) = \tfrac{1}{2} [K(t + 1) + K(t)] \tag{3}$$

The exposure is measured in person-years.
Substitution of (3) in (2) gives

$$d(t, t + 1) = D(t, t + 1) / \tfrac{1}{2} [K(t + 1) + K(t)] \tag{4}$$

The birth rate and emigration rate may be derived in an analogous fashion. The rates obtained this way are occurrence-exposure rates relating the number of occurrences to the exposure. The occurrence-exposure rate of immigration cannot be calculated since the population at risk of immigration includes all people of the world except those living in the country or region studied.

Substitution of the number of events in (1) by the number of events in (4) yields the projection model:

$$K(t + 1) = K(t) - \tfrac{1}{2} [d - b + e] [K(t + 1) + K(t)] + I$$

The time arguments associated with the rates and the number of immigrants are omitted for convenience. Reworking gives

$$K(t + 1) = \frac{1 - \tfrac{1}{2} [d - b + e]}{1 + \tfrac{1}{2} [d - b + e]} K(t) + \frac{1}{1 + \tfrac{1}{2} [d - b + e]} I \tag{5}$$

The coefficient of $K(t)$ is the growth factor. The coefficient of I is the ratio at which immigrants during the $(t, t + 1)$-period contribute to the population at the end of the period. The coefficients also provide information on the average duration of exposure. The link between projection models and models for exposure analysis provides interesting prospects for new demographic research in the field of exposure analysis (Willekens, 1988).

Note that the number of events (deaths, say) during the (t,t+1)-interval may be expressed as follows, by equation (2):

$$D(t, t + 1) = d(t, t + 1) L(t, t + 1)$$

This formulation is equivalent to the general projection model studied by Vossen (1988, p. 91). In Vossen's model, L represents the 'mass', i.e. a measure of the population at risk; d is a representation of the demographic parameter which is independent of the size and composition of the population and which needs to be predicted (In Vossen's application, the parameter is the TFR; see also Nelissen and Vossen, 1983). The prediction of the demographic parameters is the subject of the next sections.

The demographic accounting method or actuarial method for parameter estimation is used in most population projection models, including the models developed in the Netherlands (CBS model, MUDEA, PRIMOS). In recent years, the approach is being criticized by mathematical statisticians for its lack of statistical rigour. Innovations in survival data analysis and event history analysis produced new techniques which may fruitfully be utilized for estimating the parameters of demographic projection models. The assumption of the uniform distribution of events need to be replaced by a different assumption; namely, that the instantaneous rates at which the events occur are constant in the unit interval (from t to t + 1). Under this assumption, equation (5) may be written as (Van Imhoff, 1989):

$$K(t + 1) = K(t) \times exp[-m] + I \times [1 - exp(-m)] / m,$$

where $m = d - b + e$.

This approach is fully consistent with the approach adopted in event history analysis. This property may show to be significant for the development of stochastic projection models and the proper inclusion of explanatory variables (personal attributes and contextual variables) affecting the demographic rates.

5   Forecasting the components of demographic change: generalities

The accuracy of population forecasts very much depend on the ability to predict the number of births, deaths and migrations. Some models, especially the older ones, try to predict the number of events directly (see e.g McDonald, 1981). Lee (1981), in a comment on McDonald's paper, criticizes this practice since rates have a dynamics that is different from the population size. More recent methods use the insight that the variation in the number of any vital event may be attributed to changes in the size of each population category and in the category-specific rate at which the event occurs. The rates are therefore predicted separately from the 'mass'. In order to predict the rates, the population is first stratified by age and sometimes by additional attributes that are considered significantly differentiating factors. Sufficient attention to a forecasting-oriented stratification scheme may considerably simplify the hypothesis formulation, the evaluation and the monitoring. Three criteria are of predominant importance for the design of forecasting-oriented stratification schemes (see Rogerson, 1983, p. 380 and Willekens and Baydar, 1983, p.5; for a substantive discussion, see Long, 1988):

i.   homogeneity: the categories (strata) should be as homogeneous as possible with respect to demographic parameters,
ii.   stability: the categories should have a regular pattern of change and, therefore, be easy to predict,
iii. data availability: adequate data should be available for each category.

Broadly speaking, three classes of rate forecasting methods may be distinguished (see also Vossen, 1988, p. 80): explanatory methods, time series methods or extrapolation, and anticipating methods based on expectations. Explanatory methods are based on substantive theory of the causal processes at work. Most explanatory methods today are rooted in demographic or economic theory. Demographic methods emphasize the cohort versus period perspective and the inclusion of intermediate variables or demographic factors that affect the rates. For instance, it has been suggested that parity be distinguished in fertility forecasting and cause of death in the prediction of mortality. In migration forecasting, the outcome of the decision to migrate is predicted differently from the destination choice. The forecasting models rooted in economic theory emphasize two types of variable: life course variables and contextual variables. The first category of variables include variables derived from Easterlin's 'relative income hypothesis', from Becker's human capital theory and from the new home economics. The contextual variables include characteristics of the labour and housing markets. Both types of variables are generally considered exogenous, i.e. they have their own dynamics independent of the demographic processes they try to explain. A projection model that includes contextual variables is sometimes referred to as an open model (Vossen, 1988, p. 43). To be useful for forecasting, explanatory models that use contextual variables must meet several conditions (Brass, 1974): the relations should be stable and sufficiently strong, the data should be available in time and the exogenous variables should be forecast accurately. Since social and economic variables tend to change more rapidly than demographic indicators, they often prove more difficult to predict than the demographic rates they are meant to help forecast (Keyfitz, 1982a).

The time series methods lie at the opposite end of the forecasting spectrum from the demographic methods. The time series model of the Box-Jenkins type expresses the demographic rate at time period t as a linear combination of the rates at previous periods. In a pure autoregressive model, the series at time t is regressed on itself at lagged time periods. To avoid representations with many parameters (long memory), the autoregressive model can be approximated by an autoregressive moving average model (AR-MA), which expresses the rate at t as a linear combination of past observed values and errors in the prediction of the rate. In essence, time series models approach the future as a continuation of the past. "They are purely based on projections of trends from the past into the future. Time-series models produce 'atheoretical' forecasts" (De Beer, 1988b, p. 2). Consequently, the usefulness of time series methods is restricted to short-range forecasting (one or a few steps ahead). If forecasts are made for more years, they become inadequate for two reasons: (i) the forecasts tend to converge towards the mean of the past observations in the long run; and (ii) the confidence intervals, a property which is considered a major advantage of the time series methods of the Box-Jenkins type (AR-MA), get too large too soon. The latter property contradicts the observed and established inertia of aggregate demographic behaviour. The AR-MA models are not appropriate for most demographic forecasting for another reason (Baydar, 1984): they are based on the assumption that there is a *stationary* stochastic process underlying the time series of observations. The techniques are oriented towards the identification of the parameters of the stochastic process and the data requirements for applying the techniques are too high for demographic data. Usually data are compiled annually for demographic variables. Considering that a minimum of fifty time point of data are required in traditional AR-MA analysis, it is often impossible to find an adequate time series.

A direct way of acquiring information on the future is to ask a sample of people what they intend to do or a group of experts which future they consider most likely. Several countries today use information on birth expectations collected in fertility surveys in preparing fertility forecasts. I am not aware of any country that uses expectations in migration forecasting, although some countries collect information on migration intentions as part of the housing surveys (e.g. the Netherlands) or in special migration surveys. Expert opinions are generally used in demographic forecasting in an informal way. Their contribution to the predicted parameter values is at least obscure. Some countries, among them the Netherlands, have a working group of "experts" that discusses the predictions of the demographic parameters initially prepared by the forecasting organization. The working group does not use formal methods, such as the Delphi technique, to reach consensus. The method is rarely used in demographic forecasting, although it is used relatively often in business forecasting.

Before discussing the forecasting of each demographic component separately, a remark on the period versus cohort issue is warranted. The demographic rates exhibit a strong age specificity. But the age profile observed during a given period is not only the effect of age, i.e. the progression through the life course. Older people are at a more advanced stage of life but also belong to an earlier generation than people at younger ages. If the effect of generation (cohort) is not separated from the effect of stage of life, the forecast may be wrong and misleading. Suppose fertility is forecast in a period when births are being postponed. Future fertility will be underestimated if the forecast is based on the age profile of any calendar year in that period. When births are being postponed, the fertility decline at young ages is already visible in the data, but not yet the rise at older ages. In order to account for the effects of changes in the timing of fertility, it is important to follow the fertility behaviour of birth cohorts. Consequently several countries (about one half of the industrialized countries, among them the Netherlands) follow a cohort approach in their fertility forecast. When different cohorts reduce fertility in response to social, economic, cultural or legal changes, the forecast based on the cohort approach will overestimate the fertility. In that case, it is better to base the forecasts on fertility profiles observed in different years (period approach). In order to be prepared for any type of change, both cohort and period effects on the demographic rates should be distinguished from the effect of age. This calls for an age-period-cohort (APC) model. Willekens and Baydar (1984) used an APC model to analyze Dutch fertility rates. The APC model is based on analytical demography and its parameters have unambiguous demographic interpretations. A problem however is that the parameters associated with the cohorts of the last few years cannot be estimated with sufficient confidence. The cohort ARIMA (CARIMA) model developed by De Beer (1985) is claimed not to have this problem (De Beer, 1988b, p. 7). The parameters of the CARIMA model have however no substantive interpretation.

The distinction between age, period and cohort effects in forecasting demographic rates may solve a number of important forecasting problems and may show to be a significant step to a model that includes explanatory variables and is embedded in demographic theory (see also Vossen, 1988, p. 126). In addition, the APC model, which has two sets of time-dependent parameters, enables short- and long-range forecasting in an unified framework. The period effects dominate in projecting a few years ahead. As the projection period gets longer, the cohort effects get more important until the period effects disappear completely in the long run (see e.g. De Beer, 1988b, p. 18). This finding explains that several authors find period models, i.e. models based on period data, perform better in short-term forecasts while cohort models, i.e. models that represent demographic change cohort-wise and use cohort data, are significantly better in long-term forecasts (see e.g Vossen, 1988, p. 94).

6   Fertility forecasting

Fertility forecasting has been the subject of much study. Recent overviews were produced at the occasion of the International Workshop on National Population Projections in Industrialized Countries in Voorburg, the Netherlands, in October 1988 (De Beer, 1988a,1988b; Bell, 1988; Ermisch, 1988).

The three classes of forecasting methods, explanatory methods, time series methods and expectations, have been studied at length in the context of fertility forecasting. Like any other repeatable event, fertility may vary in level (how often the event, i.e. childbirth, occurs) and timing (when it occurs). The level is represented by the quantum (Total Fertility Rate), the timing by the location (distribution across age, shape of fertility curve). An interesting question is whether the two components of fertility change may be forecasted separately. The answer depends on the relation between the level of fertility and the shape of the fertility curve. Miller (1986) and Bell et al. (1988) indicate at most a weak relationship in the U.S. data, suggesting the shape of the U.S. fertility curve depends little on the level of fertility. When there is no significant relationship, the TFR and the shape can be forecasted separately (Bell, 1988, p.10). Hoem et al. (1981) and Rogers (1986) do not assume the separability of the components of fertility change.

The forecasting of the shape of the fertility curve raises a dimensionality problem: the number of relative rates to be predicted is equal to the number of age groups, which can be large if single years of age are considered. Hence, the number of time series to be forecasted can be very large. To reduce dimensionality, parameterization is introduced. Hoem et al. (1981) and Rogers (1986) give an overview of functions that may be used to represent the fertility curve. The gamma distribution is among the most popular. It has three parameters only (after transformation): the starting point of the curve (e.g. the lowest age of the reproductive period – fifteen), the mean age at childbearing and the variance of the curve. The number of parameters to be forecasted is substantially reduced by the parameterization, since only the parameters of the gamma distribution need to be forecasted in addition to the TFR. The gamma distribution has widely been studied and applied (see e.g. Miller et al., 1985; Bell et al., 1988). In the Netherlands, the gamma distribution is used to reduce the dimensionality in regional population projections (Keilman and Manting, 1987). Janssen (1988) studied five parameterization schemes for Dutch fertility profiles. He concludes that, for projection purposes, the gamma and the beta distributions are to be preferred. The Hadwiger and the lognormal distributions are too sensitive to changes in the location of fertility. Janssen has a slight preference for the beta distribution because its profile is less skew and has a greater variance and therefore resembles the empirical profile better than the gamma distribution.

Parameterization not only solves the dimensionality problem, but also assures smooth shapes of the age curves of prediction of relative fertility rates. If age-specific rates are forecast by a model or procedure that does not take into account their strong relationships, the long-term forecasts may show a distribution across age that does not make intuitive sense in terms of the curve not having the same sort of smooth shape across age as historical data. Bell (1988, p. 16) refers to this as the consistency problem. His analysis shows that age-specific rates should not be forecast separately by applying univariate time series models, but a multivariate model should be used instead to account for the strong relationships between the series. Multivariate time series methods are however not applicable when the number of age groups is large. The forecasting of parameterized age profiles is a promising approach since it solves the problems of dimensionality and consistency.

To improve demographic forecasting, some authors suggest to integrate demographic and time series methods. Lee (1974, 1981) proposes to assume shapes or profiles for fertility by age or marital duration or for nuptiality by age. "Then a single fertility or nuptiality rate index, which would shift the profile up or down multiplicatively, could be modeled and forecast using time series methods. This device would compactly summarize the information in the age distribution of the population and thereby allow prior births to affect current ones with lags of up to 40 years while not requiring time series estimation of additional parameters" (Lee, 1981, p. 794). Lee (1974) assumes that the fertility age schedule has a fixed shape (say m(a), for age a), which is shifted up or down by a period-specific fertility index (say f(t), for period t). Then the age-time specific fertility rate (say g(a, t)) is *multiplicatively separable* in age and time, and can be approximated as g(a, t) = f(t) m(a). The f(t)-term is forecasted using time series methods. Carter and Lee (1986) pursuit Lee's (1981) suggestion of an analogous development of a joint model for fertility by age and nuptiality by age. The nuptiality schedule is assumed to be multiplicatively separable in age and time; the fertility schedule is multiplicatively separable in marital duration and time. Several stochastic time series methods are explored for forecasting the t-terms. This leads to a joint forecast of nuptiality and marital fertility. The forecasting performance of the Lee-approach depends on the separability of age and time, i.e. on the age profile remaining constant.

The model suggested by Lee is a simplified version of an APC model. The Lee-model includes two effects: age and time (duration, period) (AP). Age and time are statistically independent. In the APC model, the effect of time is represented by two variables: period and cohort. In it, the age profile is independent of time, i.e. of period and cohort effects. The period effects catch the short-term fluctuations while the cohort effects picture variations over longer periods. In the Lee model, the age effect confounds the effect of cohort differences. Stochastic times series methods (AR-MA) have also been used for extrapolating the period effects and the cohort effects into the future (Willekens and Baydar, 1984).
A variation on the APC model is due to Page (1977), who follows earlier work by Henry, Coale and Coale and Trussell. In her study of *marital* fertility in Sweden, she distinguishes the effects of age, duration of first marriage and period *and* the effects of age-period and duration-period interactions. For a recent application of the Page model, see Rodriguez and Cleland (1988). The authors also briefly mention a few extensions of the model.

The stochastic time series methods, the AP model of Lee and the APC model all start from the same basic belief, that the future is a continuation of the past and can therefore be predicted by a proper investigation of patterns of change in the past. Although demographic patterns and overt behaviour exhibit considerable inertia, there is more to the future than could be observed in the past. A direct way of acquiring information on the future is to ask people about their intentions and/or experts about their views. Several countries use fertility survey data for forecasting fertility. Most use the data in an indirect way, but Australia, the United Kingdom and the Netherlands use the information in a direct way (Van de Giessen, 1988, p. 9). Although the use of birth expectations for forecasting purposes is intuitively appealing, their forecasting performance has been questionable until recently. Women, particularly young and childless women, generally overestimate the number of children they will have during their lifetime. The overestimation occurred in particular in the 1960's and early 1970's and could be as high as 30 per cent (Van de Giessen, 1988, p.2). The reason is that women do not have a fixed target regarding the total number of children they want to have (Lee, 1980). The desired family size may change as women grow older, partly because they find the future not to be as they had visualized at younger ages. Two countries (the Netherlands and Australia) which use birth expectations data for forecasting, adjust the survey results downward to discount the overestimation (De Beer, 1988a, p. 13). Birth expectations data are potentially very useful for forecasting. They may point to behavioural changes that will eventually result in changes in trends. They may also provide early warnings for changes in the timing of fertility. But expectations should be interpreted in a proper context. A woman forms expectations of the basis of information available at the moment and of her perception of the future. Both the information and the perception are likely to change as a woman collects new information and events occur that could not be foreseen. To interpret birth expectations, they should be situated within the context of human development during the life course.

To improve the prediction of fertility, a number of strategies may be suggested (Willekens, 1985b, p. 293):

i.   Distinguish between cohort and period fertility.
ii.   Distinguish between completed cohort fertility and the timing of births within a cohort. The ultimate completed fertility may be related to birth expectations.
iii. Exploit the regularity in age schedules of fertility rates (use graduation or the relational model).
iv.   Control for the effects on fertility of parity and other attributes of the women.

7   Mortality forecasting

Unlike childbirth, death is a nonrepeatable event. In addition, it occurs to everyone with certainty. What remains uncertain is the timing of the event. Two classes of methods for forecasting mortality may be distinguished: extrapolation methods and methods based on epidemiological and biomedical research. A comprehensive review of mortality forecasting methods is given by Olshansky (1988). In this section, the extrapolation methods are reviewed first, followed by methods based on the underlying processes.
    The extrapolation methods are reviewed by Pollard (1987) and Keyfitz (1982b). The simplest method extrapolates the mortality rate for each age, using an age-specific improvement factor. The method is popular with actuaries and the most commonly used extrapolation assumes a geometric improvement of mortality at different ages (Pollard, 1987, p. 56). Most extrapolation methods take advantage of the regularity in the age profiles of mortality rates. They differ in the way they summarize the age profile. The analytical methods, which are sometimes referred to as 'laws of mortality' or graduation techniques express the age-specific mortality rates or a transformation of the rates as a function of age. The first parameterization was suggested by De Moivre in 1725. In the eighteenth century, little was known of the course of mortality and De Moivre hypothesized that, from a group of children born during the same year, a fixed number would die every year until the entire cohort had expired. The implied survival function is a linear function of age. Precisely one hundred years later, Gompertz proposed a mortality function reflecting the hypothesis that man's ability to resist death decreases with age at a constant rate. He could therefore summarize the mortality profile in two parameters only. The Gompertz model had of course its weaknesses. It could not model the mortality

rates at young ages (below fifteen, say) and it overpredicted mortality at advanced ages. Several authors improved on the Gompertz model at the cost of additional parameters (for a review, see Keyfitz, 1982b). The state-of-the-art is represented by the model proposed by Heligman and Pollard (1980) covering the whole age range. The model has eight parameters. Instead of forecasting the mortality rate of each age separately, the parameters of the 'law of mortality' are predicted. The advantage of this approach is that the regular shape of the mortality profile is not lost in the forecasting. McNown and Rogers (1988) use stochastic times series models (Box-Jenkins) to extrapolate the parameters of the Heligman-Pollard model fitted to mortality schedules of the United States for the years from 1900 to 1983. A graduation technique which remained relatively unknown in demography, but has a considerable potential is due to the Italian statistician Petrioli. Petrioli (1975, 1988) introduces a function, resistance to death, which is obtained from the survival function and can be graduated with a three-parameter curve. Petrioli's model fits remarkably well. The technique warrants further investigation.

An alternative method does not involve graduation, but expresses the set of age-specific mortality rates or a transformation of the rates as a modification of a standard profile. The Brass (1971) relational model belongs to this class of methods. It specifies a linear relationship between the logit transformations of two survival functions (probabilities of surviving to various ages), one of which is used as a standard. The intercept of the linear relation is related to differences in the 'level' of mortality (life expectancy), while the slope relates to differences in the shape. Mortality forecasting involves assigning future values to the intercept and the slope. The Brass model has been applied in the Netherlands by Van Vianen (1983) in a study of the mortality decline since 1900 and by Van Poppel (1987) to describe and forecast mortality schedules of 44 regions as part of the MUDEA project (Van Poppel, 1987). Sometimes, the Brass relational model is unable to predict the survival probabilities at extreme ages sufficiently accurate. Zaba (1979) and Ewbank et al. (1983) corrected this shortcoming at the cost of additional parameters.

A final extrapolation method summarizes the mortality schedule in terms of the life expectancy at different ages an extrapolates the life expectancies. This method is adopted by the Netherlands Central Bureau of Statistics in their national population forecasts.

The analytical and relational models are usually estimated using period (cross-sectional) data. The age profile exhibited by period data however confounds the effect of generational differences. Pollard (1987, p. 58) lists studies which found that generation curves exhibit a greater degree of regularity. These studies are dated (1920's and 1930's); in recent times, this regularity has not been observed at the same extent. Manton (n.d., p. 31) reports that period mortality schedules tend to overestimate cohort mortality rates. This is particularly so when part of the cohort is eradicated by a war. Since relatively healthy persons are selected for active service, they suffer great losses, while less healthy people are more likely to survive. This adverse selection leads to an overestimation of true mortality some decades later (Dinkel, 1985, p. 95). The selection is also in effect when mortality is studied by cause of death.

Both cohort and period effects can be significant components of mortality change, especially when mortality is distinguished by cause of death. Many authors today rely on APC analysis to separate the period form the cohort effects in time series of mortality schedules (for a list of references, see Willekens and Van Poppel, 1986, p. 3). In the Netherlands, the Netherlands Institute for Preventive Medicine applied APC analysis to times series of age-specific mortality data (Van Nooten, 1985). The parameterization and forecasting of mortality schedules which confound the effects of generational differences may produce misleading results. The cohort effects should therefore be isolated before the age schedule is parameterized.

A major drawback of the extrapolation techniques is the complete absence of substantive information on the forces shaping the mortality change. Recently, epidemiological and biomedical research results are increasingly being used to improve the mortality forecasting. A preliminary step in the right direction is the projection of mortality by cause of death. Mortality projections by the separation of causes of death have in fact been performed since the 1940s (Pollard, 1987, p. 65). Today, about half of the industrialized countries consider cause of death in mortality forecasts. Since 1974, the United States Social Security Administration considers age-specific mortality rates by cause; since 1981 the mortality rates are projected for each of ten causes separately using the geometric progression approach (Manton, n.d., p. 30). Alderson and Ashwood (1985) present the results of a cause-of-death specific forecast of mortality rates of the elderly in England and Wales. The authors also provide a very useful review of methods of mortality forecasting for the elderly.

Although the cause-of-death specific forecasts are able to predict a reversal of mortality patterns, as they did in the 1960s when a rise of mortality at high ages was predicted, their forecasting performance is limited. To improve our ability to predict mortality, in particular mortality due to given causes or mortality of given subpopulations, the aggregate patterns of mortality change must be related to the underlying individual level physiological and behavioural processes generating those changes by affecting the risk levels and to the ability to control the processes through medical care. The behavioural factors relate to life styles such as food habits, hygiene and income-related hazardous life styles. Mackenbach (1988, p. 150, p. 223, p. 250) suggests that life style change is at least as important in explaining mortality decline as measured by the increase in life expectancy than medical care and the introduction of new medicines, such as antibiotics. The effect of life style variables on future mortality is expected to be significant (Beeck et al., 1989, p. 6).

Manton (n.d.) endorses the use of health process models, which include parameters for the onset and progression of chronic diseases. Ideally, the parameters of the model should be estimated from longitudinal data. Frequently, such data are not available. In that case, Manton (1985) suggests an intermediate approach. The disease process is modelled by a stochastic compartment model, which is a multistate model where certain changes in morbid state are unobserved. The functional dependence of the parameters of the model (transition rates; rate of onset, rate of progression) on time and age is specified on the basis of biomedical research; the parameters are estimated from a time series of age- and cause-of-death-specific mortality rates (see also Manton and Stallard, 1984).

8 Internal migration forecasting

In comparison to fertility and mortality forecasting, the prediction of internal migration raises several additional problems.

First, the problem of definition. A migration is usually defined as a change in usual residence involving the crossing of an administrative boundary. The concept of usual residence, however, is frequently not well defined although it generally involves some reference to a duration of residence or to an intention to stay for a minimum number of months (Willekens, 1982a). The reference to 'administrative boundary' introduces a spatial dimension in the definition of migration. The administrative area could be a municipality, as in the Netherlands; a county, as in the United States; or a province, as in Canada. Changes of residence within the geographical unit is not considered to be a migration. A change of usual residence, irrespective of the distance, is referred to as a move or relocation.

The second problem is the measurement problem. The event of migration is frequently not recorded directly but indirectly by a comparison of the places of residence at two points in time. The points in time are generally a fixed number of years apart (usually one or five years). To distinguish between the measurement of events and the approximation of the events by a comparison of the place of residence at discrete time intervals, the terms migration and migrant are used. In the Netherlands and most countries of Europe, the migrations are recorded as part of the population register. Most other countries derive migration statistics from the census or survey question "Where did you live n years ago?". In the Netherlands, the migration information from the Labour Force Survey (AKT) is of this type (with n = 1). What is being measured in this case is the migrant status, not the occurrence of a migration. The differences in measurement (observation plan) require different methods for estimating the parameters of the migration forecasting model.

The third problem is the fact that migration is subordinate to other life events, such as household formation, housing change and job change. Since the occurrence of a migration very much depends on the occurrence of other life events, migration should not be predicted without reference to the other life events. In other words, migration should be predicted within a life course context. The PRIMOS model, for instance, predicts the migration associated with housing factors, separately from the general (structural) migration (Brouwer, Gordijn and Heida, 1984). In addition, population groups that are particularly prone to migration should be treated separately. The U.S. Bureau of the Census, for instance, forecasts the migration of college students and members of the Armed Forces separately from the migration of the general population (Wetrogan, 1988b).

Recent reviews of the methods that are being used to prepare the (pseudo-) official migration forecasts include Eichperger (1984), who focuses on the Netherlands, and Ledent (1986), who reviews the experience in the USA and Canada. Drewe and Rodgers (1976) review some earlier work.

In analyzing and forecasting migration, it is useful to distinguish between level, timing and direction of migration. The level of migration is represented by the number of migrations during a given interval; the *timing* relates to the distribution within the interval. The interval may be defined in terms of calendar years or years of life. The first approach is adopted in all commonly available migration forecasting models. It is typically a period perspective. The next generation of migration forecasting models, which account for the close relation between migration and other life events, are likely to adopt a life course and/or cohort perspective. The timing of migration over the life-span exhibits a remarkable regularity, which constitutes the basis for the parameterization of profiles of age-specific migration rates and the parameterized projections using the model (e.g. parameterized) migration schedules. Rogers and Castro (1981) found that the age profile of migration rates can be described by a linear combination of double exponential functions, representing a pre-labour force component, a labour force component and a post-labour force component (see also Rogers, 1986). The parameterization may benefit from a decomposition of migration by cause (Rogers and Castro, 1984). Since 1981, model migration schedules are used in England to project migration between the 108 local authority areas within England. For the 1981-based projection round, the Department of the Environment, which is responsible for the internal migration assumptions used in the local area population projection, developed, with the help of consultants, a computerised model to determine the assumptions about migration within England (Bates, 1982; Bates and Bracken, 1987). The model is still being used (see Armitage, 1986). In the Netherlands, model migration schedules are being used as part of the MUDEA population projections (Drewe and Rozenboom, 1988; Willekens et al., 1989). The parameterization of migration profiles results in a substantial data reduction. The double exponential functions which are currently used to describe the profiles have an important disadvantage, however. The method is a curve fitting (graduation) technique and the parameters have no straightforward demographic interpretation, which complicates the prediction of future parameter values.

The methods for migration forecasting differ in the way the *direction* of migration is treated. Early projection methods focused on net migration, while recent methods predict migration by area of origin and area of destination, i.e. gross migration flows. The rationale for predicting gross flows instead of net migration is that the outmigration from a geographical area depends not only on that particular area but also on each and all of the other areas that constitute the potential destinations. In addition, gross flows lend themselves to a behavioural interpretation. The factors that determine the decision to leave a particular region may not be the same as the factors that determine the choice of destination. Gross migration flows are an essential ingredient of the multiregional cohort-component method for the projection of the population by region of residence. When origin-destination-specific migration is considered by age and other personal attributes, such as gender, the amount of data becomes too large to handle in forecasting, provided that all these data are available. Some countries, e.g. the United States and Sweden, have used simplified versions of the gross-flow method in their subnational population projection models. The 'migrant pool'-method, as the method became known, assumes that the choice of destination is independent of the origin. In the PRIMOS model, which is being used in the Netherlands, the choice of destination depends on the origin, but the dependence structure is the same for all ages (Brouwer et al., 1984, p. 294). These approaches and other simplifications of the gross-flow method can be expressed in a modeling framework, as loglinear models. Parameterization of the spatial pattern of migration in terms of loglinear models is of a recent date. It is however a useful approach to both data reduction and indirect estimation of missing flow data (Willekens, 1982b; Nair, 1985; De Jong, 1985).

Two classes of methods for projecting the direction of migration may be distinguished: extrapolation methods and explanatory models. Migration expectations or intentions are not used in forecasting, as far as I am aware. The extrapolation of a time series migration flow data is seldom encountered since (i) time series data are only very recently becoming available and (ii) ARIMA-type of models are difficult to apply due to the brief period covered. Willekens and Baydar (1986) propose an alternative strategy for time-series analysis of place-to-place migration data. First, the migration data are decomposed into three components: a level component (national number of migrations of migration rate), a generation component (share of a particular area in the total number of outmigrations) and a distribution component (distribution of the outmigrants of a particular area over all possible destinations). Second, an exploratory analysis of each component is performed to identify the major regularities and irregularities in the data structure. Third, a generalized linear model (GLM) is specified to describe the data structure. Particular attention is paid to the time-dependence of the parameters. If a component (e.g. generation component) remains relatively stable, the parameters associated with it are independent of time. Fourth, the model parameters are estimated and the model is validated. Finally, the time-dependent parameters are extrapolated. The authors decide on logit models to describe the generation and the distribution components. The models are fitted to data of the Netherlands on migration between municipalities classified by degree of urbanization.

Explanatory models have a long history in migration research. Most explanatory analyses are at the macro-level and involve some type of a spatial interaction or gravity model. In 1885, Ravenstein formulated the observed empirical regularities as 'laws of migration'. The gravity type laws formulated a crude answer to the questions why people migrate, what the migrant's characteristics are and what the pattern of internal migration is. Lee (1966) provides a more explicit attempt at theory formulation. He views migration as an outcome of a decision-making process. Four sets of factors enter directly into the decision making:

i.   push factors: factors associated with the area of origin;
ii.   pull factors: factors associated with the area of destination;
iii. intervening factors: obstacles associated with the movement itself; and
iv.   personal factors: characteristics of the potential migrant.

These factors constitute the basic elements of any spatial interaction model. The modern version of the spatial interaction model of migration is due to Alonso (1978). The Alonso model received much attention in the migration literature. Ledent (1986) uses the model to forecast interregional migration in Canada. The model includes three types of variables:

i.   'site' variables: attributes of the areas of origin and destination;
ii.   'situational' variables or systemic variables describing the relative position of each
       region within the system of regions and its effect on the total migration flow
       generated and attracted; the variables are analogous to 'potential' variables (Op 't
       Veld et al., 1984, p. 179);
iii.   accessibility variables describing the relative position of one region with respect
       to a particular other region.

The PROMIRES model, developed by Op 't Veld et al. (1987) includes similar types
of variables. Note that the Alonso model does not include personal factors, such as life
course variables. It addresses the spatial dimension only. Since persons in different stages
of life perceive the attributes of regions and the 'distance' between regions differently,
it should be useful to add a life course perspective to the Alonso model. A few ideas on
how this may be accomplished are given in Willekens (1985a). The ideas are derived
from Los' (1979) work on transportation demand forecasting. The forecasting model is
a two-stage model. In a first stage, migration is predicted on the basis of a behavioural
model. The model is a discrete choice model, based on the value-expectancy theory of
the migration decision-making process and on the formal representation of this theory.
Migration is viewed as the outcome of a process in which the expected value or utility
of an alternative location is maximized. The choice probabilities generated by the
behavioural model, constitute preliminary predictions of migration. These 'ex ante'
predictions are based on the preferences of the potential migrant without consideration
of the constraints. In a second stage, the choice probabilities are adjusted to satisfy
constraints that are given exogenously. The constraints may refer to observed stable
migration patterns or other regularities in the macro-dynamics of the spatial population
system. The outcome of the second stage constitute the 'ex post' predictions. The further
development of a migration forecasting model that includes the micro-dynamics of
individual behaviour over the life course and the macro-dynamics of the population and
socio-economic system may benefit from recent research by Weidlich and Haag (1988)
on the emergence of a universal structure of macro-dynamic behaviour when at the
micro-level very different processes exist and interact. It may further benefit from
research on multistate proportional hazard models, in which the rates of transition
between stages of life (e.g. migration) are related to personal attributes (covariates) and
contextual variables (for a recent discussion of prospects, see Gill, 1988). The precise
way in which the various recent research results may be utilized to improve migration
forecasts needs to be investigated.

9   International migration forecasting

International migration has been traditionally treated as subordinate to fertility and
mortality in national population projections. Two main reasons are often stated to support
this practice: the low level of migration and/or the scarcity of migration statistics. In a
recent review paper on methods used by statistical agencies in projecting external
migration, George and Perreault (1988, p.2) state three reasons for projecting interna-

tional migration as a separate component: (i) the direct contribution of immigration/emigration to population change and sex/age structure; (ii) the influence of immigration on the ethnic and cultural composition of the receiving countries; and (iii) the indirect effect of immigration through natural increase in the receiving country. The authors conclude that the forecasting of international migration is considered to be the most hazardous among the components of population change, mainly because of data problems, unpredictable labour demands and socio-economic and political conditions in the sending and receiving countries. The forecasting problem is further complicated by the fact that the number and composition of inflows are determined to a great extent by the ever-changing immigration policies of the receiving countries (George and Perreault, 1988, p. 20). As a consequence, the prospects for extrapolation techniques are limited at this stage and most countries use very simple extrapolation techniques to predict external migration for one or a few years ahead.

An explanatory model of international migration was developed by Nelissen (1983) among others. Nelissen, studying the Netherlands, included population and economic variables for the Netherlands, the countries of origin of immigrants and the countries of destination of emigrants. The model resembles the explanatory models of internal migration.

The potential for judgmental forecasting and scenario analysis is significant instead. In the Netherlands and in the most recent (1985) population projection of Canada, a judgmental approach is adopted to forecast external migration. The opinions of experts and administrators at the concerned government departments were used in addition to the annual immigration target levels fixed by the government.

In order to improve the quality of international migration forecasts in the short run, the following steps have been suggested:

1. Stratify the migrants to obtain relatively homogeneous strata. The stratification may be on the basis of nationality, the legal/ illegal dichotomy, etc.
2. Distinguish between immigration and emigration.
3. Distinguish types of migration: family reunion, labour migration, return migration, economic and political refugees, etc.
4. Take into account migration policies and targets of other countries that traditionally receive the same categories of migrants.
5. Improve the data base and develop methods for the indirect estimation of international migration and methods to improve the comparability of migration statistics.
6. Use techniques of judgmental forecasting (e.g Delphi).
7. Develop alternative scenarios.
8. Coordinate immigration forecasts with the most important sending countries. Such a coordination was recently established between Canada and the United States.

Several of these items are included in the immigration and emigration forecasts that are currently being prepared by the NIDI in cooperation with the Netherlands Central Bureau of Statistics and the National Physical Planning Agency.

10   Categorical population forecasts

Categorical population forecasting is the forecasting of a population that is categorized by one or more personal attributes in addition to sex and age. Place of residence is such an attribute. The attribute variable can generally take on a limited number of values, which makes it a categorical variable. The people with the same value of the attribute variable constitute a subpopulation or population category. Categorical population forecasting involves the forecasting of the size of every subpopulation. Three approaches may be distinguished. The first approach predicts the total population change and allocates the predicted total to the various subpopulations without reference to the components of change. It is a top-down approach. The allocation procedure varies from a simple ratio to a complex allocation algorithm. The changes in the share of each subpopulation are forecasted exogenously to the population. The perspective on change, adopted in applying this class of methods, is one of comparative statics. In most demographic applications, relatively simple ratio methods are used (for a review, see Pittenger, 1976; Ter Heide, 1981; and Willekens and Baydar, 1983, pp. 23ff). Examples of the top-down approach are the headship rate method of household projection, the school-enrollment ratio method of educational projection and the labour force participation rate of labour force projection. An up-to-date overview of these methods is provided in the forthcoming Manual XI of the United Nations (1989) on the integration of population variables into development planning.

The second approach predicts the size of each subpopulation separately and aggregates the predicted subpopulations to obtain the total population. It is the bottom-up approach. The advantage of the bottom-up approach is that the differential demographic behaviour of each subpopulation can be taken into account in projecting the population. The disadvantage is that the summation of the subpopulations may differ from an exogenously prepared projection of the total population. This approach is commonly used in countries with a federal structure (Canada, USA, Federal Republic of Germany). Each region (province, state, Land) prepares its own population projection; the national population is the sum of the regional populations, sometimes adjusted for the overestimation. The overestimation may be attributed to two factors. The first is that regional authorities are inclined to overestimate their future populations. The second factor is the aggregation bias: when a heterogeneous population is projected by projecting the subpopulations followed by a summation, the result is always higher than what would have been found by projecting the population without recognition of its heterogeneous subpopulations. Keyfitz (1985a, pp. 14ff) demonstrates the aggregation bias with a simple numerical example. Rogers (1976) and Gibberd (1981) identify conditions under which perfect aggregation will result.

The third approach emphasizes the linkages between the subpopulations: subpopulations grow or decline because of their internal dynamics and because people move between subpopulations. Because of the movement, the subpopulations must be forecasted simultaneously. The most simple model for projecting a set of interacting subpopulations is the Markov model. Rogers extends the Markov model to a components-of-change model by including natural change (fertility and mortality) (Rogers, 1968) and adding the age dimension, which results in the multiregional cohort-component model (Rogers, 1975; see also Rogers, 1985). Multiregional projection models are increasingly being used for regional population forecasting. In the Netherlands, the National Physical Planning Agency stimulated research and development of the multiregional projection model by supporting the MUDEA project (Willekens, 1984a; Willekens and Drewe, 1984; Drewe et al., 1988; Willekens et al., 1988). Other countries have implemented multiregional methods or are starting to do so. Rees and Willekens (1986) compare the Dutch and the English methods and experiences. The experience in the United States is reviewed by Willekens and Wetrogan (1987) and Wetrogan (1988a). Kupiszewski (1988) reviews and evaluates the practice in Poland. The experience of seven countries is evaluated in Willekens (1990).

The United Nations uses a version of the top-down approach to prepare rural-urban population projections (United Nations, 1987, pp. 35ff). For some years, the organization is considering a switch to the multiregional model. Lack of adequate data and software, the need to use an identical projection method for all countries of the world, and inadequate funding to prepare for the switch inhibits the transition to a new method. The sponsoring of a new Manual on Subnational Population Projection, which reviews methods that are currently in use and that demonstrate the potential of the multiregional approach, is an important step.

The techniques that were initially developed to study a population disaggregated by place of residence, can be applied to a population disaggregated by any personal attribute. To express the general applicability, the denomination 'multiregional' demography was changed into 'multistate' and 'multidimensional' demography. Schoen (1988) refers to a population disaggregated by a personal attribute as a multigroup population. The multistate method is sometimes referred to as the flow model and the matrix method. Since 1970, the CBS prepares population projections by marital status (since 1970 for females and since 1980 also for males). Espenshade (1985) presents multistate projections of the U.S. female population by marital status. Not all the multistate models that currently exist are developed within the context of multistate demography. Some authors extended the Markov model by including age, independently of Rogers. The SKILL model is a good example. It was developed by the Netherlands Central Planning Office to forecast the education and labour supply (see e.g. Kuhry and Passenier, 1986). The model predicts the flow of children through the educational system, in addition to the entries and the graduations, on the basis of the student flow statistics published annually by the Central Bureau of Statistics.

A particular case of a categorical population is one which is disaggregated by family or household type. Because of its relevance, the state-of-the-art of family and household forecasting models is reviewed in a separate section.

The up-to-date approach to categorical population projection involves the multistate cohort-component model. The projection of multistate or multigroup populations raises a number of problems not found in traditional projections. Most relate to the representation and measurement of the interdependence or transition (flow) structure in the multistate population. The issues involved in forecasting interregional (place-to-place) migration also arise in forecasting the interstate (state-to-state) transfers in any multistate population. The distinction between migration (event) and migrant (person), for instance, has its analogue in any multistate projection model. Event-based models consider the direct transfers between states. The data consists of movements and the model parameters are occurrence-exposure rates, i.e. ratios of number of occurrences of a given event to the total duration of exposure. Frequently, the transfers between states are recorded indirectly by comparing the states occupied at two consecutive points in time. These data, which are referred to as transition data, are generally census or survey data on the states occupied at the time of the census or survey and one or five year prior to the census or survey. Occurrence-exposure rates cannot be estimated from these data directly, since the number of occurrences are unknown. However, the data permit the inference of transition probabilities conditional on survival. The multistate projection model that results will be referred to as a person-based model. The data availability greatly affects the estimation of the parameters of the projection model. Rees (1986) discusses demographic accounting techniques for the derivation of projection models from different types of data.

Any demographic projection model projects the population from one point in time (t) to a later point in time (t+1). The projection interval is discrete, although the processes underlying population change are continuous. The model specification and, in case of an event-base model, the parameter estimation depend on the assumption one makes about the behaviour of the processes within a projection interval. In the demographic accounting tradition, it is assumed that, within a unit interval, a given event occurs at a constant probability density. If the event results in attrition, such as in the case of death, the survival function is linear. Nearly all projection models currently in use have been developed in the demographic accounting tradition. The assumption of constant probability density may occasionally result in unrealistic transition probabilities, when the length of the unit interval is too large (see e.g. Gill and Keilman, 1989). To avoid this problem, it is assumed that, within a unit interval, the intensity or instantaneous rate of transition is constant instead of the probability density. If the event results in attrition, the survival function is exponential. Recently, Van Imhoff (1989) developed a multistate population projection model that allows for international migration and is based on the assumption of piecewise constant intensity (constant within unit intervals). The intensity is a conditional density. The description of the behaviour of the process within the unit interval in terms of the intensity is fully consistent with the approach adopted in event history analysis (see Section 4).

The personal attribute, on the basis of which a population is stratified into subpopulations, is a categorical variable. Sometimes, the categories imply a certain ordering or ranking. For instance, the educational system is divided into several grades. A student is either promoted to a higher grade (usually the next), is not promoted and stays in the same grade or leaves the educational system because of graduation, drop-out, migration or death. The grades, which constitute the categories of the attribute variable, are ordered. Analogously, the female population may be divided into subpopulations on the basis of the number of children women have given birth to (parity). Parity is a categorical variable having ordered categories. In order to forecast a population which is disaggregated on the basis of an ordinal variable, a method may be used which slightly differs from the multistate method. Since transitions are possible in one direction only, the direction of a transition does not need to be predicted. All that is required to project a population is the initial distribution and a set of rates of progression. The grade method of educational forecasting and the parity progression method of fertility forecasting (Feeney, 1985) belong to this class of methods.

11 Family and household forecasting

Demography traditionally deals with individuals and most of demography deals with unrelated individuals. Populations are categorized on the basis of personal attributes and individuals with the same set of attributes are assembled into a subpopulation. But individuals are not unrelated. They develop and cherish various types of relationships. Some of the relationships are biologically determined, such as the parent-child (consanguineal) relationship. Most relationships originate in the basic need for social contact and social (and sometimes economic) support. The form of the relationship is influenced by normative, legal and economic constraints. Particularly significant for population research and policy are partnership arrangements, which include legal marriage, and living arrangements. The formation, growth and dissolution of the primary groups, that are established by these relationships, are the subject of family and household demography. Two conferences, one in December 1983 and the other in December 1984, were instrumental in establishing family and household demography as a new subfield of demography. The first conference was organized under the auspices of the International Union for the Scientific Study of the Population (Bongaarts et al., 1987), the second under the auspices of the European Association for Population Studies (Keilman et al., 1988).

Demographers have for long investigated the biological relationships, mainly in the context of the study of reproduction and kinship (for an illustrative review, see Keyfitz, 1985a, Chapters 10 and 11). A mathematical theory has been developed to infer the genealogies and the structure of overlapping generations from given regimes of fertility and mortality. The inference typically assumes that the population consists of one sex only and is stable (i.e. in the steady state or in a dynamic equilibrium). When these assumptions are not practical, such as in the projection of number of kin, or when additional variables are considered, such as marital change and migration, the mathematical theory falls short and microsimulation provides a way out (Reeves, 1987; Bartlema, 1988).

Conjugal relationships, i.e. the formation and dissolution of marital unions, have been studied in the context of nuptiality analysis. The great majority of studies do not simultaneously investigate both male and female behaviour. Instead, they focus on the female population and assume that males are abundantly available and behave precisely the way prescribed by members of the female population. If a marriageable male is not indifferent between the attributes of females, the demographer is faced with the difficult 'two-sex problem', which cannot be dealt with by conventional methods of nuptiality analysis. If, on the other hand, marriageable males are in short supply, some members of the female population are unable to marry and face a 'marriage squeeze'. The 'demography of individuals' is not well equipped to deal with these severe problems. What is needed is a demography of groups, i.e. of interacting individuals, or a 'demography of relationships'. Schoen (1988) presents and reviews neat mathematical solutions to the two-sex problem and proposes a method to assess the significance of the marriage squeeze. Keilman (1985a,b) discusses the problems in the context of forecasting, and illustrates the issues using the 1980-based population forecasts of the Netherlands. Van Imhoff (1988) recently showed that Schoen's solution to the two-sex problem (harmonic mean) is a special case of a more general solution of least square optimization.

Montgomery et al. (1988) and Willekens (1988a) present behavioural (micro-demographic) solutions to both problems. The establishment of a partner relationship is viewed as the outcome of a search process, the search for a partner. The process has two essential parameters: (i) the arrival rate of potential partners, i.e. the frequency with which possibilities for establishing a relationship arise, and (ii) the decision rule governing the acceptance or rejection of potential partners. The process is analogous to the labour market process matching jobs and people. The search process has been studied extensively in labour economics (for a review, see Mortensen, 1986).

Family and household demography is particularly relevant to forecasting. "A prime use of family demography is forecasting ... Whether to guide the market or to aid government planning, such forecasts are the more important the more the family and household constitution of the population is changing. And never has the household constitution of nations and localities changed so rapidly as in recent decades" (Keyfitz, 1987, p.9). Traditionally, the numbers of households of different types (size) were projected on the basis of ratios of the number of household heads to the number of persons. The headship rate method was first used for projection during the Second World War by the U.S. Bureau of the Census. Initially, the rates were by age and sex; marital status was added later (for a review of the method, see Kono, 1987; Linke, 1988). The headship rate concept can be expanded in a number of ways to characterize the heads of household and to accommodate the non-heads (see e.g. Akkerman, 1985; Pitkin and Masnick, 1987).

In recent years, the ratio method has been replaced by dynamic models, which bring into focus the transitions between household categories. Two classes of dynamic models may be distinguished: event-based models and person-based models. In the event-based models, the changes in the household or family structure are related to life events, such as leaving the parental home, marriage, divorce, childbearing, entry into cohabitation, etc. The person-based models focus on the *position* in the household or family; they describe the changes in household and family structure in terms of the positions persons or households (families) have in the household (family) typology at two points in time. If the category, a person or household (family) is in at the end of the period, differs from the category at the beginning of the period, a transition has taken place. The transitions may involve multiple life events or may be a consequence of different types of life events. Most of the dynamic household projection models are person-based. They include

PRIMOS (Heida and Gordijn, 1985), LIPRO (Keilman and Van Dam, 1987; Van Imhoff and Keilman, 1989), the model developed by Rima and Van Wissen (1987, pp. 99ff), WODYN (Hooimeyer and Linde, 1988, pp. 103ff), the model developed by Harsman, Snickars and Holmberg for the Swedish Building Research Council (Holmberg, 1987) and the model developed by Murphy (quoted by Corner, 1987). The REHDY model, which categorizes the population by household position *and* region of residence, also belongs to this class of models. All these models are based on multistate demography, either implicitly (PRIMOS, Swedish model, Murphy model) or explicitly (LIPRO, Rima-Van Wissen model, WODYN, REHDY). The state-space consists of a set of household categories or, in the case of REHDY, a set of household categories and regions. Corner (1987), Keilman (1988) and Ledent et al. (1986) provide recent reviews a dynamic household models. After a review of five models, Keilman (1988, p. 135) concludes that "the multidimensional (multistate) approach holds considerable promise for the future of modelling household behaviour."

Event-based models have primarily been used for projecting the family status, i.e. the type, size and composition of the family. The basic question these models address is how families evolve as a consequence of patterns of fertility, mortality, marriage and divorce. The typical approach is to follow a cohort of individuals as they age, experience life events and, as a consequence, pass through several stages of the family life cycle. Examples of event-based models are Kuijsten (1986), Bongaarts (1987) and Zeng Yi (1990). The models are constructed with the same basic technique used in the calculation of multistate life tables. Except for the Kuijsten-model, they are rooted in multistate demography. Bongaarts predicts the number and composition of nuclear families and estimates the changes of the family composition over the life course; Zeng Yi focuses on nuclear and extended families.

The conventional multistate life table and projection models assume that the demographic events that occur within a unit time interval, are uniformly distributed over the interval. This assumption, which is equivalent to the assumption of piecewise constant probability densities, may cause difficulties when different events may occur within the same unit interval (e.g. marriage and childbearing). In that case, assumptions need to be made about the sequence of the events. These problems disappear when a somewhat different approach is adopted. Instead of assuming piecewise constant probability densities, the instantaneous rates of transition are assumed to be piecewise constant. In that case, the theory of competing risks can be readily applied. Such an approach was followed by Willekens (1988a) in an event-based model and Van Imhoff (1989) in a person-based model. The event-based model is a stochastic process model which simulates the passage of cohort members through the life course; it focuses on the timing of the life events and the length of time that is being spend in each stage of life. The model includes behavioural factors: individuals have a choice to make a transition or not. The decision rules are modelled explicitly. The life course is viewed as a realization of a stochastic process and a set of decision rules. The transition rates (hazard rates) may easily be related to explanatory variables such as personal attributes and contextual variables. The model can also easily be transformed into a microsimulation model by adding a random number generator to decide whether a cohort member, to whom a given rate of transition or decision rule applies, will actually make a transition within the next unit time interval. Galler (1988) and Nelissen and Vossen (1988) project households by microsimulation; behavioural factors (decision rules) are however not included yet. A major advantage of microsimulation is that it can incorporate more personal attribute variables with a greater set of attribute values. This is an important advantage since "it provides a flexible tool for the development of behavioural hypotheses and their application to simulation and forecasting" (Galler, 1988, p. 158). A disadvantage is that the incorporation of so much detail requires the estimation of a large number of parameters. The data are frequently inadequate for the estimation of hundreds of parameters, unless parameterization is used (Land, 1986, p. 896). Microsimulation may be a promising tool, but it seems that the technique has not advanced much since its introduction in the social sciences by Orcutt (see e.g Orcutt et al., 1976). Land (1986, p. 896) recommends an evaluation of the forecasting performance of microsimulation in comparison to other methods to predict the future.

Household projection models have come a long way. The current models try to describe the life courses of individuals and the formations and dissolutions of relationships as realistically as possible by linking observed behaviour to underlying random and behavioural processes. Chance and choice are two aspects found in any life course. The operation of chance and the decision rules people use in making choices in directing their lives determine not only the future of individual life courses but also the future of the population. The models that explicitly include chance and choice mechanisms are still in a very preliminary stage. The consideration of a behavioural component (decision rules) does however provide an opportunity to embed the model in a theory of demographic behaviour. It brings the art and science of forecasting closer to the ultimate aim; namely, the discovery of a truly behavioural way of estimating the future.

12 Predictability of demographic processes [1]

Many of the issues raised in the previous sections relate, either directly or indirectly, to the *predictability of demographic processes*. To what extent are future developments in key demographic parameters foreseeable? When the answer indicates that the predictability of demographic parameters is only limited, is that only a temporal situation, or is it inherent to population processes? How do researchers cope with such a (temporary or permanent) limited predictability? And how do the users of demographic forecasts and scenarios cope with it? These are only a few of the questions that arise when one considers the relatively poor quality of population forecasts that were produced in industrialized countries after World War II. Very clear evidence of a limited predictability of population processes at the national level was recently given at an international workshop on National Population Projections in Industrialized Countries (Cruijsen and Keilman, 1989): although most industrialized countries were faced with a similar shift in their demographic regime since the 1960s, there is wide variation in the demographic future between these countries. Some countries predict a continuation of the trends observed

---

[1] This section is written by Nico Keilman.

over the past decade: low fertility, increasing voluntary childlessness, decreasing mortality rates, a steady influx of immigrants etc, while other developed countries expect rising fertility levels or no influence of external migration.

The issue of the predictability of demographic processes is a multi-faceted issue. Below we shall discuss a number of the aspects involved. Topics covered include the sources, representation and measurement of uncertainty and strategies to deal with uncertainty: monitoring and scenario analysis.

What are the *sources of error* of population forecasts? Hoem (1973) and Keyfitz (1977) were the first authors to discuss this issue, see also Willekens (1984c, p. 373). They mention sources like errors in observed trends, errors in the jump-off population, rounding-off errors, randomness of the demographic process involved, errors in values of exogenous parameters, sudden shifts in parameter values and inaccurate model specification. The most common forecasting errors in the practice of cohort component modelling are errors in values of exogenous parameters. Historical forecasts in many industrialized countries were way off the mark mainly because assumptions for birth rates, death rates and migration parameters were incorrect.

Several authors have expressed forecasting uncertainty by way of *statistical models*, to gain insight in *ex-ante errors*. Among the early contributions were Pollard (1966), Sykes (1969), Feichtinger (1971), and Schweder (1971). More recent work extending the early approaches is that of Alho and Spencer (1985), Cohen (1986), Pflaumer (1984, 1986) and Keyfitz (1985b). A recent review is given by Cohen (1985). The general conclusion from these studies is that the randomness of the population process has only limited impact on forecasting errors.

An entirely different approach was stimulated by work of Keyfitz (1981) and Stoto (1983). They studied *ex-post errors* in historical forecasts, by comparing the results of these forecasts with actually observed trends. Their conclusion that the band between the high and the low variant of the total population size represents approximately a two-thirds confidence interval was confirmed for the Netherlands (Keilman, 1983) and for the USA (Long, 1987). More refined analyses study ex-post errors in age structures, in births, deaths and migrations, etc. (see Ahlburg, 1982; Schreurs, 1989). Apart from the question for which forecast indicator we wish to study the error patterns, the question is how to *measure* the accuracy. The literature gives a large number of measures: mean error, mean percentage error, mean absolute error, root mean square error, Theils U, to name a few. Ahlburg (1982) and Armstrong (1985) discuss several of them.

A recent new line of enquiry that may have great potential for the study of the predictability of population processes is that of *non-linear deterministic systems*. The idea, which stems from weather forecasting, is that reality is inherently non-linear. Some non-linear systems, for instance systems with underlying differential equations of the logistic type, behave erratically in certain critical areas of their parameter space. Such systems may display stable equilibrium behaviour, but once their parameters have surpassed so-called bifurcation points, their behaviour becomes essentially unpredictable. It is not a possible random component in the model that causes unpredictability, but it is the non-linear nature of these deterministic systems.

This field is relatively new in demography. Wachter and Lee (1989) and Bonneuil (1989) give first attempts.

An important issue in the study of the predictability of population processes is the possible contribution of behavioural theories and, related, explanatory models based on these theories. Most authors argue that the poor performance of forecasting models is due to our incomplete knowledge of reality. Progress will be made when we put more effort in explanatory behavioural theories. Others concur with this viewpoint and argue that human behaviour cannot be explained. Boudon (1986) is the most prominent one in his analysis of theories of social change. His conclusion is that there are no good grounds for accepting a deterministic representation of social change. Individuals have a variety of possible actions, and this makes processes describing human behaviour essentially unpredictable. It would be of great value to try and apply Boudon's analysis on demographic processes.

Finally we mention strategies to cope with the situation in which we accept that the future cannot be predicted. A first strategy is to keep a check of population development by a regular (yearly, say) comparison of the predicted and realized population. The functions and implementation of monitoring are discussed by Gordijn et al. (1984). In the Netherlands, the CBS monitors the national population forecasts. A second strategy is scenario analysis. In that case, one produces internally consistent pictures of reality to explore the future and to assess the impact of unpredictable events on population processes of interest. The scenario approach has a long tradition, stemming from the early 1950s at the Rand Corporation. It has been applied in the Netherlands by Becker and his group at Utrecht University in future studies in the fields of regional developments, and health and mortality studies. Vossen (1988, pp. 131ff) applied scenario analysis to assess the impact of demographic change on social security.

We have to accept uncertainty in demographic processes, either only temporary, or as a structural aspect. Meanwhile, as no single approach would produce error-free forecasts, we should not rely on only one such approach, but instead we should combine the results of several approaches and minimize risks of missing the targets (for a review of how the U.S. Bureau of the Census integrates forecasting approaches, see Long, 1985).

13 Conclusion and research needs

The state-of-the-art review demonstrates that demographic forecasting has been a very active domain of research during the past decade. Dutch scholars were and are major contributors. They contribute not only to the international scholarly literature, but also to the improvement of the practice of demographic forecasting both in the Netherlands and abroad. It was not by accident that the first International Workshop on National Population Projections in Industrialized Countries, organized under the auspices of the U.N. Economic Commission for Europe and with financial and organizational support of the U.S. Bureau of the Census, an important contributor itself to the art and science of demographic forecasting, was held in the Netherlands. Scholars at the U.S. Bureau of the Census and in Holland have been coordinating their research efforts, through the NIDI, for several years. Dutch scholars are also cooperating with scholars in European countries, both bilaterally and multilaterally. The international study of the impact of demographic change on social security, which has been organized by the International Institute for Applied Systems Analysis in Austria, calls on Dutch scholars for the development of the household projection model. Through the United Nations system, Dutch scholars contribute to the training of professionals, predominantly from the Third World, in the use of improved demographic forecasting methods. The exploration of demographic futures has become an internationally recognized and appreciated trademark of Dutch demography.

To explore and forecast the future, we need an appropriate technology, consisting of methods, models and software. The technology should, as much as possible, be based on the substantive understanding of the processes that shape the demographic future and of their dependence structure. Before identifying research needs, a few observations are in order.

a. Although the interest of users of demographic forecasts is in the future size and composition of the population and, maybe, the number of demographic events, the processes that determine the population change are active at the micro-level, i.e. the level of the individual, family or household. Socio-economic variables do not affect population variables directly; their effect is mediated by biological and/or behavioural processes at the micro-level. These processes are developmental processes: the biological activity and the behaviour at any given stage is, at least in part, determined by the history of the process.

b. Because of the developmental nature of demographic processes at the micro-level, people with common significant historical experiences ('Schicksale') during important periods of their lives are likely to exhibit similar patterns of demographic behaviour. They may also respond similarly to contextual changes. In other words, the effect on behaviour of sudden changes in the context in which a person lives, is mediated by his or her experiences. This forms the basis for generation or cohort effects. Because of their very nature, cohort effects level out the influence of concurrent factors. Cohort effects are significant for explaining long-term patterns of behaviour; period effects explain short-term variations around long-term patterns.

c. Humans can think prospectively. Their behaviour is not only determined by their past (experience) and present (actual context), but also by their view of their own future and the future of the socio-economic system in which they live. The role of the future as a behavioural determinant increases with the growing ability to control the occurrences of demographic events and the increasing societal expectation to behave rationally.

d. Many processes that underly demographic events are active long before their existence is manifested by the occurrence of the event. The ability to predict the events
   will substantially improve if one can reveal the latent processes, identify the risk
   factors and diagnose the risk levels. Exposure analysis (with the aid of intermediate
   variables) and cause-specific analysis should be considered as first steps in an effort
   to characterize the processes demographic events are associated with.

From these general observations one may derive that the next generation of demographic forecasting models should focus on the biological and behavioural processes that
underly observed patterns of demographic behaviour. The rate at which an event occurs
at any point in time should be related to the current position of the process, to factors
representing the current personal and societal context (i.e. personal attributes, contextual
variables), and to factors that summarize the effects of the history of the process and of
past experiences. In addition, for behavioural processes, the rate of occurrence of an
event should be related to prospective factors. In short, the next generation of demographic forecasting models are likely to be models of *developmental processes*, the
demographic events are part of. *Instead of forecasting the population, we may be
forecasting the lives of people, in particular the number and patterning of life events.*
The models are also likely to have a provision for the impact of chance and choice on
demographic behaviour. In addition, they are likely to make explicit how the effect on
population of changes in the socio-economic, cultural, technological and legal contexts
are mediated by micro-level processes. The design of such models requires the integration of recent advances in analytical demography, hazard rate analysis (event history
analysis) and contextual analysis. The model design should be based on considerable
theoretical and empirical research. The research should be forecasting-oriented, i.e. focus
on unconditional causal relations or on relations that are conditional on particular
changes in contextual variables.

To substantially improve the demographic forecasting performance, research is
needed in five domains.

a. Cohort-component model (population projection model)
b. Methods for the analysis of demographic time series
c. Use of information on attitudes, expectations and intentions
d. Predictability of demographic processes
e. Forecasting with limited data.

a   Cohort-component model (population projection model)

Most population projections today are done using the cohort-component model developed by Leslie in the 1940's, a variant of it or an extension such as the multistate
model. The basic assumptions on which projection models are based have not changed
during the past fourty years. The Leslie-type model is not suited to include many of the
innovative features listed above. The model developed by Von Foerster provides a much
better base for the next generation of population projection models. Unlike the Leslie-

model, it is a model of a continuous-time process that enables the integration of age, period and cohort factors, as Preston and Coale (1982) have shown. It provides therefore a model that could be used for short-term projections and long-term projections and produce consistent results. In the short run, the period effects will dominate; the cohort effects take over gradually as the projection is further in the future. The Von Foerster model has never been used for projection and forecasting, only for analysis (stable population; it has shown to be very useful in the indirect estimation of demographic parameters and for assessing the impact of international migration on the future population of the receiving country). In addition, the link with APC analysis has never been made explicit. The mathematics is much more complicated (partial differential equations) and beyond reach of most demographers. Consequently, much research remains to be done, but the result is expected to remove a number of methodological issues that trouble statistical agencies and others involved in projection (e.g. period versus cohort perspective, isolation of true age patterns for graduation purposes, etc.). The structure of the Von Foerster model is comparable to this of a time-varying semi-Markov model. This observation may have some very interesting implications for the representation of random variation.

b   Methods for the analysis of demographic time series

A demographic time series is a series of age-specific data on events or rates. Since the future is to some degree a continuation of the past, improved methods for time series analysis may result in better forecasting. The time series methods should be such that the results can easily be integrated in the cohort-component model. Since the Von Foerster-model enables to move along each of the age, period and cohort scales, it provides for the opportunity to directly relate changes in parameter values to age (life course), cohort (historical) and period (concurrent) factors. The time series methods should be able to isolate these factors. The isolation is not only useful in its own right, but is also important if one wishes to parameterize the age schedule. In the past, the age schedule to be parameterized was disturbed by either period or cohort effects since no satisfactory technique was generally available to separate the effects of age, period and cohort. As a result, much attention was paid to find out which effect dominated. If the period effect is dominant, the age profiles measured cross-sectionally exhibits a more regular pattern than the age profiles associated with given cohorts. Consequently, a period perspective is called for. If, on the other hand, differences between cohorts dominate, age profiles measured cross-sectionally may change erratically. A cohort perspective is then more appropriate. If the period and cohort effects are removed from the age schedule, the age profile is insensitive to the perspective adopted. It is this age profile that should be parameterized. The time-dependence of the parameters of the parameterized schedule can be attributed to the effects of differences between periods and cohorts and of their interaction. The period effects dominate in the short run.

c   Use of information on attitudes, expectations and intentions

At the micro-level, life events are outcomes of complex biological and behavioural processes. The study of behavioural processes that precede demographically relevant life events has been very limited in the context of forecasting. The number of events are not predicted on the basis of an in-depth diagnosis of behavioural processes in a sample of people. If information on behavioural processes is collected for the purpose of forecasting, it is usually limited to preferences or expectations about the outcome.

Forecasting may benefit from information on behavioural processes, since increasingly demographic events are results of choice instead of chance. Fertility control is almost perfect. Mortality control is increasing, mainly due to the awareness of risk factors and risk levels. As the significance of life style variables for mortality is growing, as Beeck et al. (1989) suggest in the case of accident mortality, the controllability of the timing of death (age at death) increases, not directly but by the controllability of the risk level. As the controllability of the occurrence of life events and their timing increases, demographic forecasting may benefit from information on whether and when people expect to have a child, to migrate or to change the life style that is considered to affect mortality (risk factors and risk level). Information on expectations and intentions and, to a lesser degree, on attitudes may provide insight in the impact of behavioural processes, in particular the impact of prospective variables, on demographic behaviour. A good recent review of the role of expectations in fertility forecasting is given by Van de Giessen (1988). The review shows that women nowadays seem to be able to provide rather accurate fertility forecasts on the aggregate, much better than twenty years ago. This observation is itself worth further investigation.

The subject of the proposed research is the predictive performance of information on attitudes, expectations and intentions. A theoretical and analytical framework needs to be developed that integrates the factors affecting the formation of expectations and intentions at given stages of a person's life course, and the factors that cause the views to change. The factors include preferences, constraints and information. Several hypotheses should be formulated and tested using sequences of cross-sectional surveys and, if possible, longitudinal data. Birth expectations may be studied using the National Fertility Surveys (GO), migration intentions may be investigated using the Housing Surveys (WBO). Specialized surveys may be used to study the predictive performance of intentions with respect to leaving the parental home and living arrangement. In addition, new data may have to be collected.

d   Predictability of demographic processes

The general tone of this paper has been optimistic: if we understand ongoing processes, we can predict their outcome. This will probably be true in most cases, even if behavioural patterns change significantly. Other authors are less optimistic. Boudon (1986), for instance, suggests that the great number of factors that affect human behaviour makes it unpredictable (see Section 12). Weidlich and Haag (1988, p. 2) take an intermediate position. The behaviour of individuals may be unpredictable, but because individuals do not exist in a vacuum but *interact* with each other, the behaviour of the aggregate (population) is predictable.

The issue of predictability has never been studied in the context of demographic forecasting. The situation is different however in weather forecasting. At the Social Science Research Council Conference on Forecasting in the Social and Natural Sciences in 1984, Somerville presented a paper on the predictability of weather and climate. He states: "In recent years, the concept of predictability has come to be recognized as a central theme of modern theoretical meteorology. ... In principle an adequate theory of predictability provides a description of the best forecast which will ever be possible, one whose skill is restricted only by the intrinsic limitations of the physical system under consideration. Such a predictability theory can thus provide a kind of ideal standard against which the actual present-day skill of real forecasting may be measured. This type of comparison can reveal the extent to which current forecasting methods must be improved for their skill to reach the ultimately attainable level and it may also suggest useful directions of research toward reaching that goal. ... In this way, predictability theory plays a role similar to that of an existence proof, which is not a solution to a mathematical problem, but rather a statement that there is such a solution, and sometimes also a helpful guide to finding it" (Somerville, 1984, p. 1). Weather forecasting may show demographic forecasting how to enhance its transition from being an art to being a science.

e Forecasting with limited data

In actual forecasting, the predictability is frequently not determined by the intrinsic limitations of the system but by the lack of adequate data. This is particularly true in categorical population forecasting, such as the forecasting of minorities and household forecasting. It is also true in international migration forecasting and the forecasting of Third World populations. Since there is a general consensus that the Netherlands will remain an immigration country, the forecasting of international migration and of the population size and composition of the sending countries is likely to become an essential component of the forecasting of the population of the Netherlands. With the borders in Europe disappearing, the size of Europe in the world population declining, the graying of Europe and the rapid population growth in North and Central Africa, our ability to forecast the size and the composition of the population in the Netherlands may one day very much depend on our ability to forecast the size and composition of the population in Europe and sending countries in the Third World. To develop that ability, methods need to be developed to accurately forecast population and demographic events when data are limited. It may also be useful to establish a data bank.

Recent research following the Preston and Coale (1982) analysis of the Von Foerster model indicates that the Preston-Coale analysis, which became known as the 'variable r method', may provide a unifying framework for the indirect estimation of many demographic parameters. Parallel to the development of the next generation of the cohort-component model (see a), estimation methods should be developed for limited data situations. The state-of-the-art of the research on methods for the indirect estimation of demographic parameters in the context of forecasting has not been reviewed in this paper. Reviews are provided by the United Nations (1983, 1984). Al-Aukyli and Masser (1985) illustrate the preparation of population projections in case of limited data. Willekens (1982b) reviews methods that may be of use when categorical (multistate) population projections need to be prepared with incomplete data. Nair (1985) and Ramachandran (1988) apply some of the techniques in a Third World context.

References

Ahlburg, D.A. (1982), How accurate are the U.S. Bureau of the census projections of total live births?, *Journal of Forecasting*, 1, pp. 365-374.

Ahlburg, D.A. (1987), Population forecasting, in: S. Makridakis and S.C. Wheelwright, eds., *The handbook of forecasting*, second edition, New York: Wiley, pp. 135-149.

Akkerman, A. (1985), The household-composition matrix as a notion in multiregional forecasting of population and households, *Environment and Planning A*, Vol. 17, no. 3, pp. 355-371.

Al-Aukyli, H. and I. Masser (1985), The development of a data base for national population projections in Iraq, *Population Bulletin of ECWA*, no. 26, pp. 63-92.

Alderson, M. and F. Ashwood (1985), Projection of mortality rates for the elderly, *Population Trends*, no. 42, pp. 22-29.

Alho, J.M. and B.D. Spincer (1985), Uncertain population forecasting, *Journal of the American Statistical Association*, 80 (390), pp. 306-314.

Alonso, W. (1978), A theory of movements, in: N.M. Hansen, ed., *Human settlement systems*, Cambridge, Mass.: Ballinger, pp. 197-211.

Armitage, R.I. (1986), Population projections for English local authority areas, *Population Trends*, no. 43, pp. 31-40.

Armstrong, J.S. (1985), *Long range forecasting: from crystall ball to computer*, second edition, New York: Wiley.

Arthur, W.B. and J.W. Vaupel (1984), Some general relationship in population dynamics, *Population Index*, Vol. 50, no. 2, pp. 214-226.

Bartlema, J.D. (1988), *Developments in kinship support networks for the aged in the Netherlands*, Tilburg, Katholieke Universiteit Brabant, 1987, 302 pp. (reeks Sociale Zekerheidswetenschap; nr. 3), Ph.D. Dissertation, Tilburg.

Bates, J. (1982), *Developing the migration component of the official sub-national population projections*, Final report prepared by Martin Voorhees Associates for DPRP3 Division of the Department of the Environment, London.

Bates, J. and I. Bracken (1987), Migration age profiles for local authority areas in England, 1971-81, *Environment and Planning A*, Vol. 19, pp. 521-536.

Baydar, N. (1984), *Issues in multiregional demographic forecasting*, Ph.D. Dissertation, Vrije Universiteit, Brussels.

Beeck, E.F. van, J.P Machenbach, G.J. van Oortmarssen, J.J.M. Barendregt, J.D.F. Habbema and P.J. van der Maas (1989), Scenarios for the future development of accident mortality in the Netherlands, *Health Policy*, Vol. 2, pp. 1-13.

Beer, J. de (1985), A time series model for cohort data, *Journal of the American Statistical Association*, Vol. 80, no. 391, pp. 525-530.

Beer, J. de (1988a), *Methods of fertility projections*, Paper presented at the International Workshop on National Population Projections in Industrialized Countries, October 1988, Voorburg, the Netherlands.

Beer, J. de (1988b), *Time series models for forecasting fertility*, Paper presented at the International Workshop on National Population Projections in Industrialized Countries, October 1988, Voorburg, the Netherlands.

Bell, W.R. (1988), *Applying time-series models in forecasting age-specific fertility rates*, Paper presented at the International Workshop on National Population Projections in Industrialized Countries, October 1988, Voorburg, the Netherlands.

Bell, W.R., J.F. Long, R.B. Miller and P.A. Thompson (1988), *Multivariate time series projections of parameterized age-specific fertility rates*, Research Report No. 88/16, Statistical Research Division, U.S. Bureau of the Census, Washington, D.C.

Berkien, J. and N.W. Keilman (1988), *The interdependence of migration and household dynamics: a multidimensional approach*, Paper presented at the workshop on "Multistate Demography: Measurement, Analysis, Forecasting", Zeist, the Netherlands.

Bernstein, P.L. and T.H. Silbert (1984), Are economic forecasters worth listening to?, *Harvard Business Review*, Vol. 62, no. 5, pp. 32-40.

Bongaarts, J. (1987), The projection of family composition over the life course with family status life tables, in: J. Bongaarts, T. Burch and K. Wachter, eds., *Family demography*, Oxford: Clarendon Press, pp. 189-212.

Bongaarts, J. (1988), *Modelling the spread of HIV and the demographic impact of AIDS in Africa*, Working Paper no. 140, Center for Policy Studies, The Population Council, New York.

Bongaarts, J., T. Burch and K. Wachter, eds. (1987), *Family demography. Methods and their applications*, Oxford: Clarendon Press.

Bonneuil, N. (1989), Conjoncture et structure dans le comportement de fécondité, *Population*, Vol. 44, no. 1, pp. 135-157.

Boudon, R. (1986), *Theories of social change: A critical appraisal*, Cambridge: Polity Press.

Brass, W. (1971), On the scale of mortality, in: W. Brass, ed., *Biological aspects of demography*, London: Taylor and Francis, pp. 69-111.

Brass, W. (1974), Perspectives in population prediction: illustrated by the statistics of England and Wales, *Journal of the Royal Statistical Society A*, Vol. 137, pp. 532-583.

Brouwer, J., H.E. Gordijn and H.R. Heida (1984), Toward unravelling the interdependency between migration and housing stock development: a policy model, in: H. ter Heide and F.J. Willekens, eds., *Demographic research and spatial policy. The Dutch experience*, London: Academic Press, pp. 287-307.

Cannan, E. (1895), The probability of cessation of the growth of population in England and Wales during the next century, *Economic Journal*, Vol. 5, pp. 505-515.

Carter, L.R. and R.D. Lee (1986), Joint forecasts of U.S. marital fertility, nuptiality, births and marriages using time series models, *Journal of the American Statistical Association*, Vol. 81, pp. 902-911.

Cohen, J.E. (1985), *Mathematical demography: Recent developments in population projections*, Paper presented at the IUSSP International Population Conference, Florence, June 1985.

Cohen, J.E. (1986), Population forecasts and confidence intervals for Sweden: a comparison of model-based and empirical approaches, *Demography*, Vol. 23, no. 1, pp. 105-126.

Corner, I.E. (1987), Household projection models, *Journal of Forecasting*, Vol. 6, pp. 271-284.

Cruijsen, H.G.J.M. and W.D. van Hoorn (1983), Prognose 1980, een gevoeligheidsanalyse van het rekenmodel, *Maandstatistiek van de Bevolking*, Vol. 31, no. 12, pp. 20-30.

Cruijsen, H.G.J.M. and N.W. Keilman (1984), *Prognose van de bevolking van Nederland na 1980*, Deel 2: Modelbouw en hypothesevorming, The Hague: Staatsuitgeverij.

Cruijsen, H.G.J.M. and N.W.Keilman (1989), *National population forecasts in industrialized countries: Main findings of an international workshop*, Paper prepared for the Conference of European Statisticians Seminar on Demographic Projections, September 1989, Balatonöszöd, Hungary.

Dinkel, R.H. (1985), The seeming paradox of increasing mortality in a highly industrialized nation: the example of the Soviet Union, *Population Studies*, Vol. 39, pp. 87-97.

Drewe, P. and H.M. Rodgers (1976), *Interregionale migratie en spreidingsbeleid*, Deelrapport 2: Onderzoek naar vooruitberekeningsmodellen voor de interregionale migratie in Nederland, Instituut voor Stedebouwkundig Onderzoek, Technische Hogeschool Delft, Memorandum no. 13.

Drewe, P. and H.J. Rosenboom (1987), *Trendrapport binnenlandse migratie*, Intern Rapport no. 49, The Hague: NIDI.

Drewe, P., L. Eichperger, N.W. Keilman, F.W.A. van Poppel and F.J. Willekens (1988), *Multiregional population projection in the Netherlands*, Paper presented at the workshop on "Mulstistate Demography: Measurement, Analysis, Forecasting", Zeist, the Netherlands.

Eichperger, C.L. (1984), Regional population forecasts: approaches and issues, in: H. ter Heide and F.J. Willekens, eds., *Demographic research and spatial policy. The Dutch experience*, London: Academic Press, pp. 235-252.

Ermisch, J. (1988), *Explanatory models for fertility projections*, Paper presented at the International Workshop on national Population Projections in Industrialized Countries, October 1988, Voorburg, the Netherlands.

Espenshade, T.J. (1985), *Multistate projections of population by age and marital status*, Proceedings, International Population Conference of IUSSP, Florence, Vol. 4, pp. 151-162.

Ewbank, D.C., J.C. Gomez de Leon and M.A. Stoto (1983), A reducible four-parameter system of model life table, *Population Studies*, Vol. 37, no. 1, pp. 105-127.

Feeney, G. (1985), *Parity progression projection*, Proceedings, International Population Conference Florence, Vol. 4, pp. 125-136. Liege: IUSSP.

Feichtinger, G. (1971), *Stochastische Modelle demographischer Prozesse*, Lecture Notes in Operations Research and Mathematical Systems no. 44, Berlin: Springer-Verlag.

Foerster, H. von (1959), Some remarks on changing populations, in: F. Stohlman, ed., *The kinetics of cellular proliferations*, New York: Greene and Stratton.

Galler, H. (1988), Microsimulation of household formation and dissolution, in: N.W. Keilman, A.C. Kuijsten and A.P. Vossen, eds., *Modelling household formation and dissolution*, Oxford: Clarendon Press, pp. 139-159.

George, M.V. and J. Perrault (1988), *Methods of projecting external migration*, Paper International Workshop on National Population Projections in Industrialized Countries, October 1988, Voorburg, the Netherlands.

Gibberd, R. (1981), Aggregation of population projection models, in: A. Rogers, ed., *Advances in multiregional demography*, Research Report RR-81-6, Laxenburg: International Institute for Applied Systems Analysis, pp. 177-193.

Giessen, H. van de (1988), *Using birth expectations information in national population forecasts*, Paper presented at the international workshop on National Population Projections in Industrialized Countries, October 1988, Voorburg, the Netherlands.

Gill, R. (1988), *Multistate life tables and regression models*, Paper presented at the workshop on "Multistate Demography: Measurement, Analysis, Forecasting", Zeist, the Netherlands.

Gill, R.D. and N.W. Keilman (1989), On the estimation of multidimensional demographic models with population registration data, *Mathematical Population Studies*, Vol. 2, no. 2.

Gordijn, H.E., H.R. Heida and H. ter Heide (1984), Monitoring migration and population redistribution, in: H. ter Heide and F. Willekens, eds., *Demographic research and spatial policy. The Dutch experience*, London: Academic Press, pp. 95-110.

Heida, H. and H. Gordijn (1985), *Het PRIMOS-huishoudensmodel; analyse en prognose van de huishoudensontwikkeling in Nederland*, The Hague: Ministerie van Volkshuisvesting, Ruimtelijke Ordening en Milieu.

Heide, H. ter (1981), *Demographic distribution functions*, Paper contributed to the 19th General Population Conference of the IUSSP, Manila.

Heligman, L. and J.H. Pollard (1980), The age pattern of mortality, *Journal of the Institute of Actuaries*, Vol. 107, pp. 49-80.

Hobcraft, J. and R.J.A. Little (1984), Fertility exposure analysis: a new method for assessing the contribution of proximate determinants to fertility differentials, *Population Studies*, Vol. 38, no. 1, pp. 21-42.

Hoem, J.M. (1973), Levels of errors in population forecasts, *Artikler fra Statistisk Sentralbyrå*, nr. 61, Oslo.

Hoem, J.M., D. Madsen, D. Nielsen and E.-M. Ohlsen (1981), Experiments in modelling recent Danish fertility curves, *Demography*, Vol. 18, pp. 231-244.

Holmberg, I. (1987), Household change and housing needs: a forecasting model, in: J. Bongaarts, T. Burch and K. Wachter, eds., *Family demography*, Oxford: Clarendon Press, pp. 327-341.

Hooimeyer, P. and M.A.J. Linde (1988), *Vergrijzing, individualisering en de woningmarkt. Het WODYN simulatiemodel*, Utrecht: Elinkwijk (Ph.D. Dissertation).

Huddleston, J.V. (1983), Population dynamics with age- and time-dependent birth and death rates, *Bulletin of Mathematical Biology*, Vol. 45, no. 5, pp. 827-836.

Imhoff, E. van (1988), *A general characterization of consistency algorithms in multidimensional demographic projection models*, Paper presented at the workshop on "Multistate Demography: Measurement, Analysis, Forecasting", Zeist, the Netherlands.

Imhoff, E. van (1989), The exponential multidimensional demographic projection model, *Mathematical Population Studies*.

Imhoff, E. van, and N.W. Keilman (1989), *Current and future dynamics in the living arrangements of the elderly: with an application to the Netherlands*, Paper presented at the International Population Conference "Aging of population in developed countries", Prague.

Janssen, A.J.M. (1988), Gemodelleerde vruchtbaarheidspatronen in de vooruitberekening van geboortenaantallen, in: G.A.B. Frinking and J.H.M. Nelissen, eds., *Ontgroening in Nederland*, Amersfoort/ Leuven: Acco, pp. 106-124.

Jong, P.M. de (1985), *Prediction intervals for missing figures in migration tables*, Ph.D. Dissertation, University of Groningen, Groningen, the Netherlands.

Keilman, N.W. (1983), Bevolkingsprognoses en onzekerheid, *NIDI-bulletin Demografie*, 49, pp. 1-4.

Keilman, N.W. (1985a), Internal and external consistency in multidimensional population projection models, *Environment and Planning A*, Vol. 17, pp. 1473-1498.

Keilman, N.W. (1985b), Nuptiality models and the two-sex problem in national population forecasts, *European Journal of Population*, Vol. 1, pp. 207-235.

Keilman, N.W. (1988), Dynamic household models, in: N.W. Keilman, A.C. Kuijsten and A.P. Vossen, eds., *Modelling household formation and dissolution*, Oxford: Clarendon Press, pp. 123-138.

Keilman, N.W. and J. van Dam (1987), *A dynamic household model: an application of multidimensional demography to life styles in the Netherlands*, The Hague: NIDI.

Keilman, N.W. and D. Manting (1987), *Trendrapport regionale vruchtbaarheid*, Intern Rapport no. 52, The Hague, NIDI.

Keilman, N.W. and N. Keyfitz (1988), Recurrent issues in dynamic household modelling, in: N.W. Keilman, A.C. Kuijsten and A.P. Vossen, eds., *Modelling household formation and dissolution*, Oxford: Clarendon Press, pp. 254-285.

Keilman, N.W., A.C. Kuijsten and A.P. Vossen, eds. (1988), *Modelling household formation and dissolution*, Oxford: Clarendon Press.

Keyfitz, N. (1968), *Introduction to the mathematics of population*, Reading, Mass.: Addison-Wesley.

Keyfitz, N. (1972), On future population, *Journal of the American Statistical Association*, Vol. 67, no. 338, pp. 347-363.

Keyfitz, N. (1977), *Applied mathematical demography*, New York: Wiley.

Keyfitz, N. (1979), How demographers know the present and forecast the future, in: *Institut de la Vie/IUSSP, Population science in the service of mankind*, Institut de la Vie/IUSSP, pp. 117-141.

Keyfitz, N. (1981), The limits of population forecasting, *Population and Development Review*, Vol. 7, no. 4, pp. 579-593.

Keyfitz, N. (1982a), Can knowledge improve forecasts?, *Population and Development Review*, Vol. 8, no. 8, pp. 729-751.

Keyfitz, N. (1982b), Choice of function for mortality analysis: effective forecasting depends on a minimum parameter representation, *Theoretical Population Biology*, Vol. 21, pp. 329-352. Reprinted in: J. Vallin, J.H. Pollard and L. Heligman, eds., *Methodologies for the collection and analysis of mortality data*, Liege: Ordina Editions (for IUSSP), 1984, pp. 225-243.

Keyfitz, N. (1985a), *Applied mathematical demography*, second edition, New York: Springer-Verlag.

Keyfitz, N. (1985b), A probability representation of future population, *Zeitschrift für Bevölkerungwissenschaft*, Vol. 11, no. 2, pp. 179-191.

Keyfitz, N. (1987), Form and substance in family demography, in: J. Bongaarts, T. Burch and K. Wachter, eds., *Family demography*, Oxford: Clarendon Press, pp. 3-16.

Kono, S. (1987), The headship rate method for projecting households, in: J. Bongaarts, T. Burch and K. Wachter, eds., *Family demography*, Oxford: Clarendon Press, pp. 287-308.

Kuhry, B. and J. Passenier (1986), *SKILL: a forecasting model for education and labour supply*, European Community Symposium, Selecta Reeks, The Hague: Stichting voor Onderzoek van het Onderwijs.

Kuijsten, A.C. (1986), Advances in family demography, *Publications of the NIDI and the CBGS*, Vol. 14. The Hague: NIDI.

Kupiszewski, M. (1988), *Accuracy of the Polish single- and multiregional demographic forecasts and projections*, Paper presented at the workshop on "Multistate Demography: Measurement, Analysis, Forecasting", Zeist, the Netherlands.

Land, K.L. (1985), *Methods for national population forecasts: a critical review*, Proceedings, First Annual Research Conference, U.S. Bureau of the Census, Washington D.C., pp. 251-270. Revised version published as "Methods of national population forecasts: a review", *Journal of the American Statistical Association*, Vol. 81, no. 396, pp. 888-901.

Ledent, J. (1986), Forecasting interregional migration: an economic-demographic approach, in: A.M. Isserman, ed., *Population change and the economy: social science theories and models*, Dordrecht: Kluwer-Nijhoff Publ., pp. 53-77.

Ledent, J., Y. Péron and D. Marissette (1986), *Dossier de recherche relatif à l'elaboration d'un modèle de projection des ménages et des familles*, Cahiers Techniques, Bureau de la Statistique du Québec, Québec.

Lee, A. (1966), A theory of migration, *Demography*, Vol. 3, pp. 47-57.

Lee, R.D. (1974), Forecasting births in a post-transition population: stochastic renewal with serially correlated fertility, *Journal of the American Statistical Association*, Vol. 70, pp. 607-617.

Lee, R.D. (1978), New methods for fertility forecasting: an overview, *Population Bulletin of the United Nations*, no. 11, pp. 6-11.

Lee, R.D. (1980), Aiming at a moving target: period fertility and changing reproductive goals, *Population Studies*, Vol. 24, pp. 205-226.

Lee, R.D. (1981), Comment on McDonald's (1981) paper, *Journal of the American Statistical Association*, Vol. 76, pp. 793-795.

Leslie, P.H. (1945), On the use of matrices in certain population mathematics, *Biometrika*, Vol. 33, pp. 183-212

Leslie, P.H. (1948), Some further notes on the use of matrices in population mathematics, *Biometrika*, Vol. 35, pp. 213-245.

Liaw, K-L. (1986), Spatial population dynamics, in: A. Rogers and F. Willekens, eds., *Migration and settlement. A multiregional comparative study*, Dordrecht: Reidel Publ. Co., pp. 419-455.

Linke, W. (1988), The headship rate approach in modelling households: the case of the Federal Republic of Germany, in: N.W. Keilman, A.C. Kuijsten and A.P. Vossen, eds., *Modelling household formation and dissolution*, Oxford: Clarendon Press, pp. 108-122.

Long, J.F. (1984), U.S. national population projection methods: a view from four forecasting traditions, *Insurance: Mathematics and Economics*, Vol. 3.

Long, J.F. (1985), *Integrating multiple forecasting traditions in the Census Bureau's national population projections methodology*, Proceedings, First Annual Research Conference, U.S. Bureau of the Census, Washington D.C., pp. 237-250.

Long, J.F. (1987), *The accuracy of population projection methods at the U.S. Census Bureau*, paper Population Association of America, Annual Meeting Chicago, 29 April – 2 May 1987.

Long, J.F. (1988), *Disaggregation in multiregional population projection: how far should we go?*, Paper presented at the workshop "Multistate Demography: Measurement, Analysis, Forecasting", Zeist, the Netherlands.

Los, M. (1979), *Discrete choice modelling and disequilibrium in land use and transportation planning*, Centre de Recherche sur les Transports, Université de Montréal, Montréal.

Mackenbach, J.P. (1988), *Mortality and medical care*, Ph.D. Dissertation, Erasmus University, Rotterdam.

Makridakis, S. and S.C. Wheelwright (1979), Forecasting: framework and overview, in: S. Makridakis and S.C. Wheelwright, eds., *Forecasting* (TIMS Studies in the Management Sciences, Vol. 12), Amsterdam: North-Holland, pp. 1-15.

Manton, K.G. and E. Stallard (1984), *Recent trends in mortality analysis*, San Diego: Academic Press.

Manton, K.G. (1985), Models for forecasting morbidity, in: K.L. Land and S.H. Schneider, eds. (1986), *Forecasting in the social and natural sciences*, Boston: Reidel Publ. Co.

Manton, K.G. (no date; about 1988), *A review and assessment of models for forecasting health status and life expectancy changes in the elderly population*.

Mason, W.M and S.E. Fienberg, eds. (1985), *Cohort analysis in social research*, New York: Springer-Verlag.

McDonald, J. (1981), Modeling demographic relationships: an analysis of forecast functions for Australian births, *Journal of the American Statistical Association*, Vol. 76, no. 376, pp. 782-801.

McKendrick (1926), Application of mathematics to medical problems, *Proceedings of Edinburgh Mathematical Society*, Vol. 44, pp. 98-130.

McNown, R. and A. Rogers (1988), *Time series analysis and forecasting of parameterized model schedules: mortality*, Working Paper 88-2, Population Program, Institute of Behavioral Science, University of Colorado, Boulder, Colorado.

Miller, R.B. (1986), A bivariate model for total fertility rate and mean age of childbearing, *Insurance: Mathematics and Economics*, Vol. 5, pp. 133-140.

Miller, R.B., P. Thompson, W. Bell and J.F. Long (1985), *Forecasting graduated age-specific fertility rates*, Proceedings, First Annual Research Conference, U.S. Bureau of the Census, Washington D.C., pp. 271-287.

Montgomery, M.B., P.P.L. Cheung and D.B. Sulak (1988), Rates of courtship and first marriage in Thailand, *Population Studies*, Vol. 42, pp. 375-388.

Mortensen, D.T. (1986), Job search and labor market analysis, in: O. Ashenfelter and R. Layard, eds., *Handbook of labor economics*, Vol. II, Amsterdam: North-Holland, pp. 849-919.

Murphy, M.J. (1980), *Extrapolation of current trends for forecasting population*, Working Paper no. 80-2, Centre for Population Studies, London School for Hygiene and Tropical Medicine, University of London, London.

Nair, P.S. (1985), Estimation of period-specific gross migration flows from limited data, *Demography*, Vol. 22, pp. 133-142.

Nam, C.B. (1979), The progress of demography as a scientific discipline, *Demography*, Vol. 16, pp. 485-492.

Nelissen, J.H.M. (1983), Een economisch verklaringsmodel voor de migratie van en naar Nederland, *Economisch Statistische Berichten*, Vol. 68, no. 3412, pp. 601-604.

Nelissen, J.H.M. and A.P. Vossen (1983), *Een bevolkingsprognosemodel voor de korte termijn*, NPDO-Onderzoeksrapport no. 16, Voorburg: Nationaal Programma voor Demografisch Onderzoek.

Nelissen, J.H.M. and A.P. Vossen (1988), *Applying a microsimulation model to project the future structure of families and households*, Paper presented at the IIASA Conference on Future Changes in Population Age Structures, Sopron, Hungary.

Nooten, W.N. van (1985), *Mortaliteitsonderzoek. Gebruik van log-lineaire modellen voor de analyse van trends in sterfte bij een elftal doodsoorzaken*, Leiden: Nederlands Instituut voor Preventieve Gezondheidszorg.

Olshansky, S.J. (1988), On forecasting mortality, *The Milbank Quarterly*, Vol. 66, no. 3, pp. 482-530.

Op 't Veld, A., E. Bijlsma and J. Starmans (1984), Explanatory analysis of interregional migration in the nineteen-seventies, in: H. ter Heide and F.J. Willekens, eds., *Demographic research and spatial policy. The Dutch experience*, London: Academic Press, pp. 171-200.

Orcutt, G., S. Caldwell and R. Wertheimer III (1976), *Policy exploration though microanalytic simulation*, Washington D.C.: The Urban Institute.

Page, H.J. (1977), Patterns underlying fertility schedules: a decomposition by both age and marital duration, *Population Studies*, Vol. 31, pp. 85-106.

Petrioli, L. (1975), *Modelli di mortalita. Quaderni dell'Istituto di Statictica*, Universita degli Studi di Siena, Facolta do Scienze Economiche e Bancarie, no. 17.

Petrioli, L. (1988), Tables types de mortalité à l'usage des pays en voie de développement, in: J. Vallin, S. D'Souza and A. Palloni, eds., *Mesure et analyse de la mortalité. Nouvelles approches*, Paris: Presses Universitaires de France (for INED and IUSSP), pp. 179-196.

Pflaumer, P. (1984), Die Berücksichtigung der Unsicherheit bei der zukünftigen Entwicklung der Bevölkerung und der Rentenbeitragsätze in der Bundesrepublik Deutschland, *Zeitschrift für Bevölkerungwissenschaft*, Vol. 10, no. 4, pp. 501-530.

Pflaumer, P. (1986), Stochastische Bevölkerungsmodelle zur Analyse der Auswirkungen demographischer Prozesse auf die Systeme der sozialen Sicherung, *Algemeines Statistisches Archiv*, 70, pp. 52-74.

Pitkin, J.R. and G.S. Masnick (1987), The relationship between heads and non-heads in the household population: an extension of the headship rate method, in: J. Bongaarts, T. Burch and K. Wachter, eds., *Family demography*, Oxford: Clarendon Press, pp. 309-326.

Pittenger, D.B. (1976), *Projecting state and local populations*, Cambridge, Mass.: Ballinger Publ. Co.

Pollard, J.H. (1966), On the use of the direct matrix product in analyzing certain stochastic population models, *Biometrika*, 53, 397-415.

Pollard, J.H. (1987), Projection of age-specific mortality rates, *Population Bulletin of the United Nations*, Nos. 21/22, pp. 55-69.

Poppel, F.W.A. van (1987), *Trendrapport regionale sterfte*, Intern Rapport nr. 50, The Hague: NIDI.

Preston, S.H. and A.J. Coale (1982), Age structure, growth, attrition and accession: a new synthesis, *Population Index*, Vol. 48, no. 2, pp. 217-259.

Ramachandran, P. (1988), *Subnational population projections for India: the use of incomplete data*, Ph.D. Dissertation, Sri Venkateswara University, Tirupati, India.

Rees, Ph. (1986), Choices in the construction of regional population projections, in: R. Woods and Ph. Rees, eds., *Population structures and models. Developments in spatial demography*, London: Allen and Unwin, pp. 126-159.

Rees, Ph. and F.J. Willekens (1986), *How the Dutch and the English adopted multiregional models for subnational population projection*, Working Paper no. 472, School of Geography, University of Leeds.

Reeves, J.H. (1987), Projection of number of kin, in: J. Bongaarts, T. Burch and K. Wachter, eds., *Family demography. Methods and their applications*, Oxford: Clarendon Press, pp. 228-248.

Rima, A. and L.J.G. van Wissen (1987), *A dynamic household model of household relocation. A case study for the Amsterdam region*, Amsterdam: Free University Press (Ph.D. Dissertation).

Rodriguez, G. and J. Cleland (1988), Modelling marital fertility by age and duration: an empirical appraisal of the Page model, *Population Studies*, Vol. 42, pp. 241-257.

Rogers, A. (1968), *Matrix analysis of interregional population growth and distribution*, Berkeley: University of Calfornia Press.

Rogers, A. (1975), *Introduction to multiregional mathematical demography*, New York: Wiley.

Rogers, A. (1976), Shrinking large-scale population projection models by aggregation and decomposition, *Environment and Planning A*, Vol. 8, pp. 515-541.

Rogers, A. (1985), *Regional population projection models*, Beverly Hills: Sage Publications.

Rogers, A. (1986), Parameterized multistate population dynamics and projections, *Journal of the American Statistical Association*, Vol. 81, pp. 48-61.

Rogers, A. (1988), *Parameterized multistate forecasting models of population dynamics: a time series approach*, Paper presented at the workshop on "Multistate Demography: Measurement, Analysis, Forecasting", Zeist, the Netherlands.

Rogers, A. and L. Castro (1981), *Model migration schedules*, Research Report RR-81-30, Laxenburg: International Institute for Applied Systems Analysis, Reprinted in A. Rogers (1984), Migration, urbanization and spatial population dynamics, Boulder: Westview Press, pp. 41-91.

Rogers, A. and L. Castro (1984), Age patterns of migration: cause-specific profiles, in: A. Rogers, *Migration, urbanization and spatial population dynamics*, Boulder: Westview Press, pp. 92-126.

Rogerson, P.A. (1983), Comparisons of aggregate variable forecasting using aggregate and disaggregate models, *Socio-economic Planning Sciences*, Vol. 17, pp. 373-380.

Schoen, R. (1988), *Modeling multigroup populations*, New York: Plenum Press.

Schreurs, R. (1989), *Een beschrijvende analyse van de trefzekerheid van nationale bevolkingsprognoses*, NIDI-rapport nr. 2.

Schweder, T. (1971), The precision of population projections studied by multiple prediction methods, *Demography*, Vol. 8, no. 4, pp. 441-450.

Sharpe, F.R. and A.J. Lotka (1911), A problem in age-distribution, *Philosophical Magazine*, Ser. 6, Vol. 21, pp. 435-438.

Somerville, R.C.J. (1984), *The predictability of weather and climate*, Paper presented at the Social Science Research Council Conference on Forecasting in the Social and Natural Sciences, Boulder, Colorado, June 1984.

Stoto, M.A. (1983), The accuracy of population projections, *Journal of the American Statistical Association*, Vol. 78, no. 381, pp. 13-20.

Sykes, Z.M. (1969), Some stochastic versions of the matrix model for population dynamics, *Journal of the American Statistical Association*, Vol. 64, pp. 111-130.

United Nations (1983), Indirect techniques for demographic estimation, Manual X, *Population Studies*, no. 81, New York: United Nations.

United Nations (1984), Population projections: methodology of the United Nations, *Population Studies*, no. 83, New York: United Nations.

United Nations (1987), The prospects of world urbanization. Revised as of 1984-85, *Population Studies*, no. 101, New York: United Nations.

United Nations (1989), Integrating population variables into development planning, Manual XI, *Population Division*, New York: United Nations.

Vianen, H.A.W. van (1983), Het logit model van sterftetafels toegelicht aan de daling van de sterfte in Nederland van 1900-1979, in: S. Lindenberg and F.N. Stokman, eds., *Modellen in de sociologie*, Deventer: Van Loghum Slaterus, pp. 304-315.

Vossen, A.P. (1988), *De bevolkingvooruitberekening*, Ph.D. Dissertation, Katholieke Universiteit Brabant, Tilburg.

Wachter, K.W., and R.D.Lee (1989), U.S. Births and limit cycle models, *Demography*, Vol. 26, no. 1, pp. 99-115.

Weidlich, W. and G. Haag, eds. (1988), *Interregional migration. Dynamic theory and comparative analysis*, Berlin: Springer-Verlag.

Werner, B. and S. Chalk (1986), Projections of first, second, third and later births, *Population Trends*, no. 46, pp. 26-34

Wetrogan, S.I. (1988a), *Multiregional population projection in the USA*, Paper presented at the workshop on "Multistate Demography: Measurement, Analysis, Forecasting", Zeist, the Netherlands.

Wetrogan, S.I. (1988b), *Projections of the population of states by age, sex, and race: 1988 to 2010*, Current Population Reports, Series P-25, no. 1017, U.S. Bureau of the Census, Washington D.C.: U.S. Government Printing Office.

Whelpton, P.K. (1936), An empirical method of calculating future populations, *Journal of the American Statistical Association*, Vol. 31, pp. 457-473.

Whelpton, P.K. (1947), *Forecasting of the population of the United States 1945-1975*, Washington, D.C.: U.S. Government Printing Office.

Willekens, F.J. (1982a), Identification and measurement of spatial population movements, in: ESCAP, National migration surveys, Manual X: *Guidelines for analysis*, New York: United Nations, pp. 74-97.

Willekens, F.J. (1982b), Multidimensional population analysis with incomplete data, in: K.C. Land and A. Rogers, eds., *Multidimensional mathematical demography*, New York: Academic Press, pp. 43-111.

Willekens, F.J. (1984a), *Een multiregionaal demografisch voortuitberekeningsmodel voor Nederland*, Onderzoeksrapport van het NIDI aan de Rijksplanologische Dienst, Voorburg: NIDI.

Willekens, F.J. (1984b), *Population forecasting*, Paper presented at the International Symposium on Forecasting, London.

Willekens, F.J. (1984c), Spatial policies and demographic research opportunities, in: H. ter Heide and F.J. Willekens, eds., *Demographic research and spatial policy. The Dutch experience*, London: Academic Press, pp. 355-401.

Willekens, F.J. (1985a), *Migration forecasting*, Paper presented at the Annual Meeting of the Population Association of America, Boston.

Willekens, F.J. (1985b), *Improving national population projection methodology*, Discussion, Proceedings, First Annual Research Conference, U.S. Bureau of the Census, Washington D.C., pp. 288-297.

Willekens, F.J. (1988a), A life course perspective on household dynamics, in: N.W. Keilman, A.C. Kuijsten and A.P. Vossen, eds., *Modelling household formation and dissolution*, Oxford: Clarendon Press, pp. 87-107.

Willekens, F.J. (1988b), *The impact on births, deaths and migrations of demographic rates and population size and composition. An introduction to exposure analysis*, Paper presented at the IIASA Conference on Future Changes in Population Age Structure, Sopron, September.

Willekens, F.J. and N. Baydar (1983), *Multidimensional forecasting. A systems approach*, Working Paper no. 40. Voorburg: NIDI.

Willekens, F.J. and P. Drewe (1984), A multiregional model for regional demographic projection, in: H. ter Heide and F.J. Willekens, eds., *Demographic research and spatial policy. The Dutch experience*, London: Academic Press, pp. 309-334.

Willekens, F.J. and N. Baydar (1986), Forecasting place-to-place migration with generalized linear models, in: R. Woods and Ph. Rees, eds., *Population structures and models. Developments in spatial demography*, London: Allen and Unwin, pp. 203-244.

Willekens, F.J. and F.W.A. van Poppel (1986), *Prognose van sterftes naar doodsoorzaak*, Memo, The Hague: NIDI

Willekens, F.J. and S. Wetrogan (1987), *The application of multiregional models for subnational population projections*, Paper presented at the North American Meeting of the Regional Science Association, Cleveland, Ohio.

Willekens, F.J., F.W.A. van Poppel, N.W. Keilman, Ch. Eichperger and P. Drewe (1988), *MUDEA-prognoses van de bevolking van de COROP gebieden en de vier grote steden*, The Hague: Physical Planning Agency.

Zaba, B. (1979), The four-parameter logit life table system, *Population Studies*, Vol. 33, no. 1, pp. 79-100.

Zeng Yi (1987), *Family status life table: an extension of Bongaarts' nuclear family model*, Working Paper no. 70, NIDI, The Hague.

Emerging Issues in Demographic Research
C.A. Hazeu and G.A.B. Frinking (Editors)
© Elsevier Science Publishers B.V. , 1990

Chapter 3

DEMOGRAPHIC FORECASTING: STATE OF THE ART AND RESEARCH NEEDS; A COMMENT

Nathan Keyfitz

Willekens has provided a masterly summary of where we stand on forecasting, and the directions in which we might move to do better. His thesis is that most present forecasting is extrapolation, without any pretense of understanding the underlying mechanisms; real advance from where we are now can only be based on deeper understanding.

The first of these two statements, that what is now done is extrapolation, represents present work at its best, may even be flattering to some present work. Much of what is published is one level down from that: the application of arbitrary assumptions. Taking it that the birth rate now at 1.5 children per woman will gradually move up towards replacement cannot be valled extrapolation. Yet extrapolation of birth rates that have fallen from replacement to 1.5 children in the course of half a generation, would lead to no children at all in the course of 1 1/2 further generations, and such a forecast would be totally unacceptable.

It is thus argued that the arbitrary assumption of reversion to replacement is better than extrapolation, that is does contain a theory – that replacement is the normal condition, and all that we see is temporary departures from it. Such a theory has little support in observation, but neither is there evidence against it.

My own view is that the kind of theory that will enable us to say what the birth rate will be should include such elements as the disposition of women to take their place in the labour force; the prevalence of divorce (whose danger for any particular couple is a serious discouragement to childbearing – it would leave at least one member of the couple seriously handicapped for subsequent work or remarriage); the competition of ways of using leisure time inconsistent with raising children. The trend of these has been such that we could have forecast the present low birth rates, but did not do so. One reason is that timing of such tendencies is very hard to establish. One can have a perfectly good theory with all the factors in place, but if their incidence can vary by a quarter century or so the theory is useless for forecasting to the horizons usally required.

Research needs

The Willekens paper is optimistic, in the sense that it sees the shortcomings of past forecasting efforts as corrected by research. This reviewer is less hopeful.

Consider the use of childbearing intentions. It was said thirty or more years ago, if one wants to know how many children will be born, why not ask the women who will bear them what their plans are? That is what is done to find the demand for washing machines or houses. But results have been disappointing in respect of children.

For one thing births more than five years in the future will mostly be to women not yet married, and asking girls their intentions if and when they marry is not very fruitful. Moreover responses so far have not been very effective in forecasting turning points; women tend to report to the interviewer the number of children that they see born to neighbours and older sisters. If economic fluctuations are going to determine childbearing, then it is better to look into the economic series than to directly ask the individual women, who could well be (at least in the short run) the plaything of the business cycle. For such reasons Norman Ryder, who has done as much as anyone to collect data on intentions, has been vocal in declaring that they are not helpful for forecasting.

A further line of research that could help is on demographic relations and processes, and there is no doubt that this ought to be pursued. But we must be prepared for disappointment and failure as well as for possible success.

Consider one relation that had seemed to be immutable through most of the twentieth century: the birth rate is higher at the peak of the business cycle than in the trough. To use this would require some means of forecasting the business cycle, and cycles have been becoming less and less regular, but I do not stress this point. Much more damaging is the apparent reversal of the relation during the last decade or two. Births now seem to be fewer at the peak of the cylce, rather than more. This may well be due to good business conditions providing more opportunities for wives to take jobs; when unemployment is high they stay home and might just as well use their time for motherhood. This at least was argued by Butz and Ward.

The final line of research suggested is methods of using incomplete data. It is certainly true that many errors in forecasting have been due to incomplete knowledge of the situation at the jumping off point. Better knowledge of the past, especially for the LDCs, would enable their future to be more precisely specified.

Error and uncertainty

I was somewhat surprised that the paper talks extensively about uncertainty, but says little about the measurement of its amount and effects. We may not be able easily to do anything to make forecasts more accurate, but ought to be able to say something precise about how accurate they have been. In particular, I have found that the usual way of expressing uncertainty about the future – the publication of variants – is not very helpful when a ratio is concerned, as for instance in the forecasting of social security prospects. For that something quite different, microsimulation, seems indispensable.

Minor suggestions

Willekens "The aim of forecasting is understanding" is not what the context suggests is meant, but rather that understanding is the precondition for effective forecasting. The statement that males do not affect the growth path of a population is true only where childbearing does not depend on marriage. If all childbearing is in marriage, and the population is perfectly monogamous, then males are just as important as females for childbearing; a male dominant model is just as good as the usual female dominant one.

The model attributed to Von Foerster (1959) was worked out thirty years earlier by McKendrick. (This is a mistake that I myself have made in print.)

Conclusion

I find the paper a superb treatment of its subject, and recommend it to all those who need to know what the future population will be. It shows the extensive knowledge of the literature of forecasting, and of demography in general, as well as fine judgment, that we expect of Frans Willekens. I have not referred to its strengths, that are clearly expressed and are there to be read by all, but have rather chosen to mention those few shortcomings that I perceived.

Emerging Issues in Demographic Research
C.A. Hazeu and G.A.B. Frinking (Editors)
© Elsevier Science Publishers B.V. , 1990

Chapter 4

DEMOGRAPHIC FORECASTING; STATE OF THE ART AND RESEARCH
NEEDS; A COMMENT

Leo J.G. van Wissen

1 Introduction

Only few researchers are in a position to write an article on the state of the art in
demographic forecasting. Academic specialization has a number of advantages, but one
of the main disadvantages is that many of us know only the state of the art in our own
specialized subfield. We are specialists for instance in household modeling, in migration
analysis, or in the economic determinants of demographic events. Few of us have the
broad scope of evaluating the entire field of population studies and writing an article
such as Frans Willekens has done for this occasion. All traditional and modern approaches of demographic research are treated comprehensively and the cross-links
between various approaches become visible.

Unfortunately, my knowledge of demography and demographic forecasting methods
is considerably smaller than that of Frans Willekens. My background is in the spatial
sciences: geography, transportation science and spatial economics. I am not a specialist
in either of these fields, rather I tend to concentrate on spatial models of population
behaviour in general. Demography is one important input that I use in my work. This
position forces me to focus on only a number of aspects of the paper. I will concentrate
on two things. First, since all quantitative science involves forecasting, I will try to
compare a number of modern visions in prospective modeling that can be considered to
be the 'state of the art' in geography or transportation science with the methods discussed
in the paper. To my opinion, forecasting methods in the social sciences share a number
of common themes and problems. Frans Willekens' paper serves well as the frame of
reference for evaluating future research projects in population forecasting. But I think it
is useful to be aware of different approaches offered by related disciplines since much
of the progress in scientific work is caused by what I would call 'cross-fertilization'. A
second theme that I will focus on is the forecasting of migration, since that is one of the
fields that I am quite familiar with. I will mention a few problems one is likely to
encounter when following the behavioural modeling route supported in this paper. In my
opinion, the analysis and forecasting of migration is a good example of the non-separ-
ability of life events. Migration is a household decision within a specific housing market

environment and often related to the job career of its members and the stage and developments in the life cycle. This simultaneity should be one of the focal points for future research in population studies.

2   Forecasting: some notes from related fields

Willekens' position on forecasting methods is stated by Keilman quite clearly (section 12 paper): "(..) the poor performance of forecasting methods is due to our incomplete knowledge of reality. Progress will be made when we put more effort in explanatory behavioural theories." This is an optimistic viewpoint. So far demography has been dominated by the accounting tradition. This is not surprising since the main task of demographers has always been prediction. Accounting methods are in principle ideal instruments for this task because there are no aggregation or consistency problems. Multistate demographic models and the APC model are good examples of the level of sophistication that this tradition has achieved. As long as the parameters follow a 'stable' trajectory (stable in the sense that the trajectory can be predicted by previous values of the parameter in question) there is no problem in forecasting. If, on the other hand, their time path becomes less 'stable' in the above sense, the need arises for decomposing the intertemporal variance into various parts, that can be predicted more easily using additional information on covarying variables. If the relation between the covariate and the parameter in question makes sense in some way, we call it an 'explanation'. Usually, but not always, behavioural relationships are the only ones that make sense and in the main stream of social sciences this has been the dominant line of research for a long time. Unfortunately, the main stream of social sciences has in general not been very successful in developing forecasting methods for social events. Human geographers, for example, have a long tradition in description, exploration and explanation. Theoretically, these are indeed the stages one has to go through before entering the forecasting stage. But this final step seems still quite remote for much geographical work. It appears that there is a large gap between being able to explain social events and to predict them. I will return to this topic when discussing migration forecasting methods. Demographers have taken the short route to prediction and with relatively remarkable success. The question therefore is: do behavioural theories perform better in forecasting? It might be argued that they perform only marginal better then simple trend models and that it is not worth the effort in terms of additional data collection, model specification, estimation and aggregation. The aggregation issue is in my opinion a key problem. Behavioural models are usually specified at the micro-level. While being able to explain individual behaviour, we do not yet know the macro-level consequences. We cannot simply sum over individual behavior to obtain the macro state, which is usually where we are interested in. A system at the macro level behaves qualitatively different from aggregated individual behaviour. What is needed is a behavioural rule or function that includes the effects of the macro configuration at the micro level. The solution of this type of system equations is usually quite complicated. The work of Weidlich and Haag, also references by Willekens, is a very elegant analytical solution to this aggregation problem. They use the concept of the master equation, borrowed form statistical physics, for modeling complex individual behaviour. A behavioural equation is one element in a larger model that includes both micro and macro level elements. The main idea is that, while individual behaviour might be governed to a large degree by random factors, the macro system behaviour can still be predictable. The system trajectory is determined in a deterministic way by looking at the development of the resulting mean values. This time trajectory can show nonlinear patterns, due to the feedback between the micro and macro level. The approach is in principle suited to study any dynamic system where complex feedbacks exist between the micro and the macro level.

In transportation science a similar kind of development can be observed. Behavioural theories and models have been applied extensively in the forecasting of transportation demand in the last decades (although they have never completely replaced the non-behavioural optimization methods used in transportation forecasting). But it became increasingly clear that many phenomena could not be easily explained by applying these micro based behavioural methods. In order to predict traffic flows and transportation in the presence of congestion effects, dynamic multi-level models (dynamic network assignment, dynamic route choice models) have been developed where behavioural equations form one element in a larger system.

It is easy to draw parallels with population dynamics models. The paper of Willekens is evidence that work in this direction in demography has not developed very far yet. I think that further research in population studies would be fruitful.

The approach of Weidlich and Haag has some close links with the theory of deterministic non-linear dynamics. In general, non-linear deterministic systems are macro models, where the system state is described by means of a very small number of system parameters. Although not behavioural, these models can be very relevant for population forecasting. A striking example is given by Bonneuil, also referenced in the paper, who studied the development of fertility in a large number of countries. The regularities in fertility over time, shown by his method, can be very useful, especially for prediction of long term fluctuations. We might be able to predict the process if we have discovered long term non-linear regularities, even if we do not understand it in behavioural terms.

3 Migration forecasting

Demographers have for a long time used extrapolation methods to forecast migration. In recent models based on multiproportional fitting procedures the use of historical trend and interaction parameters can be viewed as more sophisticated ways of extrapolation. Therefore, the introduction of behavioural elements in these models is new from a demographic point of view. There is a bulk of literature on the explanation of residential mobility and migration (see e.g. Clark, 1982; Clark and Van Lierop, 1986) and there is a common agreement on a number of key factors that explain residential mobility, or interregional migration. Life cycle and housing market play a dominant role in migration decisions over short distances while the labor market related reasons are more predominant in migrations over longer distances. Economists also stress the importance of income although the exact relation is difficult to measure in a highly institutionalized housing market such as the Netherlands. In many empirical applications the influence of these variables has been measured using various techniques, such as loglinear modeling, discrete choice modeling, etc. So, in principle we know why people move. The next logical step is to use this knowledge for forecasting. Various researchers, especially in the Netherlands, have done one or more steps in this direction, either at the regional level (Van Wissen and Rima, 1988) or at the national level (Hooimeijer and Linde, 1988). I will list a number of problems that one is likely to encounter here and that to my opinion are serious enough mentioning when discussing a paper that advocates a behavioural route to better population forecasting.

1 Biases in the estimation of behavioural parameters. Especially sample bias can be a serious problem since the sample used for demographic modeling is not often exactly suited to the task. An example is the use of the Dutch Housing Needs Survey (WBO) that is also used for demographic purposes.
2 The forecasting of exogenous variables. If housing market and labour market variables are important determinants of migration, then we need an estimate of the joint distribution of these exogenous variables in order to predict future migration. However, usually we only have scarce (univariate) information, even of historical trends. Therefore we need to estimate the most probable joint distribution for the prediction period. This is essentially the modelling of the aggregation scheme (for an example, see Van Wissen and Rima, 1988) and in general requires a lot of effort. Unless appropriate data bases become available, not only for historical data but also for prospective data, these difficulties are almost prohibitive for desaggregate behavioural forecasting. Fortunately, the development of geographical information systems (GIS) has become a very popular topic in recent years and could be useful for this purpose.
3 The simultaneity of the processes involved. As Willekens puts it, future population researchers "(..) may be forecasting the lives of people, in particular the number and patterning of events". Migration is one decision taken by the household in a series of events that involve the life cycle, the housing market career, the job career and many more things. If this simultaneity is not treated properly or is ignored (as is done when taking all variables except migration to be exogenous) there is a serious risk of specification bias in the model. What is usually done is to model the different events sequentially. This is in general not the proper way to go.

I entirely agree with Willekens' statement that event history analysis is the optimal way of modeling the life course of individuals and households. But the consequence of this simultaneity of various processes is that we need the simultaneous treatment of various hazards. This is an approach in demography that is to my knowledge only taken by Courgeau and Lelièvre (Courgeau and Lelièvre, 1988). Further work in this direction is a necessary consequence of the conclusion reached in the paper. The close links between these types of models with discrete choice models on the one hand and the accounting type models on the other, make it one of the most promising directions for further research.

Another consequence of this simultaneity, the mutual relations that exist in different events in the life history of individuals and households, is that it will increasingly be difficult to draw lines between disciplines who work in population studies. I think Frans Willekens has succeeded in writing one of the papers that will be on the desks of many researchers in this interdisciplinary field.

References

Clark, W.A.V. (1982), Recent research on migration and mobility: a review and interpretation, *Progress in Planning*, Vol 18, New York: Pergamon Press, pp. 1-56.

Clark, W.A.V. and W.F.J. van Lierop (1986), Residential mobility and household location modelling, *Handbook of Regional and Urban Economics*, Vol. 1, P. Nijkamp, ed., Elsevier Science Publishers.

Hooimeijer, P. and M. Linde (1988), *Demographic change, household evolution and the housing market. The WODYN-simulation model,* Ph.D., Utrecht (in Dutch).

Wissen, L. van and A. Rima (1988), Modelling urban housing market dynamics. Evolutionary patterns of households and housing in Amsterdam, *Series in Regional Science and Urban Economics*, Vol. 18, Elsevier North-Holland.

Emerging Issues in Demographic Research
C.A. Hazeu and G.A.B. Frinking (Editors)
© Elsevier Science Publishers B.V. , 1990

Chapter 5

SOCIAL CONSEQUENCES OF DEMOGRAPHIC CHANGE

Henk A. Becker

1 Introduction

1.1 Overview

Since the beginning of this century the Netherlands, like most countries in the Western world, has been confronted with *general trend reflections*.[1] These trend reflections have led inter alia to *changes in demographic behaviour*. As an example of demographic change we cite the Second Demographic Transition (Lesthaeghe and Van de Kaa, 1986; Van de Kaa, 1987). "The principal demographic feature of the second transition is the decline in fertility from somewhat above the 'replacement' level of 2.1 births per woman, which ensures that births and deaths will stay in balance and in population remain stationary in the long run, at a level well below replacement" (Van de Kaa, 1987, p.5). The beginnings of the second transition can be found in the mid 1960's. The Second Demographic Transition originated in the Second World War and the baby boom that followed it.[2]

The demographic changes involved have had *social consequences* (Van de Brekel, 1988, p. 49-87). Some of these consequences are already well known, others have not yet reached the attention of politicians and the public in general. Some examples:

– the greying of society has raised the demand for health care (Klaassen-Van den Berg Jeths, 1989);

---

[1] Trend reflection is defined as "the action of bending, turning, or folding back (recurvation) of a trend" (compare 'reflection' in Shorter Oxford English Dictionary, Oxford 1973). Trend reflection is used in this paper as a translation of the Dutch concept of 'trendbreuk'. Also the concept 'Schicksal' by Mannheim (1928/1929) is translated in this way.

[2] An overview of the trend reflections involved is presented in H.A. Becker, P.L.J. Hermkens and F. Boerman, Trendbreuken en hun demografische neerslag (Trend reflections and their demographic consequences), in H.A. Becker and P.L.J. Hermkens, 1989.

- the greening of society (Frinking, 1988) has decreased the demand for education;
- the members of the baby boom cohorts will retire from 2010 on, creating a substantial demand for new workers;
- the greying and greening of the countries of Western Europe has led to a population unbalanced in age distribution. It raises the question of whether immigration might be used "to fill the gaps" in the age distribution (Heeren, 1987).

A number of the social consequences involved aggrevate existing social equalities or induced new ones. In Sweden, for instance, differences between birth cohorts in respect of income and housing have increased since the mid-seventies (Vogel, 1988). In the Netherlands research into these developments is still at an explorary stage. We know already that incomes (Van Rijsselt and Hermkens, 1989) and housing (Van Fulpen, 1985) show changes similar to those in Sweden. The Welfare State shows increasing cohort-related inequalities but at the same time it has been instrumental in creating formal and informal *contracts* between government, other macro-actors and the population with regard to income, employment, social security, and health care. The increase in social inequality violates these social contracts, creates social tension and might lead to social conflict.

Research by demographers, economists, geographers and sociologists into the social consequences of demographic change is evidently necessary and a research programme on the subject matter involved is emerging. This new research programme already has a number of things in its favour. The subject matter can be studied quantitatively on a large scale, with data archives and survey results providing much relevant information. New ways of analyzing the data have become available, an example being event history analysis. Improvements in theory formation also strengthen the research programme viability.

Research on the phenomena involved is however seriously handicapped by a high degree of *chaos* or noise in the social systems being analyzed. The uncertainty encountered has to be dealt with by treating the processes and systems involved as relatively 'open'. This requires the use of formal theories.

1.2   Setting

The problem as formulated by the Netherlands Organization for Scientific Research (NWO) with regard to the study of the social consequences of demographic change is set out as follows:

"To what extent will demographic change influence the contents and impact of the social 'contracts' that explicitly and implicitly shape processes of (re)distribution in society, and that might lead to the emergence or continuation of (new types of) social inequality?"

The NWO Committee has elaborated this research problem further. It has pointed out that: "Demographic change in the decades to come will induce considerable changes in the numerical relationships between generations and age-categories: the employed and the unemployed; those living single, married or in other primary relationships; between adults with and without children; between the original population and migrants belonging to ethnic minorities and between city dwellers and rural populations. Individuals that belong to one or more of these social categories can often claim certain privileges like social services or financial benefits. As a rule these privileges are institutionalized in 'social contracts'. If the relationships between the social categories involved shift, contracts have to be adapted. Because government is often a partner to these contractual relationships, political decision making has to be incorporated in the analysis."

The NWO Committee has asked us to direct our paper towards an exploration of the problem in a specific number of social areas. It has also invited us to outline research priorities with regard to the problem at hand.

In this paper we decided to concentrate our attention on the following questions:

1. what is the impact of general trend reflections on demographic processes and on the pattern of generations?
2. what is the impact of demographic and related change on cohort-related choice behaviour (in a number of specified areas in society)?
3. what is the impact of societal contracts upon cohort-related choice behaviour?
4. what is the impact of demographic and related change on societal contracts?
5. what is the impact of social inequality on cohort-related choice behaviour?
6. what is the impact of demographic and related change upon social inequality?
7. what is the impact of processes of distribution on cohort-related choice behaviour?
8. what is the impact of demographic and related change on processes of distribution?
9. what political decision making is required in respect of the societal contracts and distribution processes?
10. what type of research programme is required?

Questions one to eight require a descriptive and explanatory approach. These questions can only be dealt with in a limited way within the context of this paper. The new research programme will eventually have to provide answers to these questions.

We selected the following social areas for our investigations:

a. education;
b. employment, careers, and retirement;
c. income and pension rights;
d. value orientations;
e. migration.

Because the NWO Committee has invited other social scientists to write about social security, the labour market, and the housing market, these items are not discussed here. In this paper we do not present an overall scheme of variables neither do we make an argument for our selection. Such information can be obtained on request. The same applies to influences on demographic behaviour and to forecasting methodology.

1.3 Conceptual framework

Before we can start to explore the problem formulated in section 1.2 we have to elaborate a *conceptual framework* that defines and links the main components of the problem as formalized. This framework has been summarized in figure 1.

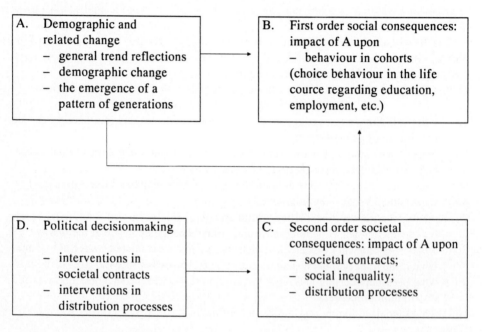

Figure 1   Conceptual framework of relationships taken into consideration in the analysis

Change

In the social sciences it is a convention to define change as a process that has a relatively heavy, long term impact and which is irreversible. Individuals, corporate actors, sometimes whole countries, experience change as a kind of unavoidable external pressure. Social scientists analyzing social behaviour from this position generally take a structuralist, non-voluntarist perspective (inter alia Gadourek, 1982).

Two types of change are relevant to our conceptual framework, firstly trends and secondly trend reflections. We are confronted in fact with general trend reflections (for example the Cultural Revolution) and specific trend reflections (for example the Second Demographic Transition).

Demographic change and its social consequences

Demographic behaviour in the strictest sense refers to birth, sexual unions, marriage, migration and death. Demographic behaviour mirrors major trend reflections (inter alia the Second Transition). *First order* social consequences of these reflections in demographic trends and also of other trend reflections, in the field of economic developments for example, are changes in life courses. These include an increase in formal education, an increase in school leavers unemployment, a decrease in income or changed behaviour on the housing market. *Second order* social consequences of demographic and related change are alterations in the pattern of social inequality or in distribution processes. Alterations in the societal contracts involved may also be partly related to demographic change, for example if the number of beneficiaries of social security provisions increase within specific cohorts.

Cohorts and generations

We follow Ryders definition of a cohort: "A cohort may be defined as the aggregate of individuals within some population definition who experience the same event during the same time interval" (Ryder, 1965, p. 845). This definition emphasizes that the 'empty' category of cohort has to be related to events that are relevant to the actors in society. We define a generation as: "A cluster of cohorts characterized by a specific historical setting, specific life courses, value orientations, behavioural patterns and with a specific generational style" (Becker, 1985 a, b; 1987 a, b; 1989 a). Since Mannheims classic essay (1928/1929) on generations in 1928 his concept has been the subject of several reappraisals. Firstly it must be borne in mind that value orientations acquired in formative years are more susceptible to change than has previously been acknowledged. Secondly we must take into consideration the fact that values acquired on biographic variables remain stable over time and that generational patterns often discriminate primarily with regard to these variables. In this paper we are not concerned with the plausibility of the pattern of generations involved (inter alia Becker, 1989 c). We take the pattern of generations as a frame of reference for the interpretation of demographic change and its social consequences.

Societal Contracts

We define societal contracts as the formal and informal obligations that confront individual and corporate actors in the Welfare State. We find formal societal contracts for instance, in the social security system. Informal societal contracts involve the expectations of actors with regard to opportunities for achieving well being and assistance in situations of need. Formalized societal contracts should been seen primarily as practical obligations not as moral requirements (Marquand, 1988).

The concept of contract has been used in the social sciences for a long time (inter alia Rousseau, Durkheim). Economics has for some years used this concept in analyzing the relationships between economic processes and private contracts (Cheung, 1969; Posner, 1986; Rosen, 1985). In the social sciences the concept appears for example in rational choice theory (Hardin, 1982, 'contract by convention'; Lindenberg, 1988). The problem formulated by the NWO Committee puts the concept in broader perspective. It looks at contracts as a complex of formal and informal obligations linking actors, both individual and corporate in the Welfare State. In order to avoid misunderstandings we call these contracts 'societal contracts' in this paper. Societal contracts are made up of formal (legal, contractual) relationships and secondly of value orientations and (informal) social norms. They also include choice behaviour, that is the behaviour actor A requires of actor B and which is based on a tacit understanding (contract by convention). The NWO Committee, by including contracts in the problem formulation stimulated the exploration of relatively new relationships with respect to the social consequences of demographic change. This concern is reflected in our present paper. The challenge has its drawbacks. We could not present a relatively integrated quantitative model, based on current research. We had in fact to explore a large number of relationships in a partly quantitative, partly qualitative way.

Social inequalities and processes of distribution

There are two aspects of social inequality (Giesen and Haferkamp, 1987; Kerstholt, 1988) which have a special relevance to our analysis. In the first place, we have to distinguish between objective inequalities and subjective perceptions of inequality. In the second place, societies acceptance of social inequality has to be taken into consideration. Both aspects give substance to the societal contracts involved. Both aspects can be described and explained in social research in a relatively reliable and valid way. The social acceptance of differences in incomes for example can be measured using the 'vignette technique', where respondents are invited to react to short descriptions of income, careers etc. (Hermkens, 1983). Social inequality in society is directly related to processes of (re)distribution. Trend reflections, inequalities related to birth cohorts, and social policy interventions reshaped the pattern of distribution in society. Dissatisfaction with the existing pattern of distribution may lead to social tension. Social tension may become social conflict if the actors involved are strong enough to launch an attack on the existing social order and if institutional restraints are inadequate to withstand such an attack.

Political decision making

An increase in social inequality or social conflict may lead to one or more actors demanding that a political decision be made. As a rule it takes a strong power position to get an issue onto the political agenda. As soon as a political decision is reached, the hazardous stage of implementation begins (Simonis, 1983). Many political decisions are not carried out at all and many political decisions are revised during implementation. Social interaction between the major actors involved may alter the contents of the decision, the resources allotted to it, or its time horizon. Rodgers (1983) provides an analysis of the characteristics of success and failure with respect to the diffusion of innovations.

1.4 Assumptions

A number of epistemological and methodological assumptions can be discerned in our conceptual framework. Below we take a closer look at these preliminary issues.

Firstly there is the question of the characteristics of the processes and systems involved. Boudon, referring to social change, distinguishes between relatively closed and relatively open situations within the social systems. Open situations show a comparatively high degree of 'disorder'. He sees two categories of generalizations corresponding to these situations. First there are laws and theories *stricto sensu* (1984, pp. 202 and 217). Laws and theories belonging to this category, which might be falsified according to the requirements formulated by Popper, are rare in sociology and other social sciences. Presumably they will remain rare because the subject matter of these disciplines shows a degree of disorder. Boudon's second category contains *formal* theories. These theories he sees as "... not in themselves directly applicable to reality, but they offer a mode of a discussion or describe ideal examples which may be useful in the analysis of certain process" (1984, p. 219; 1986, p. 207). Boudon has little faith in the search for general theories *stricto sensu*. If partial or local theories are aimed for however, some situations might be sufficiently 'closed' to make success feasible. His conclusion is that "... the only *scientific* theories of social change are 'partial' and 'local' ones" (1984, p. 220; 1986, p. 208).

Boudon does not say explicitly that "partial and local scientific theories" are concepts taken from contemporary biology. In contemporary biology the quest for universal laws no longer predominates. It yielded only vague notions for example, about 'life'. The degree of disorder found in the subject matter of biology however, does make it feasible (and relevant) to formulate laws that are restricted to a limited number of aspects and that are bound in time and space. Whenever biologists want to deal with phenomena that show a relatively high degree of disorder they use models as heuristic frames of reference. Models like these resemble the formal theories to which Boudon refers (cf. Fiske and Sweder, 1986; Outhwaite, 1987).

The second preliminary issue deals with the level of abstraction in the propositions involved. At the highest level of abstraction propositions belonging to the realm of meta theory are found. For instance rational choice theory in its most general form falls within this level of abstraction. At the second level we find theoretical propositions, for example formal theories about the emergence of social inequality or the emergence of patterns of generations. At the third level of abstraction are propositions concerning empirical hypotheses. As an example we can mention hypotheses about the unequal treatment experienced by male and female academics belonging to specific birth cohorts in Dutch universities during the seventies. At the fourth level of abstraction we find statements about observations. Explanation in a strict sense involves testing predictions derived from empirical hypotheses. These empirical hypotheses are closely connected with theoretical hypotheses and meta theories. At first sight this scheme, with propositions at four levels of abstraction, may seem obvious and rather unnecessary. However, we need it if we are to avoid a number of pitfalls. The scheme itself has been elaborated elsewhere (Becker, 1989 d).

In the empirical research projects of the research programme advocated in this paper, these assumptions have to be linked to theories closely related to demographic change and its social consequences. These are not elaborated in this paper and we refer the reader to the literature (inter alia Hernes, 1982; Becker, 1989 d).

1.5   Structure

We shall first deal with our problem by looking at the subject matter involved at the level of theoretical hypotheses. A description is given of the pattern of generations that has emerged in the Netherlands and in other Western countries and of the relationships between this pattern of generations on the one hand and societal contracts and social inequality on the other. A more elaborate version of this model of theoretical hypotheses can be found in Becker (1989 d). Other theoretical models can be used in trying to explain the relationships. As an alternative explanatory model we briefly sketch the modernization hypothesis. The subject matter is explored at this level in section 2.

In sections 3 and 4 we discuss our subject from the perspective of empirical hypotheses. We describe the processes involved by looking at the main characteristics of current research and we indicate which research hypotheses look promising. Section 3 looks at individual life courses. Section 4 focusses on phenomena related to social systems.

Section 5 is concerned with research priorities. Preconditions for a research programme are considered and possible problem areas in the research are specified.

One relatively short paper is inadequate for dealing with the subject in all its aspects. In a number of cases the reader is directed to other publications where additional information can be found.

2   Generations and social inequality

2.1   The pre-war generation

To those born between 1910 and 1930 the first severe collective experience was the economic crisis of the thirties. Massive unemployment, the dole, the hunger and poverty which affected large sections of the population are still remembered with the greatest clarity. Even those who were not directly affected by the crisis are, some fifty years later still, unable to speak lightly of unemployment. The members of the pre-war generation learned in those years that societal disorganization can lead to extremism from both left and right.

The formative period for the pre-war generation was a time when secondary education was the privilege of a happy few. If their parents were not well-to-do, they were quite often willing to make heavy sacrifices to enable their children to attend college or university. It was also common practice for parents to save money for their own old age. Sexual permissiveness was unthinkable to the pre-war generation. Birth control required practices and auxiliaries that were to many of them taboo.

When they entered the labour market members of this generation were confronted with job scarcity and low starting salaries. Once they got a job they realized that 'job satisfaction' was not an issue. Critical remarks were avoided because they ran the risk of losing their job very quickly if they appeared dissatisfied.

The Second World War probably intensified the experiences of the formative period, at least in the Netherlands. There are no indications that the Second World War changed the value orientations of members of this generation in any considerable way. To most Dutch men and woman the war was a burden on their education and their careers.

This generation carried the heaviest burden in the period of post-war reconstruction. The task was fulfilled with optimism: a better society seemed within reach. In the new Welfare State hunger, massive unemployment and lack of medical care could be abolished. To make the advent of the Welfare State possible, this generation accepted a severe delay in the growth of the incomes of most of its members. When, at the end of the fifties and the beginning of the sixties, it became apparent that economic prosperity reigned, the golden age came as a surprise to the pre-war generation. Was an economic boom possible so soon after that terrible war?

The gratitude and calm of the pre-war generation was cruelly disrupted by the developments at the end of the sixties. A generation of protesters revolted against materialism, established authority and discrimination. Clashes with the protesters particularly appalled the members of the pre-war generations when convictions established during their own formative period came under attack. The members of the pre-war generation were convinced that material progress was necessary as a safeguard against poverty and unemployment. They considered established authority necessary to avoid anarchy and chaos.

The economic crisis of the second half of the seventies has afflicted the pre-war generation in different ways. Those who had a permanent job, a house of their own and a comfortable social status did not as a rule experience much hardship. Those who lost their job were often considered too old to be given a new one, and had a hard time obtaining employment again.

In the middle of the eighties most of the pre-war generation belong to the category of 'the elderly'. If they are sixty-five and older they are probably retired. Other members belong to the category of the 'young elderly'. They all contribute to the problems experienced or foreseen with regard to 'the greying of the nation'.

2.2   The silent generation

The core of the silent generation was born in the thirties. It got its name in the late sixties. During the uprising of the young it became apparent that an earlier generation would have had just as much reason for protest. Undemocratic relationships had existed in earlier years too. The silent generation was drawn out of its quiet obscurity.

The silent generation lived through the Second World War but there is no reason to suppose that its value orientations and preferences were changed by it. After the war the silent generation had opportunities for secondary and higher education that greatly exceeded those of the pre-war generation. Grants became available on a large scale and parents were eligible for tax reductions when their children went to college or university. Even so, social barriers prevented many capable children from getting a secondary or a higher education and much talent was wasted. The sociologist Van Heek has documented this wastage in the context of the Netherlands (Van Heek, 1968).

In its formative period the silent generation had to accept and follow convential values towards sexual behaviour and attitudes towards work. The members of the silent generation entered the labour market at a time when the demand for labour was strong. Most of its members quickly found a job. Their careers acquired a velocity that was far greater than those of the pre-war generation and contained possibilities that younger generations can only dream of. Out of the four generations under consideration in this paper the silent generation has profited most from the 'golden decade', the years between 1955 and 1965. To the silent generation the golden decade came as something of a surprise. Its work ethic was high and its preferences were for a rapid career.

Economic prosperity came steadily but relatively slowly to the members of the silent generation. Maybe this gradualness in the improvement of their living conditions and the step-by-step gratification of their wants provides the key to understanding them. If ever a generation had reasons to keep silent, it was this one.

Not all members of this generation however, were lucky. Those who failed in their career were doubly disappointed, because they were failing under favourable circumstances, and some groups, such as women and homosexuals, continued to experience severe discrimination well into the sixties.

The typical members of the silent generation were and are willing to accept authority. Law and order are seen as necessary for the smooth running of society. The primary contribution of the Welfare State to the silent generation was an indirect one. Its members were not forced to save money to guard against illness or unemployment and their old age has been provided for by the social security system.

We are talking about the generation described by Schelsky in 1957 as 'sceptical'. He was referring to the younger sections of his countries population, those who were in skilled and unskilled occupation. He was struck by the lack of romantic longing for freedom and nature. There were no 'Wandervögel' anymore and in this they differed from the previous generations at a similar age. Schelsky admits that he has little empirical evidence to prove the validity of his statements, but he saw the new generation as one excelling in concreteness.

When at the end of the sixties the young started to rebel, the silent generation reacted with surprise. The fire was not directed at them, however, but at the pre-war generation. The feeling in those years was that the silent generation could build a bridge between the contestants. The silent generation never aspired to this role: the preferences of the silent generation with regard to authority and work closely resembled those of the pre-war generation.

If the pre-war and the silent generation are so similar does it make sense to continue making a distinction between them? Why not consider them as one generation? It is important to realise here that there is a major difference in the restrictions, especially the economic ones, which confronted each generation in its formative period. The silent generation had much better opportunities. Its members used them to speed up their careers and buy their houses at a far younger age. Inflation added its own bonus coming at a time when the silent generation could most profit from it.

2.3   The protest generation

The vanguard of the new generation was born about 1940 with stragglers arriving until the mid 1950's. Stories of the economic crisis of the thirties or the Second World War had little appeal to these newcomers. The new generation had been surrounded by prosperity and peace in its formative period. There was room, its members concluded, for a redistribution of wealth, for the sharing of power and for the abolition of discrimination.

The baby boom of the years directly following the Second World War resulted in swollen cohorts flooding the educational system. The reaction of the system itself was tardy and inadequate. Education became standardized, impersonal and uninspiring. This lack of inspiration and personal challenge had a major influence on the 'cultural revolution'. In the United States the civil rights movement provided a model for student revolt. In the Netherlands the student revolt came somewhat later, in 1968. The Dutch cultural revolution had its own early bird, Provo, but later took the same course as North America and other Western European countries.

The main force of the protest generation pushed through the 'cultural revolution' during or shortly after its formative period. In 1969 it was described as a 'neo-romantic' phenomenon, resembling the revolutionary romantic movements in Western Europe in the middle of the nineteenth century. Its characteristics were 'Weltschmerz', Utopian ideals about society, art, religion, and science, and an awareness of a deep chasm between ideals and reality.

In the Netherlands the years 1973-1975 marked the passing of the cultural revolution. In his research on redefinition of roles in the Netherlands in the seventies, Gadourek found a trend reflection appearing by 1975. The 'permissive society' had come to an end and a period of new rigidity with regard to work ethics and authority had set in (Gadourek, 1982).

When they entered the labour market, members of the protest generation could still find a job. But careers got slower and quite a number of them experienced periods of unemployment. In many partnerships both man and woman entered employment with the result that total family incomes often matched those of the silent generation.

The sexual revolution provided the members of the protest generation with both behavioural freedom and freedom from social control and feelings of guilt. Discrimination against woman was fought back substantially, and in certain parts of the labour market, changed into positive discrimination.

From the beginning the protest generation had a style of its own in clothes, hair, speech and general way of life, but it was never a homogeneous entity. Within the proliferation of movements some – like Provo – have acted as elites.

2.4   The lost generation

Those who are born later than 1955 constitute the lost generation. The term 'lost' springs from their unfavourable position in the labour market. The majority of this generation went through its formative period in the mid seventies and beyond. Its members saw the last days of the cultural revolution with their own eyes. They were confronted with the right-wing backlash, the law and order reaction and the coming of 'no nonsense' politics in their socially most sensitive years. At the same time they had to get used to the idea that an economic world crisis had broken out and that they would face the consequences when they left school or university. During their time in the educational system they had to work as hard or even harder than members of previous generations. Notwithstanding the difficulties considerable numbers have found jobs. Others opened small shops or started their own enterprises and many have been absorbed by the informal economy. In sexual matters the lost generation enjoys a degree of actual and moral freedom at least as generous as that of the protest generation. In this respect they are not lost at all.

Much public debate surrounds the question of the attitudes of members of the lost generation in the Netherlands, Federal Germany and other Western countries. One of these issues is the question of political orientation. Are its members accepting their present situation for example on the labour market and the housing market submissively, or are they in revolt or on the verge of revolt? Behind these questions lurks the fears of the pre-war generation; might this lost generation be susceptible to extremist propaganda and will the nightmares of the thirties repeat themselves?

A second issue is the distribution of employment. The emancipation of the elderly, especially the younger among them, requires a flexible system of retirement. Some of the more vital members of the pre-war generation would like to continue their work on a full-time or part-time basis after their 65th birthday. On the other hand the members of the lost generation have a right to work. A general shortening of the working week would be in their interest, if it were to result in a redistribution of work. A share of this would also have to be paid by the silent generation and the protest generation.

In the third place the emancipation of women is at stake. If more and more women prefer to take a job as well as running a household, this will result in a massive demand for employment particularly on a part-time basis. The same jobs which could perhaps be filled by members of the lost generations.

We conclude by making a comparison between two fictitious members of different generations. Both are male, one being Academic A, born in 1935, the other Academic B, born in 1955. What chance had the second Academic B to get a tenure position at a Dutch university, to become a full professor before he is 35 years old, to buy a house of his own and live in it free for many years because of rising house prices? Has he had the opportunity to accumulate a high lifetime income ...? Almost all these advantages were open to Academic A. They are however out of reach of Academic B. Precise research data on social inequality related to cohort membership are not yet available for the Netherlands.

2.5   *Modernization as an alternative and rival model*

The pattern of generations is not the only model available. Modernization provides an alternative model. Modernization implies an individualization of life courses (Berger, 1986). This would imply, that between and within cohorts life course variables would show less pattern, value orientation would diverge, and behavioural choices related, for instance, to political participation would follow individualized courses. In this paper this alternative, rival model is not elaborated.

2.6   *Conclusions*

The hypotheses developed at theoretical level developed in this section with respect to generations can be formulated as follows:

1. differences between and within generations, which as a result of demographic and related change have evoked and increased social inequalities;
2. the emergence and aggravation of social inequality violates societal contracts, equal opportunities being an example;
3. the violation of societal contracts evokes social tension and increases the risk of social conflict;
4. the increased risk of social conflict demands the attention of macro-actors responsible for political decision making if it is to be prevented.

These theoretical level hypotheses are restricted to the Netherlands in the period 1970-1990. Similar hypotheses may be valid for other countries in Western Europe, and for that reason international comparison becomes particularly important.

3   Cohorts and life courses

This section considers ongoing research. In some areas, for instance education, research has resulted in a detailed elaboration of differences between and within cohorts. In other areas where pensions rights are concerned for example, the differences between and within cohorts have only been analyzed in a very preliminary way, and much elaboration of detail remains to be done.

3.1   Cohorts and education

In looking for the impact of general trend reflections on demographic behaviour and the social consequences proceeding from them, we can, for example, turn to developments at the level of educational in the Netherlands.

Becker, Boerman and Hermkens (1989) have studied the development in the level of education by looking at the differences between birth cohorts. In figure 2 this development has been described for individuals born in the Netherlands between 1910 and 1955.

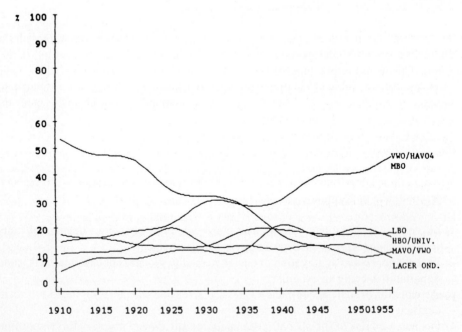

Figure 2   Educational level by year of birth; birth cohorts 1910-1955

This figure is based on data from a survey which focussed on the life situation of Dutch people in the year 1983. Data were gathered by the Central Bureau of Statistics in the Netherlands. The figure shows considerable differences between birth cohorts. The largest movements is in the number of people being educated to elementary level only. Table 1 shows that amongst people born in the period 1910-1914, 53,3 % received an elementary education only. This table shows how this percentage decreases for later birth cohorts. In birth cohort 1955-1959 just 8,6 % received only an elementary education.

Table 1   Educational level by five-year birth cohorts

	only primary	LBO	MAVO,VWO-HAVO-3k	VWO, HAVO-4, MBO	HBO, university	absolute total
1905-09	57.9%	15.1%	8.6%	10.5%	7.9%	152
1910-14	53.3%	14.8%	10.4%	17.6%	3.8%	182
1915-19	47.6%	16.3%	11.1%	16.3%	8.7%	208
1920-24	45.5%	13.9%	13.1%	18.9%	8.6%	244
1925-29	34.0%	13.1%	20.1%	21.6%	11.2%	268
1930-34	32.0%	13.3%	13.3%	30.1%	11.3%	256
1935-39	28.1%	18.9%	13.2%	28.5%	11.4%	281
1940-44	17.4%	19.3%	11.8%	30.4%	21.1%	322
1945-49	13.3%	17.6%	13.1%	39.3%	16.7%	466
1950-54	13.5%	17.5%	9.2%	40.4%	19.4%	468
1955-59	8.6%	17.8%	10.8%	46.5%	16.2%	499
total	26.0%	16.6%	12.2%	31.2%	14.0%	3346

Source: LSO83, CBS.

This trend does not appear when the figures for low-level professional education are studied. The number of people with an educational ceiling at this level remains approximately the same and ranges from 13,1 percent for birth cohort 1925-1929, to 18,9 percent for birth cohort 1935-1939. When we look at the people who have been educated at a 'mavo/havo three classes/vwo three classes'-level we see an increase up to the birth cohort 1925-1929 with a maximum of 20,1 percent. After this the percentage stabilizes at around 12 percent.

A different picture appears when participants who have finished 'havo/vwo' and 'mbo' are considered. Here we see a gradual increase. The number of people having this type of education as their highest achievement rises from 17,6 percent for cohort 1910-1914 until 46,5 percent for cohort 1955-1959. This same tendency can been seen for people who have completed a high level of professional education or university training. In the birth cohorts 1910-1914 this is just 3,8 percent, whereas for the birth cohorts of 1940-1944 it was 21,1 percent.

The developments described relate to demographic change in two ways. An increase in the level of education of men and women, under specific circumstances, leads to decreases in fertility. On the other hand a decrease in fertility means women have the opportunity to continue their educational training after they have raised (fewer) children.

When we postulate education as an interval-scale variable, and look at the average end level of education for the successive birth cohorts in figure 3, we arrive at the same conclusion. The level of education gradually increases with the later years of birth.

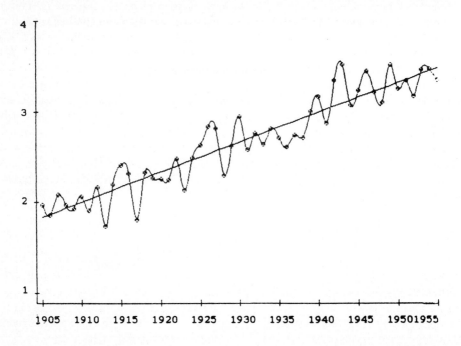

Figure 3   Educational level by year of birth; figures for birth cohorts 1910-1950 and the regression line for these cohorts

No definite answers can be given as to the social consequences of changes in educational level for the successive cohorts described above. However, we suggest that increasing educational level is the result of an increasing social demand for well-trained technical and professional people (see Blossfeld, 1987; Blossfeld and Nuthmann, 1989; Birg, Flöthmann and Reiter, 1989). The need for educated people grew with the technological advancement characteristic of modern societies. Society could no longer afford to distribute societal positions ascriptively, because of the waste of human potential. Society became increasingly achievement-based making it possible for anyone with qualifications to aspire to some position. Along with this change in general attitude, the importance of education grew. Nowadays people have acquired certain educational rights reflected in such provisions as study allowances.

The point has now been reached where everybody can seek to develop his capacities through education.

The connection between personal educational development and getting a job has changed, however. For a long time a high level of educational achievement would guarantee a high position in the labour market. Nowadays this is only partially true. The disappointing prospects facing an increasing group of well-educated people with high career expectations is a potential source of social conflict.

Until 1989 educational inequality has been defined primarily as inequality in the sense of formal education. Because of rapid economic and technical change the content of a persons knowledge and skills becomes critical. In this sense a deteriation of knowledge and skills can be spoken of and less emphasis will have to be given to crude education level. In surveys on the subject matter, respondents will have to answer questions regarding post-graduate post-experience training, to give an example. Individuals older than about 35 years are in a disadvantageous position compared to younger individuals where informatics skills are concerned because their training was not so computer centred. As a consequence of differences like these the opportunities of individuals with equal formal education show considerable variation. We hypothesize that such increases in inequalities violate the system of societal contracts because the right to equal opportunity is frustrated.

3.2 Cohorts, employment and careers

Each year individuals leave the educational system and begin to look for jobs. Cohorts with a relatively large number of individuals are in a less favourable position than cohorts with relatively few members when job opportunities are at stake. Since 1972 and the oil crisis, unemployment rates have increased in the Netherlands and in other Western European countries. Since 1972 the number of jobs available has also decreased. Blossfeld (1986) demonstrated the effects of time of entry into the labour market in the case of Germany. These discrepancies have not yet been challenged by the contents of societal contracts. Equal opportunities or related standards have not been used so far to identify social tension and the search for social conflict has taken place on a relatively small scale.

Too few areas of the labour market have been explored sufficiently for an analysis to be made which would take demographic change, social inequalities, societal contracts and tension/conflict into consideration. The academic labour market has however, in our opinion been described in such a way (Tazelaar, 1980; Van Doorne-Huiskes, 1983; Soerensen, 1989; Becker and Beekes, 1989) as to make an analysis, similar to that sketched above, possible. In this section we take this example to illustrate developments taking place and the research priorities involved.

Several trends and changes in trends can be identified in Dutch universities. In the sixties and seventies the number of academics increased from 4,000 to 18,000. There has been a small decrease in that number since 1986 (see table 2). Growth and decline mirror the baby boom and the baby bust.

Table 2   Academic staff in full time equivalents, 1963-1986

1963	5.670
–	
1968	9.526
–	
1973	13.860
–	
1983	18.462
1984	18.155
1985	18.152
1986	17.589

from: Becker and Beekes, 1989

Table 3   Development of the average age between 1963 and 1985 for several categories

	1963	1968	1973	1978	1985
Total	37.0	38.2	38.2	39.7	40.2
Males	37.0	38.2	38.3	40.1	41.0
Females	37.0	37.8	37.5	36.6	36.2
Tenured staff	40.2	43.1	43.1	43.6	45.3
Temporary staff	33.7	33.8	33.7	31.1	31.1
Fulltimers	36.5	37.8	38.0	39.4	40.2
Parttimers	40.8	41.0	39.8	38.8	38.8
Ranks					
professors (hoogleraren)	42.2	48.4	49.2	50.0	52.4
ass.-professors (uhd)	42.0	43.1	43.2	41.7	46.1
senior researchers (ud)	33.0	31.8	31.3	34.7	36.1
assistants (wet. ass.)	31.4	31.7	31.5	34.6	33.2
Facultyclusters					
Alfa	38.4	40.7	40.7	39.6	39.4
Gamma	37.7	38.1	37.0	36.7	39.5
Medicine	36.1	37.6	37.7	38.7	39.8
Beta	35.6	36.5	36.6	38.7	39.5
Technical	38.1	38.6	39.7	41.9	42.5
Agricultural	39.0	39.8	41.8	40.3	39.4

from: Becker and Beekes, 1989

The composition of university staff has changed dramatically over these years. The system has grown more and more hierarchical. At the beginning of the sixties about one-third of the staff were professors. In 1986 this figure is around ten percent. Another, partly related, change has been the trend towards more temporary staff. While the average age of permanent staff is still rising, the average age of the temporary staff is slowly declining (see table 3). As a result of this, the rise in average age of the total academic population has stopped.

The percentage of female academics has slowly increased over the years. But it remains marginal because it is almost entirely located in the sphere of temporary staff.

The system of automatic promotion after a number of years resulted in increasing numbers of academics in higher ranks. The high expenses involved led to changes in promotion rules. After 1977 the university teachers were confronted with decreasing career opportunities and this resulted in a worsening of income development. The effects on womens promotion chances have been dramatic.

As a result of several reorganisations a typical profile of university staff includes: a dual structure of temporary staff and tenured staff, the almost complete absent of mobility which results in a greying of tenured staff, lower salaries for new cohorts and a marginal position for women.

From the point of view of the system we see a flexible organisation, which has adapted itself from a system based on the characteristics of the traditional German university to a system resembling that of competitive American universities.

The price of this adaption has been paid by the individuals entering the university in recent years. This can be most clearly illustrated by developments in age structure. Between 2000 en 2010 many of the tenured staff will reach pensionable age. This will lead to a rather abrupt process of replacement. The loss in experience and knowledge can be calculated.

The trends mentioned above are the result of compound developments in demographic and social change: rising student numbers, later rising academics, the economic depression and governments rigorous retrenchment policy.

These developments refer to rules by which the internal labour market creates careers. These rules can be understood as societal contracts. The formal and informal contracts were changed for later cohorts, for example the promotion rules effective after 1977, in order to solve problems caused by the former cohorts.

In studying labour market development special attention should be given to the changing position of women in society. The emancipation of women leads to a change in the informal contracts concerning the role of women, as a group, in society. These developments are formalized as laws and affirmative action, but this does not guarantee their factual equality. Again and again it has been shown that the retrenchments of the last years have made the position of women more difficult (see Klijzing, 1989).

The academic labour market in universities shows a cohort-related inequality where the career opportunities of both male and female academics are concerned. Societal contracts have been defined in a relatively precise way. Positive action has been used to decrease the gap in opportunities between women and men, but as yet this has had little success. Social tension is evidently growing in the academic labour market at universities. For these reasons this area provides an interesting and appropriate case for further investigation. As a second step other parts of the labour market might be analysed also, taking the series of questions raised by the NWO Committee being taken as a starting point.

3.3 Cohorts, incomes and pension rights

After the second World War, and in a period of rising expectations, Dutch society was confronted with the 'Baby Boom'. This demograpic event had, has and will have, a strong influence on income development. Early in the next century the baby boom-cohorts will retire and later on they will demand a great deal of health care. Which cohorts will pay for this?

Studies of income inequality usually concentrate on differences in actual earnings. When a man or a woman enters the labour market, he/she receives a certain wage for a certain type of work until he/she reaches retirement age. Everyone in the Netherlands, on reaching the age of 65 is automatically entitled to a state pension which can be supplemented by incomes from pension funds, the amount depends upon the pension rights a worker has managed to accumulate in the course of his working life. The twentieth century has seen a wide variety of pension arrangements within the different sections of the Dutch employment market. Entitlement to a pension supplement depends largely on the pension system in force in the sector to which the employee belongs. It is presumed that the later an individual entered the labour market, the more chance he had of obtaining improved pension benefits and a correspondingly higher pension. Differences in income are, thus, not confined to differences in wage scales alone, but are also reflected in the post-employment period, the years of retirement.

It is possible to make a number of distinctions in income development during a lifetime. We can call the first phase the 'pre-income phase'. For children, there is usually no question of an income derived from labour and it is only when young people leave school and begin their working lives, that we can talk of the 'income development phase'.

A whole network of institutionalised contracts have developed in the Netherlands in connection with employment and income. These contracts contain clearly defined rights and obligations for both employers and employees regarding position-grades and the salary scales per function/training level or occupational group.

An income, in an 'active working life', is built up over a period of between 43-48 years, assuming that paid labour begins somewhere around the age of 17 years and continues up to the age of 60 or 65. This is, of course, a purely theoretical maximum and in fact, because of longer study or training periods and early retirement is often not achieved.

Nelissen (1987) has indicated a relationship between the division of incomes and age compositions. He based his findings on income data for the years 1950, 1960, 1970, and 1981 in the Netherlands. He describes a pattern of sharply rising income until the age of 40. This is followed by a period of stabilisation up to the age of about 60 years, after which there follows a fairly rapid income decline. Figure 4 presents average incomes over several years for different age groups for which inflation corrections have been made. It can be seen that the incomes for the age group 30-65 in particular rose sharply between 1950 and 1970. This was followed by a period of stagnation. The information in Figure 4 concerns cross-sectional data. Nelissen also studied the income data for generations born between 1885-1890 up to and including 1950-1955 (see Figure 5). Here again, incomes show a clear rise until about 30 years of age. The rise between the thirtieth and four[.]ieth years however, is less strong here than in the cross-sectional data. Income development continues at more or less the same level until the age of 60 has been reached, from which point it slowly begins to descend.

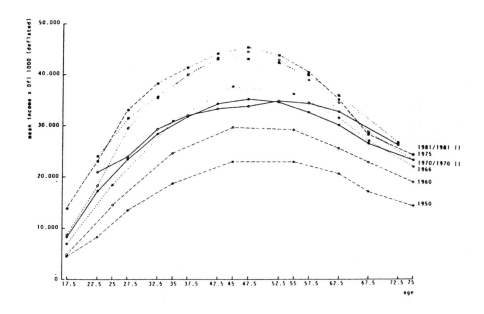

Figure 4   The relation between age and income; period 1950-1981
            Source: Nelissen (1987)

To summarize, it can be concluded that lifetime earnings for the various occupational groups follow much the same pattern. Salaries begin at a relatively low level and rise steadily over a number of years until the individual has reached the maximum appropriate to his/her salary/wage scale. In many occupations this maximum is reached somewhere between the ages of 40 and 50, or even earlier. Retirement usually entails a considerable drop in income for all groups. On average, the older age group's income is as low as that for the 30 year old age group. A well known fact arising from all income studies is that the lowest income groups include the highest proportion of both the younger (school leavers) and the older members (retired) of society.

Demographic developments such as the baby boom seem to have a strong influence on the lifetime income development of different birth cohorts and generations. Hermkens, Beekes and Rekers (1989) studying the period 1965-1985 found differences in the income development of cohorts entering the labour market in some sectors of the Dutch society. During an active working life a basis is laid for a retirement income. Between government and society there is a contract encompassing the fore mentioned state pension. This is the General Old Age Pension Act of 1 January 1957 which forms the basis of the Dutch pension system. Every tax-paying Dutch citizen receives, by law, a benefit from the age of 65 years onwards. The system is financed by those currently paying into the national Old Age Pension Fund, the so-called apportionment system. The amount of pension retired persons actually receive is, however, fairly modest. The following table will show how this old age benefit has developed over the years.

Table 4   Pension allowances according to the General Old Age Pension Act (in guilders gross per year)

	1975	1980	1985	1986	1987	1988
single people	8,507	12,737	13,922	14,087	14,060	14,039
married couples	12,049	18,385	19,733	19,867	20,348	20,283

Source: CBS, Statistisch zakboek 1985 – 1988

At this moment one in eight Dutchmen and women are older than 65 years of age. Following the demographic prognoses of the Central Bureau of Statistics this situation will change in the near future to one in four people being at or beyond retirement age. In the period 2005-2030 the baby boom birth cohorts will retire and this will increase the pressure on the publically financed pension system. At the moment little is known about the socio-economic consequences of this or what choices will have to be made.

To individuals who will have to rely entirely on a minimal old age pensions, it will mean, in reality, an enormous drop in income. For this reason many employment sectors within Dutch society provide pension facilities for their workers. Changes in the financing system of public pensions, could have a great effect on supplementary pensions.

The Dutch pension system is a rather complex 'system'. Pension systems can differ per sector, per occupational group and even per individual (Rekers and Hermkens, 1989). Contracts between pension funds and individuals regulate the supplementary pension income. However, many problems can be found in this area. There are many people who have not a supplementary pension (White spots). At this moment they number about 600,000 people. Many people do not have a sufficient supplementary pension (grey spot). These people are confronted with the fact of a 'broken pension' build up during their working live. The involvement of people with their own pension situation is very low. In order to get some information about the supplementary pension situation of different birth cohorts we cooperated closely with several pension funds.[1] Figure 5 illustrates the average annual supplementary pension situation of male and female birth cohorts born between 1910-1940 employed in the metal industry.

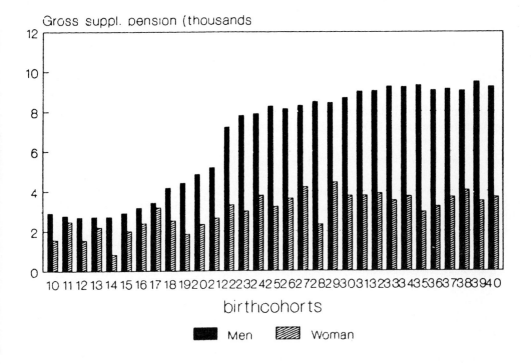

Figure 5   Supplementary pensions in 1987 in the metal industry of male and female
            birth cohorts born between 1910-1940
            Source: Hermkens and Rekers, 1989

We can see that the average annual supplementary pension of the male population shows a rise when the cohort is younger.[2] For the female population the situation is less clear. Small numbers and part-time jobs cause a more turbulent development.

---

[1] This information was gathered during the researchprogram 'old and new generations', 1989.

[2] The sudden rise of pension for the birth cohort 1922 is the result of an artificial effect caused by different populations. The birth cohorts 1910-1922 also contain people who did not retire in the sector of the metal industry.

Research in many sectors of Dutch society showed that the complexity of the supplementary pension system made it difficult to get an overall view. From the data available we were able to conclude that there are big differences both between the various sectors and within the sectors themselves where birth cohorts are concerned. The greying and greening which faces us in the future forces us to make some radical choices in the sphere of incomes. Therefore detailed research into social and financial (income) consequences seems necessary.

Where pensions are concerned societal contracts can be seen as preventing strong differences which may arise as a result of cohort membership. If fortunate cohorts exhibit their advantages in the coming years, social tension and even social conflict seems likely (Becker, 1989c). Data regarding pension rights and pension incomes will also become available in this period, mainly because a number of pension funds have been willing to provide information (Hermkens and Rekers, 1989).

3.4   Cohorts and value orientations

Each group, whether it is catogorized on the basis of age or year of birth, has a unique position in society. Its specific composition, characteristics and experiences determine the formation and change of attitudes and value orientations (Riley, 1972). Defined in this way, attitudes and value orientations reflect complex and intervening processes such as socialization, the effects of relative scarcity, ageing, and long and short term socio-historical developments.

Under the differential cohort socialization hypothesis, experiences acquired in the formative years are of major importance in the development and fixation of norms and values. As they grow older people are also influenced by their own life experiences and these effect their attitudes and values (De Jong-Gierveld and Beekink, 1989). The ageing process can be seen as a filtering process, during which access to specific societal positions and roles are regulated. Changes in values and norms can also be generated by developments in the socio-historical framework. These developments often occur over long periods and as a result they bring relatively few disruptions in trends. Beside these long term effects occasional short term effects appear influencing some or all the members of a population. These developments, whether long or short term, change the regulation processes in relation to scarce goods, services, and even positions within the social and political structure.

Informal and formal societal contracts can, to a large extent, be seen as a reflection of the value orientations of the members of a society. When differences in value orientations occur tensions about underlying normative ideas appear and societal contracts are put under pressure. This leads to objective or subjective perceptions of inequality and in the worst cases to social conflict. This is especially true for generational and birth cohort differences.

The study of longitudinal developments in attitudes and value orientations from a birth cohort perspective is comparatively recent in its developments. Researchers raise several critical questions: to what extent have attitudes and value orientations changed over long periods of time; if changes have been reported, are they equally distributed among birth cohorts; do birth cohorts cluster into broader groups and can these differences between clusters be interpreted as generational differences.

Recent empirical results provide evidence which supports the ideas of generational differences proposed by Becker (Van Rijsselt and Becker, 1989; see also De Jong-Gier-veld and Beekink, 1989, with different conclusions). Longitudinal developments in ideological value orientation for the Netherlands are described in figure 6. These consist of a social-cultural and a social-economic domain.

SPACE

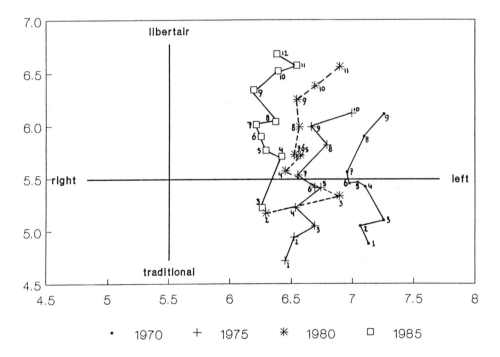

Cultural Change Surveys 1970-75-80-85

Figure 6   Scores of birth cohorts on ideological value orientation

In figure 6 value orientations of five-year cohorts are analyzed. The cohorts were interviewed in different years. The code of figure 6 reads:

1 = 1901 – 1905	7 = 1931 – 1935
2 = 1906 – 1910	8 = 1936 – 1940
3 = 1911 – 1915	9 = 1941 – 1945
4 = 1916 – 1920	10 = 1946 – 1950
5 = 1921 – 1925	11 = 1951 – 1955
6 = 1926 – 1930	12 = 1956 – 1960

The interviews took place in 1970, 1975, 1980, and 1985. The data indicate that differences between cohorts mirror the pattern of generations hypothezied in section 2, but only to a limited extent. Figure 6 is taken from the current research of Van Rijsselt.

In figure 6 clusters of birth cohorts with minimal mean differences are analyzed. A clustering of several birth cohorts can be seen as an indication for a generation. A major conclusion could be that there is a discontinuity between the Pre-war and the Silent Generation. Other empirical findings in fact confirm these results (Van Snippenburg and van Berkel, 1989).

The impact of generational or birth cohort differences on actual human behaviour has barely been studied. The hypothesis that inter-generational differences lead to social unrest or social conflict therefore remains unstudied. Scientific publications indicate however, that large demographic transitions will create great inter-generational conflicts in the near future. The emergence of new social movements, like the emancipated future 'protest'-elderly, might, to a large extent, influence the relations between younger and older people, leading for example to the adjustment of old and the implementation of new societal contracts, in a way the redistribution of such social goods as social security and employment. Cohort-related changes in value orientation can be seen as second order social consequences of demographic and related change.

3.5 Conclusions

In the four areas taken as examples we found (a) increasing cohort-related social inequality, (b) violation of societal contracts and (c) the risk of tensions or even conflict. In all cases these relationships are still hypotheses waiting for further empirical testing.

We would like to emphasize again that the four areas dealt with in this section are examples drawn from a much larger set of potential research topics. In the literature (for example Klaassen, 1989) other areas are explored in a similar way.

4 Generations and political decision making

4.1 Generations, distribution and social conflict

The pre-war generation has been the last West European generation to grow up with no expectation of state support being available in case of need. Neither did they have the notion that support could be claimed by the individual because state and citizens were bound by mutual obligations. The Welfare State has been defined as: "The type of society that is characterized by democratic institutions and by a system of state care that guarantees collective social well-being to its citizens, whilst continuing a capitalistic production system (Thoenes, 1962, p.124). The Welfare State, in Dutch 'Verzorgings-staat' ('providence state') has pledged (Schuyt, 1986, p.3):

1. to protect individuals against the risks of modern industrial society, for instance accidents during work or inability to work;
2. to guarantee a minimal income, particularly in case of illness, inability to work, unemployment or old age;
3. to provide the facilities required by citizens in order that they can participate in society. These include housing, education and health care;
4. to stimulate individual well-being, in particular by enabling individuals to follow their aspirations in life and by making it possible for them to participate in politics, cultural activities and sports.

The Welfare State, seen as a combination of societal contracts and social services, has emerged from a historical process which began at the end of the nineteenth and the beginning of the twentieth century (inter alia van Wijngaarden, 1983). Provisions in the sphere of social security for example were gradual introduced but at a very low level in Western countries. Between 1945 and 1968 the Welfare State acquired a certain maturity. Its principles were accepted on a wide scale in society, and its provisions met the formal and informal societal contracts that had emerged. Since 1968 the principles of the Welfare State have been contested and a gap has emerged between the expectations of citizens and the provisions by the state. Retrenchments in the wake of the economic recession and the rising cost of provisions, amongst which are these for the greying sections of the population, have led to this gap and its gradual widening.

In Britain, Johnson (1987) and Marquand (1988) and in the Netherlands, Albeda (1986), Van Doorn and Schuyt (1986) and Schuyt (1986) have evaluated stagnation in the Welfare State. De Swaan (1988) has tried to analyze the Welfare State by using ideas of Elias and concepts from rational choice theory. Berger (1986) has edited a book on modernization that includes an evaluation of the Welfare State. A new approach to the subject could be introduced if trend reflections in the Welfare State were to be evaluated from the perspective of (a) demographic and related change, (b) societal contracts and (c) distribution and social conflict.

4.2 Generations and migration

Several problems arised as a result of demographic and related change. These include social inequality, societal contracts, distribution processes, and social tension. Migration is also an important phenomenon in this respect and in this section we will discuss migration and its relationship to the pattern of generations.

Migration has become a major aspect of social change in the Netherlands. Political and economic refugees as well as voluntary immigrants have turned the Netherlands into a multi-ethnic society. Societal contracts oblige the Netherlands to admit refugees. Legal rules transform these obligations into demands that can be enforced. The entrance of large numbers of foreigners into the Netherlands has to be interpreted as a major demographic change. Such migration has first and secondary order social consequences.

The first wave of immigrants consisted of relatively young workers. When many members of the first wave decided to stay in the Netherlands and work towards reuniting and settling their families in their new country, the age distribution of the immigrants became more diversified because young children began to enter the country too. Meanwhile many immigrants have begun to join the ranks of the elderly, and a 'second generation' of immigrants are being educated or have entered the labour market. Esser (1989) has explored these processes for Western Germany. In the Netherlands migrants tend to be concentrated in jobs and dwellings that are vulnerable and where the risk of unemployment and slum conditions is relatively high. Migrants and their organizations appeal to societal contracts both informal and formal in order to improve their position in Dutch society (Heeren, 1987).

The age distribution of the population born in the Netherlands has become unbalanced. The processes of greying and greening imply relatively large older cohorts and relatively small younger cohorts. Could immigration 'fill the gaps' in the age distribution of the population? A policy stimulating immigration of skilled labour in specific age categories might drain the immigrants countries of origin of specialists needed at home. A further problem may be that the integration of still larger groups of immigrants might induce social tension that would grow into social conflict and have an unfavourable impact on Dutch society.

This example shows that societal contracts change very slowly, or not at all. Secondly it illustrates that we need information not only about the contents of the societal contract on a macro level but that we also need insight into the ways in which the societal contracts are internalized by the members of the cohorts involved. To what extent do different generations regard these societal contracts as being equally valid when both immigrants and the traditional inhabitants of the Netherlands are considered.

4.3 Generations, societal contracts, and political decision making

The Welfare State linked social rights to existing civil and political rights. Social rights range from the right to economic welfare and security to the more general right to share to the full in that societies heritage and to live the life of a civilized being according to the standards prevailing in that society. These rights are encapsulated in institutions, laws and (societal) contracts. The contracts between state and citizen have been influenced both by structural factors and demographic, social, economic and political developments as well as by cultural factors and ideologies, values, norms. All these contracts have effects on economic and social inequalities.

In the field of social security four types of contracts can be identified:

a. a direct contract between state and citizen (subsistence minimum);
b. between employed and unemployed (employees insurance);
c. between age groups (General Old Age Pensions Act);
d. between men and women (equal and individual rights to employment, income and social security).

As an example of contract formation and development we present a short overview of governmental policy in respect of income distribution, (social) subsistance minima and social security (Van Wijngaarden, 1986).

Since World War II three periods can be distinguished and in each period different contracts were pursued:

The 1945-1969 contract: on the road to a reasonable standard of living for everyone

In the field of income inequality and social security this contract meant the implementation of: a) a centralized wage policy effecting both the level and the structure of wages. The level was influenced by wage-freezes, by uniform wage increases and by the fixing of minimum wages. The structure was influenced by job classification and by equal pay for men and women. In addition to this civil servants pay became linked to wages paid in the market sector; b) the construction of an extensive social security system,which greatly improved employees insurance, added to the existing provisions of the general benefit acts and social assistence acts; c) progressive taxation. Both employers and employees supported this contract.

The contract of the seventies: 'levelling' and 'linking'

Many new ideas and proposals came under discussion. These included justification criteria for income differentials and a national job evaluation system. In reality little of this was accomplished because the employers no longer gave their support to the centre-left government. Two other political options did, however, yield results. Firstly 'levelling', that is a reduction of income differentials by way of taking something away from the high income groups and adding something to lower ones. The instruments employed to achieve this were: annual assessment of changes in various scales of remuneration; structural increases in minimum pay; equalisation of net minimum incomes; and the 'linking' of the social security minima to changes in the level of minimum income from work (for the results consult figure 7). Secondly 'linkage' i.e. policies designed to equalise pay for work where productivity can be directly measured with work where it cannot; and linking changes in income from work with social security benefits. One result of this was that various income groups which had previously been 'outside' the regulated income system became integrated. Among these newly 'linked' were the higher income groups, members of the professions, and the self-employed (see figure 8).

The eighties: 'delevelling' and 'unlinking', a breach of contract?

The break with the contract to achieve greater equality came as a result of complex
interdependent demographic, social, cultural, political and economic circumstances. The
centre-left government, supported by the employers stated that social security and
income distribution should be secondary to the attainment of other socio-economic
objectives. These objectives included economic growth, more employment and a smaller
financial deficit. In effect this meant the abandonment of, what was believed to be, the
wide implications of 'levelling' incomes and a 'too high' social security expenditure.
Minimum incomes were reduced and confidence in centrally directed policies diminished. Trade Unions and Employers' Organisations were once again given a major
responsibility for the distribution of income from work. Again wages were decentrally
determined by direct negotiations between Unions and employers. Consequently linkage
between remuneration in the market and in the public sector were severed. Income from
work in the market sector and government employment, and wages and transfer incomes
ceased to be equalised. It also implied a limited 'unlinking' of several groups within the
market sector. In addition social security expenditure and other entitlements were
severely reduced. The final result was 'delevelling'. Income differences between employed and unemployed as well as between the employed increased.

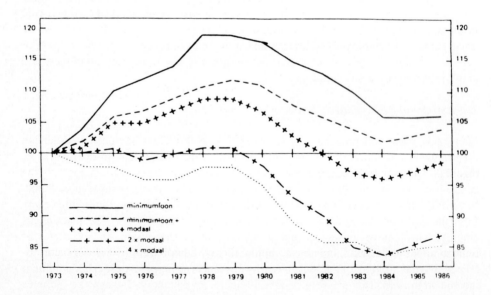

Figure 7   The effects of the 'levelling' contract
            Real disposable income, married employee in the private sector with unem-
            ployed wive, two children, excluding incidental payments.

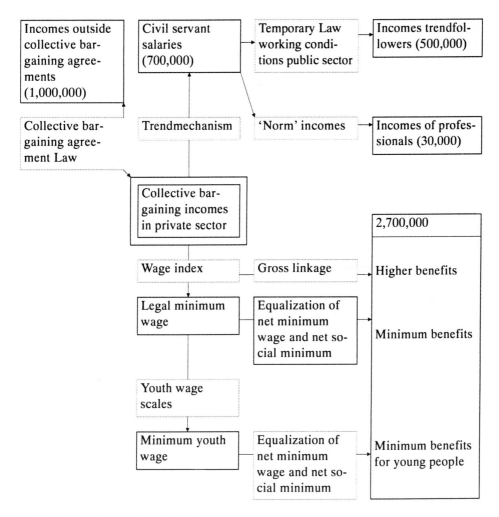

Figure 8   The 'linking' contract

4.4   Conclusions

General trend reflections and demographic change has produced a four generation pattern. Demographic and related change has a substantial impact on societal contracts and equality in society.

We have looked at generations and migration, each generation experienced the impact in a specific way.

Our second example focussed on social security and its relation to generations and gender. An overview of social security developments since 1945 clearly show impressive results in contract formation. These were: a) the minimum incomes of both employed and unemployed rose in line with general improvements in the country's welfare; b) income differentials between high and low income groups diminished; c) more and more groups were included in the regulated sphere and an increasingly uniform approach – 'linking' was implemented; d) a far reaching system of social security with a high level of benefits in comparison with other countries was developed.

In the 'eighties' these tendencies were reversed by policies designed to 'delevel', to 'unlink', and to save on social security disbursements. Should this policy be continued, the gains in equality of the seventies will soon be lost. The pressing question is: what is to be the new contract? Equal treatment and more equality between employed and unemployed, men and women, market and budget sector is receiving renewed attention. However, the processes of greying, individualization, and changes in the number of participants in the social security system and on the labour market seem to imply important restrictions on future contracts.

What have sections 3 and 4 told us with regard to problems one -nine posed in section 1? Question two, focussing on choice behaviour in cohorts and relating this behaviour to demographic and related change, has been dealt with in a preliminary way with regard to a number of areas in society, in particular the impact of the 'Second Demographic Transition'. Question three, inquiring into the impact of societal contracts on choice behaviour in cohorts, could only be dealt with as part of a discussion. Social tension and conflict, aspects of questions six and eight, could also only be answered in a limited way. The new research programme has only recently begun and it is clear that as it develops the questions raised by the NWO committee request will have to be dealt with.

5 Research priorities

5.1 Preconditions

The NWO Committee has invited the authors of papers for the workshop to elaborate research priorities. In this section we respond to this invitation. A research programme into the social consequences of demographic change already exists in the Netherlands. Our concern is that this research programme should be speeded up. What are the preconditions for such an accalaration?

Research problem

In the first place we need a problem that is sufficiently specified to enable focussed research activities. As a preliminary formulation we take the questions set out in section 1.2. The social consequences of demographic change have been sketched in more detail in Van den Brekel, 1987.

Strategy

In the second place we need a strategy to tackle the research problem involved. As a strategy we propose:

1. secondary analysis of data on life courses;
2. a survey providing overtime data;
3. a limited number of case studies considering specify relationships.

Analysis

In the third place the analytical approach to the data is important. This must contribute substantially to elucidating the problem at hand (inter alia Brass, 1989; Willekens, 1989). We propose the application of event history analysis, an already well-elaborated approach (inter alia Blossfeld, 1986, 1989; Beekes, 1989). We also propose institutional analysis, particularly with regard to the societal contracts at stake.

Explanation

In the fourth place theories are required which provide an explanation of the relationships concerned. As an overall theory, on a high level of abstraction, general rational choice theory could be used. At a lower level of abstraction theories have to be used which treat self-interest preferences and institutional requirements, including moral requirements as complementary. The application of complementary theories in the analysis of life histories and generations has been described in more detail elsewhere (Becker, 1989d). At a still lower level of abstraction the model of four generations and the modernization model can be used to provide rival explanations.

Teams, funds and facilities

Last but not least we have to look at the researchers and their professional environment. At the moment in the Netherlands a number of research teams are active in these fields. These teams need more senior and junior researchers. Both categories are to be found on the professional market or are entering the professional market soon, for example AIO's and OIO's finishing their doctoral dissertations. The teams are short of funds. The teams are also pressed for assistance, office space and computing facilities. They have elaborated social networks within the country and abroad, but these networks need strengthening.

5.2   Towards a new research programme

An acceleration and broadening of the existing research programme would imply changes that would ultimately turn the existing programme into a new one. It is necessary to ensure continuity but at the same time to stimulate a transformation into a new, less restricted research enterprise.

In the concluding section of this paper the strategy sketched in section 5.1 will be elaborated further. It is not possible however, to specify the research programme for a period of more than the first years at present.

Secondary analysis

In data archives in the Netherlands, in particular the Steinmetz Archief in Amsterdam and in the administrative data files of pension funds in particular, a number of data sets are available which would enable the researcher to analyse life courses with regard to one or more of the aspects described in section 3 of this paper. These analyses also provide information that explores relationships related to the second part of the research problem. The secondary analyses implied could start almost immediately because preliminary activities have already been completed. A specification of the data sets, variables and research problems involved can be provided at request.

Survey

The Netherlands lack a data provision comparable to the survey carried out by the Max-Planck Institute on Human Development and Education in Berlin. We propose a replica of this survey for the Netherlands, but we advocate a number of alterations in the surveys structure before it is applied.

The research project of the Max-Planck Institute has been described as follows:

"This study has the following goals: (1) to compare the temporal organizations and institutional structures of life courses; (2) to analyse the modes of operation and the effects of societal institutions, particularly, those of the schools, vocational training, the employment system, and the family as producers of individual life courses; and (3) to reconstruct a social history from the end of the Second World War on the basis of the collective histories of birth cohorts.

The life history data include information from 2,171 German respondents from the cohorts of 1929-31, 1939-41, and 1949-51. This sample is representative of the native-born German population of the Federal Republic of Germany. The objective of this data collection was to record the life histories of the respondents over every sociologically relevant area of their lives. This included social background, education, occupation, family, housing and so forth. The data were collected retrospectively by asking the respondents to reconstruct, with exact dates, their life histories in these areas. Recall errors are likely, especially if the events took place a long time ago and there are few methodological studies about the reliability of retrospectively recorded data. A general reservation with respect to the quality of such data is, therefore, plausible but it has not been empirically demonstrated. It seems, however, that data on general schooling and occupational training events as well as occupational history are relatively reliable" (Blossfeld, 1987 a,b).

We propose that a first survey on a national scale be carried out in the Netherlands in 1991, and a second survey would follow in 1995 or 1996. This second survey would cover the younger cohorts more extensively. We propose a survey in both cases of the cohorts 1925-1975. The publications by scientists working at the Max Planck Institute indicate that a survey like theirs can be used to analyse a large number of problems related to the central issue at stake. Of course, each survey has to be carefully prepared, taking into account the experiences gained in other similar projects. A specification of the research problem and the variables to be taken into consideration can be provided at request.

Case studies

A number of cases will have to be studied in depth, in order to get a balanced approach to both parts of the research problem. The first case study we propose is a survey of *academic careers*. This problem area has been explored recently both in the Netherlands (Becker and Beekes, 1989) and the United States (Soerensen, 1989) and these explorations provide a sound basis for the case study that we are suggesting. Demographic change is represented here by the differences between birth cohorts of academics. For instance the dual labour market situation is relatively unfavourable to the younger birth cohorts. University systems are characterized by numerous societal contracts, both formal and informal. The university environment becomes increasingly more restricted. These restrictions are relevant as soon as we try to explain re-definitions of societal contracts. Formal contracts like tenure are broken by the state as the central employer. Career expectations are re-defined over a period of years. The differences between cohorts leads to the hypothesis that specific generations of academics have emerged.

In the second place we propose a case study regarding *life courses of immigrants*. This case study could take place in cooperation with the research priority programme on ethnic minorities. To study the social consequences of the demographic change involved, a sample of immigrant life courses should be studied taking chains of life events into consideration and relating these events to societal contracts both formal and informal. Because a research project on this subject matter would be a relatively new enterprise, a pilot study would be necessary.

Priorities within the programme

The NWO Committee has also invited the authors of workshop papers to indicate how programme priorities might be established. Regarding research on the social consequences of demographic change we propose to take two four year periods into consideration.

In *the first four years* the secondary analysis should receive major support because of the results expected and because secondary analysis provides information necessary to later research projects. A nationwide survey would reconstruct life courses of the generation cohorts of 1925-1975. The analysis of academic careers could be used as a pilot study. Specific instances of social consequences of demographic change could be described and explained.

During *the second four year period* the secondary analysis could be continued on a lower financial basis, because its continuation would be based on prior experience. The survey would require major backing because a second wave of interviews would be due. A case study on the social consequences of demographic change related to immigration would also require funds and cooperation with the research priority programme on ethnic minorities would be required.

Research on the social consequences of demographic change must be coordinated with research on social security, housing, careers, and labour market developments. Research output regarding the social consequences of demographic change could be used as an input to future research regarding demographic development. The output concerned could also provide an input to research on demographic behaviour.

6 Summary

This paper is an attempt to answer a number of questions posed by the NWO Committee on Population Processes. These questions can be summarized as follows:

a. what are the social consequences of demographic change with specific reference to societal contracts?;
b. what research priorities are evoked by the developments involved?

In the paper we began by designing a *conceptual framework* with which we could analyse the relationships involved in the problem posed by the NWO Committee. We distinguished:

A. Demographic and related change (general trend reflections; demographic change; the emergence of a pattern of generations);
B. First order social consequences of A: impact on behaviour in cohorts (choice behaviour in life courses regarding education, employment, etc.);
C. Second order social consequences of A: impact on societal contracts, social inequality and distribution processes;
D. Political decision making and in particular interventions in societal contracts and distribution processes.

Next we sketched the *pattern of generations* that has emerged because it constitutes a synthesis of demographic and related change and provides a frame of reference when we try to look at social consequences. This pattern of generations consisted of:

a. the pre-war generation (about 1910-1930)
b. the silent generation (about 1930-1940)
c. the protest generation (1940-1955)
d. the lost generation (about 1955-1970)

This pattern of generations is presented at the theoretical level as a set of hypotheses. The hypotheses provide a frame of reference also called a formal theory (Boudon, 1984, 1986). As an alternative explanatory model modernization processes were sketched.

The following stage of our analysis concerned first order social consequences: impact on *choice behaviour by members of cohorts regarding their life course*. We related this choice behaviour as far as possible to societal contracts, old and new social inequality, and distribution processes. Our exploration of first order consequences was based mainly on current research. Promising research hypotheses were also brought to the fore.

We then outlined some aspects of second order social consequences. We discussed *societal contracts* in the Welfare State. We took the case of generations and migration. Following the questions posed by the NWO Committee we discussed societal contracts not only as the social consequences of demographic and related changes but we also discussed the dynamics of societal contracts. In this discussion we included some reflections on political decision making.

Designs for *research priorities* were presented at the end of the paper. As a starting point pre-conditions for a new research programme were stated and a number of interrelated research projects were outlined. A time perspective of eight years was taken. We advocate secondary analyses, a major social survey, and a number of case studies.

On the one hand the NWO Committee raises questions that are related to an ongoing research programme: the analysis of demographic change and generations; cohort behaviour; the dynamics of social inequality and distribution processes. On the other hand, by emphasizing societal contracts, a relatively new element is introduced and the inclusion of this aspect will lead to a relatively new research programme.

The paper emphasizes, that cooperation will be necessary between the new research programme and research regarding influences on demographic behaviour. Also cooperation is required with future demographic research, particularly the improvement of methods and the application of these methods in demographic forecasting and related research activities. In our paper developments regarding social security, and the labour and housing markets have received relatively little attention. Other papers however, deal with these phenomena in detail.

References

Albeda W., et al., eds. (1986), *De verzorgingsstaat: slopen of renoveren?*, Assen.

Becker, H.A. (1985 a), Generaties, *Hollands maandblad*, 26/4; pp. 14-25.

Becker, H.A. (1985 b), *Dutch generations today*, paper, NIAS.

Becker, H.A. (1987), *Generations and social inequality*, Utrecht.

Becker, H.A. (1988 a), Generaties en sociale dynamiek, in: W.E.A. van Beek e.a., eds., *Sociologisch en antropologisch jaarboek 1987*, Deventer, Van Loghum Slaterus, pp. 112-129.

Becker, H.A. (1988 b), *Life histories and generations, an overview of the literature*, Utrecht.

Becker, H.A. (1989 a), Generationen, Handlungsspielräume und Generationspolitik, in: A. Weymann, ed., *Handlungsspielräume*, Stuttgart: Enke Verlag.

Becker, H.A. (1989 b), Achievements in the analytical tradition in sociology, in: C.G.A. Bryant and H.A. Becker, eds., *What has sociology achieved?*, London: Macmillan.

Becker H.A. (1989 c), Cohorten en nieuwe ongelijkheden, in: J.L. Peschar, *Schijn bedriegt*, Groningen.

Becker, H.A. (1989 d), Theoretisch kader voor de analyse van levenslopen en generaties, in: H.A. Becker and P.L.J. Hermkens, eds., *Oude naast nieuwe generaties*, Utrecht.

Becker, H.A. (1989 e), Trendbreuken, cohorten en generaties, in: H.A. Becker en P.L.J. Hermkens, eds., *Oude naast nieuwe generaties*.

Becker, H.A., with F.A. Boerman and P.L.J. Hermkens (1989 e), Trendbreuken en hun demografische neerslag, in: H.A. Becker and P.L.J. Hermkens, eds., *Oude naast nieuwe generaties*.

Becker, H.A. and A.M.G. Beekes, eds. (1989), *Loopbanen van mannelijke en vrouwelijke academici aan Nederlandse universiteiten*, Utrecht.

Beekes, A., The development of cohort analysis, in: H.A. Becker, ed., *Life histories and generations* (forthcoming).

Berger, J., ed., (1986), *Die Moderne – Kontinuitäten und Zäsuren*, Göttingen.

Birg, H., E.J. Flöthmann and I. Reiter, Biographic analysis of the demographic charac-teristics of the life histories of men and women in regional labour-market-cohorts as clusters of birth cohorts, in: H.A. Becker, ed., *Life histories and generations* (forthcom-ing).

Blossfeld, H.P. (1986), Career opportunities in the Federal Republic of Germany: a dynamic approach to the study of life-course, cohort, and period effects, in: *European sociological review*, Vol. 2, no. 3.

Blossfeld, H.P. (1987 a), Entry into the labour market and occupational career in the Federal Republic, *International journal of sociology*, Vol. 17, no. 1-2, pp. 86-115.

Blossfeld, H.P. (1987 b), Labour-market entry and the sexual segretation of careers in the Federal Republic of Germany, *American journal of sociology*, Vol. 93, no. 1, pp. 1-31.

Blossfeld, H.P., and A. Hamerle, Advantages of event history analysis for life course research, in: H.A. Becker, ed., *Life histories and generations* (forthcoming).

Blossfeld, H.P., and R. Nuthmann, Transition from youth to adulthood as a cohort process in the Federal Republic of Germany, in: H.A. Becker, ed., *Life histories and generations* (forthcoming).

Boudon, R. (1984), *La place du désordre*, Paris: Presses Universitaires de Paris.

Boudon, R. (1986), *Theories of social change*, Oxford: Oxford University Press.

Brass, W., Cohort and time period measures of quantum fertility: concepts and metho-dology, in: H.A. Becker, ed., *Life histories and generations* (forthcoming).

Brekel, J.C. van den (rapporteur) (1987), *Aspecten van het bevolkingsvraagstuk*, Amster-dam, Ministerie van Onderwijs en Wetenschappen.

Chenug, S.H.S. (1969), Transaction costs, risk aversion and the choice of contractual arrangements, *Journal of law and economics*, Vol. 12.

Doorn, J.A.A. van, and C.J.M. Schuyt, eds. (1986), *De stagnerende verzorgingsstaat*, Leiden: Stenfert Kroese.

Doorne-Huiskes, J. van (1983), *Vrouwen en beroepsparticipatie; een onderzoek onder gehuwde vrouwelijke academici*, Utrecht, Ph.D., English translation: Women and labour force participation; a study of married women with an academic degree.

Esser, H. (1989), Karriere als 'Entscheidung', Stadien und Verläufe der Familienkonsoli-dierung bei Migranten, in: A. Weymann, ed., *Handlungsspielräume*, Stuttgart: Enke Verlag.

Fiske, D.W. and R.A. Sweder, eds., (1986), *Metatheory in social science*, Chicago: The University of Chicago Press.

Frinking, G.A.B. (1988), Ontgroening in Nederland, in: G.A.B. Frinking and J.H.M. Nelissen, eds., *Ontgroening in Nederland*, Amersfoort: ACCO.

Fulpen, H. van (1985), *Volkshuisvesting in demografisch en econonomisch perspectief*, Den Haag: Staatsuitgeverij.

Gadourek, I. (1982), *Social change as redefinition of roles*, Assen: Van Gorcum.

Giesen, B., and H. Haferkamp, eds., (1987), *Soziologie der sozialen Ungleichheit*, Opladen: Westdeutscher Verlag.

Hardin, F. (1982), *Collective action*, Baltimore.

Heek, F. van (1968), *Het verborgen talent*, Meppel: Boom.

Heeren, H.J. (1987), *Bevolkingsgroei en overheidsbeleid*, Leiden, Stichting Research voor Beleid.

Hermkens, P.L.J. (1983), *Oordelen over de rechtvaardigheid van inkomens*, Amsterdam.

Hermkens, P.L.J., A.M.G. Beekes and A.H.G. Rekers (1989), Inkomensloopbanen van starters 1965-1985, *Gedrag en organisatie*, Vol. 2.

Hermkens, P.L.J., and A.H.G. Rekers, Differences in pension incomes between the 1910-1940 birth cohorts, in: H.A. Becker, ed., *Life histories and generations* (forthcoming).

Hernes, G., Structural change in social processes, *American journal of sociology*, Vol. 82, no. 13, pp. 513-547.

Johnson, N. (1987), *The welfare state in transition, the theory and practice of welfare pluralism*, Brighton.

Jong-Gierveld, J. de, and E. Beekink, Changing value orientations and behaviour: a comparison between two generations of female academics, in: H.A. Becker, ed., *Life histories and generations* (forthcoming).

Kaa, D.J. van de (1987), Europe's second demographic transition, *Population bulletin*, 42, pp. 1-57.

Kam, F. de (1989), Een onbetaalde rekening, *Intermediair*, Vol. 25, 24, pp. 15-19.

Kerstholt, F. (1988), *Tussen rationele keuze en Durkheimiaanse solidariteit, over voortgang in theorie en onderzoek van sociale ongelijkheid*, Tilburg: Tilburg University Press.

Klaassen-van den Berg Jeths, A. (1989), *Zorgvoorzieningen voor ouderen, determinanten van gebruik: huidige situatie en toekomstige ontwikkelingen*, Utrecht.

Klijzing, F.K.H., Time-related aspects of male and female labour force participation status changes: the case of the Netherlands, 1977-1984, in: H.A. Becker, ed., *Life histories and generations* (forthcoming).

Lesthaege, R. and D.J. van de Kaa (1986), Twee demografische transities?, in: D.J. van de Kaa en R. Lesthaeghe, eds., Bevolking, groei en krimp, *Mens en maatschappij*, jrg. 61.

Lindenberg, S. (1988), Contractual relations and weak solidarity: the behavioural basis of restraints on gain-maximation, *Journal of institional and theoretical economics*, 144, pp. 38-58.

Mannheim, K. (1928-1929), Das Problem der Generationen, *Kölner Vierteljahresheft für Soziologie*, Vol. 7, pp. 154-184 and 309-330.

Marquand, D. (1988), *The unprincipled society*, London.

Nelissen, J.H.M. (1987), Leeftijd en inkomen, *Bevolking en gezin*, 3, pp. 53-71.

Posner, R.A. (1986), *Economic analysis of law*, Toronto.

Outhwaite, W. (1987), *New philosophies of science*, London, Macmillan.

Rijsselt, R.J.T. van, and H.A. Becker, Developments in attitudes and value orientations, a comparison between birth cohorts in the Netherlands over the period 1970-1985, in: H.A. Becker, ed., *Life histories and generations* (forthcoming).

Riley, M.W., ed., (1972), *Ageing and society, vol.3: A sociology of age stratification*, New York.

Rijsselt, R.J.T., and P.L.J. Hermkens, Income developments between 1974 and 1983: a comparison between birth cohorts in the Netherlands, in: H.A. Becker, ed., *Life histories and generations* (forthcoming).

Rogers, E.M. (1983), *Diffusion of innovations*, Glencoe.

Rosen, S. (1985), Implicit contracts, a review, *Journal of economic literature*, Sept., pp. 1144-1175.

Ryder, N.B. (1965), The cohort as a concept in the study of social change, *American sociological review*, Vol. 30, pp. 843-861.

Schelsky, H. (1957), *Eine Soziologie der Deutschen Jugend*, Düsseldorf.

Schuyt, C.J.M. et al., ed. (1986), *De verdeelde samenleving*, Leiden: Stenfert Kroese.

Simonis, J.B.D. (1983), *Implementatie van beleid als probleem*, Amsterdam: KOBRA.

Snippenburg, L.B. van, and A.B. van Berkel-van Schaik, Sociohistorical generations, constructs or reality? An empirical test of a thesis on Dutch generations in the eighties, in: H.A. Becker, ed., *Life histories and generations* (forthcoming).

Soerensen, A.B., Academic careers and academic labour markets, in: H.A. Becker, ed., *Life histories and generations* (forthcoming).

Swaan, A. de (1988), *In care of the state*, London: Polity Press.

Tazelaar, F. (1980), *Mentale incongruentie-sociale restricties-gedrag: een onderzoek naar beroepsparticipatie van gehuwde vrouwelijke academici*, Utrecht, Ph.D.

Thoenes, P. (1962), *De elite in de verzorgingsstaat*, Leiden.

Vogel, J. (1988), *Inequality in Sweden*, Stockholm: National Bureau of Statistics.

Wijngaarden, P. van (1983), *Rechtvaardige verdeling in de verzorgingsstaat*, 's-Gravenhage: VUGA.

Wijngaarden, P. van (1986), Inkomensverdelingsbeleid in de verzorgingsstaat; ontwikkeling, doelstellingen, resultaten, in: Y. Brenner, J. Reijnders, P. van Wijngaarden, eds., *Visies op verdeling*, Den Haag, pp. 93-142.

Willekens, F.J., Life table analysis of staging processes, in: H.A. Becker, ed., *Life histories and generations* (forthcoming).

Emerging Issues in Demographic Research
C.A. Hazeu and G.A.B. Frinking (Editors)
© Elsevier Science Publishers B.V. , 1990

Chapter 6

SOCIAL CONSEQUENCES OF DEMOGRAPHIC CHANGE; A COMMENT

Kees C.P.M. Knipscheer

Because of my own involvement in gerontological research I have to keep up with demographic developments in the Netherlands and in other western countries. The more I compare the Dutch situation with the demographic situation in other western European countries the more I discover the specific characteristics of our country. Especially the high birthrate between 1945 and 1965, in itself an interesting phenomenon, will continue to influence the composition of the Dutch population into the fourties of the next century.

This is one of the reasons why I read the contribution by Becker with much interest. It is not only the demographic situation itself which is of importance, the social consequencies need special attention. In this context the international discussion on 'intergenerational equity' is of primary importance (see e.g. Baum and Baum, 1980; Preston, 1985; Kingson, Hirshorn and Cornman, 1986; Pifer and Bronte, 1986; Morris, 1989). Becker elaborates the question "to which extent will demographic change influence the contents and impacts of the social 'contracts' that explicitly or implicitly shape processes of (re)distribution in society, and that might lead to the emergence or continuation of (new types of) social inequality?" He presents a number of notions on the theoretical level as well as on the empirical level. His conceptual framework appears to be a heuristic to clarify the linkages between a number of variables involved. It may be, most interesting is the combination of three broad variables under the heading of demographic and related changes (block A in figure 1 of the paper of Becker). In some way one can imagine how each of these variables by its own is related to the variables in block B – behaviour in cohorts – and to the variables in block C – societal contracts, social inequality and distribution processes –. However, the interrelationships between the three variables of block A, general trend reflections, demographic change and the emergence of a pattern of generations, remains open. From the presentation of theoretical hypotheses in section two I understand that the pattern of generations emerged as a result of demographic and related change. This implies a time-order between the variables involved and – possibly – a causal relationship. This part of the framework needs more elaboration before it can be tested empirically.

In section 3 a number of important studies are summarized and interesting data are presented. As it is shown, recent data on education, employment, income and value orientations demonstrate important findings on the age and cohort relatedness of these societal phenomena. Older cohorts have a lower average education level as younger cohorts. There is a difference in average income between cohorts, and within cohorts older agegroups up to fifty or sixty have a higher average income than younger age groups. These kind of data tell a lot about social inequalities between societal groups and do understand the origin of them. However, it is to be questioned how these data are related to demographic change. Can these kind of correlations be specified for the first and/or the second demographic transition? *Cohort related change* has to be distinguished of *demographic change related change*.

After these general comments to the contribution of Becker I would like to make some specific points on the topic under discussion in this paper. First, I agree with Becker saying that demographic change may be a consequence of general trend reflections in one or several areas of society. Looking more closely to the two demographic transitions (Lesthaege and Van de Kaa, 1986) it should be possible to trace some trend reflections which promote understanding of these demographic changes. However, my focus would be more specific on the social consequences of demographic change. I would suggest to take the four main elements of demographic behaviour as a point of departure: birth, death, marriage (or cohabitation, household formation) and migration. What are the specific social consequences of considerable changes in each of these areas?

Second, if the focus is on the social consequences related to social contracts, which seem to be an extremely important issue, these consequences have to be specified for the formal and informal social contracts under discussion. A crosstabulation like in figure 1 presents a first overview of the questions to be approached.

	birth	death	marriage	migration	total effects
child allowance					
education grants					
unemployment benefits					
preretirement regulations					
public pension					
health insurance					
informal support elderly					

Figure 1   Crosstabulation of core-elements in demographic behavioural and social (formal and informal) contracts

The formal and informal social contracts have been ordered as much as possible along the lifecourse transitions, indicating that each demographic change is specifically related to specific stages of the existing lifecourse structure. Each cell of this table needs specific attention in the context of the lifecourse trajectories set in the society. This logic along the lifecourse seem to be implied by the third point I would like to make.

Third, most of the social consequences of demographic change have a long term character (cf. the inertia of demographic processes). This implies that *it is most relevant to look over time*. For example what are the social consequences of a high birthrate between 1945 and 1965. This demographic change can be related to a number of social contracts as is demonstrated in figure 2. We all know that in the Netherlands this high birthrate is starting to have a number of social consequences in terms of the aging of the

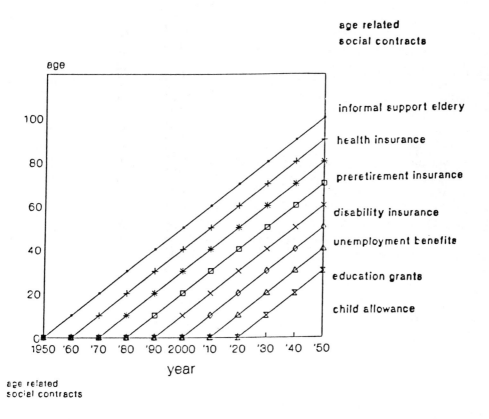

Figure 2   Cohort related change over time: the case of a high birth rate

Dutch society by the year 2010. However, another demographic change could happen between the year 1965 and 2010, e.g. a considerable raise in life expectancy. In some way this would double up the social consequences of the high birthrate between 1945 and 1965 over time. Such a second demographic change could be included in figure 2 to show the growing complexity of studying the consequences for the younger cohorts.

Fourth, demographic change never happens in a vacuum. As it is shown in the contribution by Becker several dimensions of social change may lead to demographic change and may intervene with the social consequences of demographic change. This is one of the reasons why the study of the social consequences of demographic change becomes so complex. This complexity stresses also the need for theory. At this moment I would like to refer to three theoretical notions that may be useful to the questions under discussion here. Dreitzel (1984) introduces – in his reflection on the changing relation-ships between age groups and/or generations – the "Principle of Stratified Diffusion", earlier developed in a study of Young and Willmott (1973) on the symmetrical family. "The image we are trying to suggest", they say, "is that of a marching column with the people at the head usually being the first to wheel in a new direction. The last rank keeps its distance from the first, and the distance between them does not lessen. But as the column advances, the last rank does eventually reach and pass the point which the first rank had passed some time before. In other words, the egalitarian tendency works with a time lag ...."(Young and Willmott, 1973). As Dreitzel suggests this notion of the Principle of stratified diffusion begins to work not only through the class stratification system but also through the age groups, always beginning with the young (p.25). In connection with the question of the social consequences of demographic change this is an interesting notion. How does a high birthrate relate to this priority of the young in processes of social change? How does this work out for the older generations? What is the effect of the apparent contrasting time-order in these processes?

A second theoretical contribution is recently presented by Foner (1984). She discussed a number of age conflict reducing mechanisms "that mute or avert sharp age struggles" (p.170). She gives three reasons for the existence of these mechanisms:

– "The existence of age heterogeneous groups serves to strengthen bonds among people of different ages and provides opportunities for people of different ages to influence each other, thus blunting sharp age cleavages that might otherwise arise.
– The existence of multiple forms of social stratification means that other identities – class, sex, ethnic identities, for example – often take precedence over age identities and allegiance to age peers.
– The aging process operates to mute conflict in several ways. People tend to orient themselves to the next older age stratum, anticipating the roles they will soon fill and assimilating some of the attitudes considered appropriate for these future roles." (Foner, p.171)

Considering these kind of conflict reducing mechanisms between age groups the question is *when demographic change related social inequality* (because of the violation of social contracts) has raised to a level at which these mechanisms do not work any more?

A third theoretical contribution can be adopted from Kohli (1988). He discussed lately, in analysing the challenge of an aging society to sociological theory, the traditional basis of social stratification and social inequality theory. In essence his argument is a search for a new approach of social class theories and social stratification. Originally the basis of the social class structure has been seen in the roles of the employers and the workers. Because of demographic change, industrialisation and technology this original division cannot be maintained. He is promoting to develop a broader classification scheme, including many areas of social life, and taking into account a biographical approach. The important point here is that apparently demographic change is changing the notion of social inequality itself.

A fourth, and last, comment I would like to make refers to the research priorities proposed. Two lines of research are suggested, first secondary analysis of available data and second a somewhat modified repetition of a life course study by the German Max Planck Institute in Berlin. The data which are available and the data to be gathered will allow for a number of interesting analyses, they will promote further understanding of how individual life courses are shaped by societal forces. However I am wondering if the approach proposed is focussed enough on the central question under discussion, the social consequences of demographic change. As far as I know these kind of questions have not yet been explored, less thoroughly studied. My suggestion would be to take one significant example of a demographic change and to explore it retrospectively in its early consequences and prospectively in its future consequences. This exploration should start on the macrolevel and gradually go down to the microlevel and the individual lifecourse. In my mind the Netherlands has a perfect case available in the late but pronounced decline of the birthrate at the end of the sixties.

A short elaboration on this suggestion seem to be appropriate. It is suggested to start on the macrolevel because demographic change is considered to be a macrolevel phenomenon. In this case the study of social consequences of demographic change looks for the societal reactions to it, assuming societal reactions are not the same as the sum of individual reactions. The study of the societal reactions asks for a socio-historical approach, wondering when the society became aware of it, how its first reaction to it was, who was commenting on the phenomenon, how these reactions were related to the actual socio-economic situation, what kind of political reactions have been considered including the societal implications of these reactions.

The more this approach will differentiate for specific agegroups, socio-economic classes and gender, the more it will become possible to say something about the consequences demographic change on the individual level. My suggestion to take the late but pronounced decline of the Dutch birthrate at the end of the sixties as a point of departure for a study of the consequences of demographic change implies a clear preference to take as focus a specific demographic change. It would be possible not to take a specific demographic change as focus but e.g. a specific historical period and try to understand it – among others – from the viewpoint of demographic change or a specific phenomenon, e.g. early retirement in the context of demographic change. However, given the question of the study of the consequence of demographic change a focused approach seem to be preferable. The decline of the Dutch birthrate as around 1970 is suggested because of its steep decline over a short period of time. The Netherlands is one of the few developed countries with such a 'sharp' change. The consequences of it will reach up to 2050. A longterm attention to the consequences of this demographic change will serve future generations over decades. It seems to be possible to integrate this focus with other priorities in the demographic research programme.

References

Baum, M. and R.C. Baum (1980), *Growing old, a societal perspective*, Englewood Cliffs N.J.: Prentice-Hall Inc.

Dreitzel, H.P. (1984), Generational conflict from the point of view of civilisation theory, in: Garms-Homolova, V., E.M. Hoerning and D. Schaeffer, *Intergenerational Relationships*, New York: C.J. Hogrefe, Inc., pp. 17-26.

Foner, A. (1984), The issues of age conflict in political life, in: Garms-Homolova, V., E.M. Hoerning and D. Schaeffer, *Intergenerational Relationships*, New York: C.J. Hogrefe, Inc., pp. 170-175.

Kingson, E.R., B.A. Hirshorn, J.M. Cornman (1986), *Ties that bind, the interdependence of generations*, Washington, D.C.: Seven Locks Press.

Kohli, M. (1988), Ageing as a challenge for sociological theory, in: *Ageing and Society*, 8, pp. 376-394.

Lesthaege, R. and D.J. van de Kaa (1986), Twee demografische transities?, in: Kaa, D.J. van de, and R. Lesthaege, eds., Bevolking, groei en krimp, *Mens en Maatschappij*, 61.

Morris, R. (1989), Challenges of aging in tomorrow's world: will gerontology grow, stagnate, or change, in: *The Gerontologist*, 29, 4, pp. 494-501.

Pifer, A. and L. Bronte, eds. (1986), *Our aging society, paradox and promise*, New York: Carnegie Corporation.

Preston, S. (no date), Children and the elderly in the U.S., *Scientific American 251*, no. 6.

Young, M. and P. Willmott (1973), *The symmetrical family*, London: Routledge and Kegan Paul.

Emerging Issues in Demographic Research
C.A. Hazeu and G.A.B. Frinking (Editors)
© Elsevier Science Publishers B.V. , 1990

Chapter 7

THE MICROECONOMIC THEORY OF HOUSEHOLD FORMATION AND DISSOLUTION: STATE-OF-THE-ART AND RESEARCH PROPOSALS

Jan H.M. Nelissen

1 Introduction

Since roughly the middle of the last century, economists and demographers have taken little interest in each other's work. This has not always been the case, however. Earlier classical economists, such as Smith (1776), Malthus (1878) and Ricardo (1911) considered population issues[1] to be of prime importance, and in their writings on the subject, economic and demographic developments are closely interwoven.

During the nineteenth century, however, economists began to attach less importance to demographic considerations, leading Jevons to conclude that: "Demography ... does not fall within the immediate scope of economics" (Jevons, 1924, p. 250). Given the shifting focus of economic research, from national welfare to entrepreneurial behaviour, and thus from long- to short-term considerations, it is not really hard to understand this declining interest in population growth. It should, however, be noted that classical economists did not initially assume that economic factors were determinants in the formation and dissolution of relationships. This is not really so surprising. Although it was of course generally acknowledged that economic factors, like socio-cultural factors, had an effect on the aforementioned processes, it was generally felt that these processes themselves could not be affected, given the impact of socio-cultural factors – the role of the church, the importance of rank and social position, etc. – on the daily lives, and therefore the socio-economic position of individuals.

This is not to say that demography as a whole had no part in economic theory; but it remained limited. The concept of a stationary (declining) population in particular continued to interest many economists (see e.g. Keynes, 1937), but generally speaking interest in demography was patchy.

---

[1] In particular population *growth*.

Traditional demography, as a natural extension of actuarial sciences, is governed by model schedules and empirical regularities and so is, in that sense, basically descriptive, with a strong emphasis on method. Demography is thus characterised by "a search for empirical regularities ... A product of such research is model schedules" (Montgomery and Trussell, 1986, p. 214) – in which greater emphasis is placed on methodology than on the impact of economic factors on demographic developments.

Around 1960 the situation changed. Two factors appear to have been responsible for this. Firstly, a number of publications by Leibenstein (1957), and in particular Gary Becker (see Becker, 1960; 1965; 1973 and 1974; and Becker, Landes and Michael, 1977), showed that it was possible to apply economic theory to themes such as fertility, and the formation and dissolution of relationships.[1] The growing interest in these behavioural models in economic demography corresponded to developments in various areas of the economy, such as life cycle theories of consumption, static theories of labour supply and the characteristics approach to consumption. Secondly, and most importantly, social developments during this same period led to greater freedom of individual choice: whether or not to have any, or more, children; whether or not to get married; whether or not to divorce. This greater freedom of individual choice increased the importance of economic and other factors, and probably also served to stimulate research into (micro) economic behaviour in households.

The United States in particular was fairly quick to undertake research into the economic determinants of household formation. Europe followed suit, but concentrated mainly on what effect economic factors had on fertility. Siegers is the only researcher in the Netherlands who has studied this subject in depth for a long time (see Siegers, 1985 and 1987). He too concentrates on fertility.[2]

The result of this development was that the household as such ceased to be considered as the traditional basic decision unit. Interest in decisions both within the household, and decisions affecting the formation and dissolution of households, is gaining pace – not simply because such decisions might have underlying economic motives, but also because of their economic implications. Marriage, for example, has many economic implications. Consider the possible advantages of a division of labour in both household work and a paid job. What is more, in a household of two (or more) people, economies of scale arise. By the same token, the economic importance of fertility and divorce cannot be denied.

Thus demographic factors clearly can affect economic decisions. The differences in female labour force participation are a case in point. Married women make up a smaller share of the female labour force than single women, and work fewer hours. Conversely,

---

[1] These publications initially received a mixed reception, by economists and non-economists alike. See Spangler (1966), Blake (1967 and 1968) and Boulding (1969) etc. Becker (1981) deals with this in greater detail.

[2] The Research Methods Department of the Social Faculty of Tilburg University has recently been conducting research into the effect of economic factors on the formation and dissolution of households.

economic factors affect demographic decisions, e.g. it is more common for unemployed young people to stay living in the parental home than is the case for their employed peers. And with ever-increasing freedom of choice with regard to marriage and fertility, it seems reasonable to assume that the effect of economic variables on decision-making in this area has increased.

There are thus grounds for viewing demographic factors as endogenous variables. We will confine ourselves in this paper to examining how the effect of economic factors on household formation can be studied. The following section considers how we can study the influence of economic factors on demographic behaviour.

Given the effect of demographic variables on economic variables and vice versa, it is clear that the two constantly interact. For example, if a woman has completed higher education, the effect of this might be a higher shadow wage than that for a woman of lower educational level, and this can result in the former wanting to have fewer children. This could eventually result in there being a higher supply of labour by more educated women, since, with fewer children, less time would need to be spent raising them.

Potential deterrents cannot be ruled out either. If, for example, many marriages end in divorce, this can affect the marriage rate as well as the content of the (informal) marriage contract, e.g. the specialist roles of partners within the household (see Lommerud, 1989).

If such a model is available, it is quite easy to examine its knock-on effects with the help of micro-simulation. Section 3 deals with the ins and outs of micro-simulation. The study concludes with a number of proposals for further research.

2   Research into the economic determinants of household formation

2.1   Introduction

It would be useful if we first defined which demographic phenomena we will be concentrating on. The NWO Committee responsible for preparing the Priority Programme on Population Studies asked me to elaborate on the theme of 'economic determinants and their effect on the formation of relationships, household development and fertility'. It was to be based on the premise that individuals have greater freedom of choice over demographically relevant behavioural alternatives.

This therefore entails examining demographic variables such as fertility, marriage and extramarital cohabitation, separation, and leaving the parental home.

All these demographic variables are affected by the fact that the behaviour of the Dutch population and the immigrant population differs markedly. This fact is generally accepted with regard to fertility (see for example Verhoef and Tas, 1987, and Van Hoorn, 1987), but is in fact equally applicable to other factors. Bearing in mind the analyses suggested in section 3, it would seem sensible not to dismiss immigration out of hand. It could also be important for 'research into future developments'[1]; please refer to the West German population forecasts, labour force participation and education, in which differences in nationality are clearly significant. See Mount (1989) for an economic analysis.

In my view mortality deserves attention too. Foreign research (see the summary by Valkonen, 1987) indicates that average life expectancy (as well as health) is related to socio-economic variables such as education, profession and income, which can have important implications when forecasting subpopulations, the demand for social security provisions, etc. (see Nelissen, 1987). We refer to Van Poppel's contribution to this volume for more information about mortality.

Marriage, marriage dissolution, extramarital cohabitation, leaving the parental home, expansion of the family by the birth of a child all constitute household formation processes in the broadest sense of the word; they are the result of decisions made by individuals, couples and households (see Burch and Matthews, 1987). Virtually all of these decisions entail supply and demand considerations and the outcome is usually decided within the household after discussion. Thus the household position can be seen as a composite good, in the sense that choices are made by weighing up a combination of factors such as privacy, economies of scale, sharing work, companionship, personal care, domestic services, independence and so on. From this standpoint the various different household formation processes become consistent with the home production theory. Because this theory can be applied to these types of decisions, it is possible to examine these facets in the same theoretical context and highlight the correlation between the different aspects (Siegers, 1987, p. 87) The following sub-section deals with this theory in greater depth, and section 2.3 examines the application of the home production theory to the aforementioned demographic phenomena.

2.2   The home production theory

Traditional neo-classical theory differentiates between the respective theories of production and consumption, in which production is generated by companies trying to maximise their profits in the market, and consumption takes place within the household, which in turn strives to maximise the utility of the acquired goods and services. And so companies sell goods and services to the households in exchange for labour and capital input. This concept has been challenged over the years for, amongst other things, its assumption that production only takes place in the marketplace. Those who subscribe to the home production theory consider home production to be no less important than market production. Gorman (1956), Becker (1965), Lancaster (1966a and b) and Muth (1966) are the main founders of the home production theory, the most important characteristic of which is that households are no longer regarded only as consumption units, but also as production units. The consequence of this is that, instead of seeking to maximise the utility derived from consumption of market goods, given their income, households

---

[1]   See Willekens' contribution to this volume.

maximise the utility derived from the final goods (or 'commodities', to use the home production theory terminology) produced in their household. These 'commodities' are the product of both time, and goods acquired in the market. What this all means is that the amount of time an individual offers on the labour market is partly determined by the decision made within the household regarding the production of commodities and their requisite home production time. In determining optimum consumption, therefore, income becomes an endogenous variable (insofar as it can be affected, given possible institutional constraints). Every decision is affected by time constraints and opportunity costs of time, and the implications thereof.

To illustrate the differences between the two approaches, we will consider them in greater depth. We will also show how demographic factors apply to this theory, and how it can be used to examine more closely the economic determinants of demographic behaviour. In so doing we will follow Gronau's line of argument (Gronau, 1986).

As mentioned before, in traditional neo-classical economics, consumers are seen as people seeking to maximise welfare in terms of utility:

$$\max U = U(X_1, ..., X_n ; L) \tag{1}$$

with budget constraints being an additional condition:

$$\sum_{i=1}^{n} P_i \cdot X_i = w \cdot (T - L) + V \tag{2}$$

where U is utility, X_i is the i-th good, P_i is the price of the i – th good, L the amount of leisure time, T the total time available (thus T – L is the working time), w is the wage rate and V is non-labour income. This gives rise to the following prerequisites for an optimum:

$$u_i = \delta U / \delta X_i = \tau \cdot P_i , \ i = 1 , \cdots , n \tag{3}$$

and

$$u_L = \delta U / \delta L = \tau \cdot w \tag{4}$$

where u_i is the marginal utility of good i and τ is the marginal utility of income. The marginal rate of substitution in consumption between goods i and j is equal to their price relationship ($u_i / u_j = P_i / P_j$) and the marginal rate of substitution between leisure time and goods is equal to the real wage rate ($u_L / u_i = w / P_i$).

Whereas the goods and services acquired determine the utility and therefore the welfare of consumers, the home production theory considers these goods and services as a derivative. According to this theory, households choose the set of goods and services which lead to maximum utility with respect to the production of finished products and the concomitant process of transformation.[1] The role of the production process implies that time inputs of households are very important. In addition to the budget, time is a limiting factor and therefore influences final choices.

As an example we examine the case of a one-period one-person household. Let Z_i be the i-th commodity, where each commodity (or activity) is a combination of time (T_i) and goods (X_i):

$$Z_i = f_i(X_i, T_i), \quad i = 1, \cdots, m \tag{5}$$

We can use the example of the mending of torn garments. This costs time and inputs in the form of fabric, thread and depreciation of the needle or of the sewing machine etc. An alternative would be to have the mending done. This costs time to take it to the mender and money to pay for the services and the material inputs used by the mender. The household will now maximise:

$$U = U(Z_1, \cdots, Z_m) \tag{6}$$

under the following conditions:

$$\Sigma P_i X_i = Y \tag{7}$$

and

$$\Sigma T_i = T \tag{8}$$

This assumes that the labour supply of the households involved is exogenous, so that T is equal to the total non-labour time. The essential condition for optimal consumption now becomes:

$$u_i = \delta U / \delta Z_i = \tau \hat{\pi}_i \tag{9}$$

where $\hat{\pi}_i = P_i \cdot x_i + \hat{w} \cdot t_i$ is the shadow price of commodity i, $x_i = \delta X_i / \delta Z_i$ and $t_i = \delta T_i / \delta Z_i$, are the marginal inputs of goods and time in the production of Z_i and $\hat{w}$ is the shadow price of time.

---

[1] There are differences in interpretation between Lancaster and Becker in respect to the way in which market goods are transformed within the household into final goods, in particular the extent of 'jointness' in production. We follow Becker's approach. For further analysis see Pollak and Wachter (1975) and Atkinson and Stern (1979).

The optimum combination of inputs in the production of Z_i is determined by the well-known condition that the marginal rate of substitution in production is equal to the price relationship:

$$(\delta Z_i / \delta T_i) / (\delta Z_i / \delta X_i) = x_i / t_i = \hat{w} / P_i \tag{10}$$

It follows that the demand for goods is a derivative question. This is in fact dependent on the demand for commodities, on the share of the market input costs in the total costs of producing this commodity and on the elasticity of the substitution of goods and time. This elasticity is extremely important and because of it, an increase in income has an effect not only on income but also on price so that the household may be inclined to purchase ready-made goods instead of producing them itself. Even within the household itself it is no exaggeration to say: time is money. This latter concept can best be seen if we no longer consider the decision to supply labour as an exogenous factor, but as a decision variable within the household. Income can then be increased at the expense of the time devoted to the household. Instead of the two conditions (7) and (8), one single condition suffices:

$$\Sigma \; P_i \cdot X_i = W(Z_n) + V \tag{11}$$

where Z_n represents paid employment and $W(Z_n)$ the wage. The optimum condition for Z_n now becomes:

$$u_n = \delta U / \delta Z_n = \tau \cdot [P_n \cdot x_n + \hat{w} \cdot t_n - W'] \tag{12}$$

where $W' = \delta W(Z_n) / \delta Z_n$ is the wage rate. The shadow price of time, $\hat{w}$, (where work is measured in units of time $t_n = 1$) is equal to

$$\hat{w} = W' - P_n \cdot x_n - u_n / \tau \tag{13}$$

In other words, the shadow price of time differs from the average wage w whenever the latter differs from the marginal wage, that is to say if market inputs are necessary in order to go to work (e.g. transport costs, child care etc.) and if work provides utility directly to the individual. If the marginal wage rate is equal to the average wage rate $(W = w)$ i.e. the marginal market inputs can be disregarded and if there is no direct positive or negative utility attributed to employment outside the home, then the value of time is also equal to the wage rate.

It is also easy to distinguish leisure time from home production time, since the latter can be seen as a substitute for paid employment. See Gronau (1977) for a more detailed analysis.

Thus the home production theory as formulated is practicable for economic analysis in various fields. In the following section we shall deal in more detail with the analysis of several demographic phenomena. We see this theory primarily as an analytical device, in which we focus on the distinction between consumption and production.

2.3   The application of the home production theory to demographic phenomena

One generally speaks of new home economics when applying the above theory to demographic phenomena. This approach was first used by Becker. Since the application of the above on unpaid production within the household can be placed within a single theoretical framework, this theory is perfectly suited to explicit modelling of the mutual relationship between events affecting the family, such as marriage, marriage dissolution, family size, leaving the parental home, division of labour within the household, supply of labour by the individual household members.

It is essential for the application of the present issue (see Silber, 1981) that:

a. there is a utility function applicable to each household, which describes the interdependent interests of its various members;
b. the factors comprising the utility function are made up of so-called commodities, which may also be non-material factors;
c. the activities within the household can be described by means of a production function, using goods and time as factors;
d. substitution is possible between goods and time expended within the household, taking into account a 24 hourly restriction on time.

On this basis the various family members can weigh up how much time is spent in the household and how much in the labour market. Bringing up children costs time which implies that the utility of having a(n) (additional) child (which could be one of the commodities in the utility function) must be balanced against the decrease in utility of having less time to spend in the household and in the labour market. Similar considerations are also possible for other household decisions.

A more generalized theoretical formulation of the various household formation processes was done by Ermisch (1981), but in its present form is a static one-period model. The matching problem does not arise and does not contain any bargaining elements which is why we have chosen to make an inventory of the various applications. This makes it clearer where the problems lie and where closer analysis is desirable.

2.3.1   Fertility

The most important starting point in the analysis of fertility within the new home economics theory is that children are produced not in the marketplace but at home. Production (bringing up) and consumption (utility, pleasure) take place in one and the same household. In that sense, children are to be viewed as a commodity in terms of the home production theory. Becker expected that this commodity would behave as a durable good, in which the number of children increases as income is greater (so that there is a positive income effect).

We would prefer to have the following variables featured: the age of the mother at the time of birth of the first child, the ultimate family size and the birth intervals. Taking this aim as a starting point, it would be logical to begin with a discrete-state continuous-time stochastic process. This type of model does not exist in this field, although the first useable stages of development towards that goal have been in existence for several years. The so-called static one-period fertility models are reasonably well developed. These link up closely with the home production theory, they illustrate the thought processes used and in fact are the furthest developed for the application of the fertility theory as compared with other demographic phenomena. We shall examine a model (Edlefsen, 1980) which more or less links the static and the dynamic analyses and finally we shall consider a few steps towards the required dynamic model. The following is based mainly on Montgomery and Trussell (1986, sections 5 and 6).

The one-period static models only explain the ultimate family size. Supposing that the utility of a household is a function of the number of children N, the amount of leisure time T_l and the amount of commodities consumed X, so that

$$U = U(N, T_l, X) \tag{14}$$

N can be seen as a choice variable and for simplicity's sake can be assumed to be continuous. Let w be the wage rate in the market for the woman and Y the husband's income (considered as exogenous). The time available to the household is divided into leisure time T_l, child care T_c and market work T_w so that

$$T = T_l + T_c + T_w \tag{15}$$

Child care is considered to cost time (T_c) and money (E_c). Given n children, there are several possible combinations of E_c and T_c which yield the same number of n units of child care. The way in which the utility function is formulated at present means that the household is indifferent with respect to the choice of these combinations and their quality. Their only problem in this context is to find that combination which involves the lowest costs. This problem can be solved in two ways.

In the first stage, for each (meaningful) n, we check which is the cheapest combination of E_c and T_c, thus:

$$\min_{T_c, E_c} \quad w \cdot T_c + E_c \text{ subject to } g(T_c, E_c) = n \tag{16}$$

where g is a child care production function. The solution leads to a set of conditional demand functions $T_c(w, n)$ and $E_c(w, n)$ and a cost function:

$$C(w, n) = w \cdot T_c(w, n) + E_c(w, n) \tag{17}$$

which has the property that $\delta C(w, n) / \delta w = T_c(w, n)$.

Now we come to the second step which involves searching for that family size (N), which maximizes utility with T_1 and X as other variables:

$$\max \ U(N, T_1, X), \ \text{s.t.} \ X + C(w, N) + w \cdot T_1 - Y - w \cdot T = 0 \tag{18}$$

Using comparative statics one can derive verifiable hypotheses. The model is easily developed. In Butz and Ward (1979) the influence of Y on N also depends on the scope of the woman's supply of labour. Some ideas have been provided for incorporating the costs of child care arrangements.

The above specifications lead to problems when testing empirically, in the sense that as opposed to theoretical cases, one generally comes up against a negative income effect. This has led to the incorporation of the notion of child quality. This can be classified quite simply (see Becker and Lewis, 1973). To that end, it is assumed that there is a joint production function, which is implicitly defined by $g(T_c, E_c ; n, q) = 0$. The function g gives the level of child care and the minimum monetary expenditure necessary to bring up n children with a given quality q. In fact, the function g is a combination of household production characteristics and ranking in order of preference with respect to the combinations (T_c, E_c) which yield a certain quality q.

The problem can now be phrased as follows. In the first stage now:

$$\min \ w \cdot T_c + E_c \ \text{s.t.} \ g = 0 \ \text{for} \ N = n \ \text{and} \ Q = q \tag{19}$$

This leads to a cost function $C(w; n, q)$ with the characteristic that $\delta C / \delta w = T_c(w; n, q)$. Given the cost function, we can now tackle the second step. This involves maximizing $U(X, T_1, N, Q)$, subject to the budget constraint (which is not linear in N and Q in Becker and Lewis) and the time constraint.

The essence of this development is that if the parents derive utility from quality, an exogenous increase in, for example, the spouse's income, exerts an influence on quantity as well as on quality.

The disadvantage of this type of one-period models is that they are only able to determine the ultimate family size. A first extension to the modelling of the timing of births within the context of one-period models can be found in Cigno and Ermisch (1989). However, here uncertainty is neglected. Models which take this into account could in principle be developed, but the problem is that they rapidly become mathematically unmanageable which in turn makes the derivation of verifiable hypotheses unfeasible. However, some progress can surely be anticipated.

Before we consider these (dynamic) models we shall first examine a model proposed by Edlefsen (1980) which performs the role of a link function. This model is actually a static model for birth timing and spacing. The starting point is that parents take decisions about the approximate timing of births in addition to the number of children desired. It is also important because it takes into account the possibility that the opportunity costs of a birth remain in existence during the lifespan of the child. This happens if one assumes that the wage which one receives at a certain age is dependent on experience. Consequently, a break (possibly part-time) in one's career, for example in order to bring up children, will continue to have a negative effect on the earned income received.

Edlefsen also assumes that there is a perfect capital market, that the parents choose the age at which they have their first child as well as the total number of children and that the raising of each child means a total withdrawal from the labour market during a period β, such that given N children one does not work during $S = \beta \cdot N$.

Let the wage function at age a be given by:

$$\ln w(a) = \alpha + \delta \cdot E(a) \tag{20}$$

where E(a) is the accumulated experience at age a.

For a potential reproductive lifespan of length T, full wealth is then given by:

$$F(\alpha, p) = \int_0^T w(a) \cdot \exp[-r \cdot a] \cdot da = \int_0^T \exp[\alpha + (\delta - r) \cdot a] \cdot da \tag{21}$$

Here, $\exp[\alpha + \delta \cdot a]$ is the wage earned by an individual, if employment has never been interrupted, and where r is the interest rate. So if one decides to have a first child at age a0, and to have a total of N children, which means that one will not participate in the labour force during the period $S = s$, then the lifetime earnings will be:

$$\int_0^{a0} \exp[\alpha + (\delta - r) \cdot a] \cdot da + \int_{a0}^{a0+g} 0 \cdot da + \int_{a0+g}^T \exp[\alpha + \delta \cdot (a - s) - r \cdot a] \cdot da =$$

$$\int_0^{a0} \exp[\alpha + (\delta - r) \cdot a] \cdot da + \exp[-\delta \cdot s] \cdot \int_{a0+g}^T \exp[\alpha + (\delta - r) \cdot a] \cdot da \tag{22}$$

The opportunity costs of the strategy N children from age a0, C(a0, s) are then:

$$C(a0, s) = \int_{a0}^{a0+g} \exp[\alpha + (\delta - r) \cdot a] \cdot da + (1 - \exp[-\delta \cdot s]) \cdot$$

$$\int_{a0+g}^T \exp[\alpha + (\delta - r) \cdot a] \cdot da \tag{23}$$

This is analogous to the cost function C(w, N) in the static model, yet non-linear in a0, the age at which the first child is born, and N=s / β. So, from a cost perspective alone, it would be best to have children as late in life as possible. The relationship between the opportunity costs on the one hand, and on the other hand the benefits which one can derive from having children at a young age, giving young parents more time to enjoy them, is strained. This can be realised by opting for a utility function U=U(a0, N, X), with a non-positive $\delta U / \delta a0$ relationship. The duration of the birth interval could possibly also be incorporated in the utility function. Another possibility lies in the wage function.

If this function increases exogenously, independently of the factor age, then the aforementioned assumption with respect to the utility function is not necessary. Moffit (1984) deals with the matter in more detail.

The above model can be fairly easily adapted. For example, the wage function can be generalised (for an alternative approach, see Ward and Butz, 1980) and the time invested in children can vary depending on the age and parity. The process is once again analogous to that of the one-period static models.

In addition to the Edlefsen model, various other statistical analyses exist in this field, all of which are very sophisticated. However, they all have the shortcoming that they are ad hoc, and that they do not take account of the fact that we are dealing with sequential decision-making under uncertainty, as described in, for example, Heckman, Hotz and Walker (1985) and Newman and McCulloch (1984), who opt for the hazard rate approach. The problem does not so much lie in writing such a model down in the form of a model, but in deriving verifiable hypotheses from it. For the sake of clarity, we will sketch such a model in the following (see Montgomery and Trussell, 1986, pp. 260-261).

Let us imagine that the household income at age a, Y_a, is exogenous and that no savings are made (a wholly imperfect capital market). The budget restriction within any random period would then be:

$$Y_a = X_a + p \cdot N_a \tag{24}$$

where X_a is the consumption of a composite commodity, and p is the unit price of a child. Let the indirect utility function V at age a be dependent on the number of children at that age, N_a, and a function $\varepsilon(u)$, which gives the disutility ascribed to contraceptive use at efficiency level u, where $1 - u$ is the probability of conception. For simplicity's sake we have also assumed that the constraints are implicit in V. Let the objective function of the household be:

$$\max \; E_0 \sum_{a=0}^{T} V[N_a, \varepsilon(u_a)] \cdot [1 + r]^{-a} + S(N_T) \tag{25}$$

where maximisation takes place over $\{u_t: t = 0, 1, ..., T, \; u^* \le u_t \le 1, \text{ for all } t\}$. Here, u^* is the household level of fecundity and $S(N_T)$ is a terminal value function which gives the utility over the lifecycle after the reproductive period, given N_T children. E_t indicates that the expectation is based on the information available at time t. Define:

$$J[N_t, t] = \max_{\{u\}} \; E_t \cdot \sum_{a=t}^{T} V[N_a, \varepsilon(u_a)] \cdot [1 + r]^{-a} + S(N_T) \tag{26}$$

then $J[N_t, t]$ is the maximum utility which can be reached during the other $T - t$ periods of the reproductive life phase, given N_t children at age t. As we know, a recursive equation which describes the path of $J[N_t, t]$ exists. If the definition of u_t is one minus the probability of conception, then this function can be written as:

$$j[N_t, t] = \max_{u_t} \; E_t \cdot V[N_t, \varepsilon(u_t)] \cdot [1 + r]^{-t} \; +$$

$$\max_{\{u\}} \; \{u_t \cdot J[N_t, t + 1] + (1 - u_t) \cdot J[N_t + 1, t + 1]\} \tag{27}$$

This expression characterises an optimum. However, without any further assumptions it is not very practical. The most promising methods seem to be those of Wolpin (1984), who tries to solve the problem via a backward approach, and Newman (1985) who explicitly defines the function V. The method via the principle of optimality (Bellman, 1957) is central to this.

In the foregoing we have dealt primarily with models which only consider fertility to be an endogenous variable. However, it needs no saying that labour supply, income and fertility can not be explained independently of one another. In one-period static models this is more or less standard as far as fertility and labour supply are concerned (starting with Willis, 1973), but the combination with an endogenous income is still scarce. Note also that the labour supply and income of men are considered to be exogenous. This should be questioned, especially nowadays, and does not seem right from an economic theoretical point of view either (take, for example, the division of labour).

For the rest, we have concentrated on economic factors alone. Again, it needs no saying that non-economic factors, such as altruism, social norms, model behaviour and the like are at least equally as important. The first attempts at including such variables were made by, among others, Easterlin (1966), Leibenstein (1974 and 1975) and Turchi (1975). It would be desirable to extend these models with variables which do not traditionally belong to the field of economy. The work of Bagozzi and Van Loo (1987) deserves special attention in this respect. Siegers will deal with these factors in greater detail in his contribution to this volume.

If we review existing literature in this field, we can conclude that most effort has been put in explaining the ultimate family size via static one-period models, but that there is no complete model in the sense of a simultaneous model for the relevant decision variables, including the incorporation of non-economic variables. As for the dynamic variables, we can say that this development is still in its infancy, whereby the greatest problem, apart from data problems, seems to be the lack of suitable models which can also be estimated.

2.3.2 *Marriage*

The economic theory of marriage has two basic premises. First of all, the premise that marriage and the choice of a partner are generally voluntary choices, which means that the preference theory can be applied. An important consequence of this premise is that we may assume that people who get married expect they will derive greater utility from marriage than from remaining single. The second premise is that there is a marriage market, flowing from the fact that many men and women compete as they seek mates. On the basis of these principles, the theory explains why most adults are married and why a sorting of partners takes place on the basis of education, welfare and other material and non-material characteristics.

We will try to elucidate the above by first presenting the theory as described in Becker (1973 and 1974). Next, we will briefly deal with the developments in theory since then.

We will first restrict ourselves to two persons, a male M and a female F, who have the choice of either getting married to each other or remaining single. We assume that they will only get married if both derive benefit from doing so, in terms of utility. Each household is assumed to have a production function which relates the total output of that household Z, an aggregated commodity, to various inputs:

$$Z = f(x_1, ..., x_m; t_1, ..., t_k; E) \tag{28}$$

where x_i are market goods and services, t_i are time inputs of k different household members and E are environmental variables. The 'full' income constraint is:

$$\sum^m p_i \cdot x_i + \sum^k w_j \cdot t_j = \sum^k w_j \cdot T + v = S \tag{29}$$

where w_j is the wage rate of the j-th household member, p_i is the price of the i-th good, T the time endowment, v property income, and S full income. If l_j is the time spent on the market, the following applies to all household members:

$$l_j + t_j = T \tag{30}$$

We assume that a reduction in total output of the household, Z, results in a deterioration for at least one member of the household, and not in an improvement for any member. This means that it is to everyone's advantage to maximise Z. For this, the following prerequisites must be met:

$$(\delta Z / \delta t_i) / (\delta Z / \delta t_j) = w_i / w_j, \quad 0 < t_i, \ t_j < T \tag{31}$$

$$(\delta Z / \delta t_i) / (\delta Z / \delta t_j) = \mu_i / w_j, \quad 0 < t_j < T, \ t_j = T \tag{32}$$

$$(\delta Z / \delta x_i) / (\delta Z / \delta t_j) = p_i / w_j, \quad 0 < t_j < T, \ x_i > 0 \tag{33}$$

where $\mu_i (\geq w_i)$ is the shadow price of the time of i. So, each household member needs to allocate his time over market and non-market sectors in the right proportions. This allocation is determined by equations (31) to (33). The member with the highest wage rate will also be the one who participates most in the market. Equation (33) applies to single persons.

Now, if Z_{m0} (Z_{0f}) is the maximum output for M (F) as single persons, and m_{mf} and f_{mf} their income if they had been married to each other, a prerequisite for them to get married would then be:

$$m_{mf} \geq Z_{m0} \text{ and } f_{mf} \geq Z_{0f} \tag{34}$$

The total income produced within marriage is then $m_{mf} + f_{mf}$, which is the total output of the marriage. A prerequisite for marriage is then:

$$m_{mf} + f_{mf} = Z_{mf} \geq Z_{m0} + Z_{0f} \tag{35}$$

In the foregoing, non-material commodities such as love, emotional ties and the desire to raise children play an important role. After all, without this type of commodity one would expect people to live together in as large groups as possible with a view to the concomitant economies of scale. In such cases, non-material elements apparently play a negative role. One can thus also conclude that economies of scale are not sufficient reason for men and women, for example, to decide to live together. The above shows how effective the home production theory is as an instrument of analysis in economic demography. The most important explanation for the benefits which marriage brings, is the complementarity between M and F. A more detailed analysis shows that a rise in other income v increases the incentive to get married, and if the wage rate of the woman is lower than that of the man, the economic gains from marriage become smaller as the woman's income rises (Becker, 1973, pp. 821-822).

Let us now describe the situation in which n M's and n F's want to get married. We can draw up a pay-off matrix which gives the maximum household commodity output for each (M_i, F_j)-combination. There are now n! possible different combinations of all men and women. Each sorting has its own total output Z^k, given by:

$$Z^k = \sum_{i \in M, j \in F} Z_{ij}, k = 1, \cdots, n! \tag{36}$$

Now if we give (one of) the sorting(s) which has the highest output indices on the main diagonal of the pay-off matrix, then:

$$Z^* = \sum_{i=1}^{n} Z_{ii} = \max_k Z^k \geq Z^k \text{ for all } k \tag{37}$$

If everyone were to choose the partner who maximises his income from commodities, then the optimal sorting would have the characteristic that persons who are not married to each other, can not marry each other and benefit from it unless someone else suffers from it. This means that the optimal sorting lies in the core. So, for all i and j:

$$m_{ii} + f_{jj} \geq Z_{ij} \tag{38}$$

where m_{ii} is the income of a marriage between the i-th M and the i-th F (analogous with f_{jj}).

The theory of optimal assignments (see, for example, Koopmans and Beckman, 1957) can be applied to this. The marriage market thus chooses the maximum sum of outputs over all marriages, just as in competitive product markets the sum of outputs is maximised over all companies.

The above analysis can also explain why certain traits (such as intelligence, level of education, aggressiveness, beauty, wage rate, etc.) can be positively or negatively correlated between partners. See Becker (1973, pp. 825-836).

From (38) and the condition that the output to be distributed over both partners is equal to the joint output:

$$m_{ij} + f_{ij} = Z_{ij} \tag{39}$$

we get, in the case of total negotiability, the distribution of the output over the partners. We can then simply derive:

$$Z_{ii} - \text{Max}_k (Z_{ki} - Z_{kk}) \geq m_{ii} \geq \text{Max}_k (Z_{ik} - Z_{kk})$$

$$Z_{ii} - \text{Max}_k (Z_{ik} - Z_{kk}) \geq f_{ii} \geq \text{Max}_k (Z_{ki} - Z_{kk}) \tag{40}$$

However, in view of the discrete character of Z_{ik} this distribution is not unique. If Z_{ik} becomes continuous, the solution is unique. The same applies when there are a sufficient number of men (women) with the same traits for a competitive equilibrium. In that case, supply and demand curves can also be derived. This also applies when we abandon our assumption that all n men and women get married. This is reflected, albeit only qualitatively, in Becker (1973, pp. 838-839).

Becker (1974) looks into the influence of love and caring about what happens to the partner, on the marriage output. He does this by incorporating the commodity consumption of the partner in the utility function (which gives us interdependent utilities). We can then show that individuals who care about each other are more likely to get married than the same kind of people who do not care about each other. However, Becker does not deal with the possibility of joint consumption, which limits the transferability of utility. The introduction of joint consumption commodities can be easily effectuated by assuming the existence of household public goods (see Lam, 1988; Ermisch, 1981 and Manser and Brown, 1980, also use this, as will be shown later on). This explains the possibility of positive assortative mating on wages, which is difficult in Becker's analysis, but which in practice is often the case. The possibility exists because an increasing difference in income between partners leads to an increase in gains from specialisation, and to a decrease in gains from the joint consumption of public goods.

Ermisch adopts a slightly different approach (1981), which does not focus on the consideration of cohabitation by two potential partners (who know each other), but which deals with the question as to which household size individuals choose, rather than with the choice of a specific person. The individual in question thus weighs up matters such as privacy, economies of scale, and the possibility of home production. In both the utility function and in the equation for the production of commodities, Ermisch explicitly introduces the number of adults belonging to the household. For the rest, the analysis is more or less analogous with that in the static one-period fertility models. We will therefore not go into it here. The treatment of the privacy aspect seems to be the most important element. Another advantage is that Ermisch's model can be quite simply verified. This can not really be said of the other models presented here.

However, Becker – like Ermisch – hardly deals with the timing aspects of marriage and the role played by uncertainty, also in terms of the probability of divorce – see also the next section. Keeley (1977) gives an analysis of the determinants of age at first marriage by combining the home production theory, the theory of search (see Alchain, 1969, and Stigler, 1961 and 1962) and the introduction of the search for a spouse in Becker's work. The decision to marry is thus divided into two parts. First, the individual decides whether or not to enter the marriage market, and then the search for a partner begins. Age at first marriage is thus determined by the determinants of entry and the duration of the search. Both entry and duration are in their turn determined by the gains of marriage and the costs of search.

Keeley assumes that the share of an individual in the total potential output of marriage is a random variable which depends on the distribution of the characteristics of the potential partners. He or she knows the relevant moments of this distribution. However, a search has to be made in order to be able to make any draw at all. Via a sequential search model, decisions are then made as to whether one will, or will not accept an offer. It has been assumed that individual search behaviour does not influence the distribution of marriage offers, and that offers have a zero durability, an infinite horizon. The marriage market is only entered if the expected gains from searching are at least equal to the costs, which depend on individual characteristics.

If $\hat{m}$ is the maximum possible offer, m_0 the minimum acceptable offer, and if the distribution of income from marriage is $f(m)$, then the probability that someone who is searching will receive an acceptable offer is:

$$\alpha = \Pr(m_0 \leq m \leq \hat{m}) = \int_{m0}^{\hat{m}} f(m) \cdot dm \tag{41}$$

and the expected value of an acceptable offer is:

$$h = E(m \mid m_0 \leq m \leq \hat{m}) = (1 / \alpha) \int_{m0}^{\hat{m}} m \cdot f(m) \cdot dm \tag{42}$$

Since the probability of finding a partner is α in each period, the expected number of periods one will spend searching for a partner will be $D = (1/\alpha)$.

If marrying brings higher gains than remaining single, then the expected benefit is:

$$W = (1/r) \cdot [\alpha \cdot h + r \cdot (S - C)] / (r + \alpha) \tag{43}$$

where S is the single commodity income, C the direct cost of search, and r the discount rate. The optimal acceptance wage m_0, which maximises the expected output, is derived from:

$$\alpha \cdot (h - m_0) / r = m_0 - (S - C) \tag{44}$$

This means that an offer of m which is smaller than $(S - C)$ will be refused. If m is bigger, there are two possibilities. One can either opt for a assured income flow amounting to m for the rest of one's life, or one can continue searching. This latter option is chosen if the expected income of continuing one's search (W) is at least as high as the present value of the current offer, i.e. m/r. In short, the acceptance wage m_0 is chosen such that:

$$m_0/r \leq W \tag{45}$$

and

$$\alpha \cdot (h - m_0) / r \geq m_0 - (S - C) \tag{46}$$

Equation (46) says that the marginal benefit from search is at least equal to the marginal cost of search.

The income flow of a single person is equal to S/r, whereas the expected income flow in the event of marriage is m_0/r, so that a single person will enter the marriage market when, and only when:

$$S \leq m_0 = [\alpha \cdot h + r \cdot (S - C)] / (\alpha + r) \leq \hat{m} \tag{47}$$

The above has shown that the marriage process can be conceptualised in the same manner as searching for a job. For an empirical application it would be advisable to replace the assumptions by more realistic ones, in particular those which relate to the age independence of S and C, the threshold m_0, the number of offers, income, costs, and the infinite horizon, but the basic structure of the model can still be used. Montgomery and Trussell (1986, pp. 233-237), among others, give a more general description. On the basis of this model, Keeley determines the expected effect of a number of variables. However, data regarding an individual's entry into the marriage market and the search process are very scarce. For age at marriage, Keeley (1979) solves this by using a model schedule for the age pattern of first marriage (see for example, Coale, 1971) and by explaining the scale parameters with the aid of socio-economic variables.

A first empirical estimation of the mating function – without using the search framework – has been carried out by Boulier and Rosenzweig (1984). They also abandon the assumption that the traits individuals bring to the market are exogenous. This assumption entails that non-observable traits (for the researcher) such as beauty, intelligence, aggressiveness, etc., are not correlated with the observed traits, such as level of education, for example. When applied to data gathered in the Philippines in 1973, we see that by disregarding the possibility of heterogeneity, incorrect conclusions are drawn. This also supports the hypothesis that education, marital search, and spouse selection can not be determined independently (see also Parsons, 1980, for a theoretical treatment of this issue), and that they are directly or indirectly influenced by the parent's income, the endowed traits of offspring, costs of education and marriage market conditions.

From the above, it is clear that the marriage and labour markets are interdependent. After all, the market conditions regarding the process of marriage influence the value of the time spent in the home. Until recently, attention was hardly paid to this aspect. Grossbard-Shechtman (1984) gives a first theoretical treatment of the subject. She concludes, among other things, that labour force participation of married women is determined for a part by the sex ratio of those eligible for marriage, that changes in income have a greater influence on women than on men, that group differences in patterns of the division of labour in households influence the elasticity of female labour supply, and that a positive correlation between achievement in markets for labour and household activities can further explain the backward-bending supply of labour. However, an empirical application has not (yet) taken place.

When the utility functions of various (potential) household members differ, it is not always possible to bring them together in an aggregated function, as in fact required by the above analysis. Moreover, the distribution of the gains from marriage is not always fixed. This problem can be solved by placing the decision-making problem in a bargaining framework, and then applying the game theory. Manser and Brown (1980), for example, operate in this manner. The problem of optimization is determined for each individual in the familiar way[1], whereby a distinction is made between shared and non-shared goods. An efficiency parameter is also applied, representing personal characteristics which could be valued as positive or negative within a marriage. A unique solution exists among the conditions stipulated (individual utility function is strictly quasiconcave, it rises monotonously in all arguments of the function, has continuous partial derivatives, and the utility function is independent of marital status). The utility possibility frontier (UPF) can be derived from the corresponding contract curve. Gains from marriage exist if the utility in the unmarried state lies within this UPF. If two individuals benefit from marriage, then it is assumed that these two agree on the bargaining rules to be applied. This means that it is no longer necessary to assume that a household utility function exists. The utility functions of the individuals must still be known however. The marriage bargain can be considered to be a two-person non-zero

---

[1]   See e.g. section 2.3.4.

sum game, whereby a cooperative game approach seems to be most suitable. Manser and Brown illustrate this by applying a non-cooperative model, the Dictatorial model. As for the symmetrical bargaining models, the Nash and Kalai-Smorodinsky models are applied. The bargaining approach can also be applied in the case of interdependent utilities.

Stochastic dynamic decision models in this field are still in their infancy. Matsushita (1988) gives an example in which the consumption path and the marriage decision problem with an uncertain income are solved for a simple two-period model via dynamic programming.

From the above we can conclude that the economic theory of marriage is still more or less virgin territory. Empirical applications in this field are, contrary to fertility studies, very scarce, on the one hand because data are sadly lacking, and on the other hand because the theories are still in their early stages of development.

2.3.3   Divorce

The economic theory of divorce, developed by Becker, Landes and Michael (1977), is a logical extension of the economic theory of marriage. Here too, the preference theory plays a central role, and everyone tries to maximise the expected utility. The formal model is analogous with the marriage model, albeit that the decision is now not whether one wants to remain single or marry, but rather whether one wants to remain married, or again become single. Divorce will take place if the expected utility of divorce (possibly followed by remarriage) is bigger than the expected utility of staying married.

Even if complete certainty exists with regard to the future, it is possible that the decision to end a marriage in divorce is made. On the other hand, the realised utility of marriage can, over time, deviate from the expectations prior to marriage. This can be incorporated in the model via the introduction of uncertainty, as a result of which deviations between expected and realised utility may arise. In other words, we may assume that for this group of people the outcome of marriage in terms of utility was less favourable than they had expected prior to marriage, or else that developments had taken place which made the divorced state more beneficial than the married state.

Divorce in cases of comprehensive information is an answer to declining utility during marriage. Uncertainty adds a separate dimension to this, because divorce is then no longer necessarily an anticipated decision, but rather the result of unexpected events.

It needs no saying that all decisions are imbued with uncertainty. Even after a prolonged engagement or premarital cohabitation, uncertainty remains as to one's own needs and the needs of one's partner, the possibilities of helping each other in times of need, and one's personal wishes with respect to raising children, etc.

It seems reasonable to assume that a large majority of divorces are the result of uncertainty and unanticipated developments, and that they would thus not take place in a world where all developments can be anticipated with absolute certainty. Since divorce goes hand in hand with considerable emotional and financial costs, one may assume that people would prefer to remain single rather than marry if they expect to get divorced within a few years time. Incomplete information can never raise the gains from marriage above those derived from an optimal sorting (i.e. gains in the event of perfect information), and so in most cases it will lower the gains. The actual sorting will thus also deviate from the optimal sorting.

In the above, divorce has been approached from the perspective of one of the partners only. The analysis does not change if both partners gain from getting divorced. If this is not the case, divorce will only take place (if mutual compensations are both possible and free) if the combined income in the case of a continuation marriage is expected to be smaller than the sum of the two individual incomes after separation. After all, if the total income upon marriage continuation is greater than in the case of divorce, and if one of the partners wants to get divorced, then the partner who wants to remain married can compensate the other, assuming of course that the distribution of income between the two partners is flexible. If this is not the case, one could charge 'costs' for transferring welfare from one partner to the other.

Incomplete information about possible gains of the partner do, of course, play a role in the divorce process. Peters (1986) shows which different decisions which can be made as result of incomplete information, as compared with a situation in which one has comprehensive information about the possibilities of the partner. If the permission of both partners is needed for a divorce, asymmetrical information will lead to fewer divorces than is efficient from the point of view of utility maximisation. If, however, divorce is a unilateral process, more divorces will take place than is desirable from an efficiency point of view. Note that by testing the model we can draw the conclusion that information is symmetrical, which is contrary to what one would expect on the basis of contract literature (see Hart, 1983). Peters explains this as follows: "First, the nature of interaction in marriage makes it more difficult to conceal information than would be true of more impersonal relationships. Second, there may be ties such as the presence of children that continue after the relationship has terminated" (Peters, 1986, p. 453).

As indicated above, the decision to get divorced, or not, is partly determined by the marriage strategy. Persons who have a low threshold value m_0 (see equation 41), will generally find a partner who will yield a relatively low utility which is, moreover, only slightly higher than the utility of remaining single. This means that even at the slightest provocation, divorce will become a viable alternative. Research has also shown that unexpected events, such as being made redundant, will increase the probability of divorce or bring divorce closer, see for example Sander (1986), and for a review, Nelissen and Van den Akker (1988, section 4.2). Institutional changes in the income sphere, e.g. an extension of the rights of (divorced) women regarding social security payments, can also influence the process. See Groeneveld et al. (1980), and again Nelissen and Van den Akker (1988).

Persons with high search costs will marry relatively earlier, thereby increasing the probability of divorce. The probability of divorce will also be increased if people remain single until an advanced age and therefore lower their minimum acceptable offer, m_0.

After all, a decrease in m_0 results in a greater probability of a mismatch and a greater deviation between real and optimum matching traits; it thus reduces the expected gains from marriage.

During marriage, people invest in various commodities and a kind of labour speciali- sation takes place. A number of commodities can be divided in the case of divorce, others can not. The latter are known as marital-specific capital, and include, for example, children, and the fact that after a certain period of time people know more about the habits and attitudes of their partners. The presence of such capital limits the possible gains from divorce. So, gains from marriage as compared with the benefits of being single are partially determined by the degree of labour specialisation and the degree to which marital-specific capital investments have been made. This explains the negative effect of the presence of young children on the probability of divorce. Empirical research (Hunter, 1984) clearly shows the important effect of the presence of children. The division of marital-specific capital over the partners, insofar as it exists (such as children), and the arrangements which are made as to how this capital should be 'used' is also important, of course (see also Weiss and Willis, 1985).

Note however, that the presence of marital-specific capital from a former marriage can impose constraints on remarriage (such as the presence of children from a former marriage or lasting contacts with the ex-partner); see Koo, Suchindran and Griffith (1984).

The possibility of divorce also influences the formation of marital-specific capital and thus the stability of marriage. An increase in the probability of divorce (exogenous or not), as a result of the effect of higher wages for women and increased female labour force participation, for example, will reduce the degree of labour specialisation within marriage and the investment in marriage-specific capital. This in its turn will increase the probability of divorce. In this manner self-consolidating vicious circles may be formed. With the aid of a theoretical model, Lommerud (1989) deals with the effect of the possibility of divorce on the degree of labour specialisation within marriage.

All studies in this field (known to me) are one-period models. Studies which analyse the probability of divorce by duration of marriage, such as the study by Hunter (1984) and Morgan and Rindfuss (1985), clearly show that multi-period models are to be preferred in this case. As Becker, Landes and Michael (1977) emphasized, it is worth mentioning that marriage is also an investment in the sense that the partners get to know each other; this process takes place in particular during the first years of marriage, and it means that the role of various explanatory variables changes over time. Hunter (1984, p. 67), for example, shows that fulltime labour force participation by women during the first year of marriage raises the probability of divorce during that year. Later, the effect is no longer significant. According to Morgan and Rindfuss (1985), a difference in level of education between two partners has the same effect.

Of course, institutional, sociological and psychological factors also play a role in the divorce process. Institutional elements are dealt with, for example, in the aforementioned study by Peters (1986). Huber and Spitze (1980) look into the influence of sociological factors by adding sex-role attitudes and the household division of labour to Becker's model. For lack of data, direct empirical testing is not possible however.

2.3.4 Leaving the parental home

The process whereby young people leave the parental home can also be analysed with the aid of the home production theory. However, very few studies are based on this framework. Romeijn (1983) explains that this may be the result of the fact that leaving the parental home was long thought to be a matter of tradition. Only recently views on this matter have changed.

Almost all applications have an ad-hoc character. The most sophisticated one is the contribution by McElroy (1985). She opts for a Nash bargaining model of family behaviour, in which employment, consumption and household membership are jointly determined. A Nash bargaining model is more general than more common neo-classical approaches. Since this model also has empirical applications, we will here present it as an example of the application of bargaining models (see also section 2.3.2).

A youth is expected to maximise his utility function – commodities and leisure time being the arguments – with a non-convex budget set as a constraint. The budget set is made up of two subsets. One is related to his own full income, the other to the constraints flowing from the fact that he belongs to a household. As a member of the parental household, his consumption and leisure time are determined as the outcome of a two-person (the younger on the one hand and the older on the other) non-zero sum game with a Nash solution (see Nash, 1953). The process of optimization can be divided into two steps. In step one, the maximum utility as a single person is compared with the maximum utility as a member of the parental family. In step two, we opt for the strategy which yields the highest utility. The interaction between the utility functions of the parents and the youth, together with their budget constraints, determine the youth's choice. This means that the parents and the youth jointly determine whether or not the youngster will leave the parental home and whether or not he will take on employment. In mathematical terms, this can be expressed as follows:

A youth acts to maximise utility

$$U = U(Z, L) \tag{48}$$

subject to a time constraint $L \leq T$ and a budget constraint $w \cdot (T - L) + I = p \cdot Z$ which together yield the full income constraint:

$$w \cdot T + I = w \cdot L + p \cdot Z \tag{49}$$

The youth can work in the marketplace at wage rate w:

$$w = w(X) \tag{50}$$

If the youngster is not a member of his parents' household, then the maximisation of (48) subject to (49) leads to an optimum consumption level $Z_0 = [w \cdot (T - L_0) + I] / p = Z_0(I, p, w, T)$ and optimum leisure time $L_0 = L_0(I, p, w, T)$. The suffix 0 indicates that he forms a one-person household. Substitution gives the maximum value of the indirect utility function:

$$V_0 = U[Z_0(I, p, w, T), L_0(I, p, w, T)] = V_0(I, p, w, T) \tag{51}$$

where V_0 is homogeneous of grade zero in I, p and w. With an interior solution, the supply function for hours of market work, H_0, given by Roy's identity, becomes:

$$H = H_0(I, p, w, T) \tag{52}$$

With a corner solution, the youth's reservation wage (w_0^*) is the maximum market wage in the case of exactly 0 hours of work:

$$w_0^* = \max[w: H_0(I, p, w, T) = 0] \equiv R_0(I, p, T) \tag{53}$$

The asterisk indicates that he does not work. The maximum utility if he is on his own and not working is given by:

$$V_0^* = V_0[I, p, R_0(I, p, T), T] = V_0^*(I, p, T) \tag{54}$$

Let us now look at the maximum utility which can be obtained if the youth lives with his parents. We here assume that consumption and leisure allocation are jointly determined in accordance with a Nash solution to a two-person non-zero sum game as specified by McElroy and Horney (1981). The parents and the youth then jointly maximise a Nash criterion function subject to the household budget constraint. This Nash criterion function is then as follows:

$$N = [U_p^p.y - U_p] \cdot [U_p^y.y - U_y] \tag{55}$$

where $U_p^p.y$ is the utility which the parents assign to the joint household of parents and child, $U_p^y.y$ is analogous for the youth, U_p is the utility which the parents assign to a household without a child and U_y the utility which the youth assigns to an independent household. From this, we can again derive a system of commodity demands and labour supplies, and after substitution, we can determine the maximum utility. The decision is then made by comparing the utility in the parental household with the utility of independence.

This implies that the youth's non-wage income, as well as that of the parents, also form part of the Nash criterion, which in its turn implies that the non-wage income of the household has to be disaggregated. As a result, the non-wage income of the parents also becomes an argument in the labour supply function of the youth. Moreover, each possible shift parameter in (51) or (54) also appears in the household commodity demand and labour supply system.

With the aid of the above, we can derive a system of equations, on the basis of which we can specify and optimize a likelihood function (see McElroy, pp. 298-304).

3   Microsimulation

Interest in more detailed information with respect to population structure and the socio-economic situation of the population is still growing. The desire to be able to carry out government policies as best one can is of particular importance. Both the general public and policy-makers want to gain maximum insight into the costs and consequences of changes in government policies, such as for example in the social security or tax systems. For this, we must have knowledge of the household structure, possible interaction between various household members, and the influence of changes in the state of one or more household members on the situation and decisions of other household members. In a family household, for example, comprising a man, a woman and children, a change in the tax system which results in a tax increase for the woman, will influence the labour supply of both the man and woman. In most cases, this influence will be strongest on the labour supply of the woman, but the labour supply of the man is also influenced (see for example Cigno, 1988). This has (negative) repercussions on human capital formation by the woman, and so in the long term it will have a negative effect on her potential income (as compared with a situation in which the tax system does not change).

As shown in table 1, micro-models are the most appropriate instruments for an analysis of this type of problem. With the aid of micro-models, we can incorporate so-called first-order and second-order effects (direct and behavioural effects, respectively). This method also yields ideal information on the distribution of the effects. This type of model can not be used to process so-called third-order effects (also known as cyclical effects). This can be solved in practice by constructing a (limited) macro-model around the micro-model (see, for example, Orcutt et al., 1976; Hansen et al., 1987). The model dynamics are also often limited because the structure is recursive. This problem can be alleviated by restricting the period of analysis to a week or a month instead of a year (see, for example, Bennett and Bergmann, 1986).

Table 1   Characteristics of three types of models

	Micro	Meso	Macro
Possibility of incorporating:			
– direct effects	good	good	average
– behavioural effects	good	good	average
– cyclical effects	bad	good	good
– distribution	good	average	bad
– model dynamics	bad	bad	good

Source: Van de Stadt et al. (1989)

Common meso- and macro-models can not be disaggregated such that the information needed – in particular the distribution of the effects, especially if knowledge of the other household members is needed – can be provided.

The microsimulation approach was proposed by Orcutt (1957), as was the first application (see Orcutt et al., 1962). The essence of microsimulation lies in the programme which focusses on multi-actor, multi-level and multi-process synthesis (Caldwell, 1990). For this, a bottom-up strategy is applied. The state representation of the components of the system of interest forms the basis of each modelling strategy. As the name suggests, the micro-level representation of individuals in terms of social, economic and demographic characteristics, together with other possible relevant spatial and activity attributes, forms the basis of microsimulation (Clarke, 1986). The information with respect to individuals, for example, is stored in the form of lists which are updated (list processing). An example of such a list is given in figure 1. The advantage of list processing as compared with storage via an occupancy matrix for example – the method which is used for macrosimulation, among other applications – is that the storage space needed is relatively very small, also in the case of a limited number of variables.

Label 1	Age group 2	Specific age 3	Sex 4	Marital status 5	Race 6	Educa-tion 7	Occupa-tion 8	Part or full-time job 10	No. of weeks worked in pre-vious year 11	Wage earned in pre-vious year 12	Multiple of wage median 13
1058.1	4	30	male	divorced	white	3	11	1	52	5110.11	1.40
2069.1	2	21	male	single	white	2	19	0	0	0.00	0.00
2187.1	3	25	male	married	white	4	16	1	52	4842.06	1.27
2187.2	2	23	female	married	white	4	3	1	52	3635.18	1.11
2206.1	8	54	male	married	white	4	3	1	52	8914.73	1.25
2206.2	9	55	female	married	white	2	3	1	52	7567.65	1.05
2206.3	3	28	female	single	white	2	21	0	52	0.00	0.00
2206.4	4	33	male	single	white	2	16	1	52	4069.80	0.98
2206.5	1	20	male	single	white	2	21	0	0	0.00	0.00
2728.1	7	46	male	married	white	4	11	1	52	3461.27	0.91
2728.2	6	41	female	married	white	2	18	1	52	4225.86	1.24
2728.3	2	21	female	single	white	2	6	1	52	3875.89	1.22
3031.1	11	69	male	married	white	4	20	0	0	0.00	0.00
3031.2	10	60	female	married	white	4	21	0	0	0.00	0.00
3039.1	7	46	male	married	white	2	14	1	52	6804.96	1.34
3039.2	6	42	female	married	white	3	7	1	52	5142.55	1.28
3039.3	1	12	female	single	white	1	0	0	0	0.00	0.00
4092.1	6	44	male	divorced	white	3	9	1	52	7495.00	1.33
4107.1	4	34	female	divorced	black	4	20	0	0	0.00	0.00
4107.2	1	7	male	single	black	1	0	0	0	0.00	0.00
4521.1	7	45	male	married	white	3	15	1	52	3693.00	0.91
4521.2	6	42	female	married	white	3	20	–	–	–	–
4521.2	1	11	female	single	white	1	0	–	–	–	–
4521.4	1	7	female	single	white	1	0	–	–	–	–

Source: Clarke (1986, p. 249)

Figure 1   A list of individuals and some of attributes

So how is microsimulation applied in practice? A microsimulation model comprises a micro-database of micro-units (individuals, at least if we restrict ourselves to a microsimulation model for the household sector, which will be the case in the following) and a micro-model. The micro-data refer to characteristics of the micro-units, such as age, marital status, income, labour force participation, etc., in the case of persons. With the aid of the micro-model, the characteristics of each of the micro-units are adapted in each period (preferably by applying behavioural assumptions) such that a representative continuation of the sample is obtained at the end of each period. This process is called ageing of the population, as given schematically in figure 2. To illustrate this, we will take the modelling of mortality. The decision whether an individual will or will not die is simulated with the aid of the probability of dying using the Monte Carlo method. For example, for a 77-year-old divorced woman the probability of dying was 6.75 percent in 1968. We then randomly draw a number from the uniform [0,1]-distribution. If this number is smaller than or equal to the probability of dying of 0.0675, the woman is expected to die. If the number is larger, the woman will live. If she dies, we then investigate whether she had children who have now become orphans.

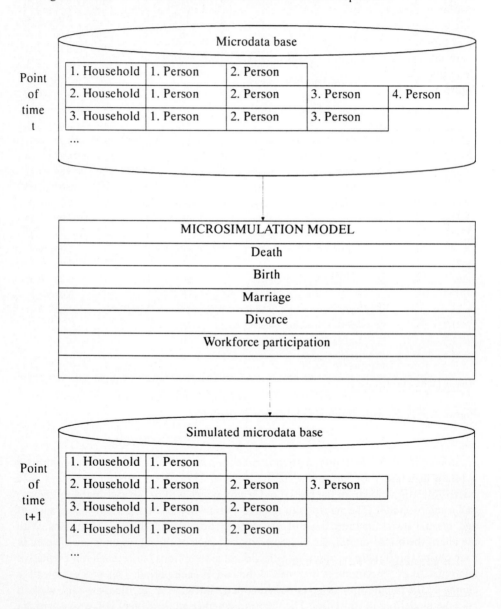

Figure 2   The principle of microsimulation

The micro-model should ideally comprise behavioural assumptions for the relevant processes, such as birth, migration, marriage, income formation etc. In general, the parameters of the relationships should be estimated. The micro-database itself is often used as the source of information. In other cases, external data are needed, and in other cases again, precise information is available, as for example, in the case of institutional rules or laws. The behavioural hypotheses are applied to all persons in each period, insofar as they are subject to the changes described by these hypotheses, in order to be able to determine the situation a period later. So, determination of the situation a period later takes place via simulation, and not via analysis of the system.

In this manner, we can create a database which reflects the (developments in the) demographic and economic structure of the population. A stylised example is given in figure 3.

		1986 (Sample Data)						1987 (Aged Data)			
			Household 1						*Household 1*		
ID	Age	Sex	Marital Status	Job	Income	ID	Age	Sex	Marital Status	Job	Income
P1 1	47	M	married	yes	38000	P1 1	48	M	married	yes	38000
P2 2	44	F	married	no	0	P2 2	45	F	married	no	0
P3 3	20	M	single	yes	23000	P3 4	16	M	single	no	0
P4 4	15	M	single	no	0						
			Household 2						*Household 2*		
P1 5	79	F	widowed	no	14000	P4 3	21	M	married	yes	25000
						P5 8	19	F	married	no	0
			Household 3						*Household 3*		
P1 6	37	M	married	yes	32000	P6 6	38	M	married	yes	35200
P2 7	38	F	married	no	0	P7 7	39	F	married	yes	14175
P3 8	18	F	single	no	0						
			Household 4						*Household 4*		
			:						:		

Source: Hellwig, 1988

Figure 3   An example for microsimulation

The advantages of microsimulation are:

1. Microsimulation takes place at the level at which most decisions are made, namely that of micro-units. Aggregation is therefore unnecessary and the concomitant prob-

lems can be avoided. So, there is no need to translate behavioural relations at the micro-level to the macro-level. This is especially important in the field of social sciences, because aggregation of theories to the macro-level has not been realised, or very restrictive assumptions have been made. See, for example, Kirnan (1989).

2. Modern social scientists break problems down into manageable parts. This leads to problems when trying to put the parts together again. In many cases, the quantitative revolution in social sciences has resulted in a strengthening of the imbalance of analysis over synthesis. Microsimulation can contribute to the reverse (see Caldwell, 1989).

3. There is hardly any loss of data. In principle, all micro-data can be used. As a result, there is a great deal of available information, and there is full representation and treatment of the heterogeneity in household and individual characteristics. One can, for example, generate the income distribution in a particular year; this is practically impossible with macro-models. In this manner we can also gain insight into the question as to how many and which households are affected by specific measures in, for example, the social security system, and how this influences further behaviour (see, for example, Bekkering et al., 1986, for such processes in the field of tax legislation).

4. The most complicated interrelationships can be described; in such cases paramount importance is attached to the explicit treatment of dynamics in simulating the system. For example, the determination of eligibility for a social welfare benefit or for a rent rebate is relatively easy with the aid of the microsimulation model. It can also determine its effect on, for example, the labour supply of various household members.

5. It is relatively easy to maintain consistency, which is a general methodological problem in, for example, modelling household and family dynamics (see Galler, 1988).

6. Assumptions and hypotheses with respect to the micro-units can be introduced or changed at any time.

7. The method is intuitively appealing because it uses existing units (e.g. individuals).

It goes without saying that microsimulation also has a number of drawbacks:

1. The behavioural hypotheses are often based on insufficient knowledge (such as the behavioural hypotheses which form the basis of demographic decisions).

2. Large databases are needed, or have to be simulated. In the Netherlands, such databases are limited. One of the available databases is the Socio-Economic Panel, but in view of the costs involved, it can hardly be used.

3. The construction and maintenance of microsimulation models requires large-scale investments in manpower, computer capacity and computer time.

4. In addition to variance related to the specification of the initial sample population, Monte Carlo variability (see Orcutt et al., 1976; chapter 11) results from the sampling approach to selecting the members of the model population whose characteristics change. By repeating the runs, we can gain deeper insight into the magnitude of this phenomenon (see Orcutt et al., 1976; and Nelissen, 1989).

A practical drawback is that all microsimulation models only have a limited number of behavioural responses, particularly in the field of household formation. In the case of the Netherlands, this problem could be solved for the demographic factors in such models, by carrying out the proposals for further research related to section 2; these will be put forward later. Once this has been done, countless exercises are possible with the aid of microsimulation models, not only in the field of demography, but also with respect to labour supply, income, social security or the lack thereof, consumption, etc. An interesting asset is that cyclical effects can be analysed, such as the effect of the increased probability of divorce on the labour supply of married women, the resulting drop in household activities by women, which in its turn will lead to reduced specialisation within the household, and this development will influence the probability of divorce, etc.

4   Conclusions and research proposals

In the foregoing, we have given a general overview of research into the significance of economic determinants of demographic behaviour. Almost all applications are based on the home production theory, either implicitly or explicitly. The greatest asset of the home production theory is that the decision-maker is confronted with constraints, and that costs are allocated to these constraints (e.g. the opportunity costs of time), which means that assessments can be made in terms of prices (i.e. costs) instead of utility, and thus that measurable variables can be used. We must not forget of course, that the theory of home production is an analytical tool, and that the distinction between consumption and production is essential to analyses of work in the home.

We have not paid explicit attention to extramarital cohabitation, but it can be dealt with in the same manner as marriage. In doing so, one can also explain why extramarital cohabitation has become more widespread, as shown in Becker (1981) and Ferment (1989), for example.

As shown in our overview, most applications are in the field of fertility. In the case of marriage, divorce and leaving the parental home, bargaining and search models have to be introduced because of the fact that more than one party is involved. Ermisch more or less circumvents this problem, but this results in a number of restrictions. Application of the game theory is possible in the field of leaving the parental home and divorce, but is a great deal more difficult in the case of marriage because of the huge number of potential partners.

Another problem is that a large majority of models are static one-period applications, as a result of which spacing and timing are lost. This can be solved in dynamic multi-period models, but such manageable models are lacking, although a few initial attempts at designing such models have been made.

All in all, there is not yet a "body of empirically tested, quantitatively stable estimates of the major behavioural relationships suggested by the theory... (but we) do have a growing capacity to generate hypotheses about both large and small questions concerning family behaviour and its consequences within a theoretical framework that is a logically coherent part of the main corpus of neoclassical economic theory" (Willis, 1978, p. 78).

On the basis of the foregoing, we can formulate a number of proposals for further research.

In the field of fertility, we saw that most attention has been paid to partial static one-period models and that dynamic models are still in their infancy. This leads to the following research questions:

- Although dynamic multi-period models are to be preferred in the long term, research in the field of static, one-period models must continue. In addition to giving information on the ultimate family size, these models can throw light on the role played by different variables. For this, a simultaneous model must be developed to explain at least the number of children, the labour supply and the income of both the man and the woman.
- Incorporation of sociological and psychological variables seems desirable. We refer the reader to studies by Kapteyn (1977), Alessi and Kapteyn (1985) and Kapteyn and Woittiez (1987) into habit formation and interdependent preferences. This approach should preferably be included.
- Measurement of the factor quality poses a serious problem which has, as yet, not been solved.
- Very little is known about the decision-making process regarding the number of children and the timing of births. However, it is very important that we know more about this process with a view to further developing theory and in particular to giving a correct specification of the dynamic models.
- Unexpected events, such as for example when one of the partners is made redundant, can influence the decision-making process. Very little is known about the magnitude of these types of effects.
- The degree to which contraceptives are used and their reliability, are also important data for dynamic models (an element of uncertainty, and as a representation of the biological aspects of reproduction). Panel data in this field, in combination with data such as those of the Socio-Economic Panel (SEP) of the Netherlands Central Bureau of Statistics (CBS) are needed.
- The various possible choices, and the actual choice made with respect to the (T_c, E_c)-combinations (see equation 16) in combination with labour supply and income have never been studied, yet they are of vital importance to static one-period models. Heckman's study (1974) is a first step in this direction.
- Following from the above, research into the distribution of T_c, T_m and T_l is important. In the economic analysis of fertility, T_c plays a crucial role via the opportunity costs.
- The continued development of dynamic multi-state models is of course most interesting of all. All the elements which we wish to incorporate in one-period models should also be incorporated in the dynamic multi-state models.

The economic theory of marriage is still more or less virgin territory. Contrary to fertility, empirical applications in this field are almost entirely absent, on the one hand because only very few data are available, and on the other hand because theories are only just being developed. Possible future research in this field should focus on:

- In order to further develop theory, we need more knowledge of the decision-making process. Is the division into two phases justified?
- An elaboration on Ermisch's model seems to be the most wise step to take at the moment. This could be done on the one hand by including various economic variables, and on the other hand by further differentiating by age and sex of the household members.
- The empirical application of search theory poses problems because not one (e.g. wage), but several observed variables are included (wage, education, age gaps, attractiveness, characteristics, etc.). It is not entirely clear how the multivariate nature of the problem can be solved in the search process, or be included in a decision-making variable (m_0) or commodity.
- As reflected in the above, there is still very little knowledge with respect to all the variables which play a role. More attention ought to be paid to institutional factors (see Hannan, 1982, pp. 70-71). The same is true for psychological factors. Phelps (1988) made a step in that direction, building on Becker's theory of altruism in the family to social interactions in the workplace, by using motives measured by social psychologists. Further research is needed, however.
- The bargaining framework has not yet been sufficiently developed for researchers to derive verifiable hypotheses from it. Montgomery and Trussell (1986, p. 240) point out that this may be attributed to the poor structure of these models.
- Further work needs to be done on the development of dynamic multi-period models, including the role of uncertainty.
- Labour supply, income, education, marriage and fertility have not yet been simultaneously modelled. These processes can not, however, be seen in isolation. In view of the importance which is attached to raising children by potential partners, it is surprising that simultaneous models for fertility and marriage do not even exist.

As is the case in the economic theory of marriage, research in the field of the economic theory of divorce is also sadly lacking. This brings us to the following proposals for further research:

- Knowledge of the decision-making process is limited. It is not known which role bargaining plays. For this, we need to know more about the distribution of the utility within the household and the possible redistribution when divorce becomes a realistic option for one of the partners.
- Although divorce is considered to be a bargaining process, we did not come across any bargaining models in the literature on the subject. This may be attributed to the limited knowledge we have of the decision-making process.
- In view of the role which (a)symmetrical information plays in the outcome of the bargaining process, research into the degree of symmetry between the knowledge of the partners' perceptions seems important.
- How important is the role of marital-specific capital in divorce? What is done with it in the event of divorce, such as for example the role of children (see Weiss and Willis, 1985)?

- It needs no saying that the decision to get divorced is not independent of fertility, marriage, etc. These processes need to be simultaneously modelled. For this, other relevant variables will also have to be endogenised.
- As a natural extension of the above, dynamic multi-period decision-making models will have to be developed in the future. However, in the field we have dealt with, no attempts in this direction have yet been made.
- It is also important that we gain more thorough knowledge of the division of labour within the household, in particular with respect to the decision-making process. To which extent does the possibility of divorce in the future and the concomitant insecurity play a role (see Lommerud, 1989)?
- Sociological and psychological variables have as yet hardly been incorporated in empirical research. Interdependence variables are very important in this context.
- What is the influence of the presence of marital-specific capital out of a former marriage on the possibility of remarriage?

As mentioned in the foregoing, research in the field of leaving the parental home largely has an ad hoc character. We would like to put forward the following proposals for further research:

- In view of the common notion that leaving the parental home is a matter of tradition, research into the decision-making process in this field would be very useful.
- This is linked to the role of education. Should education be included as an endogenous variable in this context? Note that participation in education does not play a role in McElroy's analysis.
- What are the differences between on the one hand youngsters who first leave the parental home as single persons and then marry, and on the other hand those who leave the parental home in order to marry?
- It would be a natural extension of the research questions in the preceding subsections, to try and develop a multi-period model which focusses on leaving the parental home, marriage, fertility and divorce, but which also includes the socio-economic variables which play a role. A first step in this direction would be to develop a simultaneous multi-period model for leaving the parental home and marriage.
- Which role does the division of labour within the parental home – between parents and children – play in the decision to leave the parental home?
- We are, of course, again in favour of including socio-psychological and socio-cultural explanatory variables. How can this be achieved?

As for the proposals for further research in the field of microsimulation, I will here restrict myself to demographically oriented issues. Other research proposals can possibly be derived from the contributions to this volume by Becker, Siegers, Hooimeijer, Van Imhoff and Van Poppel. This yields the following proposals:

- Microsimulation offers the possibility, via the incorporation of behavioural equations for household formation and dissolution, of studying the future Dutch household structure. The inclusion of such equations implies that demographic trends can not be seen in isolation. However, in standard – macro – household models, incorporation of socio-economic factors is hardly feasible from a practical point of view.

- Microsimulation has hardly been used as a forecasting instrument. Emphasis has primarily been placed on evaluation. However, in my view microsimulation would serve as a very effective forecasting instrument, in particular, for example, in the scenario approach (see for an application, Nelissen and Vossen, 1989). This method would also be very effective in forecasting small-sized subpopulations, a process which often creates problems when using more common methods, especially distribution methods (see also the contribution to this volume by Willekens). This approach is also useful for larger subpopulations, such as for example the distribution by level of education and position on the labour market, where behavioural relationships play a role. Another possibility would be to study the degree to which microsimulation is able to produce a complete population forecast.

- If the behavioural equations in the field of household formation and dissolution are known, we can determine the extent to which demographic trends have been determined by socio-economic changes in recent decades. For example, to which extent can the baby boom and the baby bust be explained by socio-economic trends?

- Conversely, we can also put the question as to how trends in household formation and dissolution have influenced economic factors, such as labour supply, income distribution (see, for example, Orcutt et al., 1976, chapter 15), etc.

- What is the effect of trends in household formation and dissolution on the distribution of births across various socio-economic categories. Is this development leading to a social schism in this field?

- This raises the question, in combination with an endogenisation of the factor education, as to which educational structure this leads to in the long term. After all, participation in education depends for a part on the parental background.

- If household formation and dissolution are determined for a part by economic background variables, this raises the question as to how the fact that this process is not neutral – with respect to economic variables – influences labour force participation, the demand for social security benefits, the insecurity of subsistence, consumption, and – via, for example the cumulative influence of a Social Accounting Matrix (see Cohen and Van Tuyl, 1989) – final demand, investments, etc.

- Microsimulation is an ideal tool in research in the field of life histories, in particular if one wishes to study demographic developments in combination with socio-economic factors.

- In section 2, the division of labour within households was dealt with on several occasions. With the aid of microsimulation, we can determine the influence of changes in female and male labour supply and in income trends on the household division of labour. Microsimulation can also provide an answer to questions regarding the degree to which changes (possibly partly influenced by economic factors) in the probability of divorce have contributed to changes in the labour supply of married women and thus in the aforementioned division of labour (see also Lommerud, 1989).

- Microsimulation can, for example, be used to develop a labour supply-neutral tax system (see Cigno, 1988) or to determine the effect of the proposals put forward by the Oort Committee (with respect to tax legislation) and the Dekker Committee (with respect to health care) on household formation and dissolution.

It seems worthwhile to map out a plan of action. First of all, a more consistent application of static one-period models in the demographic fields distinguished in the foregoing is desirable; Ermisch's model (see Ermisch 1981, 1985 and 1988) could serve as a point of departure. This would have to include the endogenisation of relevant socio-economic variables. A second project would be the application of bargaining models in studies of divorce and leaving the parental home, and possibly also in fertility studies. Thirdly, dynamic multi-period models could be developed, provided that we gain more insight into the decision-making process of individuals. For this, research into life histories is essential. Similarly, the mating process would have to be included in studies of marriage. Game-theory approaches are probably not very useful considering the state of the art in the field of game theories. Finally, the research proposals could be carried out with the aid of microsimulation.

References

Alchian, A. (1969), Information costs, pricing, and resource unemployment, *Western Economic Journal*, 7, pp. 109-128.

Alessi, R. and A. Kapteyn (1985), *Habit formation and interdependent preferences in the almost ideal demand system*, Research Memorandum FEW/208, Tilburg: KUB.

Atkinson, A.B. and N.H. Stern (1979), *On labor supply and commodity demands*, SSRC programme taxation, incentives and the distribution of income, No. 1.

Bagozzi, R.P. and M.F. Van Loo (1987), Individual and couple tastes for children: theoretical, methodological, and empirical issues, *Journal of Economic Psychology*, 8, pp. 191-214.

Becker, G.S. (1960), An economic analysis of fertility, in: National Bureau of Economic Research, ed., *Demographic and economic change in developed countries*, Princeton: NBER, pp. 209-231.

Becker, G.S. (1965), A theory of the allocation of time, *Economic Journal*, 75, pp. 493-517.

Becker, G.S. (1973), A theory of marriage: part I, *Journal of Political Economy*, 81, pp. 813-846.

Becker, G.S. (1974), A theory of marriage: part II. *Journal of Political Economy*, 82, pp. S11-S26.

Becker, G.S. (1981), *A treatise on the family*, Cambridge/London: Harvard University Press.

Becker, G.S., E.M. Landes and R.T. Michael (1977), An economic analysis of marital instability, *Journal of Political Economy*, 85, pp. 1141-1187.

Becker, G.S. and H.G. Lewis (1973), On the interaction between the quantity and quality of children, *Journal of Political Economy*, 81, pp. S279-S288.

Bekkering, J.M., Y.K. Grift and J.J. Siegers (1986), *Belasting- en premieheffing en de arbeidsmarktparticipatie door gehuwde vrouwen; een econometrische analyse*, The Hague, Ministerie van Sociale Zaken en Werkgelegenheid.

Bellman, R.E. (1957), *Dynamic programming*, Princeton: Princeton University Press.

Bennett, R.L. and B.R. Bergmann (1986), *A microsimulated transactions model of the United States economy*, Baltimore/London: John Hopkins University Press.

Blake, J. (1967), Income and reproductive motivation, *Population Studies*, 21, pp. 185-206.

Blake, J. (1968), Are babies consumer durables? Critique of the economic theory of reproductive motivation, *Population Studies*, 22, pp. 5-25.

Boulding, K.E. (1969), Economics as a moral science, *American Economic Review*, 59, pp. 1-12.

Boulier, B.L. and M.R. Rosenzweig (1984), Schooling, search, and spouse selection: testing economic theories of marriage and household behavior, *Journal of Political Economy*, 92, pp. 712-732.

Burch, T.K. and B.J. Matthews (1987), Household formation in developed societies, *Population and Development Review*, 13, pp. 495-511.

Butz, W. and M. Ward (1979), The emergence of countercyclical U.S. fertility, *American Economic Review*, 69, pp. 318-328.

Caldwell, S.B. (1990), How can microsimulation help develop better theories?, in: D.A. Wolf, ed., *Recent developments in microsimulation: an international perspective*, Washington D.C.: Urban Institute Press.

Cigno, A. (1988), *The economics of household formation and marriage*, Mannheim, Invited Paper ESPE Conference, 23-25 June, 1988.

Cigno, A. and J. Ermisch (1989), A microeconomic analysis of the timing of births, *European Economic Review*, 33, pp. 737-760.

Clarke, M. (1986), Demographic processes and household dynamics: a microsimulation approach, in: R. Woods and P. Rees, eds., *Population structures and models: developments in spatial demography*, London: Allen & Unwin.

Coale, A.J. (1971), Age patterns of marriage, *Population Studies*, 25, pp. 193-214.

Cohen, S. and J. van Tuyl (1989), *Growth and equity effects of changing demographic structures in the Netherlands*, Paper ESPE Conference, 8-10 June 1989, Paris, Université de l'UAP, Bouray sur Juine.

Easterlin, R.A. (1966), On the relation of economic factors to recent and projected fertility changes, *Demography*, 3, pp. 131-153.

Edlefsen, L. (1980), *The opportunity costs of time and the numbers, timimg and spacing of births*, Paper presented at the September 1980 meeting of the Population Association of America.

Ermisch, J.F. (1981), An economic theory of household formation, *Scottish Journal of Political Economy*, 28, pp. 1-19.

Ermisch, J.F. (1985), Minimal household units: a new approach to the analysis of household formation, *Population Studies*, 39, pp. 33-54.

Ermisch, J.F. (1988), An economic perspective on household modelling, in: N.W. Keilman, A.C. Kuijsten and A.P. Vossen, eds., *Modelling household formation and dissolution*, Oxford: Clarendon Press, pp. 23-40.

Ferment, B. (1989), The influence of economic factors on household formation, in: R.L. Cliquet et al., eds., *Population and family in the low countries*, VI, The Hague/Brussels: NIDI/CBGS, pp. 55-75.

Galler, H.P. (1988), Microsimulation of household formation and dissolution, in: N.W. Keilman, A.C. Kuijsten and A.P. Vossen, eds., *Modelling household formation and dissolution*, Oxford: Oxford University Press, pp. 139-159.

Gorman, W.M. (1956), A possible procedure for analysing quality differentials in the egg market, Ames: Iowa States College (reprinted in *Review of Economic Studies*, 47, 1980, pp. 843-856).

Groeneveld, L.P., N.B. Tuma and M.T. Hannan (1980), The effects of negative income tax programs on marital dissolution, *Journal of Human Resources*, 15, pp. 654-674.

Gronau, R. (1977), Leisure, home production and work – the theory on the allocation of time revisited, *Journal of Political Economy*, 85, pp. 1099-1123.

Gronau, R. (1986), Home production – a survey, in: O. Ashenfelter and R. Layard, eds., *Handbook of labor economics*, volume I, Amsterdam: Elsevier, pp. 273-304.

Grossbard-Shechtman, A. (1984), A theory of allocation of time in markets for labour and marriage, *Economic Journal*, 94, pp. 863-882.

Hannan, M.T. (1982), Families, markets, and social structures: an essay on Becker's A treatise on the family, *Journal of Economic Literature*, 20, pp. 65-72.

Hansen, H.-J., E. Klein and D. Mannel (1987), *Das makroökonometrische Modell des Sfb3; Version 5.0*, Sonderforschungsbereich 3 Arbeitspapier Nr. 238, J.W. Goethe-Universität Frankfurt und Universität Mannheim.

Hart, O. (1983), Optimal labor contracts under assymetric information: an introduction, *Review of Economic Studies*, 50, pp. 3-35.

Heckman, J. (1974), Effects of child-care programs on women's work effort, *Journal of Political Economy*, 82, pp. S136-S163.

Heckman, J.J., V.J. Hotz and J.R. Walker (1985), New evidence on the timing and spacing of births, *American Economic Review*, 75 (2), pp. 179-184.

Hellwig, O. (1988), *Micromodelling the Australian household sector; a proposal*, Department of Statistics and Econometrics, Darmstadt: Darmstadt Technical University.

Hoorn, W.D. van (1987), Het kindertal van Turken en Marokkanen in Nederland, *Maandstatistiek van de Bevolking*, 35 (9), pp. 15-20.

Huber, J. and G. Spitze (1980), Considering divorce: an expansion of Becker's theory of marital instability, *American Journal of Sociology*, 86, pp. 75-89.

Hunter, K.A. (1984), Marital dissolution: an economic analysis, *American Economist*, 28, pp. 63-68.

Jevons, W. S. (1924), *Die Theorie der Politischen Ökonomie*, Fisher, Jena (translation English edition from 1871).

Kapteyn, A. (1977), *A theory of preference formation*, Ph.D. Dissertation, Leiden.

Kapteyn, A. and I. Woittiez (1987), *Preference interdependance and habit formation in family labor supply*, Research Memorandum FEW/262, Tilburg: KUB.

Keeley, M.C. (1977), The economics of family formation, *Economic Inquiry*, 15, pp. 238-250.

Keeley, M.C. (1979), An analysis of the age pattern of first marriage, *International Economic Review*, 20, pp. 527-544.

Keynes, J.M. (1937), Some economic consequences of a declining population, *Eugenics Review*, 29, pp. 13-18.

Kirnan, A. (1989), The intrinsic limits of modern economic theory, *Economic Journal*, 99, pp. 126-139.

Koo, H.P., C.M. Suchindran and J.D. Griffith (1984), The effects of children on divorce and re-marriage: a multivariate analysis of life table probabilities, *Population Studies*, 38, pp. 451-471.

Koopmans. T.C. and M. Beckman (1957), Assignment problems and the location of economic activities, *Econometrica*, 25, pp. 53-76.

Lam, D. (1988), Marriage markets and assortative mating with household public goods, *Journal of Human Resources*, 23, pp. 462-487.

Lancaster, K.J. (1966a), A new approach to consumer theory, *Journal of Political Economy*, 74, pp. 132-157.

Lancaster, K.J. (1966b), Change and innovation in the technology of consumption, *American Economic Review*, 56, pp. 14-23.

Leibenstein, H. (1957), *Economic backwardness and economic growth*, New York: John Wiley.

Leibenstein, H. (1974), An interpretation of the economic theory of fertility; promosing path or blind alley?, *Journal of Economic Literature*, 12, pp. 457-479.

Leibenstein, H. (1975), The economic theory of fertility decline, *Quarterly Journal of Economics*, 89, pp. 1-31.

Lommerud, K.E. (1989), Marital division of labor with risk of divorce: the role of 'voice' enforcement of contracts, *Journal of Labor Economics*, 7, pp. 113-127.

Manser, M. and M. Brown (1980), Marriage and household decision-making: a bargaining analysis, *International Economic Review*, 21, pp. 31-44.

Malthus, T.R. (1878), *An essay on the principle of population*, London: Reever and Turner (eighth edition).

Matsushita, K. (1988), *Uncertain income and the marriage decision*, Mannheim, Paper ESPE Congress, June, 23-25.

McElroy, M.B. (1985), The joint determination of household membership and market work: the case of young men, *Journal of Labor Economics*, 3, pp. 293-316.

McElroy, M.B. and M.J. Horney (1981), Nash-bargained household decisions: toward a generalization of the theory of demand, *International Economic Review*, 22, pp. 333-349.

Moffit, R. (1984), Profiles of fertility, labour supply and wages of married women: a complete life-cycle model, *Review of Economic Studies*, 51, pp. 263-278.

Mont, D. (1989), Two earner family migration. A search theoretic approach, *Journal of Population Economics*, 2, pp. 55-72.

Montgomery, M. and J. Trussell (1986), Models of marital status and childbearing, in: O. Ashenfelter and R. Layard, eds., *Handbook of labor economics*, volume I, Amsterdam: Elsevier, pp. 205-271.

Morgan, S.P. and R.R. Rindfuss (1985), Marital disruption: structural and temporal dimensions, *American Journal of Sociology*, 90, pp. 1055-1077.

Muth, R.F. (1966), Household production and consumer demand functions, *Econometrica*, 34, pp. 699-708.

Nash, J.F. (1953), Two-person cooperative games, *Econometrica*, 21, pp. 128-140.

Nelissen, J.H.M. (1987), The redistributive impact of the general old age pensions act on lifetime income in the Netherlands, *European Economic Review*, 31, pp. 1419-1441.

Nelissen, J.H.M. (1989), *Microsimulation of household and education dynamics*, Discussion Paper No. 89/3, Growth Dynamics Institute, Rotterdam: Erasmus University.

Nelissen, J.H.M. and P.A.M. van den Akker (1988), Are demographic developments influenced by social security, *Journal of Economic Psychology*, 9, pp. 81-114.

Nelissen, J.H.M. and A.P. Vossen (1989), Projecting household dynamics: a scenario-based microsimulation approach, *European Journal of Population*, 5, pp. 253-279.

Newman, J. (1985), *A stochastic dynamic model of fertility*, Tulane University.

Newman, J.L. and C.E. McCulloch (1984), A hazard approach to the timing of births, *Econometrica*, 52, pp. 939-961.

Olsen, R.J. (1988), A review of 'models of marital status and childbearing' by Mark Montgomery and James Trussell, *Journal of Human Resources*, 23, pp. 577-583.

Orcutt, G.H. (1957), A new type of socio-economic system, *Review of Economics and Statistics*, 58, pp. 773-797.

Orcutt, G.H., S. Caldwell and R. Wertheimer II (1976), *Policy exploration through microanalytic simulation*, Washington D.C.: Urban Institute.

Orcutt, G.H., M. Greenberger, A. Rivlin and J. Korbel (1962), *Micro-analysis of socio-economic systems: a simulation study*, New York: Harper Row.

Parsons, D.O. (1980), The marriage market and female economic well-being, *Journal of Mathematical Sociology*, 7, pp. 113-138.

Peters, H.E. (1986), Marriage and divorce: informational constraints and private contracting, *American Economic Review*, 76, pp. 437-454.

Phelps, C.D. (1988), Caring and family income, *Journal of Economic Behavior and Organization*, 10, pp. 83-98.

Pollak, R.A. and M.L. Wachter (1975), The relevance of the household production function and its implications for the allocation of time, *Journal of Political Economy*, 83, pp. 255-277.

Ricardo, D. (1911), *The principles of political economy and taxation*, New York: Dutton (first edition, 1819).

Romeijn, J.W. (1983), Het verlaten van het ouderlijk huis, *Bevolking en Gezin*, 1983-2, pp. 273-290.

Sander, W. (1986), On the economics of marital instability in the United Kingdom, *Scottish Journal of Political Economy*, 33, pp. 370-381.

Siegers, J.J. (1985), *Arbeidsaanbod en kindertal. Een micro-economische analyse*, Ph.D. Dissertation, Groningen.

Siegers, J.J. (1987), Economische verklaringen van het kindertal, in: Koninklijke Vereniging voor de Staathuishoudkunde, ed., *Demografische veranderingen en economische ontwikkelingen*, Leiden/Antwerpen: Stenfert Kroese, pp. 89-124.

Silber, J. (1981), La théorie économique des ménages et l'étude des phénomènes démographique, *Population*, 3, pp. 557-576.

Smith, A. (1776), *An inquiry into the nature and causes of the wealth of nations*, Dublin.

Spengler, J.J. (1966), The economist and the population question, *American Economic Review*, 56, pp. 14-24.

Stadt, H. van de, R.D. Huigen and C. Zeelenberg (1989), Inkomenseffecten van de Oort-voorstellen, *Economisch Statistische Berichten*, 74, pp. 524-528 and 537.

Stigler, G.J. (1961), The economics of information, *Journal of Political Economy*, 69, pp. 213-225.

Stigler, G.J. (1962), Information in the labor market, *Journal of Political Economy*, 70, pp. S94-S105.

Turchi, B.A. (1975), *The demand for children: the economics of fertility in the United States*, Camdridge, Mass.

Valkonen, T. (1987), Social inequality in the face of death, in: Helsinki: EAPS, ed., *Plenaries European Population Conference 1987*, pp. 201-261.

Verhoef, R. and R.F.J. Tas (1987), Demografie van de niet-Nederlandse bevolking in Nederland, *Maandstatistiek van de Bevolking*, 35, no. 3, pp. 23-39.

Ward, M.P. and W.P. Butz (1980), Completed fertility and its timing, *Journal of Political Economy*, 88, pp. 917-940.

Weiss, Y. and R.J. Willis (1985), Children as collective goods and divorce settlements, *Journal of Labor Economics*, 3, pp. 268-292.

Willis, R.J. (1973), A new approach to the economic theory of fertility behavior, *Journal of Political Economy*, 81, pp. S14-S64.

Willis, R.J. (1987), What have we learned from the economics of the family, *American Economic Review*, AEA Papers and Proceedings, 77, pp. 68-81.

Wolpin, K. (1984), An estimable dynamic stochastic model of fertility and child mortality, *Journal of Political Economy*, 92, pp. 852-874.

Emerging Issues in Demographic Research
C.A. Hazeu and G.A.B. Frinking (Editors)
© Elsevier Science Publishers B.V., 1990

Chapter 8

THE MICROECONOMIC THEORY OF HOUSEHOLD FORMATION AND
DISSOLUTION: STATE-OF-THE-ART AND RESEARCH PROPOSALS;
A COMMENT

John F. Ermisch

The paper is a fine survey of the economics of the family and the household, which
concludes with a long list of proposals for further research. My comments focus on the
links between the subject areas (e.g. marriage, fertility, etc.) and their implications for
research.

It is somewhat odd to begin the discussion of applications of the home production
theory with fertility. The larger amount of research in this area may be the justification
for starting with fertility, but this mode of presentation can obscure important links
between marriage decisions and fertility, which affect the interpretation of economic
influences on fertility. It is the conventional practice to use the characteristics of spouses,
particularly their wages or expected wages, to explain variation in fertility among
couples. But assortative mating in the marriage market means the spouses' characteristics
are endogenous. For instance, if the gains from specialization are relatively important in
marriage decisions, then high wage men would tend to marry women with a comparative
advantage in home activities, including child-rearing. A positive association between
family size and the man's wage may, therefore, be partly the result of assortative mating,
and not fully the result of choosing family size subject to the spouse's earning capacities.

Furthermore, when some variables, like husband's income, are measured with error,
assortative mating may explain what may appear to be anomalous findings. For instance,
in a recent study of variation in family size in Britain, I find that, after controlling for the
wife's wage at marriage and a measure of her husband's lifetime earnings, there a positive
relationship between family size and the wife's educational attainments in conjunction
with errors in measuring husband's wealth (see Ermisch, 1989).

Lam (1988) also shows that his extension of Becker's model of assortative mating to
the case of joint consumption economies (household public goods) applies to household
formation decisions, independent of whether there is a 'market' for household members
(i.e. to joint living arrangements in general). Depending on whether joint consumption
economies or gains from specialization dominate, joint households are more likely to be
formed by people with similar or different wages respectively. In either case, the wage
dispersion in the household is endogenous. Yet, as Lam notes, "empirical research
regularly uses the economic characteristics of individuals living together to explain
economic behaviour", including consumption and labour supply decisions.

While flattered by the attention given to my model of household formation (Ermisch, 1981), I do not think of it as a generalized formulation, as suggested on different pages. It focuses on whether a 'family unit' or individual should live with other family units or individuals. The family units result from other demographic decisions, particularly marriage, fertility and divorce, which are themselves influenced by economic factors along the lines suggested in Nelissen's survey. Thus, as I elaborate more fully in Ermisch (1988), I view the resulting household composition as the outcome of family formation and dissolution decisions, which result in a population of family units and individuals, and household formation decisions by this population.

The former decisions, say marriage, would be modelled differently, taking into account assortative mating, from household formation decisions, to which my model is more applicable. This two-stage approach is particularly appealing for empirical modelling of household formation and composition.

It is, therefore, somewhat misleading to discuss the Ermisch (1981) model in the context of marriage. It was never meant to apply to marriage decisions, nor has it been applied this way. For instance, Ermisch and Overton (1985) examine the household formation decisions of elderly *married couples*.

The author provides an extensive list of further research, but while there are many oversimplifications in our theoretical models and gaps in our empirical research, we do not need to solve all of these problems. Existing models can often be usefully applied to particular issues, like the causes and implications of the growth in one parent families, for which the economics of marriage and divorce are particularly relevant, or the implications of child care subsidies for fertility. The models may be improved in ways particular to these applications, and in that way more general progress is made. In my view, the substantive issue dictates the methods of analysis and the ways in which existing models need to be adapted or replaced by one emphasizing a different perspective. Thus, research priorities need to be set on the basis of the importance of the substantive issues: it is then clearer how the tools (theoretical models and statistical methods) need to be developed in order to address these issues.

Reference (not cited in chapter 7)

J.F. Ermisch (1989), Purchased child care, optimal family size and mothers' employment: theory and econometric analysis, *Journal of Population Economics*.

Emerging Issues in Demographic Research
C.A. Hazeu and G.A.B. Frinking (Editors)
© Elsevier Science Publishers B.V. , 1990

Chapter 9

THE MICROECONOMIC THEORY OF HOUSEHOLD FORMATION AND
DISSOLUTION; STATE-OF-THE-ART AND RESEARCH PROPOSALS;
A COMMENT

Jozef M.M. Ritzen and Hendrik P. van Dalen

1 Introduction

The Dutch author Godfried Bomans once told an anecdote about himself joining an
angling club. On his very first fishing day he wanted to make a good impression, so he
arrived at the canal with a sophisticated telescope fishing rod, ready to start practising
his newly acquired sport. As newcomers are always watched with malicious pleasure by
the 'old boys', so was Bomans watched by some experienced members of the angling
club. He was constructing his fishing rod which at full size far outsized the width of the
canal. The treasurer of the club, who could not resist a good tease, went over to Bomans
and said: "Sir can better stand on the other side of the canal with just this rod", thereby
pointing to a fishing rod which was about one fourth of Bomans' sophisticated fishing
rod.

We have no intention of being offensive, but when we read Nelissen's overview of
the theory of household formation we get the impression that a shorter fishing rod or, to
be more precise, simpler methods and theories can achieve just as much in explaining
demographic phenomena than the high-brow economic *theory* of household formation.
This is not Nelissen's fault: it is the state of the art. However, we would have appreciated
a more critical review.

For a discussion on household formation it is important to define the notion of a
household. This is not simple. Households can be defined in different ways as shown in
a paper by Hartog and Ritzen (1989). Often a household is defined as a unit of *one* or
more persons who *share* for a longer period of time commodities which are spatially
constrained to one point (like housing) according to a general agreement. This definition
excludes boarders as part of the household of the landlord or -lady. It also excludes
institutions in which many people share housing and meals according to specific
agreements (in terms of contracts on prices paid and services rendered). The definition
given before is the 'living together' definition. Generally, one may assume utility
interdependence, in the sense of Hochman and Rodgers (1969), between persons who

constitute a household: person A will value the availability of goods and services to person B of the same household also for his or her own welfare, sometimes even as much as he or she would value such availability for himself or herself. Strong utility interdependence could be another criterion for the delineation of households. For example, children who live on their own, but are fully supported by their parents, could be part of their parents' household, according to this delineation. But according to the 'living together' definition, they are separate households.

For different purposes one might like to use different definitions. For fertility, the 'living together' definition is appropriate, as long as most children are born within wedlock. For purposes of income distribution, also the utility interdependence definition (to be proxied by voluntary transfers) could be appropriate.

This discussion on definitions is immediately related to section 2.3 in the Nelissen-paper. This section is entitled: "The application of the home production theory to demographic phenomena". This is the main thrust of the paper with half of the total pages. We miss here a *critical* review of the literature and more attention for utility interdependence (and the forces behind the formation of utilities). In our view the author relies too much on what Montgomery and Trussell (1986) have to say on household formation.

In this comment we address the following critical points of the theory of household formation. First, we consider some stylized facts, which could be used as a guideline for the economic theory of household formation (section 2). In section 3 our attention is directed at an element that is conspicuously absent in mainstream household theory: a theory of preference formation. Subsequently, we consider more in detail the need for empirical work (in section 4). Section 5 discusses simulation models. The last section (6) presents a list of research priorities.

2 Stylized facts

Nicolas Kaldor established the good tradition to start with some stylized facts before theorizing. The theory of household formation as presented by Nelissen seems to have no set of stylized facts, which it intends to explain. In our opinion, the positive theory of household formation should try to explain the following selection of stylized facts (we rely here on figures given in Montgomery and Trussell, 1986, and Ermisch and Joshi, 1987):

1. The continuous fall in fertility in all industrialized countries from around 1965 to the present.
2. Men marry consistently at a higher age than women.
3. Fertility rates differ across countries, whether these countries are developed or developing.
4. An increasing number of people in industrialized countries do not choose to marry and remain single or cohabit.

5. A continuous increase in divorce rates, where changes in propensities to divorce have occured at all ages.
6. Labour supply by women differs consistently over industrialized countries but has increased over the past thirty-fourty years. The participation of men does not differ very much over industrialized countries, while it has shown a downward trend over the past thirty-fourty years.
7. The number of generations within a household (i.e. a multi-generational household) varies inversely with the level of development of a country.

It is unclear from the paper to what extent the *economic* theory of household formation can contribute to the explanation of these phenomena. It is known (see e.g. Zimmermann, 1985, and Tzannatos and Symons, 1989) that the stylized fact of fertility decline can be satisfactorily explained. A theory of household formation that can explain more of the stylized facts presented above is however more desirable.

Although economic theory has progressed enormously in the field of household formation in recent years, it still misses a theory of preference *formation*. In the next section we will discuss the endogeneity of preference formation.

3 Endogeneity of preference formation

Nelissen does not mark in his survey of the economic theory of household formation the inconsistency between the pure Becker-model of household formation and its extensions, and the notions of 'love', 'caring', and 'enjoying each other's company'. We will forward endogenous preference formation as a bridge over this disturbing inconsistency. A bridge which implies *time inconsistency* of household formation. We distinguish two types of time-inconsistency here. The first time-inconsistency argument runs as follows: people form households of more persons because of the *expectations* on household production and the sharing of commodities. Once this decision has been made, preferences can start to change in the sense of increasing utility interdependence among the members of the household. The basis of the original decision is then no longer sound. This is a time inconsistency problem, which only disappears if people also have expectations on how their preferences will change. The second time-inconsistency argument is found in Kydland and Prescott (1977). It refers to the design problem of choosing a policy that maximizes social welfare over a certain planning horizon. Policy making is rarely done by one policy maker at one point in time. It is more appropriate to think of policies as being chosen at certain intervals in time by different agents. Time inconsistency of optimal plans simply means that the policies, which would have been chosen at the beginning of time and adhered to forever ('policies with commitment'), turn out to be irrelevant in a world where governments have no access to a commitment technology (contract, force). Individuals will not base their decisions on the 'policy with commitment' if a different set of policies will be chosen in the future. The design problem is then to strive for *time consistent* or *credible* policies. Nelissen notices that divorce mostly can take place under pure certainty. This could be due to the time-inconsistency of optimal plans mentioned.

An analytical difficulty with a theory of preference formation is that we have to make a distinction between time preference and the preference for the arguments of the welfare function. For matters of tractability one can treat time preference as constant, although in a macroeconomic setting endogenous time preference deserves attention (as in Epstein and Hynes, 1983). Needless to say, empirical research should use time-series analysis to detect how preferences change.

Endogeneity of preferences and utility interdependence are mentioned in the paper and in the conclusions. However, they are not introduced explicitly. Preference formation becomes – as a result – the black box of household formation and research efforts should be devoted to detecting how utility interdependence evolves and develops.

4 The need for empirical work

Much of the work in the theory of household formation has proceeded by way of analogy. The most dominating theory covering all aspects of household formation is the theory of international trade. Theories of age at first marriage can be traced back to search theory of the labour market. Walras' auctioneer has a part-time job as matchmaker on the marriage market. Dissolution and divorce theories find their origins in contract or retirement theories. The wide-spread use of alimony can be interpreted as an application of the Hicks-Kaldor compensation criterion of Pareto-optimality. Household production theory resembles large parts of the theory of industrial organisation. More analogies can be given. Now the question is: what we can learn from these theories for household formation. General analytical results turn out to be very scanty, as the paper shows. Whether the theoretical framework is useful at all then depends on the empirical tests. Efforts directed at testing these analogies should have the highest priority.

The theory of household formation only offers on the one hand trivial theorems ("individuals who care about each other are more likely to get married than the same kind of people who do not care about each other", or that changes in relative prices have income and substitution effects) and sophisticated reduced form equations for estimation with variables which are often not measured. A closing of the gap between theory and measurement deserves a top ranking on the list of research priorities.

5 Microsimulation models: empty boxes?

A telling statement in Nelissen's paper is found at the end of section 3: "A practical drawback is that all microsimulation models only have a limited number of behavioural responses, *particularly in the field of household formation*"(!). This does not come as a surprise. Theory is far ahead of measurement. What is more surprising is that a lot of work is devoted to the building of *empty boxes*, as we will call these microsimulation models, whereas the work should be allocated to estimating behavioural responses. The only purpose microsimulation models serve at present is that of an accounting frame-work, which yields sophisticated extrapolations. As put forward in Nelissen's paper as one of the many lapses of knowledge is information about the decision-making process regarding the number of children and the timing of births, leaving the parental home, marriage and divorce.

Nelissen sees the *use* of microsimulation models for the analysis of alternative government policies. This step is however fraught with a lot of analytical difficulties. Even in the most simple general equilibrium models of the representative agent, questions like "how should distortionary tax rates be set?" and "how much should the government supply in public goods?" are difficult to answer. Under conditions of *endogenous* household formation and fertility decisions, fiscal policies influence the population structure and birth rates; changes which perhaps were not part of the intention of the government. An economic policy must therefore consider first the question of optimal population growth, size and structure before introducing a policy measure. Otherwise these policies are likely to be a step in the dark. The welfare economics of endogenous fertility is gaining pace (see Nerlove et al., 1987, and Nerlove, 1988) but it needs to be explored extensively before a government starts (indirectly) taxing or subsidizing births, marriages, divorces and the like.

6. Research priorities

In conclusion, we would like to propose the following plan of action for research in the field of the economics of household formation:
1. Develop *theoretical* concepts of preference formation.
2. Develop *estimation* models of preference and household formation and the micro-data for their estimation.
3. Further the understanding of the major demographic developments of nations by means of the theory and the empirical estimation of household formation.
4. Develop the *welfare* economics of *endogenous* population growth.
5. Develop microsimulation models *once* empirical relationships are firmly established.

Needless to say that this is not an agenda for a single researcher or even a single research group. It is evident that "in der Beschränkung zeigt sich der Meister".

References

Epstein, L.G. and J.A. Hynes (1983), The rate of time preference and dynamic economic analysis, *Journal of Political Economy*, 91, pp. 68-95.

Ermisch, J. and H. Joshi (1987), *Demographic change, economic growth and social welfare*, European Population Conference, Jyväskylä.

Hartog, J. and J.M.M. Ritzen (1989), Theoretical issues in size income distribution policy, in: V.L. Urquidi, ed., *Income Policies*, London: MacMillan.

Hochman, H.M. and J.D. Rogers (1969), Pareto optimal redistribution, *American Economic Review*, 59, pp. 542-557.

Kydland, F.E. and E.C. Prescott (1977), Rules rather than discretion: the inconsistency of optimal plans, *Journal of Political Economy*, 85, pp. 473-491.

Montgomery, M. and J. Trussell (1986), Models of marital status and childbearing, in: O. Ashenfelter and R. Layard, eds., *Handbook of Labor Economics*, Vol. I, Amsterdam, North-Holland, pp. 205-271.

Nerlove, M. (1988), Population policy and individual choice, *Journal of Population Economics*, 1, pp. 17-31.

Nerlove, M., A. Razin and E. Sadka (1987), *Household and economy, welfare economics of endogenous fertility*, New York: Academic Press.

Tzannatos, Z. and J. Symons (1989), An economic approach to fertility in Britain since 1860, *Journal of Population Economics*, 2, pp. 121-138.

Zimmermann, K.F. (1985), *Familienökonomie. Theoretische und empirische Untersuchungen zur Frauenerwerbstätigkeit und Geburtenentwicklung,* Berlin u.a.

Emerging Issues in Demographic Research
C.A. Hazeu and G.A.B. Frinking (Editors)
© Elsevier Science Publishers B.V. , 1990

Chapter 10

TOWARDS THE CONSTRUCTION OF INTERDISCIPLINARY
THEORETICAL MODELS TO EXPLAIN DEMOGRAPHIC BEHAVIOUR

Jacques J. Siegers

1 Introduction

Traditional demographers cannot easily be accused of being very much involved in the construction of theoretical models. On the contrary, they concentrate primarily on the search for empirical regularities. Recently, their work was described as: "a refined variant of actuarial science" (Olsen, 1988, p. 577). Such activities of advanced demographic bookkeeping are of course necessary; but they do not suffice. After all, we are never satisfied with description alone, we always want to understand the behaviour which lies behind it. And here lies the difference between on the one hand traditional, formal demography and on the other hand economics. As Laslett of Cambridge University said during the Third Annual Meeting of the European Society for Population Economics in June 1989: "Demographers try to describe the world, economists think they understand the world". This quote reflects not only the division of labour between these two disciplines, but also the pretensions with which economists have moved into the field of demography.

In this contribution I will try and show that these pretensions are, on the one hand, partly unjustified: economists don't understand demographic phenomena thàt well. But I will also try and show why the economic approach can be a great deal more fertile than it has been in the past, because it offers an excellent theoretical framework for the construction of interdisciplinary theoretical models to explain demographic behaviour.

In the following I will not deny my economic background, nor my preoccupation with explaining fertility, nor my vested interests in interdisciplinary research. With respect to the emphasis I will place on finding an explanation for fertility, I would like to add that all conclusions drawn also apply, by analogy, to an explanation for other demographic phenomena.

I will first give you a concise evaluation of the economic theory of fertility; concise, so as to avoid as much as possible any overlap with the paper by Nelissen on the economic determinants of demographic behaviour. One of the three conclusions based on my evaluation will be that the economic approach should be extended with relevant factors which do not belong to the field of traditional economics.

I will then outline a general theoretical framework, the rational-choice framework, from which interdisciplinary theoretical models can be derived to explain demographic behaviour.

Next, I will put forward some proposals for further research in which the theoretical approach propagated can be applied to explain a number of demographic phenomena which seem to deserve priority from a societal point of view.

2   An evaluation of the economic theory of fertility

The economic theory of fertility is rooted in the work of Malthus. Although it does not follow naturally from his analyses, as is generally believed to be the case (see, for example, Andorka, 1978, pp. 15-17), researchers have concluded that Malthus believed there was a positive relationship between per capita income and the number of births. However, in much empirical research this relationship has not been found; more often than not even a negative relationship has been found (Van de Kaa and Moors, 1982). This has inspired a great many authors to construct models which fit the neo-classical research programme and which at the same time are compatible with these empirical findings. In so doing, they have assumed that if sufficient other circumstances are kept constant, the underlying relationship between fertility and income will be positive, but that if income changes, another phenomenon will change too, which could undo the positive effect of income on fertility. According to Becker and his followers, it is the fact that child quality rises with income which causes the income elasticity of fertility to be very small or even negative.

Most of the economic theory of fertility forms part of the new home economics. However, the advantages which the new home economics has brought for the economic theory of fertility are still small compared with, for example, the benefits which the economic theory of labour supply has derived from its incorporation in the theory of consumer behaviour (Siegers, 1985). So, developments within economics in the field of the new home economics have been relatively limited, although I must point out of course that the new home economics was developed much more recently than the theory of consumer behaviour. Moreover, empirical testing poses problems to economists owing to the fact that, among other things, when applying the new home economics to an explanation of fertility, phenomena are introduced in the model which can not be translated into variables suitable for empirical analysis as easily as in the application of economics in the field which it traditionally covers. See for example, the problem of adequately operationalising the aforementioned concept of 'child quality'; in a recent evaluation, Willis (1987, p. 75) here speaks of an "unresolved issue".

The economic theory of fertility has been subjected to much more severe criticism than the related economic theory of individual labour supply. This may be attributed in the first place to the fact that in the former case, more stringent assumptions must be made in order to derive empirically verifiable hypotheses from theory (Siegers, 1985, pp. 195-196; Siegers, 1987, p. 114). Secondly, the role of social values and norms is deemed much more important in decision-making, by individuals and households, with regard to fertility than in decisions regarding labour supply. According to some people, the options are so limited in the case of fertility, that economic science hardly has any role to play; this field should be left to social demographers, they say (Kinsella, 1975). This is in agreement with Duesenberry's statement (1960, p. 233) that: "Economics is all about how people make choices. Sociology is all about why they don't have any choices to make". Closely linked to this second reason is a third reason, namely that a sociology of individual labour supply hardly exists (cf. Veenman, 1983, pp. 208-209), whereas social demography has a long tradition. So, criticism of the economic theory of fertility is mainly voiced by social demographers, who saw 'their' field being invaded by economists (Blake, 1967 and 1968; see also Namboodiri, 1972 and 1975, and Ryder, 1974).

Most of the criticism of the economic theory of fertility is directed at the assumptions made therein. However, for participants of the neo-classical research programme in the field of fertility, these assumptions belong to, in the terminology of Lakatos (1970), the hard core or the protective belt of this programme (Siegers, 1985, pp. 6 and 196). For this reason this criticism barely seems to have influenced the development of the economic theory of fertility.

We can say that the economic theory of fertility seems to focus predominantly on determining the extent to which the research programme is capable of explaining known phenomena, including the aforementioned negative relationship between fertility and income (Blaug, 1980, p. 248; Perlman, 1975, p. 554; Namboodiri, 1975, p. 564 and 568). Despite this verificationist tendency, the economic theory of fertility is able to throw new light on a number of demographic phenomena. I would like to mention in particular, the consequences of Willis's interaction model for the empirical analysis and interpretation of the relationship between fertility on the one hand and the level of education of men and women on the other hand; I would also like to refer to what theory has to say about the interpretation of what Schultz (1981, p. 230) has called "The classical problem that brings labour and population economics together", that is to say, the relationship between fertility and labour supply.

The application of the 'new home economics' to the explanation of fertility, yields a theoretical analytical framework from which models can be derived – with the aid of supplementary assumptions – in order to answer specific research questions (see Siegers, 1985, p. 198 and the references therein). Nevertheless, very few models which can actually be used in policy-making have as yet been developed. This is true in particular for the Netherlands, where the economic analysis of fertility is still in its infancy. In fact, this is the case for economic explanations of demographic behaviour in general, as can be illustrated by the fact that of the nine papers in the field of demographic changes and economic developments, which were submitted to the Koninklijke Vereniging voor de Staathuishoudkunde in 1987 on the occasion of its 125th anniversary, seven dealt with the economic consequences of demographic phenomena and only two tried to give an explanation for these phenomena (Kapteyn, 1987). So, what should be given priority in future research?

Economic theory in the field of fertility has, until now, paid relatively little attention to the decision-making process of (potential) parents. Still, this process is a crucial factor in explaining both the present and the ultimate number of children. During one's lifecycle, the restrictions one faces change constantly. These restrictions can be both exogenous (for example, involuntary unemployment) and predetermined endogenous (for example, the present fixed costs of a household depend for a part on whether it has bought a house in the past; another example: the current earning capacity depends for a part on investments made in the past in human capital, including experiences gained during employment, and so it depends on past labour force participation, and on the interruption of one's career to raise children; Groot et al., 1988). Strictly speaking, almost every current restriction comprises a predetermined element (so, the probability of involuntary unemployment is determined for a part by the job one has chosen in the past, which in its turn may have been determined by the desired number of children, and the probability of involuntary childlessness is partly determined by delayed pregnancies in the past). With given preferences, behaviour will change as restrictions change during the course of one's life. However, restrictions and behaviour are not the only aspects which change during a lifetime; the preferences themselves change too. Both the preferences with respect to the timing of births and those with respect to the ultimate number of children change over time. Even if the desired timing and the desired ultimate number of children do not change, the preferences will at least become more defined during one's lifecycle (see e.g. Veevers' study on voluntary childlessness, 1973), until preferences and reality coincide, or else until those involved are forced to reconcile themselves to the facts (see also the mental incongruence theory, Tazelaar, 1980).

Against this background, we can formulate three related research priorities (Siegers, 1987, p. 118; see also Siegers, 1980):

a. extending the economic analysis by introducing relevant factors which do not belong to the traditional field of economics (Cramer, 1986, p. 50: "Extending the analysis with non-economic factors has priority over a further refinement of the theoretical specification" – translation by JJS).
b. research into the question how the system of preferences, restrictions and behaviour changes during the lifecycle, and into the question which determinants are responsible for these changes.
c. construction of theoretical models which can be translated into empirical estimating models which can be used in policy.

I will now try and explain the first research priority.

3 The rational-choice framework

Micro-economic analysis, including the aforementioned economic theory of fertility, is in fact a specification of the rational-choice framework. I call to mind that this framework has been derived from a social theory of behaviour, which assumes that human behaviour can be explained with the aid of the 'preferences – restrictions – behaviour' scheme. It is assumed that human beings are led by preferences, and that they strive for maximum realisation of these preferences. As a result of restrictions, they can never fully realise all their preferences, and so they have to make choices. The resultant of this choice process is behaviour.

The central thesis of my paper is that the general, rational-choice framework offers an ideal opportunity to combine the advantages of both economics and the other social sciences, namely to enrich the rather bare but formal and elegant economic models with psychological and sociological insights. Also, biological aspects can easily be incorporated in this framework.

Before I go into more detail about this thesis, I must answer the question why interdisciplinary research is needed; after all, an interdisciplinary approach is not an end in itself. I will give an example to illustrate my point.

An economist who is interested in finding an explanation for fertility will use income and relative prices as the major determinants in his analysis. For a sociologist, on the other hand, the central variables are likely to include norms and values. Both types of variables are probably closely related, partly because common 'third' factors influence both of these types of variables. As a result, the effect of one of these types of variables also reflects, in a separate analysis, the effect of the other type of variable, and it needs no saying that this will lead to incorrect scientific and policy conclusions. This example also illustrates that a multidisciplinary approach cannot replace an interdisciplinary approach.

How can the general, rational-choice framework be used to explain demographic behaviour, such as for example, fertility (see for the following Siegers and De Jong-Gierveld, 1989). For this, the 'preferences – restrictions – behaviour' scheme derived from the framework serves as a starting point. In applying this to a specific research question, both the specific preferences and the specific restrictions which are generally analysed within economics, as well as the specific preferences and the specific restrictions used within the other social sciences, are included (see also Turchi, 1989). So, data collection can be directed towards the gathering of information which enables more relationships to be identified within one model than was possible until now, thus allowing more behavioural aspects to be endogenised in the theoretical model and the derivative empirical estimating models (Siegers, 1989b). However, this does not detract from the fact that I do agree with those authors (such as Tazelaar, 1989) who say that we should strive for parsimonious models, since the essence of modelling is that it helps us to see the wood through the trees. And parsimony seems especially to be a necessary element in a research strategy which is aimed at explaining more than one behavioural aspect.

The first step in the application of the rational-choice framework, with a view to explaining fertility, is the construction of the preference functions for both potential parents. Two general, final preferences could be physical well-being and social approval (Lindenberg, 1989). From this point of view income or economic independence, leisure and having children (Niphuis-Nell, 1981; Den Bandt, 1982; Rozendal, Moors and Leeuw, 1985) are lower level preferences, i.e. preferences which serve as instruments to realise the general preferences mentioned; we can thus speak of a hierarchy of preferences (Bagozzi, 1984). This build-up of final and intermediary preferences is entirely analogous with the relationship between commodities on the one hand and the factors of production, time and market goods, on the other hand in the new home economics. Similarly, the functional relationships between final and intermediary preferences can, by analogy with the new home economics, be called production functions. However, in this case the functions are not technical production functions which describe the technical production process through which time and market goods are transformed into commodities, but they are social production functions which describe, for example, how social approval, that is to say status, behavioural confirmation and positive affect, can be obtained from, among other things, norm conformity, occupation and income (Lindenberg, 1989, pp. 4-5).

If we translate the 'preferences – restrictions – behaviour' scheme into a specific model and if we know two of the three parts of the scheme, and thus of the model, we can derive the third part. So if we know everything about the preferences and everything about the restrictions we can derive the resulting behaviour. Let us look, for example at the neo-classical theoretical models of behaviour such as consumption analysis, labour supply, and fertility. In empirical analyses, however, at least in much economic and sociological research, we observe behaviour and restrictions, and preferences are only there by implication. This raises the question whether we can try and 'observe' preferences and incorporate these preferences into our economic and sociological models. Of course, if we do so, we 'observe' all three parts of the 'preference – restrictions – behaviour' scheme and risk introducing inconsistencies. But do we not have to search for such risks and can we not learn from these possible inconsistencies, with a view to improving our models? The objection could be raised that the measurement of preferences is not an easy task (see, for example, Burch, 1989; Deven, 1989; Spiess, 1989). However, this is also true with respect to the measurement of restrictions (such as income and prices, let alone shadow prices) and behaviour (see, for example, the measurement problems with respect to labour supply or with respect to the allocation of time in general). So, I am not much impressed by the measurement problems with respect to preferences nor by the problems of conceptualisation.

When we measure preferences for the sake of improving our models, it seems necessary that both economists and social psychologists should want to know more than they want to know now. In other words, economists should be more interested in preferences than they find acceptable by the standards of the perceived hard core of the neo-classical research programme. And social psychologists should be more interested in improving economic and sociological models than, as has been customary until now, to merely state that the assumptions which underlie these models, regarding the preferences, appear to contradict the results of psychological research. We all know that; what we need to find out is how we can make good use of this knowledge.

In most economic analyses of household decision making, it is assumed that both partners strive to maximise one joint final preference function. However, such a complete harmony of interests does not seem very plausible. This assumption also precludes an extension of the analysis to explain, for example, household dissolution. It would thus seem better to use a separate preference function for each partner. This raises a difficult yet interesting problem, namely the mutual adjustment of behaviour by both partners. The drawback of game theoretical solutions is that they do not guarantee Pareto-optimal solutions (see, for example, Kooreman, 1986). That is to say, they generally give rise to a state of equilibrium in which it is possible that somebody can better his or her position without this being at the expense of the position of the partner. This hardly seems plausible in a family context. On the other hand, the incorporation of Pareto-optimal solutions by viewing the household final preference function as a convex combination of the final preference functions of both partners, only yields tractable, closed-form behavioural equations when a rather restricted specification is applied to the individual final preference functions, namely the Stone-Geary specification (cf. Kooreman, 1986; Grift and Siegers, 1989).

The second step in the application of the general rational-choice framework is the formulation of relevant restrictions: values and norms (partly related to attitudes of network members including somebody's partner), expected and received support from network members (for example, for the realisation of wishes with respect to a paid job; see Tazelaar and Sprengers, 1985), education, labour market situation, market prices (including wage rates), time, biological factors (Moors, 1974, pp. 119-129; Rozenzweig and Schultz, 1985), etc. As for the restrictions, we must distinguish between actual restrictions on the one hand, and perceived restrictions on the other hand. This can be illustrated by the (expected) underestimation by young women of the increased probability of a miscarriage and the decreased probability of the realisation of the desired fertility when delaying pregnancy after the age of about 25 years (see for more on these age-specific probabilities Moors, 1986). But a subjective assessment of the situation also applies with respect to traditional economic variables such as income (especially future income), and prices, as well as matters such as the availability of day-care facilities. Information plays an important role with respect to the discrepancy between perceived and actual values of variables. Information is in fact itself the outcome of a production process where time, market goods and the nature and size of social networks are the production factors.

The third step in applying the general rational-choice framework is to relate the preferences and restrictions to each other in a single theoretical explanatory model. The behavioural equations can be derived by maximising the preference function, given the restrictions. In order to be able to test and estimate the theoretical model, it needs to be translated in an empirical estimating model which can be statistically analysed. The results of such analyses can then be used to improve the theoretical model.

Once the parameters of the theoretical models have been estimated, the models can be used for simulation analyses, for example, to evaluate policy measures. This can be illustrated by the following example. Let us assume that we want to know what the effect will be of tax or social security measures on (the timing of) male and female labour supply and their fertility. From the model estimation in the analytical phase, we know the parameters which indicate how the wage rates of men and women as well as their social security benefits and non-wage income, if any, influence the (timing of) male and female labour supply and fertility. Changes in the tax or social security systems give rise to changes in the wage rates and in any social security benefits and non-wage income received; these changes can be calculated with knowledge of the institutional regulations. Next, we can determine the effect on the (timing of) male and female labour supply and fertility with the aid of the behavioural parameters estimated during the analytical phase (see, for example, Bekkering, Grift and Siegers, 1986; Grift and Siegers, 1988).

4 Proposals for further research

Strictly speaking, every kind of demographic behaviour can be studied with the aid of the rational-choice framework I have just presented. In the following, I will give a number of possible applications to issues which could prove to be important both from a scientific and from a societal point of view.

a. Decision-making processes within the household.
   A natural extension of what I said earlier about the mutual adjustment of behaviour between both partners within a household is the need for more in-depth research into decision-making processes. The game-theoretical approach in particular seems to offer good possibilities (Horney and McElroy, 1980; Manser and Brown, 1979), allowing us to determine if, and to which extent non-Pareto-optimal states of equilibrium exist in practice, and if they do exist, under which circumstances such situations arise. Unless one assumes that partners are entirely altruistic (in the every-day meaning of the word, and not in the sense described by Becker (1981) and his followers), much demographic behaviour is a matter of negotiation, to a greater or lesser degree. Moreover, this approach also allows us to throw light on the introduction of altruism in the Beckerian sense to explain demographic behaviour.
b. The interrelationship between female labour market behaviour and fertility.
   It is often suggested that the increased labour force participation of women in the Western world has played an important role in reducing fertility, and that fertility may continue to decrease if the growth in female labour force participation persists. However, it can be questioned whether this causality is as strong as many people believe. This means that we cannot be sure that measures aimed at creating greater opportunities for women to combine parenthood and paid labour will actually in-

fluence fertility, and if they do, what the influence will be. In order to be able to answer this question further, theoretical and empirical interdisciplinary research will have to be carried out into the relationship between female labour-market behaviour and fertility (including the aspects of timing and spacing); this can be done along the lines sketched in the foregoing (see Siegers and De Jong-Gierveld, 1989). Research into the question how the relevant preferences, restrictions and behaviour change during the lifecycle, and into the question on which determinants these changes are based (see also Bulatao and Fawcett, 1983) would be particularly relevant.

c. The demand for day care.

Very little is known about the determinants of the demand for various forms of day care (for descriptive studies, see Wilbrink-Griffioen, Van Vliet and Elzinga, 1987, and Suij, 1987). The question as to the extent to which behaviour on the demand side is influenced by rationing (especially in the case of public day-care facilities, all of which have long waiting lists) and by social values and norms, constitutes a difficult problem. To which extent can various forms of day care be substituted for various social categories and income groups of women (see for example Hinde and Ermisch, 1989), and what are the consequences for the labour force participation of women and their fertility?

d. The supply of day care.

One does not have to be an economist to understand that the actual use of various forms of day care is the resultant of supply and demand. The supply side comprises day care offered by family and friends, by private commercial institutions, including firms, and day care offered by non-profit organisations, whether government-subsidised or not. Each of these components of the supply of day care need to be studied in more detail. The rational-choice framework can be applied to the supply behaviour of individual family members and friends, but it can also be used to trace the effects of the trend found in the public sector of withdrawing in favour of the private sector, and thus of leaving the realisation of day-care facilities to negotiations between employers and employees and their respective organisations. With the aid of the rational-choice framework we can analyse this behaviour and determine to which extent we may assume that only the costs and benefits for the negotiating partners themselves play a role in these negotiations, and that the costs and benefits for society as a whole are insufficiently reflected in the outcome of the negotiations (see Siegers, 1989a, and Schippers and Siegers, 1989). The rational-choice framework can also be used to analyse the behaviour of municipalities in order to explain the supply of public day-care facilities per municipality. It is generally believed that the presence of a woman or several women on the municipal council and/or among the Mayor and Aldermen influences policy in this respect. For example, in Sweden a positive relationship has been found between the supply of public day-care facilities and the percentage of women in municipal councils (Gustafsson and Stafford, 1988, esp. p. 19). We can obtain a systematic analysis of the supply of public day-care facilities by application of the interest function approach developed by Van Winden (1983), and its application at the level of municipal policy, as developed by Renaud and Van Winden (see Renaud, 1988, and Renaud and Van Winden, 1988) and by incorporating the factor gender in this approach.

e. The fertility of immigrant women in the Netherlands.

Research conducted by Schoorl (1989 and forthcoming) has shown that the fertility of immigrant women – of Turkish and Moroccan origin – which fertility deviates strongly from that of Dutch women, drops after these women settle in the Netherlands. This downward adjustment is generally viewed as a shift of the preferences of these women. However, in accordance with the rational-choice framework described, another explanation is also possible. Let us assume that the final utility function of the women in question comprises only two arguments: physical well-being and social approval. Let us also assume that the social production function that describes the production of social approval includes children (possibly: boys in particular) as production factors, where the relative weight of this factor is a function of social pressure. This social pressure is believed to be a great deal stronger in the country of origin than in the Netherlands, which means that we may expect fertility to decline, even if preferences remain constant. Other aspects in the sphere of restrictions also play a role of course, such as the availability and cost of contraceptives, the wider range of economic opportunities and the concomitant repercussions for divorce and fertility, and the like (see Schoorl, 1989, and forthcoming). These factors and their interrelationships can be analysed through further research along the lines of the interdisciplinary framework I have sketched.

f. Household formation and dissolution.

The interdisciplinary application of the rational-choice framework seems to be an adequate instrument to explain household formation and dissolution. If one has knowledge of economic analyses of such demographic behaviour, it is very clear that my earlier remark that economic models are relatively bare is in fact very true here (see for example, Fulop, 1980, and Becker, 1981). By extending the analyses along the lines I have described, one can gain more insight into current and future developments in household formation and dissolution, that is to say, in demographic behaviour which has far-reaching consequences for society.

g. The relationship between demographic trends and social security (see Siegers, 1989a).

In the Netherlands, empirical research into the relationship between demographic trends and social security has been more or less limited to statistical simulations of the effects of, for example, a changing age structure of the population on future macro-financial consequences for the social security system, assuming that behaviour will remain constant, or that it will change according to a fixed trend, as for example in the case of divorce. Such research is necessary, but it does not suffice. For example, if the frequency of divorce continues to increase, female labour-market behaviour will be affected (partially in anticipation of such a trend). Similarly, the trend towards smaller families will (partly through the declining size of kinship networks; see Bartlema, 1987) influence behaviour, as will the greying of the population. The resulting changes in behaviour, including feed backs to demographic behaviour, will affect the demand for social security received through the public and private sector. What we need here are interdisciplinary, theoretical and empirical simulation analyses of premiums paid for, and benefits received from social security by individuals and households during their lifecycle. This implies the need for research into:

- labour-market behaviour, in particular with respect to the formation and depreciation of human capital, in relationship to income and asset formation, as well as in relation to social security premiums and social security benefits;
- household formation and dissolution, in particular in relationship to eligibility for, and level of social security benefits;
- the greying of the population, especially with respect to the effects produced via the labour market (see also Van Altena et al., 1989), and with respect to the demand for facilities (see, for example, Vollering and Nijkamp, 1988).

5 Conclusion

Keeping in mind Laslett's quote which I gave at the beginning of my paper, one can say that what I have proposed in the foregoing is not without pretensions. I have said that the construction of interdisciplinary theoretical models is a necessary and fertile scientific activity for explaining demographic behaviour. However, I also hope to have shown that a great deal of effort is still needed before we will really understand even only the demographic part of the world.

References

Altena, A.R. van, J. Plantenga, J.J. Schippers and J.J. Siegers, *Demografische ontwikkelingen en het functioneren van de arbeidsmarkt. Een vergelijkende studie naar het overheidsbeleid in Duitsland, Frankrijk en Zweden*, Den Haag: Organisatie voor Strategisch Arbeidsmarktonderzoek (forthcoming).

Andorka, R. (1978), *Derminants of fertility in advanced societies*, London.

Bagozzi, R.P. (1984), A prospectus for theory construction in marketing, *Journal of Marketing*.

Bandt, M.L. den (1982), *Vrijwillig kinderloze vrouwen*, Deventer.

Becker, G.S. (1981), *A treatise on the family*, Cambridge, Mass.

Bekkering, J., Y.K. Grift and J.J. Siegers (1986), *Belasting- en premieheffing en arbeidsmarktparticipatie door gehuwde vrouwen. Een econometrische analyse*, Den Haag, Ministerie van Sociale Zaken en Werkgelegenheid.

Blake, J. (1967), Income and reproductive motivation, *Population Studies*, November.

Blake, J. (1968), Are babies consumer durables? Critique of the economic theory of reproductive motivation, *Population Studies*.

Blaug, M. (1980), *The methodology of economics*, Cambridge, Mass.

Bulatao, R.A. and J.F. Fawcett (1983), *Dynamic perspectives in the study of fertility decision-making: successive decisions within a fertility career*, International Population Conference Manilla, 1981, Volume I, Luik, IUSSP.

Burch, Th. K. (1989), *De gestibus confusi sumus: with illustrations from the Canadian Fertility Survey*, Paper presented at the Workshop "Female labour market behaviour and fertility: preferences, restrictions, and behaviour", Organised by Nederlands Interdisciplinair Demografisch Instituut and Centrum voor Interdisciplinair Onderzoek van Arbeidsmarkt- en Verdelingsvraagstukken, University of Utrecht, held at Den Haag, April 20-22.

Burg, B.I. van der, J. van Doorne-Huiskes, J.J. Schippers and J.J. Siegers (forthcoming), Loopbaanverschillen tussen mannen en vrouwen binnen arbeidsorganisaties: een structureel-individualistisch verklaringsschema, *Sociologische Gids*.

Cramer, J.S. (1986), Het economisch onderzoek in de toekomst, in: H.M. Jolles, A.P. Plompen and H. Weijma, eds., *Vijftien wetenschappen vijftien jaar verder*, Den Haag.

Deven, F. (1989), *Shortcuts as pitfalls? Ways of measuring childbearing preferences and intentions*, Paper presented at the Workshop "Female labour market behaviour and fertility: preferences, restrictions, and behaviour", Organised by Nederlands Interdisciplinair Demografisch Instituut and Centrum voor Interdisciplinar Onderzoek van Arbeidsmarkt- en Verdelingsvraagstukken, Utrecht University, held at Den Haag, April 20-22.

Duesenberry, J.S. (1960), Comment in: *Demographic and economic change in developed countries*, Princeton.

Fulop, M. (1980), A brief survey of the literature on the economic analysis of marriage and divorce, *American Economist*.

Grift, Y.K. and J.J. Siegers (1988), *Supply determinants of part-time work of Dutch married women: the influence of taxes and social premiums*, Paper presented at the Second Annual Meeting of the European Society of Population Economics, Mannheim, June 23-25.

Grift, Y.K. and J.J. Siegers (1989), *Estimating an individual utility labour supply model with a family budget constraint and with Pareto optimal outcomes*, Paper presented at the Third Annual Meeting of the European Society of Population Economics, Bouray sur Juine, June 8-10.

Groot, L., J.J. Schippers and J.J. Siegers (1988), The effect of interruptions and part-time work on women's wage rate: a test of the variable-intensity model, *De Economist*.

Gustafsson, S. and F. Stafford (1988), *Day care subsidies and labour supply in Sweden*, Paper, Arbetslivcentrum, Stockholm/Institute for Social Research, University of Michigan.

Hinde, P.R.A. and J.F. Ermisch (1989), *Women's earning capacity and childbearing*, Paper presented at the Third Annual Meeting of the European Society of Population Economics, Bouray sur Juine, June 8-10.

Horney, M.J. and M.B. McElroy (1980), *A Nash-bargained linear expenditure system: the demand for leisure and goods*, Research Memorandum, Center for Mathematical Studies in Business and Economics, University of Chicago.

Kaa, D.J. van de, and H.G. Moors (1982), Social status, social structure and fertility. A critical review with special reflections on the Netherlands, in: *Population et structures sociales*, Leuven.

Kinsella, R.P. (1975), A note on the new home economics, *International Journal of Social Economiscs*.

Kooreman, P. (1986), *Essays on microeconometric analysis of household behaviour*, Ph.D. Dissertation, Katholieke Universiteit Brabant, Tilburg.

Lakatos, I. (1970), Falsification and the methodology of scientific research programmes, in: I. Lakatos and A. Musgrave, eds., *Critisism and the growth of knowledge*, London.

Lindenberg, S.M. (1989), *Social approval, fertility and female labor market behaviour*, Paper presented at the Workshop "Female labour market behaviour and fertility: preferences, restrictions, and behaviour", Organised by Nederlands Interdisciplinair Demografisch Instituut and Centrum voor Interdisciplinair Onderzoek van Arbeidsmarkt- en Verdelingsvraagstukken, University of Utrecht, held at Den Haag, April 20-22.

Manser, M. and M. Brown (1979), Bargaining analyses of household decisions, in: C.B. Lloyd, E.S. Andrews and C.L. Gilroy, eds., *Women in the labor market*, New York.

Montgomery, M. and J. Trussell (1986), Models of marital status and childbearing, in: O. Ashenfelter and R. Layard, eds., *Handbook of labor economics*, Amsterdam.

Moors, H.G. (1974), *Child spacing and family size in the Netherlands*, Leiden.

Moors, H.G. (1986), Moeder worden op oudere leeftijd: een nieuwe trend?, *Demos*, February.

Namboodiri, N.K. (1972), Some observations on the economic framework for fertility analysis, *Population Studies*, July.

Namboodiri, N.K. (1975), Review of T.W. Schultz, ed., Economics of the family. Marriage, children and human capital, *Demography*, August.

Niphuis-Nell, M. (1981), *Motivatie voor ouderschap*, Deventer.

Olsen, R.J. (1988), A review of "Models of marital status and childbearing" by Mark Montgomery and James Trussell, in: Handbook of Labor economics, eds. O. Ashenfelter and R. Layard, *Journal of Human Resources*, 23, no. 4.

Perlman, M. (1975), Review of T.W. Schultz, ed., Economics of the family. Marriage, children and human capital, *Demography*, August.

Renaud, P.S.A. (1988), *Studies in applied political modelling*, Ph.D. Dissertation, University of Amsterdam.

Renaud, P.S.A. and F.A.A.M. van Winden (1988), *Gemeentefinanciën en gedecentraliseerde besluitvorming*, Leiden.

Rosenzweig, M.R. and T.P. Schultz (1985), The demand and supply of births: fertility and its life cycle consequences, *American Economic Review*, December.

Rozendal, P.J., H.G. Moors and F.L. Leeuw (1985), *Het bevolkingsvraagstuk in de jaren '80*, Voorburg.

Ryder, N.B. (1973), Comment, *Journal of Political Economy*, March/April, Part 2.

Schippers, J.J. and J.J. Siegers (1989), Gemeenschapscreches, bedrijfscreches en de segregatie tussen mannen en vrouwen op de arbeidsmarkt, *Sociaal Maandblad Arbeid*, June.

Schoorl, J.J. (1989), *Fertility adaption of Turkisch and Moroccan women in the Netherlands*, Paper prepared for the IUSSP General Conference, New Delhi, September 20-27.

Schoorl, J.J., *Fertility and contraception of Turkisch and Moroccan women in the Netherlands*, Ph.D. Dissertation, University of Pennsylvania (forthcoming).

Siegers, J.J. (1985), *Arbeidsaanbod en kindertal. Een micro-economische analyse*, Ph.D. Dissertation, Groningen University.

Siegers, J.J. (1987), Economische verklaringen van het kindertal, in: A. Kapteyn, red., *Demografische veranderingen en economische ontwikkelingen*. Preadviezen voor de Koninklijke Vereniging voor de Staathuishoudkunde, Leiden.

Siegers, J.J. (1989), De economische theorie van het individuele arbeidsaanbod:van statische naar dynamische analyse, *Maandschrift Economie*.

Siegers, J.J. (1989a), *Gebruik van de sociale zekerheid*, Paper presented at the Workshop on the Research Programme 1990/1991 of the Commissie Onderzoek Sociale Zekerheid (COSZ), Den Haag, May 30.

Siegers, J.J. (1989b), *Summary report*, Presented at the Workshop "Female Labour market behaviour and fertility: preferences, restrictions, and behaviour", Organised by Nederlands Interdisciplinair Demografisch Instituut and Centrum voor Interdisciplinair Onderzoek van Arbeidsmarkt- en Verdelingsvraagstukken, University of Utrecht, held at Den Haag, April 20-22.

Siegers, J.J. and J. de Jong-Gierveld (1989), *Het arbeidsmarktgedrag van de vrouw en haar kindertal*, NWO Research Proposal, Economisch Instituut/Centrum voor Interdisciplinair Onderzoek van Arbeidsmarkt- en Verdelingsvraagstukken and Nederlands Interdisciplinair Demografisch Instituut, Utrecht/Den Haag.

Spiess, E. (1989), *Motivation of reproductive behavior and the professional motivation of women*, Paper presented at the Workshop "Female labour market behaviour and fertility: preferences, restrictions, and behaviour", Organised by Nederlands Interdisciplinair Demografisch Instituut and Centrum voor Interdisciplinair Onderzoek van Arbeidsmarkt- en Verdelingsvraagstukken, University of Utrecht, Held at Den Haag, April 20-22.

Suij, G.N.C. (1987), *Op de kleintjes letten*, Den Haag.

Tazelaar, F. (1980), *Mentale incongruenties – sociale restricties – gedrag. Een onderzoek naar beroepsparticipatie van gehuwde vrouwelijke academici*, Ph.D. Dissertation, University of Utrecht.

Tazelaar, F. (1989), *Predicting work and family size decisions over time: the multifold effect of restrictions*, Paper presented at the Workshop "Female labour market behaviour and fertility: preferences, restrictions, and behaviour", Organised by Nederlands Interdisciplinair Demografische Instituut and Centrum voor Interdisciplinair Onderzoek van Arbeidsmarkt- en Verdelingsvraagstukken, University of Utrecht, held at Den Haag, April 20-22.

Tazelaar, F. and M. Sprengers (1985), *Een sociaal-strukturele en een cognitief-motivationele verklaring van de reacties van werklozen op ontslag*, Final ZWO Report, Vakgroep Theoretische Sociologie en Methodenleer, University of Utrecht.

Turchi, B.A. (1989), *How economics, psychology and sociology might produce a unified theory of fertility and labor force participation*, Paper presented at the Workshop "Female labour market behaviour and fertility: preferences, restrictions, and behaviour", Organised by Nederlands Interdisciplinair Demografisch Instituut and Centrum voor Interdisciplinair Onderzoek van Arbeidsmarkt- en Verdelingsvraagstukken, University of Utrecht, held at Den Haag, April 20-22.

Veevers, J.E. (1973), Voluntarily childless wives, *Sociology and Social Research*, April.

Vollering, A. and P. Nijkamp (1988), *Size and distribution of expenditures on amenities for aged people*, Paper presented at the Second Annual Meeting of the European Society for Population Economics, Mannheim, June 23-25.

Wilbrink-Griffioen, D., I. van Vliet and A. Elzinga (1987), *Kinderopvang en arbeidsparticipatie van vrouwen*, Den Haag, Ministerie van Sociale Zaken en Werkgelegenheid.

Willis, R.J. (1987), What have we learned from the economics of the family?, *American Economic Review*, Papers and Proceedings, May.

Winden, F.A.A.M. (1983), *On the interaction between state and private sector*, Amsterdam.

Emerging Issues in Demographic Research
C.A. Hazeu and G.A.B. Frinking (Editors)
Elsevier Science Publishers B.V. , 1990

Chapter 11

TOWARDS THE CONSTRUCTION OF INTERDISCIPLINARY
THEORETICAL MODELS TO EXPLAIN DEMOGRAPHIC BEHAVIOUR:
A COMMENT

John F. Ermisch

It is hard to disagree with the case made by Siegers for interdisciplinary theoretical models. It would be unscientific to do so. Furthermore, the framework he suggests as the foundation for a broader theoretical model is bound to appeal to an economist like myself. Nevertheless, the 'preferences' part of the tripartite scheme is more problematic than this paper suggests.

For economists, preferences refer to a *preference ranking*. Suppose, for example, that we are concerned with combinations of family size (f) and parental consumption (C). Economists assume that parents can rank in order of preference any two combinations of F and C, call them A = (F_A, C_A) and B = (F_B, C_B): either A is preferred to B; B is preferred to A; or parents are indifferent between A and B. Assuming that this ranking satisfies some criteria (for example, A preferred to B and B preferred to D implies A preferred to D), the preference ranking can be represented by an ordinal preference (utility) function of F and C such that when A is preferred to B, A receives a higher functional value, etc. Thus, the combination of F and C that maximizes this function subject to the constraints on choice (restrictions) is preferred to all other combinations satisfying these constraints. From observing behaviour and these constraints, economists can make inference about the preference ranking.

This concept of preferences differs quite dramatically from that used by psychologists and sociologists, as the workshop recently organized by Siegers and De Jong-Gierveld (NIDI, the Netherlands, 1989) made clear. This ranking concept of preferences also makes their measurement particulary difficult, as the ranking covers an infinite number of comparisons of combinations of F and C. That is an important reason why economists prefer to parameterize preference functions and estimate these parameters from information on choice and constraints.

Perhaps I am just lacking imagination in this regard. As I recall, attempts have been made by Van Praag to incorporate preferences in the calculation of equivalence scales. So perhaps more progress can be made here than I suspect, but the paper under discussion certainly leaves us in the dark about how the gaps between economists' idea of preferences and those of other disciplines and between idea and measure can be closed.

Emerging Issues in Demographic Research
C.A. Hazeu and G.A.B. Frinking (Editors)
© Elsevier Science Publishers B.V. , 1990

Chapter 12

TOWARDS THE CONSTRUCTION OF INTERDISCIPLINARY THEORETICAL MODELS TO EXPLAIN DEMOGRAPHIC BEHAVIOUR; A COMMENT

Siegwart M. Lindenberg

*"The economic approach can be a
great deal more fertile than it has
in the past, because it offers an
excellent theoretical framework
for the construction of interdisciplinary theoretical models
to explain demographic behaviour"*
J.J. Siegers

1 Introduction

Periodically, there is a cry for more integration of the socio-economic sciences. In the past, these cries have not had much success. Will it be different now? This is the major question to be answered in the following pages.

The motto sums up the major message by Jacques Siegers (1990) and it leads directly to his proposal how this goal can be reached: a) extend the economic analysis by introducing relevant factors which do not belong to the traditional field of economics; b) analyse life-cycle changes of the system of preferences, restrictions and behaviour, and find the determinants of these changes; and c) construct theoretical models which can be translated into empirical estimating models and thereby used in policy decisions.

These proposals sound so eminently reasonable that it is difficult to imagine that any intelligent reader would disagree. Yet, so far all pleas for interdisciplinary work in the socio-economic sciences have sounded eminently reasonable and yet had no marked success. Why should it be different now? Siegers' own (implicit) answer to this question is that the use of the rational choice framework, in which behaviour is explained by the 'preference-restrictions-behaviour' scheme, "offers an ideal opportunity to combine the advantages of both economics and the other social sciences, namely to enrich the rather bare but formal and elegant economic models with psychological and sociological insights." But what is new about the 'preference-restrictions-behaviour' scheme? It is and has been the basis of micro-economic modelling. Why, then, has the economic approach not been much more fertile for the explanation of demographic behaviour in the past? Why have the three research proposals offered by Siegers not been adopted long ago, given they have been suggested before and are taken to be eminently reasonable? Why would anyone succeed now if none has succeeded in the past? Only if these questions can be answered will we know whether we should take Siegers' proposals as yet another cry in the desert or as the outline of a fertile new programme to be followed.

Anticipating the result of the investigation, my answer is yes, there are good reasons to believe that the integration of the socio-economic sciences will work now even though it has failed in the past. And the better these reasons are understood the more likely that the endeavour will succeed.

The major issues I will look at in my investigation[1] are first, changes in the relation between economics and sociology; second methodological advances regarding bridge assumptions, the method of decreasing abstraction and behavioural economics; third, theoretical advances regarding social production functions and ought-implies-can dynamics.

2   The relation between economics and sociology

In the last years, the convergence between sociology and economics has advanced by leaps and bounds, reversing a secular trend of divergence, erasing a longstanding tacit division of labour between them and heading towards news form of cooperation and competition.

This change did not occur over night but whereas it started about thirty years ago, it only picked up momentum in the last ten to fifteen years, which is quite a short time given the long history of divergence and the tenacity of the conventional division of labour: tidy models and rational behaviour for economics, non-rational behaviour and messy social reality for sociology. This division worked well for both sides. It exempted economists from gathering and analysing data that their models could not have dealt with (such as data on religion, tradition, ideology, self-sacrifice, mass appeal, issues of fairness, norms, complex interactions, networks, power relations, self conceptions and reference groups) and it excused the sociologists from formulating rigorous theories. This

---

[1]   Most of the following points have been dealt with in some more detail in Lindenberg 1983a (which is partially reproduced in Lindenberg 1985b, and Lindenberg, 1985a).

arrangement also had a conservative influence on the development in each field because it forced economists and sociologists alike to stay well within the boundaries of their spheres of research (market versus non-market). Even if they would have liked to stray into the area of the other, it would have been incompatible with the division of labour, because at least by implication, scholars in both disciplines had to assume that man is dual-natured and that the rational side come to the fore in the market place and the non-rational side in all non-market relations.

By scientific standards, this arrangement was quite precarious because it was wrought with internal contradictions. The behavioural theories in both disciplines were elaboration of either rational or non-rational man and they could not cope with dual-natured man. No theory within neo-classical economics could specify the conditions under which man the rational maximiser would turn into non-rational man. For traditional sociology, the only way to cope with dual-natured man was to make rational behaviour itself a norm that governs roles in the market place, which left the problem unsolved how somebody who is able to behave like rational man in the market place can be restricted to non-rational behaviour in all other social relations.

The scientific problems inherent in the assumption of dual-natured man are so volatile that in all likelihood they would have exploded long ago had it not been for some extra protective belts around the cores. In economics, the main protection consisted of the high costs of giving up what was becoming increasingly *more* important for the professional self-image of the well-trained economist: rigorous model building. True, there where cries for more consideration of sociological insights, but they were no threat to the protective belt. More likely, these cries were themselves part and parcel of the protective strategy by having all the markings of a periodic ritual to be performed mainly in obligatory articles for state-of-the-art-conferences.[1] Why only ritual cries? Because – due to the existing division of labour – there really was no methodological instrument to make any kind of systematic use of sociological insights in micro-economics.

In sociology, the situation was quite different. Here, the major stabilization of the arrangement with economics came from a second frontier which turned out to be the major battle ground for sociologists. An understanding of this frontier, although it was established long ago, is the key to the understanding of the of the new situation today. The discipline that has emerged as 'sociology' (and which I call 'traditional sociology' for ease of identification) is the result of a considerable competition of approaches for the explanation of social behaviour and other social phenomena in the late 19th and early 20th century. This can be nicely traced in Sorokin's account of social theories of that

---

[1] See for example Krupp (1966); Huppes (1979) ; Bell and Kristol (1981). At times entire book is devoted to this purpose (for example, Thurow; 1984).

period (Sorokin, 1964 [originally 1928]). There were approaches that modelled social mechanisms as analogies to physics (especially mechanics and thermodynamics) such as L. Winiarsky's theories on "le mécanique sociale" and on "l'énergie sociale"[1]. There were attempts to link social theory to meteorology by explaining varieties of social phenomena by differences in climate. As a prominent example of this approach one can single out E. Huntington's theories on "the character of races" and on "civilization and climate"[2]. Biology figured large as a possible basis for sociology, as exemplified by P. Lilienfeld's "Die menschliche Gesellschaft als realer Organismus", 1873, and some blatantly racial versions of this school for which G.V. de Lapouge (with "Les sélections sociales", 1896) is an outstanding example[3]. Psychology was also used as the theoretical foundation of sociology, with G. Tarde's "La logique sociale", 1895, as a famous example. There is also an instictivist variant of the psychological school whose most prominent author may be W. McDougall with his "Introduction to Social Psychology", 1923[4].

In this fierce competition, slowly but surely, yet another approach seemed to have won out against all others: the radical view, not found in any other discipline, that social behaviour and all other social phenomena were themselves caused by social phenomena and only by social phenomena. The success of this approach was in no small part due to the apparent weaknesses of the other approaches. The strategy used by sociologists to expose these weaknesses was four-fold. First, they fashioned a model of man that would maximally support the radical view, viz. role-playing man[5], by rendering social behaviour completely dependent on social influences. Second, in contrast to the other approaches, they presented their view as an 'autonomous' discipline, not grafted on to some other field of research, and therefore truly new and worthy of being taught in universities. Third, they maintained that every explanation of social phenomena that ignored the full causal impact of other social phenomena was seriously flawed and needed to be redressed by a discipline that was not already committed to the explanation of non-social phenomena of one kind or another. Fourth, they developed a tradition of empirical research inspired both by anthropology and the handling of census data, thus ranging from participatory observation and secondary analysis to survey methods and multivariate analysis.

---

[1] Referenced and described in Sorokin, 1964, pp. 23ff. Winiarsky's work is a prime example of "theorizing by analogy" in the late nineteenth century.

[2] Both works were published in 1924 (see Sorokin, 1964, pp.138ff).

[3] See Sorokin, 1964, pp. 200ff and pp. 234ff.

[4] See Sorokin, 1964, pp. 636ff and pp. 608ff.

[5] To be more precise, the model of man comes in two versions which I have named SRSM (Socialized, Role-playing, socially Sanctioned Man) and its watered-down version OSAM (Opinionated, socially Sensitive, Acting Man). The first sort of man is playing roles into which he or she has been socialized, and inner (conscience) and outer sanctions see to it that behaviour does not deviate from the role expectations. The second sort of man had been invented to make role-playing man fit for large survey research: he or she has an opinion (or attitude) about everything and acts accordingly, but due to the social sensitivity of man, his/her opinions are the product of social influences.

"In this way, sociologists attacked views about the determinative influence of biological characteristics (e.g. race and ethnic origin) on criminal behaviour, on intelligence, on ways of thinking, on achievement motivation, on social organization and inequality. They attacked each and every explanation of social phenomena by instinct, by biological given sentiment or by biologically determined state of mind (such as the explanation of the incest taboo by instinct, the explanation of the institution of the family by the ubiquitous sentiment of jealousy, the explanation of suicide by mental illness, or the explanation of religion by 'primitive mind'). In a similar vein, they took on all explanations that failed to acknowledge social determination explicitly (such as historical explanations based on 'great men', all explanations based on human preferences that failed to acknowledge the social influences on human goals and values, all explanations of social inequality based on 'natural' individual characteristics and motivation, as for instance talent and laziness). Finally, they locked horns with generally held views that failed to take the complexity of social determination into account. Thus, they would show that conflict is not at all bad since it also produces solidarity, that crime is not at all bad because it reinforces common values, that informal networks would form around formal organizational structures, that many social phenomena are unintended consequences of human action and thus much more complex than most people thought they are" (Lindenberg, 1985a, pp. 246).

Whereas economics was too powerful a science to be attacked in earnest, virtually every confrontation with other (and weaker) sociologically 'naive' views, would see sociology come away the winner. The success was attributed to the underlying model of man, so that by implication every view less radical than that (say, a theory mixing biological and social factors as causes of social phenomena) was hereby deemed 'sociologically naive', a battle cry that could be heard for many decades. Of course, sociology was helped in this success by the link of the Third Reich with an extreme racism.

This account also carries the key to the contemporary development. First of all, traditional sociology was an empirical *debunking* science which experienced its greatest triumphs in its battle against 'sociologically naive' competitors . Secondly, the battle ax, sharpened in successful combat, was the particular sociological model of man: role-playing man. Non-rational man was thus central to all the successes and was not easily being abandoned. Unable to subdue economics (and, for the reasons given above, safe from its competition) sociologists thus also had to live with dual-natured man and with a mutually reinforcing but scientifically precarious division of labour. How precarious this arrangement was became apparent when traditional sociology had virtually soaked Western culture with its message. This point was dramatically marked in many Western societies in the sixties by the passing into adulthood of the first generations that had grown up in a thoroughly sociologized culture. In an unequal fight, the remnants of the 19th century were brushed aside by an unholy alliance of sociologist gurus with youth movements. After that there was simply no 'sociologically naive' competitor left and debunking had run out of targets. Shortly thereafter the triumphant traditional sociology had itself run out of steam. Its sharp ax of success, role-playing man, turned out to be a blunt instrument indeed when the task had shifted from demonstrating *that* social phenomena were determined by other social phenomena to showing *how and why* that was supposed to be the case. In 1981, Irving Kristol, a renowned professor of social thought, observed that "there simply does not exist a body of knowledge that permits sociologists to talk with more authority about society than someone who may never have received sociological training" (Kristol 1981, p. 202). Dual-natured man had finally become a fatal liability, at least to sociologists.

In the sixties a growing number of sociologists were beginning to look for a model of man that could revitalize theory formation. At first, many hit upon what looked like a compromise between the rational and the non-rational sides of man: behavioural propositions based on learning theory[1]. But, for reasons to be discussed below, it turned out that this compromise does not lend itself to theory formation beyond the small group.

In response to that, many continued the search and found in the seventies another compromise: the rational man of economics, but tempered or 'bounded' by limits to knowledge and information processing capacity. Eventually this new *homo socio-economicus* was dubbed RREEMM[2] (an acronym for resourceful, restricted, expecting, evaluating, maximizing man). 'Rational man' thus entered for the first time a discipline that was rich with traditions of empirical research and rich with insights that had not been theoretically integrated systematically due to the paucity of role-playing man as a theory of action. It thus also opened a door for the systematic use of results from economics in sociology. Both these points are illustrated by what happened to social network research. A sophisticated methodology and a huge amount of empirical material on social networks had been accumulating over the years in sociology, but due to the severe theoretical limits of role-playing man, not much interesting theoretical work had been done with social networks. After rational man entered the sociological scene, theoretically interesting network studies began to mushroom. Theoretical ideas from economics on the use of scarce resources and on investment behaviour could now be easily connected to sociological aspects. For instance, social networks can now be seen as 'social capital' for the procurement of information, social support and other services; thus people are also likely to invest in the building and maintenance of social networks, but there are important investment differences between weak and strong ties because the conditions for use and maintenance are quite different, etc. In short, due to the paradigmatic shift, existing insights can be theoretically unlocked and used in the context of a strong research tradition. This situation had never existed before.

The convergence did not come from sociology alone. Since dealing with institutions was incompatible with the aim of rigorous model building, it had ended up on the sociological side of the division of labour. Some outstanding theoreticians, like Schumpeter and Hayek, objected to this arrangement long before the days of convergence, but most economists did not. But slowly things changed. There was no sign that politics did

---

[1] George Homans (1961) may have been the most influential author in this respect (see also Opp, 1985).

[2] See Meckling 1976 and Lindenberg, 1983a).

not affect markets. To the contrary, it seemed that politics became ever more interwoven with markets in the budding welfare states, and so dealing with institutions became increasingly more important to a broader segment of economics itself, leading to various forms of a new political economy. In turn, this development greatly facilitated the new developments in sociology in the seventies (see Lindenberg, 1985b). Thus prepared, economists also moved rapidly into traditional sociological areas, such as the family, health care, crime, discrimination, higher learning and arts, when it became clear that the sociological success story had ended. The so-called 'economic imperialism' is nothing but the flamboyant end of the old division of labour. In its wake there came an increased awareness that the insights sociologists had accumulated on these non-market terrains would be extremely useful if they only could be 'unlocked' for economic theorising. We have seen that this unlocking is taking place within sociology, but there are considerable methodological problems connected with the dove-tailing of model building and empirical content and they will be discussed in the following section.

3   Bridge assumptions versus behavioural economics

With the waning of the old division of labour and with rational man beginning to become a unifying model of man in the socio-economic sciences, it is not surprising that much attention shifted to the discussion of rational man him- or herself. The most famous voice in this discussion may be Herbert Simon (see Simon, 1959). In Europe, Popper's philosophy of science, with its emphasis on depth in explanation, had been brought to bear on the social sciences by the pioneering works of Hans Albert, and his criticism of neo-classical model of man as a mere 'logic of choice' was widely discussed (see Albert, 1967 and 1984).

By now criticism of the neo-classical model of man has become more or less institutionalised, with its own journals and societies. The most outspoken of these efforts has become known under the name of 'behavioural economics', although divergent groups are associated with this term[1]. The controversy centers around the following point: if we know that the various versions of rational choice theory are strictly speaking empirically false or empty, should we or shouldn't we replace them by more realistic psychological theories? The proponents of behavioural economics say we should replace rational choice theory because time and again we find that certain predictions from this theory are contradicted or at least not confirmed in psychological experiments. Proponents of neoclassical economics say we should not replace rational choice theory because it allows us to use the construction of clear and understandable models with clear and testable implications, and even if some of these implications are contradicted by experimental evidence, holding on to rational choice theory is still better than losing the strong guide of general deductive reasoning in exchange for a plethora of more realistic

---

[1]   There are mainly three groups: the Carnegie group around Simon, the Michigan group around Katona, and the Oxford group around Marshak and Shackle (see Earl, 1988).

but also more complex and less general theories of specific phenomena. For the possibility of theoretical integration in the socio-economic sciences, this controversy is of utmost importance because there is no use trying to apply economic models in various non-market areas (especially demography) if they cannot become more realistic. But if, by trying to make them more realistic, the advantages of model building are lost, then there is little reason to turn to economics to begin with. In order to make the controversy more intelligible, it is helpful to look at the conditions for theory-guided research in some more detail.

The capacity for theory-guided research may be pinpointed by the right juxtaposition of two kinds of issues dimension: major/minor and common/unique (see Figure 1).

issues

		common	unique
issues	major	type 1	type 2
	minor	type 3	type 4

Figure 1   Relevant issues dimension for theory guided research

Major issues of a problem are those issues that, if ignored, will prevent an adequate problem solution; *minor* issues of a problem are those issues that are not major and that, if dealt with, may improve the quality of the problem solution. *Common* issues are those that are common to the great variety of problems dealt with in a field, to be distinguished from those *unique* to a subclass of problems in that field[1]. What deductive model building in micro-economics does is focus on type 1 issues, i.e. to address the common issues in a great variety of problems (say, shifts in relative prices given human resourcefulness), under the assumption that thereby it also addresses the major issues of all these problems. Type 2 issues (if any) are dealt with by creating subclasses of type 1 issues (like inventing a new sort of costs, such as transaction or information costs). Type 3 and type 4 issues are incidental. This strategy is made possible by an action theory that is clearly geared

---

[1]   These distinction are clearly not operational analytical distinctions. Often only hindsight will be able to tell whether we are dealing with one or another kind of issue. But for our purposes this is not really damaging because we are dealing with a heuristic process (that of theory-guided research) in which the distinctions of issues will be revised in an ongoing process of conjectures and critique.
    At this point, it should be mentioned that the importance of theory-guided research for (micro) economists can also be gleaned from the fact that some would rather solve the (apparent) dilemma between theory-guided research and empirical content by dropping causal analysis altogether and turning to a hermeneutic solution. That this way out is mistaken has been convincingly shown by Albert (1989), but it demonstrates another (curious) result of the convergence between economics and sociology.

to the common issues and, judging by the success of micro-economics in the past, to major issues as well. The strong tradition of theory-guided research in this discipline comes from this strategy. But two problems can arise. First, by moving into new subfields, the frequency of type 1 issues may decline, thereby reducing the theoretician's ability to guide research. In that case the theory may have to be adapted to reduce the frequency of type 2 issues, and here the exchange with the new kind of sociology has proved to be a fruitful path to take. Second, because of the strong focus on type 1 issues for the sake of theoretical guidance of research, the other kinds of issues may be too much neglected, rendering the results (i.e. the explanations) too far removed from reality. Behavioural economists have singled out this problem and they suggest to improve the quality of explanations by doing away with the distinctions between major and minor issues, because it is exactly the neglect of these minor issues that keeps the explanations so removed from reality. Thus the vehicle used to make the distinction between major and minor, viz. utility theory, has to go and it has to be replaced by realistic psychological theories. Once this is done, the psychological theories will also offer more room for unique issues because certain psychological variables (such as self-confidence) may only become relevant in a subclass of problems (such as decisions under great uncertainty). Why will this suggestion not work and what can be done about the dilemma apparent in the controversy?

Although the problems are far from being solved, there has recently emerged a clear methodological lead as to how the dove-tailing of model building and empirical content can be achieved. This lead has profitted greatly from the bad experience in traditional sociology of working without a strong deductive heuristics. Let us look at the major points of this lead[1]. This boils down to a neglect of the difference between the primary focus of a discipline (its *analytical* primacy) and the tools to deal with the primary focus (its *theoretical* primacy).

In economics and sociology, the main task is to analyze social systems. In other words, the analytical primacy is focussed on social systems. In order to explain social systems and related social phenomena, both disciplines have to make use of theories of action; i.e. the theoretical (or explanatory) primacy is focussed on the individual. Thus the two primacies refer to two different levels. There is analytical interest in the individual but only a instrumental interest for coming up with explanations on the social systems level. In psychology, the situation is different. Here both analytical and instrumental (theoretical) interests focus on the individual. Given that the analytical primacy in both cases is different, different requirements are placed on the 'individual' theories in psychology on the one hand and in economics and sociology on the other. Let us distinguish between two kinds of theories dealing with individuals, indicated by individual 1 and individual 2, respectively, according to the scheme in Figure 2:

---

[1] For more detail, see Lindenberg, 1981, 1983a and 1985a, and Wippler and Lindenberg, 1987.

	psychology	economics and sociology
analytical primacy	individual	social system
theoretical primacy	individual 1	individual 2

Figure 2   Different primacies for psychology versus economics and sociology

Making this distinction shows that many suggestions by behavioural economists and other critics of neo-classical economics boil down to the (implicit) claim that individual 1 theories are not only more realistic than individual 2 theories (this is not controversial) but that they will work better than individual 2 theories no matter what the analytical primacy is. And it is exactly this claim that is unfounded.

Let us look at a list of reasonable requirements for an individual 2 theory:

(1) It must not require much information about each individual to whom it is applied; (2) It must allow us to model institutional and social structural conditions as defining intermediate goals and constraints of action; (3) It must allow psychological (including physiological) theories to influence its assumptions. For example, the information processing capacities of individuals must not be fixed by axiom; (4) It must allow us to express our degree of ignorance explicitly. Thus it must allow us to introduce simplifying assumptions in such a way that they can be replaced with more complex assumptions as our knowledge increases (method of decreasing abstraction). Via this capability, requirement (3) has an explicit means of being satisfied; (5) It must be well corroborated as a theory that explains behaviour of human beings in the aggregate, inclusive of resourceful behaviour.

Let me briefly elaborate each point. First, many individual 1 theories require much information per individual (for example the learning history or the personality traits). The more information per individual a theory requires, the less likely that it can be used for large aggregates for the simple reason that the necessary information becomes harder to come by. The 'watering down' of such theories in order to apply them to aggregates, such as in a psychiatric theory of crime (rates), covertly reintroduces the distinction between major and minor issues but this time not for the sake of theory-guided research (i.e. to increase type 1 issues) but as a way to solve a technical problem of measurement. More importantly (point two), because the primacies lie on different levels in economics and sociology, a theory of action in these fields must allow the *simultaneous* attention to these two levels. This requires an approach considerably different from psychology. For example, profit maximization can be seen as a human motive or drive but then it is part of an individual 1 theory, directing attention to psychological dynamics of the individual rather than connecting the individual and the system's level. An example of an individual 2 approach would be to focus on the structural aspect of 'profit' (as based on an institution that assigns the right to the residual) and then link this to the individual level by assuming that due to the institutional arrangement, profit has become an instrumental goal to individuals with the right to the residual and with rewards positively correlated to the size of the residual. Under additional structural assumptions (say concerning the dependence of other valued outcomes on the amount of profit) the instrumental goal 'profit' becomes so overriding that it can be assumed to be the main maximand. Thus, for an individual 2 context, we must be able to link the systems level and the individual level not only after dealing with the individual level (say, in a micro-to-macro step) but *while* dealing with this level. This is very difficult, if at all possible, with individual 1 theories. The assumption we use to make this link are called *bridge assumptions*. In effect, these bridge assumptions allow type 2 (i.e. major and unique) issues to be connected to type 1 (i.e. major and common) issues. Some methodological problems connected with this point will be elaborated in somewhat more detail in the section on social production functions below, but first we have to deal with the other three requirements.

The third and fourth requirements are related to the problem of bridge assumptions and have to be dealt with simultaneously. The third requirement refers to the claim that advances in individual 1 theories must be able to influence theorising in economics and sociology. But how can that be done without replacing individual 2 theories by individual 1 theories? If the answer to this question is: by bridge assumptions, then the next problem is how the deductive advantage of model building (with its requirements of simplification) can be preserved if ever more bridge assumptions render models increasingly complex.

The essential feature of bridge assumptions is that they enter as *auxiliary* assumptions rather than as a proxies for the main theory. For example, every utility theory must assume something about the individuals' information concerning relevant events. We can assume that individuals are completely informed and if we see that the results are too unrealistic, we can replace this bridge assumption by a more realistic one, say that the individual infers probabilities of event occurrences from objective frequencies; if the results are still not satisfactory, this, in turn, can be replaced by still more realistic assumptions about particular biases in the process of inference, etc. There is also a price to be paid for the more realistic bridge assumptions: the more complex they are, the more they will violate the first requirement because they will require increasingly more information. In addition, we simply may not know enough to formulate a more realistic bridge assumption and yet, we would be able to get on with the limited knowledge we have. For these reasons, bridge assumptions are to be introduced according to the *method of decreasing abstraction*: as simple as possible and as complex as necessary. Behavioural economists would be pleased to see inference biases brought into the theory, and indeed it may improve the quality of the explanation at hand. But they would also suggest that the unrealistic utility theory be *replaced* by a more realistic psychological theory and this is exactly where they neglect the conditions for theory-guided research and the possibilities offered by the method of decreasing abstraction. No matter how complicated a bridge assumption gets, it remains an auxiliary hypothesis for a *simple* utility theory. For the ability of theory to guide research, this distinction between a simple theory and (possibly) complex auxiliary assumptions is essential because a complex theory would draw research into a preoccupation with the same complexities (like inference biases) no matter what problem on the system level needs to be solved, i.e. it would neglect the distinctions between major versus minor and common versus unique issues. With the help of the method of decreasing abstraction, we can hold on to the crucial research guiding function of theory with its strong emphasis on type 1 issues, while at the same time we also bow to the requirement of increased empirical content by additional bridge assumptions, stepwise approximating reality (thus moving from type 1 to type 2 and if there are problems of connecting type 2 issues to type 1 issues then we will have to add bridge assumptions concerning type 3 issues which will allow us to connect them with the remaining type 2 issues and , possibly, to add some type 4 issues as well). How far we have to go with this decreasing abstraction depends on the problem and not on some *apriori* nomological standard.

The fifth requirement, that the individual 2 theory must be well corroborated as a theory that explains behaviour of human beings in the aggregate, does decidedly not mean that the action theory must withstand all sorts of tests designed for individual 1 theories. Rather, it requires that the individual 2 theory must indeed have proven time and again that the issues common to a great variety of problems are also the major issues. And this is where price-theory has done much better in traditional 'economic' applications than in many non-market application. On this point improvement is clearly necessary (see section 4 below). But will it come from behavioural economics? Because behavioural economists ignore the distinctions between major versus minor and common versus unique and thus they don't address this problem. Clearly, the big contribution by behavioural economics to model building can be made in another area: providing well researched bridge assumptions, ordered by decreasing abstraction and flagged by indices of robustness. This is also very necessary because of problems generated by the old division of labour. The old package that bundled "collective, non-rational, moral, values and sanctions" and the one that bundled "individual, rational, instrumental, preferences and constraints" had each fallen apart but the language that had developed on the basis of the old division of labour and thus on the basis of these packages was hopelessly inadequate. Few, if anybody, had dealt with the problems that fell between the packages, such as the relation between morality and utility or between value and preference. According to what has been said above, at least a good deal of the solutions to these problems should come in the form of bridge assumptions (for example on framing).

It can now be seen, how theory-guided research and the nomological claims of behavioural economics can be reconciled. The theory of action must be simple and address the common issues but there must be a systematic possibility to deal with the minor and unique issues in order to improve the quality of the explanation, as needed. This can be done by using bridge assumptions and the method of decreasing abstraction. But in order to have knowledge about the robustness and concreteness of bridge assumptions, there should be a branch of research geared to the generation of this knowledge. Behavioural economists may eventually focus more on this task as is done already by some economic psychologists (see Lea et al., 1987) and by some sociologists (see for example Tazelaar and Wippler, 1985). Research on 'framing', i.e. on the effects of the definition of the situation on choice, for the use in individual 2 theories is also well under way (see for example Lindenberg, 1989a). On the other hand, model builders should be familiar with this research in order to try to incorporate it into the 'standard' theory so that this theory can remain simple *and* viridical enough to ensure a high frequency of type 1 issues.[1]

4.1   Social production functions

"An explanation of preferences... is necessary if social processes are to be explained. All social sciences aim to do this" (Opp, 1985, p. 236). One can only agree with him, because without an explanation of preferences, choice theories remain mute on a large area of social reality or they open the doors to ad hoc theorising about changes that are exogenous to the theory. Opp's assessment refers already to the new times of convergence. Indeed, when sociology and economics began to converge, it seemed to some an ideal marriage because at least in one point, the two were said to be complementary. Whereas economists studied constraints and took preferences as given, sociologists studied preferences (values) and dealt with constraints (i.e. alternatives and their outcomes) mostly implicitly (i.e. as part of role expectations). But due to the old division of labour, the euphoria was premature, since the complementarity was more an illusion than reality.

Due to role-playing man, sociologists had approached preferences not from the standpoint of choice under constraints but from the standpoint of social control. How is behaviour socially determined? By *socializing* an individual in such a way that he will want to do what he is socially expected to do. Thus 'wanting' was removed from choosing and was (if socialization was successful) itself a sign of social constraint or control. The desired (preference) was socially engineered to coincide with the desirable (value). This did not fit utility theory. Nor did utility theory fit into a social control context. Without a solution to the explanation of preferences, the usefulness of rational choice theory in non-market areas would be quite limited. But this is only half the story because without a solution to the social control aspect, important aspects of the development of constraints will also be missed.

Let me begin with preferences. Recent developments do offer a likely solution. They center around a change in economics that had come about as a response to non-market applications, and can be summarised by a shift from man the consumer to man the producer. This shift has been propagated by Gary Becker who, based on the shift from consumer to producer, had also instigated the new home economics framework that he and others apply to the family and labour market participation. What is so important about this shift is that it allows preferences to appear entirely in an instrumental context whereby they would have to be explained as part of the social structure and thus as part of the given constraints.

---

[1]   Rachlin (1980) and De Alessi (1983) for this view of the standard theory of action in economics.

This feat is accomplished by the assumption of two kinds of preferences (see Stigler and Becker, 1977): *universal* preferences (goals) that are identical to all human beings and therefore need no explanation, and *instrumental* preferences for the means that lead to the ultimate goals which are in fact constraints and can thus be explained in a constraint driven approach. Technically speaking, there is only one utility function for all mankind but there are systematically different production functions for different kinds of people. Buying a particular good is now not an act of consumption but the purchase of a means of production, such as a record for the production of music pleasure.

Needless to say, this approach fits nicely into the bridge assumption methodology outlined above, because the specification of production functions can be seen as providing bridge assumptions about instrumental preferences. So far so good. But without a specification of what the ultimate goals are, the old danger of ad hoc theorising looms large and little has been gained. For this reason, Becker's approach was further developed into what may be called the 'social production function approach' (see Lindenberg, 1984a, 1984b, 1986b, 1989b). Taking the lead from Adam Smith, it was assumed that there are at least two ultimate goals: physical well-being and social approval[1]. They are aspired by everybody, and therefore the means people have to reach these goals are of utmost importance to them, so important that a systematic threat to these means may cause a revolution (see Lindenberg, 1989c). These means vary with social position and are called 'social production functions'. They work like standard operating procedures and the clearer role expectations are formulated and sanctioned the clearer the social production functions[2]. When the positive and/or negative sanctions connected to the expected behaviour become less and less, then the individual will look for alternative means of getting physical well-being or social approval. And since the individual is assumed to be resourceful he or she will actively look for alternatives rather than remain within the role-expectations until somebody tries to resocialize him or her. For example, in a traditional industrial social structure with segregated gender roles, the man has his job and his life style as sources of social approval, the woman has making a home and the raising of the children as sources of social approval. When making a home and raising children yield less and less social approval, women will seek to change their social production functions, for example by entering the labour market if they have not done so already for the sake of money (physical well-being). This approach can be applied to demographic questions on number of children and of labour market participation (see Lindenberg, 1989b). Here, the difference between the old and the new situation is quite apparent. In sociology, it has been known for a long time that social approval is an important reward connected to holding a job (see for example Morse and Weiss, 1955), but due to 'role-playing man', this insight was not theoretically worked into a theory of labour market participation until the model of man in sociology changed to RREEMM.

---

[1] Loss-avoidance may be a strong candidate for a third universal goal, see Lindenberg, 1989a.

[2] Note that role expectation are here literally taken to be normative expectations concerning behaviour of a person in a particular position. They do not imply that individuals follow these expectations because they have learned to do so in the process of socialization.

4.2   The ought-implies-can dynamics

Let me finally turn to the social control aspect that figured so prominently in the traditional sociological approach of eliminating choice from theoretical consideration. Once choosing man (RREEMM) is brought into sociology, one can relate norms to choice by establishing links with each element of RREEMM. For example, norms specify situations in which resourcefulness is positively or negative sanctioned and thus made more or less likely; norms are restrictions by influencing outcomes positively or negative; they have a strong influence on what is expected in a situation; they function as standards for evaluations; and they specify situations in which maximizing behaviour should take a particular form (like being able to verbalize the process of weighing the alternatives or being spontaneous). These links are very useful in the sense that they make it quite clear that there is not one but may ways in which norms and choice connect. Still, there is a whole area of the control aspect not covered by these links and that is what may be called the *ought-implies-can dynamics*.

In traditional sociology, society is seen as a functional whole in which conformity to role expectations serves to uphold the functioning of society. As a prerequisite for conformity, people must be able to meet role expectations in such a way that they do not have to violate one norm in order to follow another. To the degree to which a society does not meet this prerequisite it is pathological and there is a strain towards reestablishing the prerequisite (see Merton, 1957). Thus people must be able to do what is expected of them, otherwise the expectations cannot possibly be met and we reach a state of factual normlessness or 'anomie'.

This seems very plausible, but theoretically it is poorly worked out because there is no mechanism specified that would counteract anomie. Is it still necessary to try to specify such a mechanism when one does not use role-playing man but choosing man (RREEMM) as model of man? Up to now, this aspect has received least attention from either sociologists or economists. But consider the following argument that is also important for demographic issues.

Due to the boundedness of rationality (especially due to genuine uncertainties), people have no way of weighing the costs and benefits of all alternatives open to them. This is especially the case with alternatives that create long-term commitments, like the choice to have a child. People will generally assign a low net-utility to long-term commitments in a contingent world. In other words, they will avoid getting into such long-term commitments (cf. Birg et al., 1989). However, some choice situations that involve these commitments have positive externalities (public good aspects), such as investing in a long-term education or having a child. People will not choose to take on these commitments and the public good will not be produced, i.e. society will have a shortage of experts and of children, to stay within our example. When there are strong externalities within a group then there will be norm-entrepreneurs (say, a government, or writers, religious leaders, pressure groups etc., as the case may be) who will try to establish norms for certain categories of people to choose the long-term commitment alternatives. Why would norm-entrepreneurs be willing to take the trouble? Since everybody will be better off if the public good is produced, the norm-entrepreneurs can claim the credit for the improvement and will thus stand to gain even more than the general public.

Once a norm for long-term commitment decisions has been established, the decision situation changes from one of uncertainty to one of conformity (see Lindenberg, 1983b) which means that the long-term commitment and the uncertainty surrounding it does not enter the decision in any prominent way. Thus we can expect that virtually in every society, having a child, investing in long-term training or education and other long-term commitments with high uncertainty will be normatively expected from certain categories of people in that society. Such norms will have entered the social production functions of these people.

Taking on a long-term commitment because it is societally expected creates secondary externalities if one does not keep to the implied commitment. Thus, if the child is not brought up or if the training is not finished, the public good will not be produced. Again norms will be introduced about keeping to the commitment. Neither of these norms would yield higher levels of the public good if people could not conform to them. But then, if the public good is not produced, the norm-entrepreneurs cannot claim credit for improving the situation. It is thus in their interest also to mobilize collective resources to make norm conformity possible. If the possibilities for norm conformity deteriorate later on without decline of the positive externalities, then there is an opportunity for new norm-entrepreneurs to work towards improvement of the situation. As long as there are strong public good gains from normatively regulating long-term commitments, there is likely to be an ought-implies-can dynamic, that is a political process of shifting resources towards the conditions for norm-conformity regarding (covert) long-term commitment decisions. It should clear that this dynamic connection between norms, choice and the distribution of resources is something that had fallen between economics and sociology in the old situation and thus could not be studied. Much remains to be done in the exploration of the ought-implies-can dynamics, but a beginning has been made.

5 Conclusion

Siegers is right that "the general, rational choice framework offers an ideal opportunity to combine the advantages of both economics and the other social sciences, namely to enrich the rather bare but formal and elegant economic models with psychological and sociological insights" (Siegers, 1990). But we have seen that there are specific reasons why this will work now whereas it has not worked in the past. These reasons are rooted in the convergence between sociology and economics, in methodological advances concerning the method of decreasing abstraction, and in theoretical advances concerning social production functions and the ought-implies-can dynamics. Understanding these changes is important for implementing Siegers programme suggestions because they go to the heart of what is meant by "combining the advantages of both economics and the other social sciences".

References

Albert, H. (1967), *Marktsoziologie und Entscheidungslogik*, Neuwied: Luchterhand.

Albert, H. (1984), Modell-Denken und historische Wirklichkeit: zur Frage des logischen Charakters des theoretischen Ökonomie, pp. 39-61 in: H. Albert (Hrg.), *Ökonomisches Denken und soziale Ordnung*, Tübingen: J.C.B. Mohr (Siebeck).

Albert, H. (1989), Hermeneutik als Heilmittel? Der ökonomische Ansatz und das Problem des Verstehens, *Analyse und Kritik*, 11, pp. 1-22.

Bell, D. and I. Kristol, eds. (1981), *The crisis in economic theory*, New York.

Birg, H., E.-J. Flöthmann and I. Reiter (1989), *Biographic analysis of the demographic characteristics of the life histories of men and women in regional labour-market-cohorts as clusters of birth cohorts*, Institute for Population Research and Social Policy, Universität Bielefeld.

De Alessi, L. (1983), Property rights, transaction costs, and x-efficiency: an essay in economic theory, *American Economic Review*, 73, pp. 64-81.

Earl, P.E., ed. (1988), *Behavioural economics*, Vols. I and II, Aldershot: Edward Elgar Publishing Co.

Homans, G. (1961), *Social behavior. Its elementary forms*, New York: Harcourt, Brace & World.

Huppes, T., ed. (1976), *Economics and sociology: towards an integration*, Leiden: Nijhoff.

Kristol, I. (1981), Rationalism in economics, pp. 201-218 in: D. Bell and I. Kristol, eds, *The crisis in economic theory*, New York.

Krupp, S.R., ed. (1966), *The structure of economic science*, Englewood Cliffs, N.J.

Lea, S.E.G., R.M. Tarpy and P. Webley (1987), *The individual in the economy*, Cambridge: Cambridge University Press.

Lindenberg, S.M. (1981), Erklärung als Modellbau: Zur soziologische Nutzung von Nutzentheorien, in: W. Schulte, ed., *Soziologie in der Gesellschaft*, Bremen: University Press, pp. 20-35.

Lindenberg, S.M. (1983a), The new political economy: its potential and limitations for the social sciences in general and for sociology in particular, in: W. Sodeur (Hrsg.),

Ökonomische Erklärung sozialen Verhaltens, Duisburg: Verlag der Sozialwiss. Kooperative, pp. 1-68.

Lindenberg, S.M. (1983b), Utility and morality, *Kyklos*, 36, no. 3: pp. 450-468.

Lindenberg, S.M. (1984a), Normen und die Allokation sozialer Wertschätzung, in: H. Todt (Hrsg.), *Normengeleitetes Verhalten in den Sozialwissenschaften*, Schriften des Vereins für Socialpolitik, Neue Folge Bd.141, Berlin: Duncker&Humblot, pp. 169-191.

Lindenberg, S.M. (1984b), Preference versus constraints, *Journal of Institutional and Theoretical Economics*, 140, pp. 96-103.

Lindenberg, S.M. (1985a), Rational choice and sociological theory: new pressures on economics as a social science, *Journal of Institutional and Theoretical Economics*, 141, pp. 244-255.

Lindenberg, S.M. (1985b), An assessment of the new political economy: its potential for the social sciences and for sociology in particular, *Sociological Theory*, 3, 1, pp. 99-114.

Lindenberg, S.M. (1986), Individual economic ignorance versus social production functions and precarious enlightenment, *Journal of Institutional and Theoretical Economics*, 142, pp. 20-26.

Lindenberg, S.M. (1989a), Choice and culture: the behavioral basis of cultural impact on transactions, pp. 175-200 in: H. Haferkamp (Hrsg.), *Social structure and culture*, Berlin: De Gruyter.

Lindenberg, S.M. (1989b), *Social approval, fertility and female labor market behavior*, paper presented at the Workshop "Female labout market behaviour and fertility: preferences, restrictions, and behaviour", Organised by Nederlands Interdisciplinair Demografisch Instituut and Centrum voor Interdisciplinair Onderzoek van Arbeidsmarkt- en Verdelingsvraagstukken, Den Haag, April 20-22.

Lindenberg, S.M. (1989c), Social production functions, deficits, and social revolutions: pre-revolutionary France and Russia, *Rationality and Society*, 1, 1, pp. 51-77.

Meckling, W. (1976), Values and the choice of the model of the individual in the social sciences, *Schweizerische Zeitschrift fur Volkswirtschaft und Statistik*, 112, pp. 545-559.

Merton, R. (1957), Social structure and anomie, in: R. Merton, *Social Theory and Social Structure*, Glencoe: Free Press, pp. 131-160.

Morse, N.C. and R.C. Weiss (1955), The function and meaning of work and the job, *American Sociological Review*, 20, pp. 191-198.

Opp, K.D. (1985), Sociology and economic man, *Zeitschrift für die gesamte Staatwissenschaft/Journal of Institutional and Theoretical Economics*, 141, pp. 213-243.

Rachlin, H. (1980), Economics and behavioural psychology, in: J.E.R. Staddon, ed., *Limits to action*, New York: Academic Press, pp. 205-236.

Siegers, J.J. (1990), *Towards the construction of interdisciplinary theoretical models to explain demographic behaviour*, this volume.

Simon, H.A. (1957), *Models of man*.

Simon, H.A. (1963), Economics and psychology, in: S. Koch, ed., *Psychology, a study of science*, New York: McGraw-Hill.

Sorokin, P. (1964), *Contemporary sociological theories*, New York: Harper.

Stigler, G. and G.S. Becker (1977), De gustibus non est disputandum, *American Economic Review*, 67, pp. 76-90.

Thurow, L. (1984), *Dangerous currents, the state of economics*, New York.

Tazelaar, F., and R. Wippler (1985), Problemspezifische Anwendung der allgemeinen Theorie mentaler Inkongurenzen in der empirischen Sozialforschung, pp. 117-179 in: G. Büschges und W. Raub (Hrsg.), *Soziale Bedingungen, individuelles Handeln, soziale Konsequenzen*, Frankfurt: Lang.

Wippler, R., and S.M. Lindenberg (1987), Collective phenomena and rational choice, in: Alexander, J., et al., eds, *The micro-macro link*, Berkeley: University of California Press, pp. 135-152.

Emerging Issues in Demographic Research
C.A. Hazeu and G.A.B. Frinking (Editors)
© Elsevier Science Publishers B.V. , 1990

Chapter 13

THE ECONOMIC CONSEQUENCES OF DEMOGRAPHIC CHANGE

Evert van Imhoff

1 Population economics

Economics is the science which studies human behaviour as a relationship between ends and scarce means that have alternative uses. This definition covers such a wide range of human behaviour that there are hardly any aspects of behaviour left of which economists do not have something to say. Today, even the economists themselves seem to be aware of their imperialistic tendency to expand their domain into the areas hitherto considered to be the exclusive playground of fellow disciplines (e.g. Hirshleifer, 1985). Human behaviour seems almost everywhere to involve at least some allocation of scarce resources.

Thus, it should not come as a surprise that economists, at least recently, have paid quite a lot of attention to various aspects of demographic phenomena. The field of *population economics* has by now become an established sub-discipline of economics, with its own subject code in the Journal of Economic Literature, and its scientific societies and journals (Van Praag, 1988).

The objects studied by population economics can roughly be divided into two categories. The first category, which one might call '*economic demography*', consists of an explanation and analysis of demographic phenomena using economic theories. That is, demographic behaviour (like fertility, marriage and divorce, household formation and dissolution, etc.) is explained as the resultant of the inherent conflict between unlimited desires and finite resources. This area of population economics is discussed extensively in the papers by Siegers and Nelissen in this volume.

The second category, which I usually refer to as '*demographic economics*', takes the demographic phenoma as such as given, and studies its effects on economic variables. That is, it studies the way in which the demographic situation affects the demand for and supply of scarce resources, and the way in which these changes in demand and supply in their turn affect human behaviour and social welfare. It should be stressed that these changes in demand and supply are not restricted to the market sector of the economy: the consequences for the public sector, in which either demand or supply, or both, are determined through collective decision-making processes, are studied as well (e.g. Ritzen, 1983).

It is this latter interpretation of population economics on which I will concentrate in the present paper.

2   Economic aspects of demographic phenomena

In the 1980s the Netherlands (as well as many other, mostly industrialized countries) can be considered to be in the middle of a transition phase between two situations of (more or less) constant population growth. Since the end of the 1960s the annual number of children born has decreased dramatically. Today's population projections indicate that the number of births will remain approximately constant until about 1995 and will decrease even further in the years after.

This decline in the number of births causes the population to age, in two respects. First, when the growth rate of the number of births is constant for a period long enough for the population to be stable (i.e. to have a constant age structure), the proportion of the elderly in the total population is permanently higher than before the start of the fertility decline. This is the long-run ageing effect. Second, during the transition phase there is a period in which the elderly stem from higher growth-rate cohorts than the younger generations, rendering the proportion of the elderly in the total population higher than it is in the final stable population. This is the transitory ageing effect. The transitory ageing effect of the fertility decline is, of course, larger than the long-run ageing effect.

In studying the economic consequences of demographic change, this fundamental distinction between transitory and permanent effects has to be constantly kept in mind.

The *age structure* of the population has important economic consequences of various kinds. Indeed, if one would restrict the number of explanatory variables to one, age would be the most appropriate candidate for the analysis of many different phenomena (and not only in economics). Consumption, labour supply, savings, eligibility for social security, demand for health care, are but a few of the many economic variables that are to a large extent determined by the age structure of the population.

Although changes in the age structure constitute the most visible aspect of the present demographic development, other aspects also have far-reaching economic consequences. First, the *growth rate of the population* itself is one of the main determinants of the savings and investment rate, as physical capital, needed to equip the labour force, and educational facilities, needed to prepare the young to enter this same labour force, as a proportion of national output, depend on the rate at which the labour force grows.

Second, other dimensions of the population concept play a role in the economic process, for example *spatial aspects* of the population, that is, the way in which the population is distributed over countries, or over national regions. Another important dimension is the way in which the population is grouped into households. Household formation and dissolution behaviour is an area which is rapidly gaining interest in demography, with many potential applications in economics and other sciences (Keilman e.a., 1988). Obviously, the *household structure* of the population is very important for various commodity markets, like housing, and also for certain areas of public policy, like social security (Van Imhoff and Keilman, 1989). A somewhat related component of the relevant demographic situation is the structure of kinship networks, nowadays subject to significant and far-reaching changes as a result of fertility decline (Bartlema, 1987).

From the previous discussion we can see that there are numerous mechanisms through which demographic developments affect the economic situation. Population economics being a relatively new science, only limited progress has been made in tracing these various relationships, let alone that it has been able to produce a systematic and comprehensive framework within which the full interplay between demographic and economic development can be embedded. Most of the studies are only partial, analysing one or only a few of these mechanisms. In short, a lot of work remains to be done.

3 Age structure and economic behaviour

The central theoretical construct in studying the effects of demographic variables on economic development is the so-called *theory of life-cycle behaviour* (Modigliani, 1986). Individuals, in making economic decisions, take into account the effect of current decisions on their welfare position in present and future phases of their life cycle. For instance, people of working age save part of their earnings in order to be able to continue to consume after retirement from the labour force. People at the beginning of their working career are willing to forego labour income in exchange for investment in education, thus increasing their earnings capacity during the active phase of their life cycle. These and similar considerations can be used to analyse how several key economic variables, like income, consumption, labour supply, demand for education, and savings, vary with the age of the individual in question.

When the age structure of the population changes, the first-order effect on these age-dependent key variables will consist of shifts in aggregate demand and supply curves due to changes in the weights by which the various age-specific demand and supply curves are transformed into their aggregate counterparts. The computation of the direction and size of these first-order effects is quite straightforward, given estimates of age-specific demand and supply curves. For example, if the age structure becomes older due to a decline in fertility, then under ceteris paribus conditions the relative demand for education will decrease and the relative demand for health care will increase.

These last two commodities (education and health care) are typical examples of markets which are to a large extent controlled by the public sector. The supply of these and similar services is basically determined by a collective decision-making process. From a viewpoint of policy planning in the medium term, it is very important to know how demand will change in response to demographic developments. The policy makers can then review the costs and benefits of the various policy options, and then decide on the degree to which they are willing to honour these demographically induced demands.

However, in the case of commodities that are primarily distributed through private markets, the ceteris paribus conditions are virtually guaranteed *not* to be satisfied. The demographically induced changes in demand and supply will change the conditions in the market for the commodity in question, generally affecting both the equilibrium price and the equilibrium quantity. These price changes, both present and future, will act as incentives for individuals to adjust their life-cycle behaviour to the changed scarcity conditions, thus affecting demand and supply in other commodity markets as well. It is here that the economic analysis of the social consequences of demographic change truly begins (cf. Von Weizsäcker, 1988, for an analysis of this type of demographic effects on income distribution).

4 Distributional questions and the concept of time

For the economy as a whole, the demographically induced shifts in scarcity conditions and commodity prices, discussed in the previous section, have both volume effects and distributional effects. The volume effects include the level and growth rate of national output, the composition of consumption, the relative importance of factors of production, the relative size of the public versus the private sector, and the allocation of national output to investment versus consumption.

Although, in the general spirit of the papers in this volume, the emphasis will be on the distributional aspects of the economic consequences of demographic change, some discussion of nondistributional aspects cannot be avoided. By the very nature of human economic behaviour, where exchange of scarce resources in the market plays such a predominant role, distribution cannot be studied in complete isolation from volume effects. In economics, the size of the cake is not independent of the way in which the cake is distributed. For example, policy measures intended to change the distribution of income (like a progressive income tax) may have far-reaching volume effects (e.g. on the labour supply or export of capital), and vice versa.

According to Pestieau (1989), "traditional measures of income distribution encompass three sources of interrelated differences: age, inter- and intra-generational differences" (p. 5). In assessing the distributional effects of demographic change it is essential to make explicit the way in which the role of *time* is considered, in order to be able to disentangle these differences. Here there are at least four possibilities:

1. distribution is viewed as a static, i.e. time-less concept. Quantities like the size-distribution of personal income, the relative earnings capacity of trained versus untrained workers of thirty years of age, and the like, correspond to this concept.
2. distribution is viewed as a concept that takes the full life cycle of individuals into account. That is, time plays a role insofar as it affects the age of the individual. If all individuals are equal, then the welfare distribution within generations is also equal, regardless of the growth rate of the population and the level of national income per capita.
3. distribution refers to individuals of different generations. Here, the role of time is to distinguish subsequent cohorts of individuals. As an example, one could compare the welfare position of pensioners under two different demographic regimes.
4. the most elaborate concept of distribution involves a combination of the previous two. Time plays the two-part role, well known in demographic analysis, of both biological time (age) and calendar time (cohort). If under regime 1 pensioners receive a lower state pension (e.g. financed on a pay-as-you-go basis) than in regime 2, they are not

necessarily worse off under regime 1 if they had a higher wage income during their
active years and consequently were able to save more than under regime 2.

It is clear that the conclusions of the analysis of distributional issues may vary widely
depending on in which of these four ways the factor time is incorporated. This need not
be a fundamental problem, as long as one clearly defines to which time dimension one
is referring. From a theoretical point of view the fourth concept of time is the most
complete and desirable one. However, given the present state of the art, many applications are still of a partial nature, for which the preferred approach may not be feasible.

A further complication in assessing the distributional consequences of demographic
change, again related to the factor time, is caused by the fundamental difference between
transitory and permanent effects mentioned earlier. Many analyses in economics use the
approach of comparative statics. That is, for two regimes of exogenous variables, the
corresponding steady states (i.e. 'permanent' states) are calculated and compared. This
approach has its advantages, but it runs the danger of overlooking the potentially
important transitory effects generated during the transition from one regime to another
(Van Imhoff, 1989b). An illustration of the danger of the "steady-state only" approach is
provided by Verbon (1988), who demonstrates that, if the population growth rate falls,
conversion of a pay-as-you-go pension system into a capital-reserve system is not
optimal, even if the capital-reserve system is optimal in the steady state corresponding
to the lower rate of population growth.

5   An outline of research questions in demographic economics

The general question to be answered by the national research programme in population
studies insofar as it concerns the topic of the present paper is the following:

"What are the effects of the demographic trends, both present and expected to prevail
in the future, on the distribution of economic resources and welfare across economic
agents? How can these distributional effects be evaluated ? And what policy instruments can be used, and in which way, to make these distributional effects as desirable
as possible ?"

It would be an understatement to characterize this reseach question as ambitious. To
get somewhere near an answer would require a research effort of unprecedented size. An
economic model would have to be constructed that simultaneously includes:

- decisions on savings, labour supply, consumption and investment in education;
- overlapping generations, differentiated not only by age but also by family size,
  household situation, and regional characteristics;
- a public sector, with taxes and social security;
- a private sector, differentiated by at least broad categories of final products;
- an international component;

– an explicit treatment of the dynamic nature of economic and demographic development.

This is clearly too much to ask for. Yet, the list of these requirements for the 'ultimate' demographic-economic model points towards an interesting new line of research: the extension of existing general-equilibrium models (see Shoven and Whalley, 1984, for a review) to include both overlapping generations and the dynamic role of time.

In the meantime, there are many components in this all-encompassing scheme which need to be tackled by research projects more limited in scope and of a more partial nature. The results of these studies would add greatly to our as yet still rather limited insight into the demographic-economic relationships, and can at a later stage be incorporated into the framework of the dynamic general-equilibrium model.

In the remainder of this section I will list and discuss some of these research topics which in my view are among the most pressing. These topics are treated according to the sector of the economy to which they belong.

First, let us consider the *labour market*. For given age-specific labour force participation rates the effects of demographic change on labour supply can be readily computed. One question concerns the changes in labour force participation rates, especially those for (married) women, in response to fertility changes. Some work in this area has been done (Siegers, 1985, as well as numerous more recent publications) but many aspects of the relationship are still little understood.

The labour market is not a homogeneous entity. Within the total labour force, large differences exist between age groups and educational specializations. The mobility of labour with respect to both jobs and specializations is a decreasing function of age. If structural shifts in the composition of the demand for labour occur, the danger of serious long-term mismatches between labour demand and supply increases as the age structure of the labour force becomes older (Frijns e.a., 1987). More quantitative research into these issues would be very welcome, including an investigation into the role of recurrent education as an instrument to increase the mobility of labour supply.

On the demand side of the labour market, the main determinant of the composition of demand will be the structure of *consumption demand*. This demand is not only related to age (e.g. education, care for the elderly), but also to other characteristics of the population (e.g. household composition, regional distribution). Further research should yield conclusions that are somewhat more specific than "there will be an increase in the demand for nurses".

Closely related to labour supply, is the *demand for education*, educational and labour services representing in many respects two sides of the same coin. Some theoretical results on the relationship between changes in age structure and education are known from previous work (Van Imhoff, 1989a). Generally speaking, we can conclude from these results that an increased training effort is profitable to partially offset the relative increased scarcity of labour due to ageing of the population. For the purpose of educational policy, the relationship between age structure and education has to be made much more specific, including a breakdown by educational specialization (preferably linked to the demographically induced changes in the composition of consumption referred to above). Also, the role of education as a transmittor of technological innovations in an ageing society (Van Imhoff, 1988) needs further empirical foundation.

Next, we arrive at the *demand for and supply of capital*, i.e. *investment and savings*. Although there is ample evidence of substitution between capital and labour in the productive sector, the absolute demand for capital will mostly move in the same direction as the demand for labour. In the long run, a lower rate of population growth corresponds to a lower rate of investment, although the composition of investment may change (e.g. from private housing to public investment). According to the life-cycle theory of savings, the supply of capital will also change with the growth rate of the population. Since the elderly population typically consists of dissavers, a shift in the age distribution towards the older age groups tends to reduce the aggregate savings rate, which is, at least in the long run, in line with the decline in the investment rate. However, the exact nature of these changes is not well-known and quite complex, as many variables affect individual savings behaviour (rate of interest, social security, tax system, pension system, number of children). In addition, the transitory effects are much more complicated than the permanent effects. Much work in this area remains to be done.

An area in which much research *has* already been done is *public expenditures and social security*. Confronted with the threat of a severe degree of ageing of the population in the decades to come, national governments have become very worried about the consequences for their national budgets and social security systems, which explains the large number of research reports published in this area. Most of these studies adopted a very simple methodology: what would happen if everything were to remain the same *except* the age structure of the population? This one-sided approach leaves open many issues which require additional research before well-founded policy responses can be formulated and implemented. If the status-quo policy leads to substantial increases in expenditures, how are these to be financed? What will be the consequences of higher tax rates and/or social security premiums on labour supply, private savings, and other important aspects of economic behaviour? Is age structure the only important demographic variable, or do other aspects of the demographic structure perhaps affect the collective budget to an even larger extent? As far as the latter question is concerned, household structure is a potentially highly influential variable. *Poverty* varies very strongly among different household types (e.g. one-parent families). According to present demographic projections, not only will the number of retired persons increase but a much larger proportion of these retired persons will live in one-person households, significantly increasing the costs of the state pension system. In addition, these retired persons will have a much smaller kinship network for private-sector support. These and other questions are still a long way from being answered.

Finally, a very much neglected aspect of distributional consequences of demographic change is related to the *international context*. On a world-wide scale, the demographic development can be characterized as divergent: developed countries, on the one hand, experience a slow-down of population growth and a severe ageing problem; developing countries, on the other hand, are still characterized by very high levels of fertility and continue to be threatened by overpopulation. These high rates of population growth in many developing countries impose major limitations on economic growth in per-capita terms. A multi-country study would be able to investigate the effects of diverging demographic trends on international welfare distributions, and would also be able to assess the possibilities for international cooperation in exploiting the advantages and in fighting the disadvantages of fertility changes.

6   On the importance of endogenizing demographic behaviour

Throughout this paper I have treated the demographic situation and its development over time as being exogenous to the analysis. This attitude is in line with the division of labour implemented by the organizers of this volume, and I am not going to complain about that.

However, I would like to stress that research into the relationship between demographic and economic variables that follows the link of causality in one direction only (namely from demography to economics), can *at the very best* constitute only a limited, albeit important, component of the comprehensive research programme in population studies, the construction of which is the objective of the Netherlands Organization for Scientific Research.

There are two main reasons why the analysis, explanation and forecasting of the demographic trends themselves is of crucial importance to the research programme. First, it has by now become an established fact that demographic processes and economic (and social, and political) processes do not belong to more or less independent systems, but, on the contrary, influence each other in many ways. If the simultaneous nature of demographic, economic, social and political processes is not explicitly taken into account, the results of the analysis are necessarily incomplete and could well lead to rather erroneous conclusions. This is especially true if the effects of these processes are felt over a long period of time. By the very nature of demographic variables, their effects are typically a long-term affair, and so are the feedback mechanisms to which they are subjected.

Second, and even more important, an analysis of the consequences of given demographic developments is of limited interest if the causes of these demographic developments are not properly understood. If the number of single-person households is expected to increase in the near future, it is one thing to conclude that this will increase the demand for housing, but quite another thing to trace the causes of the increase (i.e. to assess the validity of the forecast), to assess its welfare implications, and, if these welfare implications are found to be negative, to propose and implement policy measures capable of reducing the welfare losses as far as possible. The central role of policy is, and will continue to be, to achieve social well-being. This goal can only be reached on the basis of a proper understanding of the forces that drive individual behaviour.

References

Bartlema, J.D. (1987), *Developments in kinship support networks for the aged in the Netherlands*, Tilburg: Katholieke Universiteit Brabant (Reeks Sociale Zekerheidsweten-schap).

Frijns, J.M.G., B. Kuhry, A. Nieuwenhuis and R. van Opstal (1987), Demografische ontwikkeling en arbeidsmarkt, in: Koninklijke Vereniging voor de Staathuishoudkunde, *Demografische veranderingen en economische ontwikkelingen*, Leiden: Stenfert Kroese (Demographic development and the labour market; in Dutch).

Hirshleifer, J. (1985), The expanding domain of economics, *American Economic Review*, 75/6 (Special Issue), pp. 53-68.

Imhoff, E. van (1988), Age structure, education, and the transmission of technical change, *Journal of Population Economics*, 1, no. 3, pp. 167-181.

Imhoff, E. van (1989a), Optimal investment in human capital under conditions of non-stable population, *Journal of Human Resources*, 24, no. 3, pp. 414-432.

Imhoff, E. van (1989b), *Optimal economic growth and non-stable population*, Heidelberg: Springer-Verlag.

Imhoff, E. van and N.W. Keilman (1989), *The impact of changing living arrangements on social security expenditures in the Netherlands, 1985-2015*, Paper prepared for the IIASA/ECE Task Force Meeting on Social Security, Family and Household in Ageing Societies, Laxenburg, March 9-10, 1989.

Keilman, N.W., A.C. Kuijsten and A.P. Vossen, eds., (1988), *Modelling household formation and dissolution*, Oxford: Clarendon Press.

Modigliani, F. (1986), Life cycle, individual thrift, and the wealth of nations, *American Economic Review*, 76, no. 3, pp. 297-313.

Nelissen, J.H.M. (1990), *The microeconomic theory of household formation and dissolution: state-of-the-art and research proposals*, this volume.

Pestieau, P. (1989), The demographics of inequality, *Journal of Population Economics*, 2, no. 1, pp. 3-24.

Praag, B.M.S. van (1988), The notion of population economics, *Journal of Population Economics*, 1, no. 1, pp. 5-16.

Ritzen, J.M.M. (1983), *Bevolking, publieke sector en economie*, Den Haag: VUGA (Population, public sector and economics; in Dutch).

Shoven, J.B. and J. Whalley (1984), Applied general-equilibrium models of taxation and international trade: an introduction and survey, *Journal of Economic Literature*, 22, no. 3, pp. 1007-1051.

Siegers, J.J. (1985), *Arbeidsaanbod en kindertal*, Ph.D. Dissertation, University of Groningen (Labour supply and number of children; in Dutch).

Siegers, J.J. (1990), *Towards the construction of interdisciplinary theoretical models to explain demographic behaviour*, this volume.

Verbon, H.A.A. (1988), *The evolution of public pension schemes*, Heidelberg: Springer-Verlag.

Weizsäcker, R.K. von (1988), Age structure and income distribution policy, *Journal of Population Economics*, 1, no. 1, pp. 33-55.

Emerging Issues in Demographic Research
C.A. Hazeu and G.A.B. Frinking (Editors)
© Elsevier Science Publishers B.V. , 1990

Chapter 14

THE ECONOMIC CONSEQUENCES OF DEMOGRAPHIC CHANGE:
A COMMENT

Pierre Pestieau

On the whole, I have no real criticism of Van Imhoff's contribution, but perhaps a slightly different emphasis might bring to light some interesting points. His paper provides a quite impressive survey of what is meant by demographic economics. He chose to allude to a large number of topics rather than to focus on a couple of issues. Doing so in less than a dozen pages is quite an achievement. In my comments, I will proceed along the same path as his paper, thus providing a separate discussion of each section.

1. The distinction between 'economic demography' and 'demographic economics' is novel to me. I am not sure that it is desirable. In my view, population economists should try to take into account the endogeneity of both demographic and economic behaviour. To put it another way, they should merge Becker and Easterlin's lines of thought; that is, new home economics and traditional demographics economics. As to prove me right, the last section of this paper argues that endogenizing demographic and family choices is a must.

   If research segmentation is looked for, I would rather advocate studying particular issues involving both demographic and economic choices while keeping everything else constant. This approach is to be preferred to the one relying on complex models taking all demographic variables as given.

2. I totally concur with the wide-ranging definition of demographic phenomena. When dealing with below-replacement fertility, one clearly has to focus on the aging structure and on the declining population size. Yet, household formation, retirement decisions, residential choices, inheritance behaviour and altruism within and across generations are also quite relevant as to their economic consequences.

   What should be explored in that respect is the adjustment lag of each demographic phenomenon. One knows that basic demographic variables move slowly whereas phenomena such as retirement choices or household patterns can vary quickly.

3. We are told that the computation of first-order effects of aging on aggregate demand and supply is straightforward. I am not so sure. First, what is meant by first-order effects? Is it the assumption of constant behaviour and prices (demand elasticities, wage and productivity pattern)? If so, measuring the effects of varying age structure is relatively easy but quite meaningless. Just to take an example, what is going to be the effect of aging on the wage structure of our societies? Even on the basis of past

experience (babyboomers entering the job market), one gets mixed answers to that question.

4. When thinking of the economic consequences of population changes and of the appropriate public policy to countervail undesirable consequences, the focus is often put on distributive questions. One indeed has the feeling that in the medium run population changes affect less the size than the sharing of the cake. In the long run, things may be different.

On this point, there is often an opposition between the ways social scientists and politicians define an equitable allocation. Let me give you an example which roughly fits the reality of many countries. I am labeling each generation by the year it starts working. I assume that each individual works during thirty years and retires for thirty years. On the table herebelow, the level of disposable income per person is given:

DISPOSABLE INCOME PER MEMBER OF EACH GENERATION

	periods				
	1920	1950	1980	2010	2040
generations					
1920	60	60			
1950		80	100		
1980			100	60	
2010				80	40

In the current period 1980, we have a perfect equality of income across ages (intragenerational disparities are here assumed away). Yet from the viewpoint of intergenerational equity, taxing the current generation of retirees and workers to build up a pension fund would make sense. Unfortunately, such a proposal would not be popular.

5. We now reach the crucial section which sketches both the themes and the methodology of future research. I am quite skeptical as to the usefulness in the near future of computational dynamic general equilibrium models à la Shoven-Whalley. Not only would they yield results which are too rough and too approximate but furthermore, they are so complex that one cannot see through them in order to understand the links between their various components.

As to the themes, an essay of this kind could not do much more than touch on selected issues. Quite clearly, judgment on what are major or minor issues depend on one's time horizon and how much the government is ready to intervene in the intra- but also in the inter-generational allocation of resources.

In my view, there is a need to understand the role of the family in the distribution of welfare. Family instability is often considered as one of the major sources of poverty. On the other hand, family altruism is at times viewed as the most efficient way to compensate for market failures towards distribution and for the retrenchment of governments in the field of social protection. What will be the role of family in an aging society? This is a still widely unexplored field. After all, the family is the locus where most demographic decisions are taken and a lot of transactions take place.

A better understanding of the relations among countries with different demographic patterns is also in order. Too often, we forget that today very few societies are aging. Some people believe factor mobility can be an answer to our demographic problems. Such an issue surely deserves more than shallow conjectures.

Also, the role of women in an aging society should get more attention. With a life expectancy much higer than that of the men (nine years in France), a rate of labour participation much lower but still increasing than that of the men, a retirement age often earlier than that of the men, their economic role is for sure going to increase. Further, those three distinctive features can be expected to change, implying in turn various economic consequences.

6. After this quick review of the paper at hand, I would like to come back to the main issue: the economic consequences of population change. When coping with it, we, economists, tend to focus on quantitative aspects. This is not surprising for our dismal social science. This is also relevant if one needs to understand what is likely to happen and what should be a good public policy. It remains, however, that a phenomenon such as the aging of a society is vowed to have various effects on the values, both ethical and cultural, which in turn will affect motivations, incentives and choices. These effects could be as important as the quantitative effects that a dynamic general equilibrium effects could yield. Unfortunately, this being said, I am unable to say what will be the direction of these effects.

This critique bears some similarity with Lucas' critique of macroeconometric forecasting. How can we forecast the future with reaction functions which reflect values and expectations of the past? My feeling is that these effects operating through changes in values affect more the volume of output and income than its distribution. Hence, the research program suggested by Van Imhoff keeps all its relevancy.

In closing, I want to make two remarks which go beyond the economic consequences of population change but concern the overall research project. First, one should not forget the old advice of Tjalling Koopmans: "don't measure without theory". In trying to understand the various interrelations between population changes and socioeconomic variables, one needs a conceptual framework from which empirical tests can then be conducted according to a consistent line.

Second, in designing policy schemes in view of countervailing undesirable consequences of aging, one should try to keep them flexible. The rigidity of policy tools and the unability of adjusting them to a changing environment are often responsible for public deficits and policy uneffectiveness. Here are two examples: mandatory retirement ages should be made a function of the age structure, and payroll taxes could vary according the branch of occupation and depend on the life expectancy observed in each of them.

Emerging Issues in Demographic Research
C.A. Hazeu and G.A.B. Frinking (Editors)
© Elsevier Science Publishers B.V. , 1990

Chapter 15

DETERMINANTS AND CONSEQUENCES OF MORTALITY IN THE
NETHERLANDS: SOME SUGGESTIONS FOR RESEARCH

Frans W.A. van Poppel

1 Introduction

The period 1870-1880 heralded the beginning of a new era in the demographic history
of the Netherlands. Revolutionary changes in the mortality pattern were a key factor in
this change.

If we assume, as others do (see Goldscheider, 1971; McNicoll, 1986) that the mortality
pattern is characterised by four main features – the mortality level and its associated age
pattern; the degree of annual fluctuation in the mortality level; the incidence of socio-
economic or geographic variations in mortality; and the cause-of-death pattern and
underlying diseases particular to the population concerned – then the fundamental
changes which have taken place since the middle of the nineteenth century can be
summarised as follows:

- human life expectancy has increased dramatically and deaths are increasingly occurring in the more advanced age categories;
- sharp annual fluctuations in the mortality rate caused by starvation and epidemics are
  largely a thing of the past;
- major internal variations in mortality – by geographic region or socio-economic
  status, for example – have for the most part disappeared;
- the cause-of-death pattern is determined by chronic, rather than infectious, disorders.

The following statistics illustrate these changes:

- Around the middle of the last century in the Netherlands, the life expectancy of men
  was 36.4 years and that of women 38.2 years. By the end of the nineteenth century,
  this had increased to 46.2 years and 49.0 years respectively; by the 1930s it was 63.7
  years and 65.3 years respectively. The most recent (1987) statistics quote average life
  expectancies of 73.5 years for men and 80.1 years for women (CBS, 1988b).
- In the middle of the nineteenth century, 18-20% of all live-born children died before
  reaching their first birthday. Infant mortality progressively declined, most noticeably

after 1880, to below 10% around 1910. Currently less than 1% of children born die in the first year of their lives.

- Whereas previously most deaths occurred in early life – up until 1900 in the Netherlands, for example, more than 25% of those who died were less than a year old – this has not been the case since the middle of the twentieth century. Since 1950, more than 50% of deaths have occurred in the 70+ age category, whereas before 1900, less than 20% of those who died had reached this age.
- Sharp annual fluctuations in mortality in the Netherlands were particularly common before ca. 1875, when epidemics and crop failures caused dramatic shifts in the mortality rate. The cholera epidemic of 1849, compounded by the failure of the potato crop, caused e.g. the mortality rate to rocket to roughly 33.0 per 1000. A year later the mortality rate reverted to its more usual level (24.5 per 1000). Similar disturbances occurred in 1826, 1847 and 1859, when the mortality rate rose to roughly 25-30% above the usual level.
- Mid-nineteenth century data on provincial variations in life expectancy indicate that male life expectancy in the western provinces was 26 to 28 years, whilst in the rest of the country it was 38 to 41 years. Similar variations in female life expectancy can be found at a somewhat higher level. The most recent provincial life tables, however, indicate that male life expectancy in Limburg is still only 1.0 year less than that in Zeeland, whilst the maximum female variation between Limburg and Friesland is only 0.8 years. Socio-economic variations were probably on a par with geographical variations in the eighteenth and nineteenth centuries, but very little data are available: Schellekens (1988) published estimations of life expectancy for the years 1726-1805 which reveal variations as high as nearly 15 years between the lowest and highest social classes in the municipalities researched. Recent data from the Amsterdam District Study (Lau-Yzerman, 1979) indicate respectable variations of about 5 years.
- Conditions attributable to micro-organisms (such as tuberculosis, bronchitis, whooping cough, measles, smallpox, cholera, diarrhoea, typhoid and typhus) caused the vast majority of deaths in the middle of the nineteenth century, but during the course of the nineteenth and twentieth centuries these diseases waned and were superceded by cancer, cardiovascular disease and other chronic degenerative diseases. Mortality is increasingly the result, not of immediately lethal events, but rather of chronic degenerative conditions. Because the population is ageing, multimorbidity is increasingly becoming a feature of mortality – with people suffering from a range of major and minor ailments which are the product of the ageing process, and which give rise to aspecific complaints.

However, the fact that the cause-of-death pattern has changed does not invalidate mortality data. They can still be extremely useful for population health status research, particularly if they are cause-specific, since they provide a very important yardstick for measuring health problems, tend to be fairly reliable and permit the study of longterm trends. Besides, they are often available for different regional units, are relatively easy to obtain and are of reasonably good quality.

The majority of the changes in the mortality pattern described above had essentially taken place by the 1950s; this is not to say that the mortality pattern remained unchanged after 1950 – quite the contrary.

Mackenbach (1988) was correct to point out that, from an age-specific point of view, there were clearly dramatic changes in mortality trends in the post-war period. Generally speaking, there were more relative changes in the mortality rate post-1950 than pre-1950, particularly in the higher age groups. There were also major changes in the cause-of-death pattern after 1950.

Given the aforementioned global developments since the middle of the nineteenth century, which issues should be researched as a matter of priority?

Four major issues come immediately to mind:
- which factors brought about the fundamental changes in mortality which took place between the last quarter of the nineteenth century and the beginning of the 1950s;
- how should demographic research respond to health pattern and mortality changes over the past decades, i.e. how should it deal with the increased significance of morbidity and multimorbidity as health indicators;
- has Dutch society's transition towards greater social and cultural homogeneity in fact eliminated mortality regime variations within social sub-groups;
- how has Dutch society assimilated the effects of the changed mortality pattern.

2   Changes in mortality in the period 1800-1950

Although fertility trends during the period of demographic transition have been extensively researched in the Netherlands, little time has been devoted to researching mortality trends during this period and even less reference made to foreign research. What little research exists is deficient in many areas and contains noticeable gaps.

Essential information of a purely descriptive nature – e.g. mortality trends decomposed by a number of characteristics – is absent. In general, the studies show a high aggregation level and use global indicators for mortality trends. Very little data are available on mortality levels before the mortality decline. The research seldom has a clear theoretical base with the result that one is forced to rely on ad hoc explanations for trends: explanatory causal models, in which the relationship between the characteristics and disease processes and death are clearly established, are for most part absent. The relative significance of the various factors which contributed to the mortality decline – improvement in living conditions, improved hygiene and sanitary provisions, advances in the field of preventive and curative medicine, and biological changes independent of human intervention – is still unclear. Specific studies at local level could provide important information in this respect. Research could be focused on the following issues.

2.1   The mortality level before the advent of civil registration

Virtually no age- and sex-specific mortality data are available in the Netherlands for the pre-1840 period. The tables of death published for the years 1828/1829 are an exception. A certain amount of data has become available in recent years concerning mortality levels and variations for the pre-civil registration period; one of the reasons for this was that mortality trends were, to some degree, taken into account in family reconstructions (Noordam, 1986; Schellekens, 1989). Research into the utility of applying indirect methods, developed for situations with incomplete data, to mortality estimation in historical demographic research should be continued. Research into the utility of life contingent contracts for mortality estimation is also desirable. Alter (1983) instigated analysis of data of this kind and applied it to Amsterdam annuities. A data inventory of widows' and orphans' benefits, funeral and insurance funds, and an evaluation of their reliability, could yield information about the mortality level and mortality trends of specific population groups in the seventeenth and eighteenth century.

2.2   Reconstruction of the mortality pattern by age and sex of individual years and birth cohorts

Although more detailed mortality data have been available since 1840, an accurate picture of the historical development of age- and sex-specific mortality rates of the Dutch population really requires a series of comparative mortality data at a national and regional level, which are not presently available.

Researchers using the national life tables for the period 1840-1940 rarely consult the original publications, since they are too far flung and not easily accessible for other reasons. The calculation methods and statistical data used in the various life tables, are not fully understood. Frequently, researchers settle for summary indicators taken from life tables for 1931-1940 (CBS, 1942) and from subsequent life tables published by the Netherlands Central Bureau of Statistics (CBS). Over the years, researchers have applied divergent methods of calculation, notably to the younger age categories – particularly for the 1840-1851 period – and to the 90-plus age category.

A better understanding of long-term mortality trends could be achieved by compiling a precise inventory of the basic data at the national and provincial level, by evaluating the methods of calculation applied in the light of current knowledge and by establishing a cross-referenced, comparative series of life tables for the period 1840-1940.

Use of the original data to compile generation life tables is also recommended. In contrast to the CBS publication (CBS, 1975), which dealt with generation mortality, it would also be useful to calculate the probability of dying for individual birth years, and to consider to what extent data for the years 1850-1870 (classified only by sex and age) could be integrated into a database classified by generation. A database of this kind could provide a springboard for the analysis of age, cohort and period effects on mortality trends. Recent attempts to visualise long-term mortality trends by age with the help of contour maps could be very usefully applied to the Dutch situation. In this way it is possible to highlight previously indistinct age, period and cohort interactions (Caselli, Vaupel, Yashin, 1985). A database of this kind could be invaluable for both historical and prospective research.

The compilation of life tables at provincial level would help considerably in understanding the background to regional variations in mortality. Historians debating the causes of regional variations and changes in mortality in the nineteenth century rarely avail themselves of age- and sex-specific mortality data. Age is only specifically taken into account when considering infant mortality. Little use is made of existing provincial life tables for the middle of the last century (1840-1851 and 1850-1859); this is partly for the reasons given above concerning life tables for the country as a whole.

Provincial life tables for the period 1860-1930 could, in principle, also be compiled; the basic information is available. The compilation of a series of uniform life tables for the Dutch provinces for the period 1840-1930 could provide the first step towards expanding our knowledge about the advent of, and shifts in, regional variations in mortality.

2.3 Causes and effects of the mortality transition in the nineteenth and twentieth centuries

McKeown has carried out the most authoritative research into the causes of mortality decline (see McKeown, 1976). Although his research concentrated mainly on England and Wales, the results are often equally applied without any adjustment, to other European countries. McKeown concentrated mainly on diseases caused by micro-organisms which he classified according to the mechanism by which the infection was carried. In the first phase, improved feeding (the result of improved distribution, new crops and farming methods) had the greatest impact on infections caused by air-borne diseases. Subsequent improvements in hygiene (water-supply, sewerage systems, refuse disposal) had a major impact on water- and foodborne diseases. In the beginning of the nineteenth century, improved feeding and, later, improved working and living conditions contributed to the mortality decline. In McKeown's view, the sole contribution of medical science, in terms of individual health care, to the decline in mortality due to infectious diseases in the nineteenth century was probably the smallpox vaccine. This situation changed after 1900, but not to a large degree. And finally, a change in the relationship between micro-organisms and humans had an impact on mortality due to a limited number of infectious diseases.

McKeown's research and conclusions provoked criticism from other researchers. Razzell (1974), referring to an earlier publication of McKeown, expressed grave reservations about the effects of improved feeding and placed greater emphasis on major changes in personal hygiene. Other authors attached greater significance to the impact of improved living standards and improved socio-economic circumstances and likewise felt that improved feeding was of less significance.

Szreter (1988) points out that "the independent role of those socio-political developments which were responsible for such hardwon improvements as those in working conditions, housing, education, and various health services" is being overlooked. "The history of food adulteration and the battle for its regulation and control" are regarded simply as an "automatic corollary of changes in a country's per capita real income." Szreter underlines the fact that nineteenth century rural and urban developments differed greatly, affected mainly by "those public health measures which combated the upsurge of diseases directly resulting from the defective and insanitary urban and domestic environments created in the course of industrialisation". Consequently, "those agencies which brought about the implementation of these preventive health measures" were a major factor in mortality decline.

Razzell's case for comparative, international research based on specific hypotheses, is still valid, but research of this kind is currently still in short supply in the Netherlands. Verdoorn's (1965) and Jansen and De Meere's (1981) conclusions are based exclusively on data from Amsterdam. Verdoorn relies heavily on the theory established earlier by Hofstee (see below) of the change in the overall cultural pattern. Although in some areas in-depth studies have taken place (see e.g. Rutten, 1985, on the increased availability of medical care; Swartsenburg, 1981, on the effects of a number of public health expenditures and Mackenbach's study, 1988, of specific twentieth century medical interventions) countless fields of research are totally lacking; specific studies – such as the research conducted by Cherry (1980) into the role of hospitals in the mortality decline process and research into the relationship between morbidity and mortality are especially needed. New developments in mortality research have already been applied to English historical data. Alter and Riley (1989), for example, published research in which they applied Manton and Stallard's heterogeneous 'frailty' model to historical data (see below). They used nineteenth century English friendly society sickness data and demonstrated that as mortality declined in the nineteenth century, so morbidity was increasing. Benedictow's (1987) interesting study of the role of the plague in decimating the European population towards the end of the Middle Ages examined which mechanisms were involved in spreading the disease. The morbidity data he had at his disposal came from material from many different sources. Using an idea developed by Schofield, he was able to gain fresh insight into the way these diseases were spread. In principle, the death statistics by location and household necessary for research of this kind are available from nineteenth century Dutch sources and could also be applied to other contagious diseases.

The fact that McKeown's work on Britain "continues to provide the only thoroughly researched empirical support for the extreme laissez-faire position, that health and welfare gains may be generated most effectively merely as a byproduct of economic growth and that government policies should therefore simply be directed at maximising economic growth alone", is one of the reasons for ongoing research into mortality decline in the nineteenth and twentieth centuries.

2.4   *Trends and causes of variations in regional mortality in the nineteenth and twentieth century*

An important implication of the socio-economic and geographic variation in mortality is that a substantial range of mortality experience exists at any given time in most societies. A mortality regime is in effect a layering of subregimes. Although very little research has been carried out into the class-specific nature of mortality decline in the Netherlands, variations in mortality by geographic region have been extensively researched.

In the nineteenth century, the Netherlands was not a homogeneous area in terms of mortality. Provinces such as Noord-Holland and Zuid-Holland, Zeeland and Utrecht exhibited particularly high mortality rates. The situation remained virtually static until about 1875. By the turn of the century, however, these provinces were amongst those areas with the lowest mortality rates in the Netherlands, and as of the first decade of the twentieth century, their mortality rates were lower than anywhere else in the country. Obviously the mortality rate gradually levelled out, but to date, the southern provinces are still characterised by high mortality rates and the western provinces by relatively low mortality rates. Which factors were responsible for the disadvantageous situation in the western provinces around 1875? And which factors were responsible for the subsequent mortality decline? How was the foundation laid for a pattern of geographical health variations which persists to this day?

Hofstee attributes the changes in regional mortality to an increased awareness of hygiene, embedded in the development of the modern cultural pattern and ascribes the high mortality in the middle of the nineteenth century in the West to the salting up of surface and ground water, the lack of good ground water and the high degree of urbanisation.

Hofstee's conclusions did not go unchallenged. Jansen and De Meere (1982) attributed the mortality decline in the West to the economic revival in the second half of the nineteenth century, which resulted in less malnutrition and a decline in mortality due to diseases of the digestive system, followed later by a drop in mortality caused by respiratory diseases. Regional variations in infant mortality – the most important determinant of overall variations – were the subject of an extensive dispute between Vandenbroeke et al. (1981) and Hofstee (1983). In somewhat oversimplified terms, whereas Vandenbroeke et al. felt that the regional variation in infant mortality was largely attributable to the breast-feeding rate, Hofstee attributed it to factors such as the quality of the drinking water, the use of supplementary feeding and soporifics and the incidence of malaria. Lesthaeghe (1983) tried to incorporate all the available data concerning different factors affecting infant mortality in the Netherlands into an explanatory model. He concluded that a step-by-step measurement of many potentially relevant variables – such as the proportion of breast-feeding women, the quality of drinking water and supplementary feeding, malaria, practices such as wet nursing, availability of medical care, level of education, hygiene, professional occupation of women, etc. – was necessary before an attempt could be made to statistically test a developed model.

Research into nineteenth century regional variations in mortality in the Netherlands, compared to that of other countries, has never quite got beyond the descriptive stage. Research based on theoretical notions as to the causes of mortality variations are the exception rather than the rule. As a result, virtually no explanatory models have been established; nor have they been tested statistically. Research of the kind conducted by Friedlander et al. (1985) and Woods et al. (1988) is absent. The data situation is partly to blame for this (on a comparative regional scale level, a great deal of data are not available for the Netherlands). The database set up in Amsterdam (Geography) which contains regional demographic and other data could be a good starting-point for this sort of research.

Mackenbach et al. (1988) pointed out that one of the problems of studies about regional mortality variations is that they focus on level variations. However, many cause-specific mortality trends are very dynamic, so that measurements taken in isolation frequently give an incomplete picture of regional mortality variations. They suggest, as others have before them, that attention be focused on geographical regions characterised not only by high mortality levels but also by slow mortality decline. Researchers into historical mortality would do well to heed this advice.

2.5 Research into a cause-of-death classification table which could be applied to nineteenth century historical research

There is another source of information which offers great possibilities for the study of mortality trends in the critical period of the last quarter of the nineteenth century, namely statistical data concerning deaths, classified by municipality and by cause of death, age category and sex.

These data are available, covering five-yearly periods, commencing 1875-1879 up to and including the period 1895-1899, with causes of death classified consistently through-out. Few researchers have availed themselves of this information to date. Swartsenburg (1981) and Hofstee (1981) are exceptions. The statistics in question are not automatically suitable for analysis. Many 'causes' were simply symptoms which could refer to a variety of diseases. Even with specific causes of death, the accuracy of diagnosis can often be questioned. The name of one disease might encompass a number of different illnesses, or multiple designations could be used for the same disease. Joint research by doctors and demographers into the exact significance of the recorded causes of death – based on data concerning the medical know-how of the time, the disease models used, seasonal patterns, and taking into account shifts in classification as a result of the cause of death classification being compiled on different, and more reliable, lines around 1900 – could provide the basis for a reliable reference system for researching trends and regional and age-specific variations in the mortality pattern in this critical period in Dutch demographic history.

2.6 Individual characteristics and probability of dying

A factor common to many of the issues dealt with here is that they all require research based on individuals and their own particular characteristics. However, because infor-mation of this kind is not available, researchers often rely on a higher aggregation level for their conclusions. Research conducted at individual level is always confined to a particular regional scale. Recently, however, steps have been taken to establish a database which would not lack this sort of information. The research proposed by the Stichting Historische Steekproef Nederlands Bevolking (Netherlands Foundation for a Historical Population Sample), to be based on a random sample of birth certificates of people born in the Netherlands between 1815 and 1920, matched by name against data from marriage and death certificates, and population and tax registers, could provide extremely useful information about Dutch mortality patterns (for the period 1815-1940), social and regional mortality variations as well as more specific issues such as maternal mortality, infant mortality, the impact of emigration on urban excess mortality, and so on. Useful data on socio-economic mortality variations could, for example, be derived from whatever data are gained concerning the relationship between social mobility (both inter- and intra-generational) and social mortality variations. If this proposal were put into effect, Dutch research could dovetail with longer-term foreign research projects in Canada, France, Sweden, Finland and Belgium. The test project proposed by the Foundation would deal with the province of Utrecht.

3 Developments in morbidity and mortality after 1950: methodological considerations

Nowadays, dying is rarely a sudden event: it is usually the culmination of a lengthy process during which the individual has suffered to a greater or lesser degree from diseases or handicaps which affect his mortality risk. It is thus a complex process (morbidity), the conclusion of which (death) cannot be studied without taking into account the process which preceded it: the population distribution of morbidity is a prime determinant of mortality risks and in turn the selection effects of mortality determine who survives with a chronic degenerative disease.

The majority of Manton and Stallard's research concentrates on the complex relationship between morbidity and mortality. Their work (Manton and Stallard, 1984a) represents a successful attempt at combining concepts and data from many different angles of research (e.g. clinical medicine, epidemiology, biostatistics) with current demographic and actuarial models. Their multidisciplinary approach was not confined to content alone; where existing demographic models proved inadequate, improvements were suggested.

Their approach centred on the development of demographic models designed to enable the effects of morbidity and mortality processes on human populations to be examined. An important feature of these models is that they are biologically realistic, i.e. the models give a realistic picture of the biological mechanisms which convey morbidity and mortality. Both authors devote much attention to the "assessment of the societal and health service implication of the results of their models". The net result of this is that the model output can be translated "in quantities that are meaningful for policy questions".

The term applied by Manton and Stallard to their attempt to develop a formal model, for integrating many different sorts of population health data with a view to analysis of the health status of the entire population is 'medical demography'. They use this term because they are essentially dealing with 'population characteristics' and because research into the population model which is the product of these population characteristics must be based on and be consistent with biomedical data and theory. Their aim is not to replace clinical, epidemiological and experimental studies, but to create an integrating structure for the various types of data and on the basis of that input and the model structures to provide specific quantitative estimates of population health characteristics.

The organising principles which should govern the development of these medico-demographic models can be summarised as follows: they must be process-oriented at the individual level, i.e. take into account the natural history of disease processes, including such factors as disease and disease-host interaction and dependency. Only by representing disease processes in this way can both their simultaneous occurrence as well as the fact that an individual can manifest a multiplicity of conditions be taken into account.
The models must also, however, be process-oriented at aggregate level. This is necessary because there are a number of mechanisms operating at population level which affect the manner in which health effects which operate at individual level become apparent at aggregate level. Two mechanisms are particularly important: morbidity and mortality selection, and the competing risk effect.

"The need to adjust for mortality selection arises because individuals in a population are usually quite heterogeneous in their susceptibility to disease processes. As a population is subjected over time to disease or mortality risks, the most susceptible persons will have the highest likelihood of being selected. If there is a high level of selection then the residual population will have a relatively lower average susceptibility to the disease. Thus, high rates of selection may cause the age trajectory of aggregate risks to deviate from the age trajectory of individual risks. Therefore, in devising a model to translate the biological mechanisms operating at the individual levels, one must ensure that the model structure can be adjusted for selection phenomena". "The competing risk effect refers to the interaction between the cause-specific mortality rates when the causes of death are classified into two or more categories. In multiple-decrement or cause elimination life-table models, the elimination of a given mortality risk affects not only the mortality rate for that risk but also the mortality rates for all of the remaining active risks.
A third mechanism that must be represented in these models is the effect of ageing on health, effects that are independent of, but may interact with, specific disease processes" (Manton and Stallard, 1984).

To date, very little research has been carried out in the Netherlands into the relationship between morbidity and mortality at population level, although a number of studies carried out by the Steering Committee on Future Health Scenarios have provided an initial impetus. Continuation of this research is recommended. Moreover, research into ways of translating this new information into instruments for optimum measurement of health is also important, since the scientific and social value of research results must surely be questionable, if the methods and instruments applied have not been tested for applicability, reliability and validity. The development of a refined set of instruments is consequently of crucial importance for progress and quality in mortality research.

3.1 Designing and analysing cause-of-death statistics for the period 1900-1990

In order to gain an accurate insight into past and present mortality trends, it is necessary to analyse very precisely which factors determine the mortality level. A first step in this direction is an analysis of the impact on total mortality of different causes of death.

If an analysis of this kind is to be of any use, it must be based on categories which are both biologically and demographically homogeneous, with the many medical causes of death being simultaneously summarised in a limited number of groups. An additional prerequisite for the evaluation of trends, certainly those of mortality, is a long series of observations.

The International Statistical Classification of Diseases, Injuries and Causes of Death (ICD) should, in principle, fulfil this function. However, since its compilation at the beginning of this century, it has been the product of a compromise between the desire to classify deaths according to the disease process which caused death (etiological classification) and the impossibility of clearly defining these processes (which frequently led to the use of anatomical criteria). Furthermore, the ICD has been revised nine times since the beginning of the century, and on some occasions the revisions were quite extensive, which begs the question of how a coherent historical series can be built up on the basis of this material.

Mackenbach has applied a cause-of-death classification to the Netherlands which produces a fairly consistent series of statistics for the period 1950-1984. He also utilised a uniform system of classification for several infectious afflictions covering a longer period (Mackenbach, 1988).

Vallin and Mesle (1988) recently completed a comprehensive research project for France, in which they designed a reclassification table for each transition in classification during the 1925-1978 period. In addition, each cause of death was recoded in such a way that it was possible to analyse the cause of death pattern both anatomically and etiologically. The results of their analysis of cardiovascular mortality in France on the basis of the reconstructed material clearly showed the utility of this kind of reconstruction – which would be most desirable in the Netherlands, both from a historical standpoint as well as with a view to future preliminary investigations.

3.2 Secondary causes of death

Analysis of mortality by cause of death, in the Netherlands as elsewhere, is usually based on the primary or underlying cause of death. However, the causes of dying are generally more complex than can be indicated by one single cause of death. Consequently the medical certificate of cause of death calls for "adventitious diseases which contributed to death, but which are not causally related to the aforementioned diseases". The CBS publishes this information as secondary causes of death. Secondary cause of death is probably established for less than half of all deaths. However, particularly in the case of people who have died at advanced age, secondary cause of death data are often available. Although it is not easy to interpret these data, their utility is, in principle, very great.

As a result of the ageing of the population, multimorbidity is a feature of an increasing number of deaths. It would thus no longer seem appropriate to describe health status solely on the basis of the underlying cause of death, when death is in fact increasingly less the product of immediately lethal events than of chronic degenerative conditions.

When primary and secondary cause of death data are viewed together, a new picture of the relative importance of different causes of death emerges. Mackenbach (1987) points out that the value of standard cause elimination life tables, too, is enhanced when they are supplemented by secondary cause of death data. Cause elimination life tables are based on the assumption that each death has only one cause and that causes of death are independent of each other. In the case of current populations, which are dominated by chronic diseases associated with the ageing process, this assumption is not, however, realistic. Death is multiply caused and causes might operate in a dependent fashion.

Information about secondary causes of death increases our insight into the interdependence of causes of death. Manton and Poss (1979) evaluated three life table models of this kind taking into account these characteristics of the current cause of death pattern.

Analyses of recent changes in the underlying and multiple cause of death mortality data provide important evidence to help select between competing current models of human mortality. One of Manton and Stallard's publications (1982), for example, examines the theory that the recent mortality reductions in the USA were due to the control of lethal sequelae (e.g. pneumonia) of certain chronic diseases and not to a reduction in the incidence rates of these conditions. Failure to find an increase in significance of pneumonia and other infectious diseases as associated causes of mortality at advanced ages have led Manton and Stallard to conclude that other explanations should be entertained.

Clearly, secondary cause of death data should also be utilised for regional and time series analyses to obtain a clearer insight into the impact of different risk factors on mortality. See, for example, Van Putten et al.'s research into breast cancer mortality in the Netherlands (1981). Before these data can be used, however, their quality must be thoroughly researched. Mackenbach makes a case for further research into the availability of the data, their further subclassification by age, sex, place of death, geographical region, etc., and the translatability of the results in terms of the impact of secondary causes of death on both the disease process and mortality process.

3.3 Heterogeneity assumptions and mortality analysis

A formerly common assumption of mortality research was

"that all those at age x are considered to have an equal likelihood of dying. In reality some persons aged x are healthier than others and hence there is heterogeneity with respect to the risk of death. Recognising heterogeneity can greatly complicate mortality analysis. One difficulty is that over time the less healthy die more quickly and thus differential mortality works to change the composition of the population with respect to dying. Standard demographic methods currently recognise the importance of population heterogeneity as evidenced by stratification of mortality analyses by such variables as age, race, sex, cause of death, geographic region, marital status... Unfortunately, stratification and standardisation are only partial responses to the problem of population heterogeneity in mortality risks ... these procedures are only applicable when the dimensions underlying heterogeneity in mortality risks are directly measurable. This is problematic because epidemiological studies of chronic disease risk factors indicate that, even given the 'best' set of risk variables, there consists considerable individual variation in the mortality and morbidity risks of chronic diseases. This individual variation leaves considerable potential for bias in actuarial measures of risk which assume homogeneity of mortality risks within population strata" (Manton and Stallard, 1984b).

Heterogeneity in mortality risks implies a selection process in which those individuals with the lowest risks have a survival advantage. The implications for standard mortality analysis of mortality selection have been researched by Manton and Stallard (1984b). They put forward techniques which can be used in different situations to suit standard mortality analyses whilst taking heterogeneity into account. To date, the scope of applications of this theory and these methods in the Dutch context has yet to be completed.

3.4 Morbidity and mortality: interrelationship at population level

We have already discussed the fact that changes in the disease and cause of death pattern resulted in mortality becoming less indicative of the population health level, hence the increasing importance of population morbidity data.

Van der Maas (1982) pointed out in an interesting article that certain types of effective and desirable medical interventions result not only in mortality reduction but also in an increase in the number of diseases within the population. One of the results of this health care paradox is that, as a result of postponing death by effective primary intervention and effective curative care – particularly in the case of acutely infectious diseases and other acute disorders – those diseases cease to occur and consequently people do not die of them. Thus average age increases as does the risk of getting a chronic degenerative affliction. Generally speaking, the most medical treatment of these afflictions can do, is postpone death due to that particular affliction, thereby protracting the disease process.

The net result of all this is that, at a given age, people have less chance of dying but more chance of needing medical treatment.

An in-depth knowledge of disease processes, based on quantitative data, and analysed demographically, should facilitate the interpretation of mortality trends and variations and the forecasting of future trends. Conversely, mortality data can also be used to obtain data about disease processes. In addition to the fact that morbidity data are becoming increasingly available from health surveys and/or special registers, work is also being done to try to make indirect estimations of morbidity patterns by means of mortality data. Based on statistical models, mortality data by cause of death and survival probability data of cancer patients, Egidi et al. (1988) made an estimation for Italy of the incidence of cancer, its lethality and the survival rate in the period 1955-1979. This sort of approach has the advantage of permitting a much clearer insight into the mechanisms which gave rise to sex- and age-specific mortality variations and a more accurate interpretation of these variations. Similar attempts were undertaken for cardiovascular diseases. Manton and Stallard (1982b) made an estimation of the prevalence of stomach cancer using another approach – based on biomedical data and mortality data. In Manton's view, multidimensional demography provides a good basis for the development of integrated morbidity-mortality models. (See the applications of multidimensional demography published by Haberman, 1983, 1984; Nour and Suchindran, 1984, and Waters, 1984.) Although no comparable applications have been published in the Netherlands, Willekens and Van Poppel (1986) have put forward a research proposal to this end.

3.5 Development and improvement of analytical methods and instruments: expectation of life in good health, cause elimination life tables

We have already discussed the important changes in cause of death specific mortality which arose over the past decades and which were accompanied by a simultaneous stagnation, and subsequent increase in, life expectancy. The interrelationship of these two developments warrants attention. Various different methods have been developed to evaluate the impact of mortality trends due to important causes of death on life expectancy. Although few applications of these methods to the situation in the Netherlands have been carried out to date (Pollard, 1988; Lopez, 1983), those that have been done have already yielded important information concerning causes of fluctuations in male and female, and period-specific, mortality variations.

Closely related to these methods are the so-called cause elimination life tables: these indicate which changes in life expectancy occur when cause-specific mortality is eliminated.

Newman(1986) put forward several supplements for situations in which cause-specific mortality is reduced rather than completely eliminated. His proposed method also allows scope for supplementing the life expectancy concept in such a way that account can be taken of the age division of the group whose mortality risks are eliminated or reduced. Finally, Newman's method also takes into account the fact that the reduction of certain causes of death has an effect on specific population groups in particular.

The interaction of different causes of death on mortality risks poses a particular problem in analysis of cause-specific mortality. The theory of competing risks commonly assumes that risks are independent of one another. In practice, however, this assumption is not always defensible. Data and epidemiological knowledge could be used to ascertain the dependency structure of competing risks.

Given the growing number of old people in the population and the changing morbidity pattern, classical health indicators are becoming increasingly inadequate. When using indicators such as the expectation of life in good health an attempt is made to take into account the fact that some of the 'bonus' years could in fact be disadvantageous for those involved because they might be years spent in a state of dependency, disease and handicaps. Sullivan was one of those who proposed the establishment of an index incorporating population mortality and morbidity levels in one single index. The key variable is variously termed 'life expectancy in good health' or 'life expectancy without handicap'. Legaré (1986) expands on this theme and applies it to Canadian data, whilst Colvez and Robine (1986) and Robine and Colvez (1984) explored the French situation in greater depth. The advantage of the index is that it is a more sensitive indicator of population health status, whilst also permitting a useful differentiation by sex, geographic region, etc.

In theory, calculations using indicators of this kind should also make it possible to examine the relationship between future mortality and morbidity trends, which has presented problems in the past. To this end, three theoretical options are available. The optimistic view presupposes that life expectancy at birth will stabilise in the short term and that mortality due to chronic degenerative disorders will shift to the higher age bracket. The more pessimistic view presupposes that mortality decline will be accompanied by an increased morbidity level. A third option is that morbidity and mortality plot a parallel course. A comparison of temporal trends in life expectancy with expectation of life in good health could assist in discovering which of the three options is most probable. The debate conducted in the USA as to the raising of the retirement age was a good example of the practical importance of information of this kind. In the report of the National Commission on Social Security, one group adopted a minority position by suggesting that "the evidence does not support any claims that longer life is equivalent to longer years of good health", whilst the majority of the commission "anticipated that increased longevity will be accompanied by a corresponding increase in active life." (Feldman, 1986).

Finding suitable data and agreeing the definition of concepts such as 'good health' pose problems. One of the problems of this index is that the calculations presuppose that the probability of dying is independent of the probability of invalidity. More precise hypotheses can in fact only be obtained by longitudinal measurement.

It would seem useful to apply the methods and concepts developed here to the Dutch situation. In terms of life expectancy in good health, data from the CBS health survey could be combined with data from death statistics. These indices could also be expanded to active life expectancies. Research in this field could be integrated with methods developed in multistate demography for the analysis of the transitions of people to and from situations of dependence and independence.

3.6   Generations and mortality trends

Although the impact on mortality trends of health-specific intergeneration variations has been recognised since the 1920s, it was not until the 1970s that a trickle, and gradually a stream, of mortality trend analyses based on this premise began to emerge. In these analyses, mortality trends are seen to be the product of the independent effects of three dimensions: age effect, period effect and cohort effect. Sometimes interactions between the age, period and cohort dimensions are also distinguished (see Barrett, 1973; Osmond and Gardner, 1982; Osmond, Gardner and Acheson, 1982; Tu and Chuang, 1983; Geddes et al., 1985; Mason and Smith, 1985, etc.).

Hobcraft et al. (1984) differentiate between exploratory or descriptive and analytic or explanatory age-period-cohort (APC) analysis. In the former,

> "the main focus is upon assessing relative goodness-of-fit of a variety of models which include terms in some or all of the three dimensions in order to find out whether explanation requires terms in all three dimensions. Unless there is clear evidence of a need for cohort effects it is of little value investing a large amount of effort in producing cohort life tables, in developing models which assume only cohort and age as sources of variation, or in collecting expensive information which is specific to cohorts for use in elaborate regression analysis to explain cohort effects on mortality. The second kind of analysis is concerned with explaining the actual sources of APC variation" (Hobcraft et al., 1984).

Most analyses carried out by demographers are exploratory. One of the problems of in-depth analysis is the explanation of discovered trends. After all, "it is not cohort membership, time period or age itself which affects mortality. Thus it is of considerable interest to seek models with biological underpinnings which explain or capture age, period or cohort variation in mortality" (Hobcraft et al., 1984).

Various models have been developed in the past decade with which age-period-cohort effects on mortality data can be traced in time series and with which indices of age, period and cohort effects can be estimated. The application of APC-models is hampered by difficulties in estimating parameters: the value of age, period or cohort effect parameters should be limited in advance. This makes the results difficult to interpret. Willekens and Baydar put forward a solution to this specification problem. (See also Willekens and Van Poppel, 1986, for a proposal geared to mortality data. See Osmond and Gardner, 1989, for an opposing view.)

There are relatively few Dutch generation-specific mortality studies, and in those that exist, the scope of the generations studied is relatively limited. The CBS generation life tables have not as yet been used for analysis. Specific studies concerning mortality caused by lung cancer (Van het Hoff, 1979) and breast cancer (Van der Putten et al., 1981) have, however, appeared, whilst Van Nooten (1985) made a study of generation mortality trends due to eleven causes of death during the period 1950-1980.

Generation analyses conducted in several countries have provided fresh insights into the background of mortality trends.

A major research preoccupation of those European countries which were actively involved in World War I was examining the health and mortality situation at advanced age, of the extensive group of men who saw active service (Caselli, 1988; Wilmoth et al., 1988). Effects of the War were also apparent in those generations whose adolescence coincided with World War I. Cohort effects need not, however, be confined to this sort of event. Wilmoth et al. (1988) studied French mortality data for the 1899-1981 period and discovered that the Spanish Flu, too, had a marked long-term effect. Generations born in the years 1918-1920 were doubly weakened by the advent of this epidemic: "new-borns, being extremely vulnerable, may have developed various complications, especially of the respiratory system, which left their after effects. Second, the Spanish flu must have been the source of numerous congenital deformations for the children of women struck ill during early pregnancy." Wilmoth finally refers to the cohorts born in the 1950-1959 period which was characterised by strikingly high mortality. It transpired that this was a phenomenon which occurred in many European countries and which was particularly marked in the Netherlands. In Wilmoth's opinion, the cause of this was "the generalisation of hospital-based childbearing. This change was accompanied by developments in obstetrical interventions which without a doubt allowed the saving of a large number of children who would otherwise have died at birth. The first cohorts thus saved may have remained unusually frail afterwards and these interventions may have provoked a certain amount of obstetrical trauma."

As a result of the past massive decline in, particularly infant and child mortality, contemporary cohorts have inherited a health history which differs greatly from that of previous generations. Many researchers wonder whether this altered risk was advantageous to the survivors, to the extent that a selection process killed the least healthy people first, or whether it was in fact more of a disadvantage, given that the survivors' health status must ultimately be negatively affected by the fact that they grew up in a period which was relatively disadvantageous to health as a whole. Empirical research has yielded no clear-cut results; only with the help of age-period-cohort models can these questions be answered.

This field of research, in addition to the proposals for reconstruction of mortality data mentioned above, should be given high priority in the Netherlands.

Further methodologically-based research is needed into two aspects of the generation-specific approach in order to calculate to what degree a relationship can be established between standard procedures used to measure period mortality on the one hand and generation mortality on the other. Translation methods for fertility and marriage have been available for some decades. It would be equally desirable to develop a set of instruments of this kind which could be applied to non-repeatable events (Dinkel, 1985).

The application of APC-models to mortality data may present new prospects for research into the use of mortality models capable of representing age-patterns by means of a limited number of parameters. If, as they grow older, different cohorts exhibit identical mortality patterns – with period effects remaining constant – then age variations can only be attributed to the physiological, psychological and social consequences of ageing. The risk of applying model age schedules to period or cohort data is that some of the age-effect might be attributed to either cohort or period effects. The application of mortality models to cohort- and period-effect adjusted mortality age patterns would probably yield better results than applying these models to non-adjusted mortality data.

4   Differentiation in mortality patterns

Although there is less differentiation in mortality patterns compared with the situation before and during the mortality transition, mortality differences still exist in a number of important areas, and new differences have arisen in other areas. The traditionally small difference in life expectancy between males and females has become much bigger. Mortality differences by ethnic origin has become an important issue as a result of the settlement in the Netherlands of large numbers of persons from countries with mortality patterns which differ fundamentally from the Dutch pattern. The traditional differentiation by age is still relevant: it allows us to identify groups which have benefited less from the mortality decline or which have increasingly been faced with rising mortality.

In a period in which large differences take place in lifestyles and, partly as a result of this, in the population structure, we can gain deeper insight into mortality trends by focussing on patterns of specific groups instead of on general trends. However, we need to pay more attention to changes which take place during an individual's life course than we have done in the past: individuals change their social class, their marital status, they move house, and the effects of such changes can be considerable. These changes can only be studied with the aid of a longitudinal analysis. Special attention has to be paid to the following areas.

4.1   Specific age groups: perinatal mortality, maternal mortality, mortality of the aged

In global terms, the Netherlands belongs to the group of countries with a very low perinatal and maternal mortality. Hoogendoorn (1986), on the other hand, states that in the past decades, the position of the Netherlands has deteriorated compared with countries such as Sweden, Norway and Denmark.

A drawback of perinatal mortality rates is, however, that they are not very reliable, particularly when compared at an international level. For that reason, Hoogendoorn's comparison has been strongly criticised (Keirse, 1987). However, part of the criticism was directed at Hoogendoorns' suggestion that insufficient involvement by clinics at delivery was one of the reasons for the delayed development in the Netherlands. Standard data on perinatal mortality can not provide an answer to such problems. A different line of research is needed, which includes, among other things, ethnic origin. Mackenbach et al. (1988; see also Mackenbach, 1988), suggest that a promising line of research would be to leave the realm of aggregate studies and to investigate individual deaths in an attempt to identify deficiencies in the availability, uptake and effectiveness of health services. Confidential inquiries have been used to obtain detailed information on the care received by the deceased. We might consider incorporating questions on the complete pregnancy history of the respondents in future family history surveys or health surveys. In the Australian Family Project (Santow and Bracher, 1988) such questions yielded extremely important and reliable information on foetal loss. Although the authors did find the usual relationship between age, gravidity and previous experience of foetal loss, their interpretation of this relationship was completely different, especially with respect to the age effect. Yet another alternative would be a longitudinal study in which a group of pregnant women are followed until one, or a few years after the birth of a child: thus, matters such as social characteristics, risk factors and complications during pregnancy and childbirth, morbidity and mortality of the mother and child could be incorporated, and related to subjects which are given priority in fertility studies.

Earlier, the results of a survey into mortality trends until 1978 among people aged over seventy were published in the Netherlands (Van Poppel et al., 1981).

These data revealed a few striking trends: mortality rates of women aged over 75 years dropped sharply, and a further increase in mortality among males seemed very likely to occur. This survey needs to be updated, and should include an analysis of changes in causes of death (Lopez and Hanada, 1982; Kivela, 1985).

4.2   Mortality differences between ethnic groups

Studies of mortality among persons born outside the Netherlands are useful for detecting particular diseases which are common among immigrants, and for investigating aetiology and validating international differences in diseases. Studies have shown that migrants tend to bring with them the particular disease risks of the old country, but these risks usually change within one or two generations, to approximate more closely the disease risks of the host country. This points to the influence of the environment and lifestyle in the aetiology of many major diseases. British studies have shown that mortality differences between migrants are strongly independent of social class differences. Mortality does, however, strongly depend on culture, as reflected in lifestyles (Marmot et al., 1984).

Marmot et al. point out that the British survey has a number of drawbacks. For example, the year of entry and the age at entry into the United Kingdom have not been incorporated. (The effects of these factors have been analysed in Australian surveys by Young, 1986b; Young, 1988.) Thus, the persistence of the differences could not be studied either. Moreover, data on the second generation, born in the U.K., are entirely lacking.

In the Netherlands, only very rough figures are available on this subject. Data published by the Netherlands Central Bureau of Statistics, the CBS, show that the (indirectly standardised) mortality rates of the Surinamese-born population living in the Netherlands are about 20% higher than the mortality rates for the total population of the

Netherlands (Tas, 1986). Among the small group born in the Netherlands Antilles, the mortality rate is 30% lower.

The results of a number of surveys conducted in the early 1980s into perinatal and infant mortality differ from one another. Data gathered in Amsterdam by Doornbos and Nordbeck (1985) show that in the years 1975-1980, the standardised perinatal mortality among children born to mothers born in Surinam or the Netherlands Antilles, was 17% higher, and among children of mothers born elsewhere outside the Netherlands was 19% higher than among children born to Dutch-born mothers. These conclusions are confirmed by data from The Hague. In Amsterdam, infant mortality among children of Surinamese origin, and even more so among children of Moroccan or Turkish origin, was much higher than among the non-immigrant population. This was not the case in The Hague. In Amsterdam, mortality was also significantly higher among Turkish and Moroccan children aged 1 to 3 years. The authors attribute the higher perinatal mortality found among immigrants to the virtual lack of medical care before, during and after childbirth, and the absence of professional maternity care at home after childbirth.

The CBS has published national data for the entire population for the years 1977-1981 (CBS, 1983a). Mortality among Turkish and Moroccan children aged 1 to 4 years was considerably higher than among the total population. This difference became smaller with increasing age. From the age of 40 years (among Moroccans) and 45 years (among Turks), the mortality level was even higher among the Dutch population. Data for 1986-1987 (Van der Erf and Tas, 1988), standardised by age, show that mortality was higher among Turkish men than, in order of importance, among the Dutch, Moroccan and other non-Dutch population. Among women, the mortality rate of both the Moroccans and the Turks is higher than that of the Dutch and other non-Dutch population. If we compare the mortality rates of the entire non-Dutch population with those of the Dutch population, we see that between 1971-1981 and 1982-1984, the mortality rate of the non-Dutch population dropped only among the under-20 age group. Among the Dutch population the decline was more general. However, in terms of average life expectancy, the differences are not very big: about 0.3 years for men and about 1 year for women. However, we must keep in mind that among the non-Dutch population who died, more than 40% came from countries which are similar to the Netherlands as far as the socio-economic and public health system are concerned (West Germany, United Kingsom, Italy, among others).

In view of the unclear situation, and keeping in mind the wishes of the Programming committee on Socio-economic Health Differences, it is desirable to focus on mortality among the non-Dutch population. We could, first of all, analyse mortality by cause of death, specified by a number of nationalities, and supplemented with information on the date of settlement. Such an analysis could be combined with an analysis of cause-of-death-specific mortality in the country of origin. Finally, it would be worthwhile determining the extent to which mortality differences are related to selective return migration by the elderly: data available at institutions such as the Social Insurance Bank could be used for this.

4.3   Differences in health and mortality by sex

Although in the early 1950s the difference in life expectancy between men and women was still more or less the same (2.6 years) as in the period 1870-1950, this difference increased rapidly after 1955. In the early 1970s, the difference was already as much as 6.0 years. It continued to rise slightly for some time, but the difference has now more or less stabilised: in 1987, it stood at 6.6 years (CBS, 1988b).

The relative mortality differences are very high between the ages of 15 and 25, and between 55 and 80 years: at these ages male mortality is more than twice as high as female mortality. In 1980-1983 excess male mortality in the age groups 65-74 years and 75-plus accounted for 31.0 and 26.3% of the differences in male and female life expectancy, respectively. Such percentages were not found anywhere else in Europe (UN, 1988).

Note that in the Netherlands, cancer of the respiratory system was largely responsible for male excess mortality. In 1984, this cause of death resulted in a 1.5-year lower life expectancy, that is 21.4% of the total difference in life expectancy. Only in Belgium was a similar level found. However, male excess mortality through accidents and violent deaths was unexpectedly low. Changes in mortality in the age groups 55-64 years, 65-74 years and 75 years and older contributed to the growing differences in male and female life expectancy by 21.1%, 40.5% and 36.7%, respectively, in the period 1950-1954 to 1980-1983.

Sex-specific differences in life expectancy are caused by a wide variety of factors (Waldron, 1985). Cultural influences on behaviour contribute significantly to these differences. In Western industrial nations, this is true in particular for the social pressures which have encouraged males to smoke more, drink more alcohol, and behave in a more hazardous fashion than women.

In the Netherlands, very little attention has been paid to such mortality differences. Van Brunschot (1980) has studied data which refer to the period up to 1975, concentrating on a description of the situation at that time. However, future research could focus on updating the description and studying in more detail the age groups and causes of death which have been responsible for the growing differences in life expectancy between men and women since the early 1950s, especially since on the one hand, important changes have taken place in the factors which are responsible for the incidence of certain diseases (growing car ownership among women, increased labour force participation by women, fewer risks associated with reproduction, increased participation by women in fitness activities, growing awareness of a healthy diet, etc.), and on the other hand because the available information on the differences between men and women with respect to the above points have become much greater.

It would be worthwhile analysing historical series of regional mortality rates (starting from the 1930s for example) in order to determine whether regional differences in the time at which sex-specific differences take place can be observed. So, supplemented with regional data on the differences between men and women in health-influencing factors, this can throw light on the factors which bring about mortality differences between both sexes. Such an approach has been followed for Belgium, for example (Poliwa, 1977).

This study showed that at the regional level, conditions of social stability have a positive influence on equal mortality risks between men and women. This result is in agreement with the outcome of research into mortality differences by marital status.

4.4 Mortality differences by marital status

In the Netherlands, married men aged 40 years have a life expectancy which is 2.5 years higher than for unmarried men of the same age, almost 2 years higher than for divorced men, and 1.5 years higher than for widowers. These differences are smaller than those found among women: at the age of 40 the difference in life expectancy between married and non-married women is about one year (CBS, 1988a).

Protection hypotheses (marriage plays a protective role, in particular among men), and selection hypotheses are often used to explain these differences (Gove, 1973). According to Verbrugge (1979), the high mortality rate among divorced people in the United States in the 1970s was the result of the higher frequency of high-risk lifestyles among this group, such as smoking, alcohol consumption, few hours of sleep, unhealthy diets, more risky driving habits, and of the occurrence of a selection process (people with health problems get divorced more often and do not remarry as frequently). Widowed persons are often in more or less the same position, but the effects are less noticeable, for various reasons. The group of unmarried people includes many who do not marry for health reasons. The neglect of symptoms and lack of care related to the absence of family responsibilities and lack of encouragement to undertake any actions which could improve one's health, in addition to time constraints are more important than high-risk behaviour. However, these factors have a positive influence on the state of health of married people.

A study carried out in the United States (Mergenhagen et al., 1985), has shown that in the past decades, excess mortality of divorced men had declined significantly, whereas excess mortality increased for most causes of death among the never-married and widowed, and among divorced women. The position of widows and widowers appears to have deteriorated in the past decades. It is not quite clear whether these changes are related to changes in the roles and lifestyles of divorced and widowed people, to changes in the demographic and socio-economic composition of both groups, or to changes in the probability of remarriage.

Whatever the reason, important changes have taken place in the United States in the position of different marital-status groups. Between the early 1950s and the late 1980s the percentage of divorced people shot up. Partly as a result of this increase, the stigma attached to being divorced has weakened somewhat, and the financial position of divorced people has improved. Social support for widowed people has improved in various places, and the position of unmarried people has also changed. They are no longer a group of people who have been negatively selected both socially and financially. It is generally expected that the number of divorced people will continue to grow strongly in the future. Many will enter into a new relationship after some time, and will either remarry or live with their partner. However, the elderly, in particular women, are less likely to do so. At the same time, the position of married people will change: the protective effects, in particular for men, will be reduced because the role of women will change, which in its turn will change the role of men. What will be the consequences of such developments for the health and mortality risks of those involved? This deserves to be studied further.

One factor which could strongly influence life expectancy in the future is the rapidly changing population structure by marital status. In view of the big differences in mortality levels between various marital-status categories signalled earlier, and in view of the changes in the structure of the Dutch population by marital status predicted by the CBS, one would expect the mortality level of the entire population to change when larger proportions of the elderly population spend part of their lives in marital states with higher mortality risks (Serow, 1987). Research in this area could be based for a part on data on mortality by age, sex and marital status gathered on a routine basis by the CBS. A simple analysis of trends through time should be carried out, incorporating a cohort approach. However, if we want to provide answers to specific questions regarding the effects of the time spent in a given marital status on mortality, special print-outs of the CBS mortality registers must be made.

It also remains to be seen whether the newly created lifestyles have a specific influence on morbidity patterns and mortality risks. The numbers involved are probably still too small to warrant statistically reliable observations. The question as to whether the health situation of widowed and divorced people differs, depending on the family burden and responsibilities, and the networks on which they can rely, has not yet been answered.

4.5   Regional mortality differences

During the past few years, the work of Mackenbach in particular, has thrown light on regional mortality differences in the Netherlands. On the basis of an analysis of mortality data by cause of death for COROP-regions in the period 1950-1984, the following can be said:

– There is a contiguous area of relatively high mortality in the south-east part of the country (parts of Gelderland and all regions in Limburg and Noord-Brabant). Other areas with relatively high mortality are Twente, the northern part of Noord-Holland and Greater Amsterdam. A belt of low mortality stretches from the north-east into the central and western parts of the country.
– Since 1950-1954, the mortality pattern has changed in a number of respects. The situation in several regions in the centre of the country has improved, whereas a trend towards a more unfavourable situation was observed in the north.
– For most causes of death, mortality was higher in the south than in the north, even more so in the 1950s than in the 1980s.

Perinatal mortality, avoidable mortality and total mortality decreased less in heavily urbanised regions, and in regions which were centrally located and had a high income. However, the opposite was true for ischemic heart disease, suggesting that there was a more rapid diffusion of new lifestyles in these regions. The faster mortality decline in regions with a high income level suggests that a widening of mortality differentials took place. Total mortality dropped more abruptly in regions where the income level had increased more strongly. The rapid dissemination of medical technology could not explain regional differences in the rate at which mortality from avoidable causes of death dropped.

Further research into the causes of the high mortality rate in the south of the Netherlands deserves high priority. Mackenbach (1988, p. 243) puts forward suggestions for a possible approach. In such research, attention should also be paid to migration processes, and to possible relationships with mortality patterns in neighbouring regions in Belgium and Germany.

Studies of regional mortality differences generally assume that the region of death is also the region in which the individual has spent most of his life. Only on the basis of this assumption can characteristics of the region be meaningfully related to mortality differences between regions. Where research was carried out into the effect of migration on regional mortality differences (Fox and Goldblatt, 1982), mortality among the group of 15 to 44-year-old males appeared to be particularly susceptible to migration. A drawback of this study was that migration could only be studied in a period of no more than five years prior to death.

4.6 Socio-economic mortality differences

Large differences in mortality resulting from the socio-economic circumstances of those involved were found as early as the nineteenth century. These differences have been most thoroughly documented with respect to infant mortality (Van Poppel, 1982a). Note that both data referring to districts classified by the welfare level of their inhabitants and data on the socio-economic position of the children's parents, show that, whereas the absolute differences in infant mortality between districts and socio-economic groups have declined with time, the *relative* differences have not become smaller since the last quarter of the nineteenth century and the mid-twentieth century.

A large number of studies in countries which can be compared with the Netherlands have shown that even today, important differences in health exist between people from different socio-economic backgrounds. These differences are reflected in mortality statistics, among other things (for an overview see Valkonen, 1987; Occupational Mortality, 1988; Socio-economic Differential Mortality, 1988).

From as early as the early 1970s, when social and economic inequality was a prominent political issue, the importance for government policy of research into socio-economic differences in the state of health of the Dutch population was also brought to the fore by demographers. Surprisingly enough, it was not until the mid-1980s, when equality had become a less important political issue, that this research attracted the attention of both academic and political circles. This raises the question as to which factors influenced this renewed attention, which factors triggered interest in this subject in the past, and how the academic and political world have reacted to the results of such research. For this, we can use an existing inventory of research carried out by demographers, statisticians and medics in the past century and a half, into socio-economic differences in infant mortality and, regarding the post-World War II period, adult mortality (Van Poppel, 1981, 1982b). Future research could focus on applying the 'issue-attention-cycle' model developed by Downs (1972) to the process of the formation of public and scientific opinions on this subject.

Dutch material on socio-economic mortality differences is still rather limited, but the conclusion is warranted that the differences in mortality observed are to the detriment of sectors of society with a lower socio-economic status. This conclusion was drawn by, among others, the so-called Zutphen study (Spruit et al., 1987), in which mortality differences by socio-economic status were found among the younger age categories in particular. Similar conclusions were drawn by the Kaunus Rotterdam Intervention study (Van Reek et al., 1986) which yielded data on the city of Rotterdam, by the comparative district study in Amsterdam (Lau-Yzerman, 1979), and by a study into perinatal and infant mortality carried out in The Hague and Amsterdam by Nordbeck (1982). Mackenbach and Van der Maas have drawn up an extensive yet rather general explanatory model for differences in mortality by socio-economic status (1987). A more detailed attempt at explaining these differences was made by Surault (1983), among others.

In their model, Mackenbach and Van der Maas distinguish four levels, running from general (the outcome of social distribution processes) to specific (health problems). An individual's social position, or factors which influence the social position, can affect his health status in a number of ways: a living environment which affects health and determines access to consumer goods, participation in the production process, access to available knowledge, values and norms and habits, access to health care, a place in social networks. These can, in their turn, have concrete repercussions for material and psychological circumstances which are directly related to processes of health and sickness. Such factors, which influence incidence prognoses, include material facilities in one's private life, working conditions and industrial relations, health behaviour and high-risk habits, adequate use of preventative and curative health care and personality traits and psychosocial stress.

The Programming Committee on Socio-economic Health Differences has already drawn up a research programme for the period 1989 to 1993 (Socio-economic Health Differences, 1988). The subjects proposed include secondary analyses of data collected for other purposes, and the design of a longitudinal study. It would be advisable to allow demographers to contribute to this research.

The subcommittee Cause-of-death statistics of the Programming Committee on Socio-Economic Health Differences has made an inventory of the possibilities of drawing up cause-of-death statistics by socio-economic characteristics. The proposal put forward by the committee is currently being examined.

Research into the relationship between socio-economic position and health should not stop at those who form part of the labour force. Far-reaching changes in the social lives of individuals affect their physical situation, and one of the most drastic events in a person's life is without a doubt the termination of employment. The physical consequences of leaving the labour force, both voluntarily and involuntarily therefore deserve to be studied in more detail. Research carried out in Canada (Adams and Lefebvre, 1980) has shown that the mortality risks dropped in the first years following retirement. In the Netherlands, Groothoff (1986) has studied the influence of disability on mortality, on the basis of data for the years 1968-1982. Mortality among those who were forced to leave the labour force was still very high, despite the fact that it was on the downturn. Future research could also focus on the influence of horizontal and vertical social mobility, incorporating factors such as lifestyle, tensions, and the like.

In the periodical surveys of opinions and attitudes of aspects of the population issue in the Netherlands, or MOAB, very little attention has as yet been paid to knowledge of, and opinions about certain causes of death, social inequality in the face of death, and the like. Attention could also be paid to the degree of verbal and actual acceptance of policy measures in the field of health care, illness and death. Both subjects could be dealt with in a new round of the MOAB survey.

5   Consequences of changing mortality patterns

"When connections between mortality reduction and social change are examined, the population analyst often reverts to demographic parochialism. In most discussions of the 'consequences' of the mortality revolution, analyses are restricted to the impact of mortality changes and variations on population growth, age structure, fertility, and to a lesser extent, on migration... Behavioural responses to mortality change comparatively easy to observe statistically and within the disciplinary overview of demographers and economic planners tend to obscure more interesting and ultimately more consequential structural effects" (McNicoll, 1986).

Until now, demographers have indeed focussed on the consequences of (changes in) mortality which can be determined with the aid of demographic and economic models.
An important theme in these studies was the influence of the mortality decline on the age structure.
The ageing of the population used to be a phenomenon which was caused primarily by the fertility decline. Where mortality dropped, this generally resulted in the juvenation of the population since young people in particular benefited from the mortality decline. However, this situation has changed. In the past few decades, mortality has also declined considerably among the elderly, and at the present moment the decreasing mortality rate is partially responsible for the ageing process. Until now, most attempts at determining the effects of a mortality decline on the ageing process were based on stable population models and population projections.
However, Gonnot (1986) applied a simple procedure to determine the extent to which the 60 to 84-year-old population in the Netherlands had grown or declined in the periods 1950-1980 and 1955-1980 as a result of changing mortality patterns. Among women, population growth through mortality decline increased with age, from about 1.2% (60-64 years) to 8.6-9.5% (80-84 years). However, the number of retired men dropped as a result of an increase in mortality.

An empirical sensitivity analysis carried out by the CBS (1983b), shows that changes in the mortality hypotheses, will influence in particular the future population size at more advanced ages. Changes of 1% in the expected mortality rates for a given year at ages between 60 and 90 years, will bring about changes which rise with age in the numbers of married, divorced and unmarried women at the end of that year; this change can vary between 1% and 20%. The numbers of widows are particulary susceptible to changes in the male mortality rate at ages between 20 and 60 years: a 1% change in the mortality rate of married men will trigger a 20% to 10% decline in the numbers of widowed women. Ekamper recently (1989) carried out an analytical sensitivity analysis of both the CBS model and the multidimensional population forecasting model.

Wunsch and Lambert (1981) have presented several scenarios of the long-term effects of mortality changes on the future structure of the Belgian population, by age and sex and by pattern of activities (school-going, employed population and working-age population, retired population, employment sectors) and of the effects on the social security system. In various scenarios, they included assumptions regarding the declining differences in mortality by social background and sex. By comparing the scenarios with the results assuming constant mortality, we see that the population continues to rise and continues to age rapidly. Scenario I also assumes an enormous increase in expenditures on pensions and health insurance. This is even stronger in scenario II. Scenario III assumes greater similarity in the current divergent age structures of various social classes, which will also result in higher expenditures on social security benefits. A similar study was recently published by Janssen (1989), who used Scandinavian relative mortality differences decomposed by level of education as the basis for the mortality scenario, but based his analysis on the Dutch demographic and socio-economic situation.

A totally different type of research includes studies which focus on the significance of the mortality decline in the past on economic growth. However, Dutch studies in this field are totally lacking. In 1973, Usher tried to assess the value of improvements in longevity as an ingredient of economic progress. Recently, his attempt was repeated by Williamson (1984). By applying the human capital theory to English data for the period 1780-1930, we see that the conventional indices of real income, which neglect the improved life expectancy, considerably underestimate the 'true' real income growth. Further research in this field is needed in the Netherlands.

Demographers have also paid a relatively large amount of attention to the results of changing mortality patterns on family structure. After all, in a given generation, the mortality level and mortality trends significantly determine the family life cycle. Young (1986) has studied the degree to which differences in family life cycle experiences of successive birth cohorts depend on the one hand on differences in mortality levels, and on the other hand on differences in other demographic factors (changing percentages of ever-married persons, of childless marriages etc.). Her study shows that there has been a considerable increase in the percentage of women who experienced the 'usual' family phases (marriage, having children, both parents remaining alive until the child leaves the parental home) between the generations born in 1860 and those born in 1940. No less than 55% of this increase may be attributed to changes in the mortality pattern. The mortality decline has also greatly influenced the duration of the period which parents spend together after the children have left the parental home. Until well into the nineteenth century, this family phase was still exceptional. Young has also examined the degree to which we can derive the percentage of married children who look after their widowed fathers or mothers. Research based on mortality patterns decomposed by region or social class supplemented with similarly specified data on nuptiality and fertility patterns can throw light on the historical differentiation in patterns of family life cycle experiences. Such information, with the exception of the general data published by Frinking (1977) and Niphuis-Nell (1974), is totally lacking.

Compared with the important changes which took place in the family life cycle during the first demographic transition, the changes in post-World War II mortality patterns have only had a marginal effect. The most important factor was the increased female mortality decline: as a result, the number of women who survived their husbands has risen considerably, and the period of widowhood has been prolonged. A large number of married men remain married until they die, and they have a companion and helper until the very last moment, whereas elderly women almost always live their last years as widows: in the year 2000 a much larger number of men aged over 60 will still be married as compared with women.

But death also affects upon family relations in another manner. If a married man or woman dies, minor children if present are partially orphaned, and if a father or mother in a single-parent family dies, the child becomes a full orphan. The Social and Cultural Planning Agency expects a considerable increase in the number of one-parent families until the year 2000 contrary to the developments of the past decades: single-parent families headed by a widower will increase from 7000 to 9000, and those headed by a widow will increase from 36,000 to 46,000 (Prins et al., 1986). The reason for this development is that the large post-war birth generations will reach an age at which they run a high risk of losing their partner by death. Since other types of one-parent families will also rise, the number of orphans will grow considerably in the coming years.

However, as the family loses ground to other life styles, and as marriage loses ground to consensual unions, friendships, and the like, the family approach will become a less valuable tool. With the aid of a simple statistical model, and without directly interviewing the elderly, Bytheway (1970) has tried to indicate for friendships, the extent to which individuals in various life phases are affected by the death of a contemporary. His study showed that in the same interval, men lose acquaintances much more rapidly and at a much higher frequency than women. It is highly probable that women become aware of the changing sex differences in mortality: after all, they lose their friends to a lesser degree and at much longer intervals than was the case among earlier generations.

As mentioned earlier, much demographic research into the consequences of mortality differences is one-sided. "Yet the consequences that are of interest here pertain not just to this arithmetic event but to its corporal and cultural antecedents: illness or injury, pain and debility, dread and hope, and so on – qualities and perceptions in part tied to the characteristics of the person and society involved, but in part tied also to the specific cause of death" (McNicoll, 1986).

McNicoll gives examples of a different approach in the field of the drop in infant mortality and mortality at more advanced ages. Due to changes in the number of people who perform certain roles and/or in the degree to which individuals give up certain roles, the normative content of those roles and of the interrelations between those roles must be adjusted. Quoting Blauner, McNicoll states that "the gradual removal of death from common experience lessens the need for reallocation of roles and dissociates reallocation from death. The institutions that coped with it would presumably tend to erode." According to McNicoll, the dwindling importance of religion can also be partly attributed to this.

In a successful attempt at comparing characteristics of the pre-industrial and the present mortality regime, Goldscheider (1971) outlines the influence of former and current mortality patterns on the family and on kinship networks, as well as on the socio-economic and religious and cultural system. When mortality rates are very high – a life expectancy of less than 40 years and a percentage of children dying in their first year of life which exceeds 20 percent – death is an omnipresent factor. Enormous yearly fluctuations in mortality as a result of failed harvests and epidemics created huge uncertainty regarding life expectancy. Death could not be explained in scientific or rational causal terms, but was 'explained away' with non-rational, sometimes mystical reasoning. Death, after all, took its toll most of all in the first years of life.

When, as is the case nowadays, life expectancy approaches 80 years and a negligible percentage of births ends in death within one year of life, death decreasingly disrupts one's daily life. And when such things do happen, the elderly living in old people's and nursing homes are primarily affected. A rational scientific vocabulary is used to explain mortality.

The degree to which someone who has died leaves behind an emptiness depends on how strongly the individual was involved in the functional activities and social life of a given group. As mortality becomes a matter of the elderly who no longer participate in the labour force and who no longer have any parental responsibilities, the disruption of one's daily life through death should dwindle. However, because of the changing character of death, the process of dying takes more time than it used to.

Historically, most deaths prevented were of a type that would have involved very short periods of illness, either because they occurred as a result of the trauma of accident or childbirth, or because they were due to an infection which either killed, or was cured in a short period of time. The elimination of these deaths and the extension of the average length of life imply that long-term illnesses would be relatively more prevalent in the society. The major causes of death in cases of low mortality involve a greater proportion of degenerative and environmental conditions that produce longer periods of incapacity preceding demise (Hull and Jones, 1986).

The declining frequency of death, and the increased concentration at more advanced ages, significantly affect our attitudes towards life. The fact that life expectancy is higher and more predictable than in the past could encourage an attitude of planning for, and looking into the future. This attitude could be strengthened by the fact that death disrupts the social networks of individuals to a lesser, and less predictable, degree. It is worth noting that the mortality decline has a disproportionately large effect on the stability of an individual's social network (Preston, 1978).

Has the changing mortality pattern also changed the definition of being old? Events which take place in the lives of people who are of the same age as the individual in question, are a crucial source of information about what is normal behaviour at that age. When acquaintances of the same age die, people are more likely to think about death in more personal terms. Death then becomes something which belongs to one's own age. When acquaintances and friends begin to die more frequently and at shorter intervals, one begins to define in these terms what is 'old' and what is 'not old'.

Among women in particular, important changes have taken place in this respect, and especially among women the term 'over-65', referring to old-age pensioners, has lost its meaning; it is not until the age of 80 or so that the word takes on negative connotations.

The process of dying has changed with the advent of modern medicine. What is known as a natural death process is becoming less common, and this has generally resulted in a prolonged deathbed, usually in an institutional environment, instead of a short deathbed in one's own surroundings.

About 60% of all people who died in 1970, and about 57% of those who died in 1984, died in a general or psychiatric hospital, in a mental home or in a nursing home. In view of the fact that between 1970 and 1984 the number of people who died at a very old age increased, one would have expected the number of people who died in an institution to have risen as well. This shift is probably related for a part to the declining number of people in such institutions, and for a part to changing attitudes regarding terminal care. Very little information is available regarding the circumstances in which people die in institutions, as compared with the situation at home. Qualitative studies were carried out among a limited population by a Belgian group of researchers (Keirse et al., 1981). They studied, among other things, the consciousness of patients that they were dying, the communication among medical staff and between staff and patients, aspects of suffering, family relations, and the circumstances in which one dies. Demographers can also contribute to such studies, in collaboration with medical sociologists.

The mortality decline has not led to a proportionate decline in the fear of death at every age, and in some situations the statistically observed mortality decline even seems to have gone hand in hand with a heightened fear of death. Can this be attributed to the fact that illness and pain, hope and fear are also all linked to a certain pattern of causes of death?

Until now, research conducted in the Netherlands into the changing meaning of death in society has been more or less anecdotal. The demographic changes described above were hardly incorporated in these studies. Studies dealing specifically with the situation in the Netherlands, such as that by Ariès and Vovelle for the situation in France, are lacking. It's high time demographers started to take the aforementioned subjects seriously, instead of making do with speculative accounts.

6 Conclusions

"So far, the orientation of demographic research has been almost exclusively on the documentation of the extent, and as far as possible precise measurement of differences in mortality levels and patterns among societies as well as within a given population" (Ruzicka, 1985). Income, profession, education, marital status, sex, ethnic origin and other factors of which we know that they are related to health and mortality differences do not in themselves have a direct explanatory power for the existence of health differentials. They are intertwined with a large complex of underlying factors.

"Social and economic processes and other factors deemed responsible for, or associated with, the observed differentials have, in a great majority of studies, been largely hypothesized. Demographers ... have by and large neglected to take account of the biological processes linking the socio-economic environment to health impairment. As yet, except where there is an external cause, death can not occur without being preceded by a shorter or longer illness, a process which is largely governed by biological forces ... Systematic investigations of mortality call for the development of conceptual frameworks which would incorporate ... the biological mechanisms involved in the processes of health impairment, some of which lead, eventually, to a fatal outcome. The concepts developed in medical science disciplines will have to be adopted in a creative fashion..." (Ruzicka, 1985, pp. 185-187).

There is increasing recognition that knowledge and understanding of mortality can not be enhanced and advanced much further unless the traditional disciplinary boundaries are crossed.

Since the early 1980s, the response to this call has been reasonably successful in the field of infant mortality in developing countries. The 'proximate determinants framework' developed by Mosley can be seen as an important step in the right direction. In this model, biologically determined disease processes in children are linked to their social determinants in the family and wider community. Proximate determinants are basic biosocial mechanisms that directly influence the risks of morbidity and mortality. These determinants include individual-level variables (such as traditions, norms and attitudes), household-level variables (income, wealth) and community-level variables (ecological environment, political economy, health system). By drawing up a coherent framework in which these proximate determinants and the independent variables can be incorporated, it becomes possible to carry out an integral analysis of biological and social determinants of infant mortality. Thus, causality and possible interactions can be specified.

Van Norren and Van Vianen (1986) have developed an adapted version of this model, in which greater emphasis is placed on the behavioural aspects of the so-called intermediate variables, and in which a number of variables have been more closely specified.

Historical research and research into present-day mortality differences and trends, would benefit enormously from developments in these and other explanatory models both for infant mortality and for mortality at more advanced ages.

The same is true for studies of closely related subjects such as the relationship between morbidity and mortality at the population level, the heterogeneity of mortality risks, primary and secondary causes of death, and generation analyses of mortality. These subjects play a prominent role in medical demography, as propagated by Manton and Stallard. In the Netherlands, research in this field is still in its infancy.

References

Adams, O.B. and L.A. Lefebvre (1980), *Retirement and mortality. An examination of mortality in a group of retired Canadians*, Ottawa.

Alter, G. (1983), Estimating mortality from annuities, insurance, and other life contingent contracts, *Historical Methods*, Vol. 16, no. 2, pp. 45-58.

Alter, G., J.C. Riley (1989), Frailty, sickness and death: models of morbidity and mortality in historical populations, *Population Studies*, Vol. 43, no. 1, pp. 25-47.

Arriaga, E.E. (1984), Measuring and explaining the change in life expectancies, *Demography*, Vol. 21, pp. 83-96.

Barrett, J.C. (1973), Age, time and cohort factors in mortality from cancer of the vertix, *The Journal of Hygiene*, Vol. 71, pp. 253-259.

Barrett, J.C. (1980), Cohort mortality and prostate cancer, *Journal of Biosocial Science*, Vol. 12, pp. 341-344.

Benedictow, O.J. (1987), Morbidity in historical plague epidemics, *Population Studies*, Vol. 41, no. 3, pp. 401-432.

Brunschot, C.J.M. van (1980), Sterfteverschillen tussen mannen en vrouwen. Een verkenning van verklaringen voor met name de Nederlandse situatie, *Tijdschrift voor sociale Geneeskunde*, 58, no. 1, pp. 14-18.

Bytheway, W.R. (1970), Aspects of old age in age-specific mortality rates, *Journal of Biosocial Science*, Vol. 2, no. 4, pp. 337-349.

Caselli, G. (1988), Les effets de génération dans les différences de mortalité et leur évolution, in: J. Vallin, S. D'Souza, A. Palloni, *Mesure et analyse de la mortalité. Nouvelles approches*, PUF, Paris, pp. 251-272.

Caselli, G., J.W. Vaupel, A.I. Yashin (1985), Mortality in Italy: contours of a century of evolution, *Genus*, Vol. XLI, no. 1-2, pp. 39-56.

CBS (1942), *Sterftetafels voor Nederland afgeleid uit de waarnemingen over de periode 1931-1940*, The Hague.

CBS (1975), *Generatie-sterftetafels voor Nederland, afgeleid uit waarnemingen over de periode 1871-1973*, Voorburg.

CBS (1983a), Sterfte onder Turkse en Marokkaanse personen in Nederland, *Maandstatistiek van de bevolking*, 31, no. 6, pp. 13-14.

CBS (1983b), Prognose 1980, gevoeligheidsanalyse van het rekenmodel, *Maandstatistiek van de bevolking*, Jrg. 31, no. 12, pp. 20-30.

CBS (1988a), *Overlevingstafels naar burgerlijke staat, 1981-1985*, Voorburg.

CBS (1988b), Sterfte 1983-1987, *Maandstatistiek van de bevolking*, Jrg. 36, no. 9, 1988, pp. 32-37.

Chernichovsky, D. (1986), Interactions between mortality levels and the allocation of time for leisure, training, consumption and saving over the life cycle, in: United Nations, *Consequences of mortality trends and differentials*, New York, pp. 126-134.

Cherry, S. (1980), The hospitals and population growth: the voluntary general hospitals, mortality and local populations in the English provinces in the eighteenth and nineteenth centuries, part 1 and part 2, *Population Studies*, Vol. 34, no. 1, pp. 59-77; Vol. 34, no. 2, pp. 251-267.

Colvez, A., J.M. Robine et al. (1986), L'espérance de vie sans incapacité en France en 1982, *Population*, 41e Année, no. 6, pp. 1025-1043.

Crimmins, E.M. (1986), The social impact of recent and prospective mortality decline among older Americans, *Sociology and social research*, Vol. 70, no. 3, pp. 192-199.

Dijk, J.P. van (1981), *Doodsoorzakenclassificaties 1750-1950*, Groningen.

Dinkel, R.H. (1985), The seeming paradox of increasing mortality in a highly industrialized nation: the example of the Soviet Union, *Population Studies*, 39, pp. 87-97.

Doornbos, J.P.R. and H.J. Nordbeck (1985), *Perinatal mortality. Obstetric risk factors in a community of mixed ethnic origin in Amsterdam*, Dordrecht.

Downs, A. (1972), Up and down with ecology, the issue-attention cycle, *The Public Interest*, 28, pp. 38-50.

Dronkers, J. et al. (1987), *Voorstel tot oprichting van de databank 'geboorte-acten Nederland 1815-1920'*, Utrecht.

Dunning, A.J. and W.I.M. Wils, eds. (1987), *The heart of the future. The future of the heart, Vol. 2., Background and Approach*, Dordrecht, 1987.

Egidi, V.A. Golini, R. Capocaccia, A. Verdecchia (1988), Une modèle d'évaluation de l'état de santé de la population à partir de mesures de la mortalité, in: J. Vallin, S. D'Souza, A. Palloni, *Mesure et analyse de la mortalité, Nouvelles approches*, PUF, Paris, pp. 425-442.

Ekamper, P. (1989), *Gevoeligheidsfuncties voor meerdimensionale bevolkingsprognose modellen met een twee-geslachten algoritme*, Groningen.

Erf, R.F. van der and R.F.J. Tas (1988), Niet-Nederlanders op 1 januari 1988, *Maandstatistiek van de bevolking*, Jrg. 36, no. 12, 1988, pp. 12-19.

Feldman, J.J. (1986), Work ability of the aged under conditions of improving mortality, in: United Nations, *Consequences of mortality trends and differentials*, New York, pp. 185-191.

Fox, A.J. and P.O. Goldblatt (1982), *Longitudinal Study: socio-economic mortality differentials, 1971-75. England and Wales*, London, HMSO.

Friedlander, D., J. Schellekens, E. Ben-Moshe and A. Keysar (1985), Socio-economic characteristics and life expectancies in nineteenth-century England: a district analysis, *Population Studies*, Vol. 39, no. 1, pp. 137-153.

Frinking, G.A.B. (1977), L'incidence de la surmortalité masculine sur le cycle de la vie familiale, in: J. Cuisenier, ed., *The Family Life Cycle in European Societies*, The Hague, pp. 277-283.

Geddes, M., C. Osmond, A. Barchielli and E. Buiatti (1985), Analysis of trends in cancer mortality in Italy 1951-1978: the effects of age, period of birth and period of death, *Tumori*, Vol. 71, pp. 101-110.

Goldscheider, C. (1971), *Population, modernization and social structure*, Boston.

Golini, A., V. Egidi (1984), Effect of morbidity changes on mortality and population size and structure, in: J. Vallin, J.H. Pollard and L.Heligman, eds., *Methodologies for the collection and analysis of mortality data*, Liège, 1984, pp. 405-448.

Gonnot, J.P. (1985), *Some selected aspects of mortality in the ECE region*, Economic Commission for Europe, Geneva, 1985.

Gove, W.R. (1973), Sex, marital status and mortality, *American Journal of Sociology*, 78, pp. 45-67.

Groothoff, J.W. (1986), *Gezondheidstoestand van de beroepsbevolking. Een studie naar de indicatoren arbeidsongeschiktheid, sterfte, gezondheidszorg*, Groningen.

Grundeman, R.W.M. (1985), *Migranten, gezondheid en kontakten met de Nederlandse gezondheidszorg. Een overzicht van ontwikkelingen in de periode 1975-1985, gebaseerd op onderzoekspublikaties*, NIPG, Leiden.

Haaften, M. van (1923), De sterftetafels, afgeleid uit de volkstellingen in Nederland, *Het Verzekerings Archief*, Jrg. IV, pp. 129-163.

Haberman, S. (1983), Decrement tables and the measurement of morbidity I, *Journal of the Institute of Actuaries*, 110, pp. 361-381.

Haberman, S. (1984), Decrement tables and the measurement of morbidity II, *Journal of the Institute of Actuaries*, 111, pp. 73-86.

Hobcraft, J. and W. Gilks (1984), Age, period and cohort analysis in mortality studies, in: J. Vallin, J.H. Pollard and L. Heligman, eds., *Methodologies for the collection and analysis of mortality data*, Liège, pp. 245-264.

Hoff, N.M. van het (1979), Cohort analysis of lung cancer in the Netherlands, *International Journal of Epidemiology*, 1979, Vol. 8, no. 1, pp. 41-47.

Hofstee, E.W. (1978), *De demografische ontwikkeling van Nederland in de eerste helft van de negentiende eeuw. Een historisch-demografische en sociologische studie*, Deventer.

Hofstee, E.W. (1981), *Korte demografische geschiedenis van Nederland van 1800 tot heden*, Haarlem.

Hofstee, E.W. (1983), Geboorten, zuigelingenvoeding en zuigelingensterfte in hun regionale verscheidenheid in de 19e eeuw, *Bevolking en Gezin*, Supplement 1983, no. 2, pp. 7-60.

Hoogendoorn, D. (1986), Indrukwekkende en tegelijk teleurstellende daling van de perinatale sterfte in Nederland, *NTVG*, 130, no. 32, pp. 1436-1440.

Hoogendoorn, D. (1987), Moedersterfte in Nederland en in enkele andere Westeuropese landen, *NTVG*, 131, no. 25, pp. 1084-1087.

Hull, T.H. and G.W. Jones (1986), Introduction: international mortality trends and differentials, in: United Nations, *Consequences of mortality trends and differentials*, New York, pp. 1-9.

Jansen, P.C. and J.M.M. de Meere (1982), Het sterftepatroon in Amsterdam 1774-1930. Een analyse van de doodsoorzaken, *Tijdschrift voor sociale geschiedenis*, Jrg. 8, no. 26, pp. 180-223.

Janssen, A.M.J. (1989), *Differentiële sterfte en de sociale zekerheidsuitgaven aan bejaarden. Vier scenario's voor de jaren 1987-2035*, Tilburg.

Keirse, M., F. Baro, K. Pauwels and M. van Nevel (1981), *Sterven van bejaarden. Onderzoeksproject in een algemeen ziekenhuis*, CBGS-rapport 46/1981, Brussel.

Keirse, M.J.N.C. (1987), Registratie en betrouwbaarheid van prenatale sterfte in Nederland, *NTVG*, Vol. 131, no. 21, pp. 891-895.

Kivela, S. (1985), Changes in mortality among the elderly Finnish population, 1951-1979, *Social Science and Medicine*, Vol. 21, pp. 799-805.

Kobrin, F.E. and G.E. Hendershot (1977), Do family ties reduce mortality? Evidence from the United States, 1966-1968, *Journal of Marriage and the Family*, 39, pp. 737-745.

Kunitz, S.J. (1987), Explanations and ideologies of mortality patterns, *Population and Development Review*, Vol. 13, no. 3, pp. 379-408.

Lau-Yzerman, A., J.D.F. Habbema, P.J. van der Maas, T. van der Bos, J.B.J. Drewes, P.M. Verbeek-Heida and J.W. Oosterbaan (1979), *Vergelijkend buurtonderzoek naar sterfte, ziekenhuisopname en langdurige arbeidsongeschiktheid in Amsterdam*, Rapport no. 1, Sterfte, Amsterdam.

Légaré, J. (1986), *Espérance de vie en bonne santé: construction et applications*, Chaire Quetelet 86, Populations Agées et Révolution grise, Louvain-La-Neuve.

Lesthaeghe, R. (1983), De borstvoeding als verklaring voor regionale verschillen in vruchtbaarheid en zuigelingensterfte; Nederland en België in het midden van de XIXe eeuw, *Bevolking en Gezin*, Supplement 1983, nr. 2, pp. 61-84.

Lopez, A.D. (1983), The sex mortality differential in developed countries, in: A.D. Lopez and L.T. Ruzicka, eds., *Sex differentials in mortality. Trends, determinants and consequences*, Canberra.

Lopez, A. and K. Hanada (1982), Mortality patterns and trends among the elderly in developed countries, *World Health Statistics Quarterly*, Vol. 35, pp. 203-224.

Maas, P.J. van der (1982), Mythen over vergrijzing en volksgezondheid, *Tijdschrift voor sociale geneeskunde*, 60, no. 23, pp. 711-721.

Maas, P.J. van der, J.P. Mackenbach and L.J. Gunning-Schepers (1987), Sociaal-economische gezondheidsverschillen: op weg naar een onderzoeksstrategie, in: *Wetenschappelijke Raad voor het Regeringsbeleid*, pp. 157-169.

Mackenbach, J.P. (1987), Secundaire doodsoorzaken, *Tijdschrift voor Sociale Gezondheidszorg*, 65, no. 16, pp. 524-528.

Mackenbach, J.P. (1988), *Mortality and medical care. Studies of mortality by cause of death in the Netherlands and other European countries*, Rotterdam.

Mackenbach, J.P. and P.J. van der Maas (1987), Sociale ongelijkheid en verschillen in gezondheid; een overzicht van de belangrijkste onderzoeksbevindingen, in: *Wetenschappelijke Raad voor het Regeringsbeleid*, pp. 59-95.

Mackenbach, J.P., A.E. Kunst, C.W.N. Looman, J.D.F. Habbema and P.J. van der Maas (1988), *Gezondheiszorg en 'vermijdbare' sterfte. Voorbeelden van het gebruik van sterftegegevens voor nationaal en regionaal gezondheidszorgbeleid*, Deel 1 en 2, Rotterdam.

Manton, K.G. and S.S. Poss (1979), Effects of dependency among causes of death for cause elimination life table strategies, *Demography*, Vol. 16, no. 2, pp. 313-328.

Manton, K.G. and E. Stallard (1982a), The use of mortality time series data to produce hypothetical morbidity distributions and project mortality trends, *Demography*, Vol. 19, no. 2, pp. 223-230.

Manton, K.G. and E. Stallard (1982b), Temporal trends in U.S. multiple cause of death mortality data: 1968 to 1977, *Demography*, Vol. 19, no. 4, pp. 527-548.

Manton, K.G. and E. Stallard (1984a), *Recent trends in mortality analysis*, Orlando, etc.

Manton, K.G. and E. Stallard (1984b), Heterogeneity and its effect on mortality measurement, in: J. Vallin, J.H. Pollard and L. Heligman, eds., *Methodologies for the collection and analysis of mortality data*, Liège, pp. 265-304.

Marmot, M.G., A.M. Adelstein and L. Bulusu (1984), *Immigrant mortality in England and Wales 1970-1978. Causes of death by country of birth*, OPCS, Studies on Medical and Population Subjects, no. 47, London.

Mason, W.M. and H.L. Smith (1985), Age-period-cohort analysis and the study of deaths from pulmonary tuberculosis, in: W.M. Mason and S.E. Fienberg, eds., *Cohort Analysis in social Research*, New York, pp. 151-227.

McKeown, T. (1976), *The modern rise of population*, London.

McNicoll, G. (1986), Adaptation of social systems to changing mortality régimes, in: United Nations, *Consequences of mortality trends and differentials*, New York, pp. 13-19.

Mergenhagen, P.B. Lee and W. Gove (1985), Till death do us part: changes in the relationship between marital status and mortality, *Sociology and social research*, no. 1. pp. 53-56.

Mosley, W.H. (1985), *Biological and socioeconomic determinants of child survival. A proximate determinants framework integrating fertility and mortality variables*, in: IUSSP, International Population Conference, Florence 1985, Vol. 2, pp. 189-208, Liège.

Nam, C. (1988), Pour une analyse des causes multiples de décès, in: J. Vallin, S. D'Souza and A. Palloni, *Mesure et analyse de la mortalité. Nouvelles approches*, Paris: PUF, pp. 351-366.

Neurdenburg, M.G. (1929), *Doodsoorzaak en statistiek*, Amsterdam.

Newman, S.C. (1986), A generalization of life expectancy which incorporates the age distribution of the population and its use in the measurement of the impact of mortality reduction, *Demography*, Vol. 23, no. 2, pp. 261-274.

Nijhuis, H.G.J., H.J. Nordbeck and S.J.M. Belleman (1985), Perinatale en zuigelingen-sterfte in Amsterdam en 's-Gravenhage. Een probleem van migranten, *Tijdschrift voor sociale gezondheidszorg*, 63, no. 10, pp. 409-414.

Niphuis-Nell, M. (1974), *De gezinsfasen*, Amsterdam.

Noordam, D.J. (1986), *Leven in Maasland. Een hoogontwikkelde plattelandssamenleving in de achttiende en het begin van de negentiende eeuw*, Hilversum.

Nooten, W.N. van (1985), *Mortaliteitsonderzoek. Gebruik van log-lineaire modellen voor de analyse van trends in sterfte bij een elftal doodsoorzaken*, NIPG, Leiden.

Nordbeck, H.J. (1982), Perinatale en zuigelingensterfte in de grote steden, in het bijzonder bij allochtonen, in: M.J. Dantz, H.A. van Geuns and H.J. Nordbeck, eds., *Verslagboek Symposium Gezondheidszorg voor ethnische minderheden*, NIPG/TNO, 's-Gravenhage, pp. 99-115.

Norren, B. van, and H.A.W. van Vianen (1986), *The malnutrition-infections syndrome and its demographic outcome in developing countries. A new model and its applications*, PCDO, The Hague.

Nour, E.L. and C.M. Suchindran (1984), Multi-state mortality by cause of death: a life table analysis, *Journal of the Royal Statistical Society*, A, Vol. 147, pp. 582-597.

NPDO (1980), *Rapport van de ad hoc werkgroep sterfte*, Voorburg.

Occupational Mortality in the Nordic Countries 1971-1980 (1988), *Statistical Reports of the Nordic Countries*, Copenhagen: Nordic Statistical Secretariat.

Osmond, C. and M.J. Gardner (1982), Age, period and cohort models applied to cancer mortality rates, *Statistics in Medicine*, 1, pp. 245-259.

Osmond, C., M.J. Gardner and E.D. Acheson (1982), Analysis of trends in cancer mortality in England and Wales during 1951-80 separating changes associated with period of birth and period of death, *British Medical Journal*, 284, pp. 1005-1008.

Osmond, C. and M.J. Gardner (1989), Age, period, cohort models. Non-overlapping cohorts don't resolve the identification problem, *American Journal of Epidemiology*, Vol. 129, no. 1, pp. 31-35.

Poliwa (1977), *Etat démographique de la Wallonie et éléments pour une politique de population*, Rapport POLIWA, Louvain-la-Neuve.

Pollard, J. (1988a), Causes de décès et espérance de vie: quelques comparaisons internationales, in: J. Vallin, S. D'Souza and A.Palloni, *Mesure et analyse de la mortalité, Nouvelles approches*, PUF, Paris, pp. 291-316.

Pollard, J.H. (1988b), On the decomposition of changes in expectation of life and differentials in life expectancy, *Demography*, Vol. 25, no. 2, pp. 265-276.

Poppel, F.W.A. van, and A. Janssen (1981), *De ontwikkeling van het sterfterisico van personen die de 70-jarige leeftijd hebben overschreden*, NIDI, Intern Rapport nr. 23, Voorburg.

Poppel, F.W.A. van (1981), A review of research into the socio-economic determinants of mortality since the Second World War, in: UNPD, WHO, CICRED, *Socio-economic differential Mortality in industrialized societies*, Vol. 1, Paris, pp. 67-76.

Poppel, F.W.A. van (1982a), Sociale ongelijkheid voor de dood. Het verband tussen sociaal-economische positie en zuigelingen- en kindersterfte in Nederland in de periode 1850-1940, *Tijdschrift voor Sociale Geschiedenis*, Jrg. 8, nr. 27, pp. 231-281.

Poppel, F.W.A. van (1982b), Differential mortality as a subject of research policy and as a theme in political discussions: the case of the Netherlands in the 70's, in: UNPD, WHO, CICRED, *Socio-economic differential Mortality in industrialized societies*, Vol. 2, Paris, pp. 49-54.

Preston, S. (1977), Mortality trends, *Annual Review Sociology*, 3, pp. 163-178.

Prins, A., K. Mesman Schultz and F. Leeuw (1986), Wezen en half wezen in Nederland. Een vergeten groep in het sociaal-wetenschappelijk beleidsonderzoek?, *Jeugd en samenleving*, Jrg. 16, no. 6, pp. 356-372.

Putten, D.J. van, J.D.F. Habbema, G.J. van Oortmarssen and P.J. van der Maas (1981), *Preliminaries for the evaluation of breast cancer screening*, Department of Public Health and Social Medicine, Rotterdam.

Reek, J. van, A. Appels, W.M. van Zutphen, F. Otten, A.J. Ten Thije, P.G.H. Mulder and F. Sturmans (1987), Mortaliteit en cardiovasculaire morbiditeit naar sociale klasse bij Rotterdamse mannen in de periode 1972-1981, *Bevolking en gezin*, 1987, no. 3, pp. 1-6.

Robine, J.M. and A. Colvez (1984), Espérance de vie sans incapacité et ses composantes: de nouveaux indicateurs pour mesurer la santé et les besoins de la population, *Population*, 39e Année, no. 1, pp. 27-46.

Rogmans, W.H.J. (1983), Voorlichting en educatie inzake veiligheid in de privésfeer: een ontwerp voor een systematische aanpak, *Tijdschrift voor sociale gezondheidszorg*, 61, no. 1, pp. 28-32.

Rutten, W.J.M. (1985), Mortaliteit en medicalisering: een regionaal-differentiële analyse van de sterfte zonder geneeskundige behandeling in Nederland, ca. 1870-1900, *Holland*, 17, pp. 131-160.

Ruzicka, L.T. (1985), Conceptual frameworks for the study of socio-biological correlates of mortality, in: IUSSP, *International Population Conference*, Florence 1985, Vol. 2, pp. 185-187, Liège.

Santow, G. and M. Bracher (1988), *Do gravidity and age affect pregnancy outcome?*, Australian Family Project, Working Paper no. 4, Canberra.

Schellekens, J. (1989), Mortality and socioeconomic status in two eighteenth-century Dutch villages, *Population Studies*.

Schoen, R. (1986), The direct and indirect effects of mortality decline on demographic variables, in: United Nations, *Consequences of mortality trends and differentials*, New York, pp. 20-30.

Serow, W.J. et al. (1987), *Research plan on marital status, differential mortality and longevity*.

Sociaal-economische gezondheidsverschillen (1988), *Een onderzoeksprogramma voor de periode 1989 t/m 1993*, Programmacommissie sociaal-economische gezondheidsver-schillen.

Socio-economic differential mortality (1988), *Seminar*, 9-12 and 13-16 September, 1986, Zamardi, Hungary, Hungarian Statistical Office, UNFPA, UNPD, WHO, CICRED, Vol. 5 and Vol. 6. s.l.

Spruit, I.P., D. Kromhout and T.J. Duijkers (1987), Sociaal-economische status; sterfte en de rol van gedrag, een studie naar beroepsklasse, roken en sterfte in Zutphen, in: *Wetenschappelijke Raad voor het Regeringsbeleid*, pp. 97-111.

Stuurgroep Toekomstscenario's Gezondheidszorg (1986), *Het hart van de toekomst. De toekomst van het hart. Scenario's over hart- en vaatziekten 1985-2010*, Utrecht/Antwerpen.

Stuurgroep Toekomstscenario's Gezondheidszorg (1988), *Ongevallen in het jaar 2000. Deel 2. Achtergrondstudies en wetenschappelijke verantwoording. Scenario's over Ongevallen en Traumatologie*, Utrecht/Antwerpen.

Surault, P. (1983), Les déterminants socio-culturels de la morbidité et de la mortalité, in: *Morbidité et mortalité aux âges adultes dans les pays développés*, Chaire Quetelet, 1982, Louvain-la-Neuve, pp. 193-243.

Swartsenburg, L.A. (1981), *Sterfte in de stad 1869-1910. Een onderzoek naar het verloop van de sterftedaling in de Nederlandse steden met behulp van de doodsoorzakenstatistiek*, Amsterdam.

Szreter, S.R.S. (1988), The importance of social intervention in Britain's mortality decline ca. 1850-1914, a reinterpretation of the role of public health, *Social History of Medicine*, Vol. 1, no. 1, pp. 1-38.

Tas, R.F.J. (1986), De demografische ontwikkeling van de Surinaamse en Antilliaanse bevolking in Nederland, 1971-1986, *Maandstatistiek van de bevolking*, Jrg. 34, no. 10, pp. 25-39.

Tu, E.J.C. and J.L.C. Chuang (1983), Age, period and cohort effects on maternal mortality: a linear logit model, *Social Biology*, 30, pp. 400-412.

United Nations (1988), Sex differentials in life expectancy and mortality in developed countries: an analysis by age groups and causes of death from recent and historical data, *Population Bulletin of the United Nations*, no. 25, pp. 65-107.

Valkonen, T. (1987), *Social inequality in the face of death*, Europaen Population Conference 1987, Jyväskylä, IUSSP, EAPS, FINNCO, Plenaries, Helsinki, pp. 201-261.

Vallin, J., F. Meslé (1988), *Les causes de décès en France de 1925 à 1978*, Paris.

Vandenbroeke, C., F.W.A. van Poppel and A.M. van der Woude (1981), De zuigelingen- en kindersterfte in België en Nederland in seculair perspectief, *Tijdschrift voor Geschiedenis*, pp. 461-491.

Verbrugge, L.M. (1979), Marital status and health, *Journal of marriage and the family*, Vol. 41, no. 2, pp. 267-285.

Verdoorn, J.A. (1965), *Volksgezondheid en sociale ontwikkeling; Beschouwingen over het gezondheidswezen te Amsterdam in de 19e eeuw*, Utrecht/Antwerpen.

Waldron, I. (1985), What do we know about causes of sex differences in mortality? A review of the literature, *Population Bulletin of the United Nations*, No. 18, pp. 59-76.

Ware, H.R. (1986), Differential mortality decline and its consequences for the status and roles of women, in: United Nations, *Consequences of mortality trends and differentials*, New York, pp. 113-125.

Waters, H.R. (1984), An approach to the study of multiple state models, *Journal of the Institute of Actuaries*, 111, pp. 363-374.

Wetenschappelijke Raad voor het Regeringsbeleid (1987), *De ongelijke verdeling van gezondheid*, Verslag van een conferentie gehouden op 16-17 maart 1987, Voorstudies en achtergronden, 's-Gravenhage.

Williamson, J.G. (1984), British Mortality and the Value of Life, 1781-1931, *Population Studies*, 38, pp. 157-172.

Wilmoth, J., J. Vallin and G. Caselli (1988), *When does a cohort's mortality differ from what we might expect?*, Paper presented at the Annual Meeting of the PAA, New Orleans.

Woods, R.I., P.A. Waterson and J.H. Woodward (1988), The causes of rapid infant mortality decline in England and Wales, 1861-1921 Part I, *Population Studies*, Vol. 42, no. 3, pp. 343-366.

Wunsch, G. and A. Lambert (1981), *Life-styles and death styles. Differentials and consequences of mortality trends*, Département de Démographie, UCL, Louvain-la-Neuve, Working Paper, no. 103.

Young, C.M. (1986a), The residential life cycle: mortality and morbidity effects on living arrangements, in: United Nations, *Consequences of mortality trends and differentials*, New York, pp. 101-112.

Young, C.M. (1986b), *Selection and survival. Immigrant Mortality in Australia*, Canberra.

Young, C.M. (1988), Ethnic differences in mortality with special reference to the effect of age and period of residence: the case of Australia, in: *Occupational mortality*, Vol. 6, pp. 252-283.

Emerging Issues in Demographic Research
C.A. Hazeu and G.A.B. Frinking (Editors)
© Elsevier Science Publishers B.V. , 1990

Chapter 16

DETERMINANTS AND CONSEQUENCES OF MORTALITY IN THE NETHERLANDS: SOME SUGGESTIONS FOR RESEARCH; A COMMENT

Godelieve Masy-Stroobant

The paper that Van Poppel prepared gives a very clear and comprehensive overview of today's state-of-art of the demographic research and methodology in the field of mortality in general. The author also identifies the numerous possible research subjects that can be undertaken given the data available in the Netherlands.

A very large scope of research subjects are thus proposed:

- An in-depth demographic analysis of the nineteenth century mortality and causes-of-death statistics, including longitudinal mortality analysis by birth cohort, regional mortality and a reappraisal of the quality of those data in order to improve their comparability over time.
- The very new methodological developments in the field of morbidity/mortality are presented, in particular the heterogeneity assumptions, the concept of expectation of life in good health, multistage analysis of the morbidity/mortality process.
- The third series of subjects is devoted to differential mortality with frequent references to the 'lifestyle' explanations of the traditionally observed differences by sex, marital status, ethnic group, socio-economic status or region of residence.

In doing so the author gives us an inventory of what a demographer can do on his own using the traditional (demographic) administrative sources of data in the field of mortality. His presentation is also operational as he identifies the feasibility of the research subjects with the available Dutch data.

But besides a more or less explicitly expressed need to update data and demographic analysis in the field of mortality, I hardly could find any structured research objective (and hence research programme) in this paper. I am truly convinced of the great importance of producing adequate, compatible and comparable measures of a demographic phenomenon like mortality, and the kind of descriptive analysis the demographer performs is invaluable. Nevertheless research on the determinants and consequences of mortality in the Netherlands needs to go a step further and initiate more causal research, opening the field to other ways of thinking, other methods and to have recourse to more comprehensive data.

The traditional distinction between infant/child mortality and mortality at the other ages is seldom present in the paper whereas descriptive and causal analysis in the field revealed their fundamental differences.

The Belgian nineteenth century history is a good illustration of the necessary distinction between both mortality and/or life periods: adult mortality and even child mortality with the only exception of infant mortality improved from the mid-seventies onwards, whereas the infant mortality rates began to drop only at the turn of the century. So did other European countries. The McKeown nutritional hypotheses refer merely to overall mortality and did not take into account the specificity of the regional and/or national infant feeding practices which possible explain the differences observed in the characteristics and the timing of improvement of the two mortality types.

The data sources currently available and their related methodology differ also fundamentally for the analysis of both types of mortality: linking birth and death records is a very common base for the study of infant mortality at the individual level, whereas linking death records and census individual data is more in use for mortality at older ages, etc. The paper contains no information nor proposals for studies based on linked records.

If we are convinced of the supremacy of health on mortality or of qualitative duration of life on quantitative duration, then some new (i.e. new for demographers) concepts like 'life style', 'life expectancy in good health', 'social support', 'family life cycles' or 'heterogeneity' often mentioned in the paper need more attention.

Those concepts need an accurate definition and their exact role in the complex process of morbidity/mortality and inequal quality or duration of life should be stated in a multidisciplinary thinking process in which sociologists, epidemiologists, economists, psychologists and demographers shoud be involved.

Moreover those concepts are often too rapidly operationalized by means of the usual identification variables currently available at the traditional administrative sources. Everybody now agrees that they are insufficient in doing so. Even the traditional causes-of-death approach in measuring the health of the population has proved to fall short.

Hence the need for setting up new information systems or trying to use the existing systems another way, namely through record linkages between medical and other administrative sources, etc.

In many instances the usual quantitative methods (including multivariate data analysis) need also to be supplemented by more qualitative approaches and observations in order to gain a better understanding of the evolution and of the characteristics (inequalities in health, possible divergences of the mortality and health evolutions, etc.) of the health and mortality process.

But the basic question remains for me the real objective of the proposed research programme: beyond the methodological exercise, why do research on heterogeneity, on life styles related to differential mortality, why measure expectation of life in good health, etc., if all those researches are not organized into specific objectives, defined as a priority for the Dutch population?

Emerging Issues in Demographic Research
C.A. Hazeu and G.A.B. Frinking (Editors)
© Elsevier Science Publishers B.V. , 1990

Chapter 17

TOWARDS A SPATIAL DEMOGRAPHY OF HOUSING

Pieter Hooimeijer

1 Introduction

The effects of demographic change on the functioning of the housing market have shown up as an important priority in various research programming studies in the mid-eighties. In the research programme on housing of the VRA-OGO (Preliminary Board of Advice on Research of the Built Environment, 1985) four demographic trends were identified having implications for the housing market: the aging of the population, the growth of the potential labour force, the decrease in household size and the increase in housing demand of ethnic minorities due to the rise in immigration. In particular, the effects of these demographic trends on the changes in housing needs, the residential mobility process and the need for management, renewal and new construction were mentioned. In the inventory on demographic research of the PCDO (Programming Board of Demographic Research, 1986) attention was drawn to research initiatives with respect to demographically defined subpopulations and their housing market behaviour.

A programming study which specifically aimed at the relation between demographic change and housing was produced by Dieleman (1984). He identified six major themes of research in this area: the production of household forecasts, the housing market behaviour of households in the reduction phase of the life cycle, the housing market position of households resulting from separation or divorce, the modelling of residential mobility and housing choice, regional variations in the housing market and the (re)distribution of housing. His recommendations for further research were based on an inventory of the research in this area, much of which originated from the research programming of (semi)governmental institutions.

Much has changed over the last five years. Some of the research questions have been answered and new issues have been raised. An overwhelming body of literature with respect to applied research in this area has been created in the Netherlands, although only a limited part of it has shown up in official (international) journals. Academic research certainly has not lagged behind. A comparatively large number of dissertations have been produced which are relevant to this field of research, often addressing more fundamental issues, but also producing operational (forecasting) models. Making or even updating an inventory of the research in this area is beyond the scope of this contribution, but is probably also redundant. Many topics are fully covered within the existing programming and receive adequate financing. Instead I will try to concentrate on a limited number of topics which are, in my opinion, fundamental to the progress in the field of housing demography.

A lot of research will not be mentioned, not because it would not be interesting, but mostly because it has been done or is progressing very well. For instance the research on the housing needs of (demographically defined) special interest groups will receive no attention in this contribution. A number of considerations has been chosen as a starting point in identifying the topics which, in my opinion, should be subject of research in the near future:

1. Demographic changes are not directly related to (aggregate) housing needs or housing market processes, but come into effect only through the changes in the number and the composition of households. Household development instead of demographic change as such, will therefore be the kernel of this expose.
2. Processes of household formation, expansion, reduction and dissolution are of course to a large extent dependent on purely demographic trends like the decline in fertility, the diverging life-expectancy of males and females etc., but are also dependent on other societal changes, particularly on changes in the provision of housing. Household development has to be studied in relation to the wider context of the housing system.
3. This context is even more important when it comes to the effects of household development on the functioning of the housing market. Housing needs and aspirations are also determined by economic developments and the effectuation of demand presupposes the availability of suitable vacancies and is limited by constraints. The interconnectedness of factors driving housing market behaviour are central to the understanding of the functioning of the housing market, including the effects of household development on this functioning.
4. Due to this interconnectedness, housing-demographic behaviour is dynamic over time and over space. Again the relations are recursive; changes in household composition in aggregate will lead to specific additions to the housing stock, while formation and (re)location decisions of households will be influenced by the composition of the housing stock.

The topics which warrant further research, will be clustered in three wider fields, which will be discussed in the following: (a) household development, (b) housing demand and residential mobility and (c) household relocation and spatial redistribution. Within each field attention will be paid to three types of research (though not necessarily in this order):

1. Descriptive and monitoring research, which is concerned with data-collection and a general representation of patterns and trends.
2. Exploratory and explanatory analysis, often leading to, or starting from theoretical concepts with regard to household behaviour.
3. Projection and simulation models, mostly aimed at forecasting or exploring future trends and states.

No a priori predominance is given to one type of research over the others. All three are necessary to advance scientific research. However, considering the nature of the research programme, the recommendations will emphasize research of type 2 and type 3.

2 Household development

One of the most striking advancements in household development research and most relevant in a housing context, is the research on household modelling in the Netherlands. At the national level approaches using state probabilities (static models) have been replaced by approaches using transition probabilities (dynamic models). Researchers from various institutes have developed dynamic household models:

- The PRIMOS model (Heida and Gordijn, 1985) has been developed at INRO/TNO, Delft, to provide estimates of the number of households in relation to the construction of new dwellings.
- The LIPRO model (Keilman and Van Dam, 1987) is in development at the NIDI, The Hague, and aims at household composition in relation to social security benefits.
- The RIWI model (Rima and Van Wissen, 1987) was developed at the Department of Regional Economics of the Free University of Amsterdam to be used in spatial planning.
- The WODYN model (Hooimeijer and Linde, 1988) has been developed at the Faculty of Geographical Sciences of the University of Utrecht to form the basis of a housing market simulation model.
- The NEDYMAS model (Nelissen, 1989) has been developed at the Catholic University of Brabant, Tilburg in the context of social security.

All these models operate nationally, except for the RIWI model which was developed for one region. With one exception they can be described as multi-dimensional, deterministic models. The population is subdivided into 'homogeneous' groups which are exposed to transition probabilities which are fixed during each interval of calculation. The transition probabilities vary for successive cohorts. In demography, this type of models is mostly referred to as macro-simulation. The NEDYMAS model is a micro-simulation model, working with a representative sample of individuals which are exposed to transition probabilities by means of Monte Carlo simulation.

Up to this moment, these models have been developed in relative isolation, partly because they originate from different contexts. Within any new field of research a phase of development in which divergent approaches are being applied is very fruitful. However this should be followed by a phase in which the results are being compared at a detailed level, evaluating the success of these approaches. Up to now only two models have been compared systematically, viz. the WODYN and the PRIMOS model (Heida, Hooimeijer and Linde, forthcoming).

A comparison of the various models evaluating the modelstructure and -methodology with respect to application in a housing context will identify the focus for further research in this area. A number of criteria with respect to the applicability in a housing context can be listed, without being exhaustive:

- The household definition should be based on cohabitation and/or housekeeping and not on civil status. The definition should allow for more than one household sharing the same dwelling.
- Housing market transactions which are a result from household transitions (e.g. vacating a dwelling because of cohabitation of two singles or because of a move into an institution) should be part of the output of the model. This implies the incorporation of the housing distribution in the state space or the data-base of the model, and the output of household events rather than household structure.
- Household positions or household characteristics in the models are often purely demographic (based on the relations among household members). However, housing market behaviour depends on other aspects as well (e.g. labour force participation, income, capital accumulation etc.). The model structure should be such as to allow for incorporation or linking of these attributes to the household characteristics per se.
- The model should produce output below the national level. The housing market is regional (or even local) rather than national.

The rational of these criteria will become clear in the next paragraphs. Here, it suffices to state that none of the models mentioned above meets all of these criteria. It should be noted that the criteria pertain to the application of household models in studying the effects on housing market behaviour, and therefore to the output of the model.

A second aspect of the phase of development of the research into household modelling is, that the attention has concentrated on the structural rather than the substantive properties of the model. In the next phase in the cycle of model construction (Kuijsten and Vossen, 1988) a rethinking of the behavioural assumptions on which the models are based is necessary, concentrating on the causes of the processes of household change. In other words this calls for exploratory and explanatory research of household develop-ment. Keilman and Keyfitz (1988) conclude that a universally valid theory is lacking and that the search for it would be a futile attempt. Instead they put forward the life course perspective as consistent framework to synthesize contributions to a theoretical expla-nation from various disciplines. Within the life course perspective the household career is linked to other careers (e.g. labour-market, health, housing). The interrelatedness with the other careers stretches the importance of this approach beyond the explanation of household development as such, because it also draws attention to other factors mediating or enhancing the effects of household development on the housing market. I will return to this issue in the next paragraph.

With respect to household development in a housing context, two kinds of life course research warrant specific attention:

The first is the study of heterogeneity in household transitions. Baanders, Van Leeuwen and Ploegmakers (1989) provide an example of such a study with respect to the leaving of the parental home. From their analysis it becomes clear that the education career should be included in household formation models, hinting at the effect that this also corresponds with diverging housing needs. Another example is the research by Filius in which the effect of the housing career on the transitions to institutions for elderly is being studied. To my knowledge no work has been done yet on the analysis of the process of cohabitation in relation to the educational and job career or on separation in relation to the fertility and job career (this should include non-married couples).

The second but closely related topic is the effect of (changes) in housing provision on household development. This issue is raised in the latest Sociaal en Cultureel Rapport (SCP, 1988). According to the calculations of the SCP, the age at which people leave the parental home has increased in the first half of the eighties, which might have been caused by the growing housing shortage in the Netherlands. However no attempt is made to analyse this causal relation. It could very well be that staying with the parents longer is not directly related to the housing shortage, but to the sharp decrease in the supply of (furnished) rooms. Another example of the effect of changes in housing provision on household development is the decrease in admission rates into institutions for the elderly, leading to a decrease in household dissolutions. The impact of changes in housing provision on household development should be subject of research in the near future, as this might uncover an important cause of non-stationarity in household development.

The study of the variation in transitions within cohorts (heterogeneity) and across cohorts (non-stationarity) is essential to the understanding and therefore the modelling of the dynamics of household development over time and over space. It is striking that changes over time have received considerably more attention than variations over space. Changes over time in household development are monitored on the basis of the Housing Needs Survey (WBO – for instance Ploegmakers and Van Leeuwen, 1985) or the Survey on Family Formation (LOG – for instance Van de Giessen, 1987).

The spatial variation is an important issue in the third aspect of the development of the research on household modelling, viz. the production of household information and household forecasts at the regional or local level. Apart from insight in the regional variation in household transitions, two more things are needed. Essential to the development is the construction of a migration model at the regional level which produces consistent output on households. I will return to this issue in the paragraph on spatial relocation. The second thing which is needed is a reliable set of household statistics at the local level. The lack of a census in this country, has left us devoid of this information. However, the production of these statistics has a high priority at the Central Bureau of Statistics, warranting no further research, although it might be wise for future consumers of these statistics to show an interest at an early stage of production.

3 Housing demand and residential mobility

The relation between the household life-cycle and the residential mobility process has been acknowledged ever since the publication of "Why families move" by Rossi (1955). However at an early stage it was argued that the effects of the job career should be taken into consideration as well (Leslie and Richardson, 1961). In the Netherlands these well established relations have led to extensive monitoring of both housing demand and residential mobility in relation to demographic and socio-economic characteristics. The Nationaal Rayon Onderzoeken (annual) and the Woningbehoefte Onderzoeken (every four years) have given rise to a wealth of descriptive studies enumerating (changes) in these patterns (e.g. Buijs and Dijkhuis-Potgieser, 1988, De Rooij and Van der Marel, 1988). The availability of these micro-data to researchers has also stimulated studies of a more exploratory and explanatory nature. Many of these studies fit into the life course perspective, which has a long tradition in mobility research and has recently gained attention in demography (see paragraph 2).

Much of this research has been aimed at uncovering the heterogeneity in housing demand and residential mobility. Some authors have concentrated on actual moves of households, implicitly treating these as 'revealed' preferences for various dwelling types or attributes. The research by Deurloo, Clark and Dieleman (Deurloo, 1987) provides a prominent example. From their multi-variate statistical analyses it appears that residential mobility and housing choice have to be understood from the interaction between the demographic, socio-economic and housing characteristics of the households. Their analyses are cross-sectional, although the theoretical framework postulates that it is the progression over the life cycle and in the job career which triggers of residential mobility. Their outcomes however conform to those from longitudinal studies (e.g. of Harts and Hingstman, 1986) linking life cycle, job career and housing career. Among starting households, the labour force participation of both partners has a decisive influence (Linde, Dieleman and Clark, 1986). The conclusion should be that the residential mobility process, linking household development to housing market behaviour, can not be understood or modelled purely on the basis of household transitions.

The relative consensus about the factors driving residential mobility and housing demand does not imply that there is no need for further explanatory research. On the contrary, the research on heterogeneity may be extensive, but covers only part of the problem. Implicit in this type of research is the assumption that housing market behaviour is demand driven. However effective demand (the actual moves from one dwelling to another) is shaped, not only by the preferences of the households, but also by the availability of vacancies and by constraints in the form of the price-mechanism or allocation rules. Many households do not end up in the dwelling of their choice. They substitute their housing preferences because of the lack of opportunities or because vacancies are not open to them. As supply conditions vary from place to place and are changing over time, they form an important source of non-stationarity in the level and direction of the residential mobility. Very little is known about this substitution behaviour of households. Income seems to be of importance as this variable is a strong predictor of actual housing choice, but a weak predictor of housing preferences (Van Lierop, 1985).

Besides income, household composition seems to be of prime importance, small house-holds suffering from a lack of suitable vacancies and discriminatory allocation rules (Hooimeijer and Linde, 1988). A better understanding of this substitution behaviour is crucial to the study of household development on actual housing market behaviour. Simulation of household decision making (for instance, using decision net techniques; Timmermans and Borgers, 1985) could provide insight at the micro level into the responses of households to a changing housing context.

A second, but closely related problem is the interdependency of cohorts of households in the provision of housing. This is the demographic counterpart of the well-known adage 'Houses filter down, while households filter up'. The shortage of dwellings suitable for the growing number of elderly households in the Netherlands, decreases the mobility rate of this group. The decreased level of mobility results in a limited turnover in the spacious sub-markets which they occupy. This has a negative effect on the mobility of younger families, causing them to remain longer in dwellings which are to small for them, thereby blocking the opportunities for young small households to move to an independent dwelling. The effects of new construction and housing allocation with respect to this trickling-down mechanism are as yet not fully understood. However the study of the effects of the differences in size of successive cohorts on this mechanism could be better performed in the context of housing market simulation models, than through explanatory research.

The development of housing market models has actually progressed along the same line as the household models. Static models using state probabilities like the model in the Trendrapport Volkshuisvesting 1982 (BSM, 1984) have been replaced by dynamic models using transition probabilities. In the Netherlands two dynamic housing market models are operational at the national level:

- the QUATRO model (Heida and Den Otter, 1988) using the PRIMOS household model as its basis, and
- the WODYN model (Hooimeijer and Linde, 1988).

Both are macro-simulation models that have been developed to study the effects of household development on the housing market. Although they do differ in specification, they share three major shortcomings from a conceptual point of view, which makes their applicability in the present form doubtful.

The first is that they only contain interactions between the household life cycle and the housing career. Neither of them contains any income variable in their state space. From the discussion of the research above it is clear that this is a serious omission. Extension of the models requires some analytical work. There is a strong relation between (changes) in age and household composition and income (changes), having a decisive impact on housing market behaviour. For instance the combination of two wage-earners into one household as a result of cohabitation is strongly linked to the entrance into the owner-occupied sector, while separation often means a reduction in income for at least one the partners involved and is often associated with a return into the rental sector. The models should be able to represent this three-way interaction of household-, income- and housing market dynamics. Much could be learned from the experience gathered in the development of the NEDYMAS model, which already contains some household/income interaction.

The second is that the substitution behaviour of household in the models is not based on any empirical research, but on a priori decision rules. This gap could be filled by the explanatory research proposed above, but the results will have to be translated into the model structure.

The third is that the models operate at the national scale completely, neither supply nor demand have been fixed locationally. With the increasing disparities in regional housing shortages, this is probably the most important drawback. A spatial disaggregation however, presupposes operational dynamic household models at the regional level.

4 Household relocation and spatial (re)distribution

Small-area population analysis and forecasting is probably the most challenging and complicated field within housing demography. It is also a field in which demographers traditionally have shown little interest. However, applied demographers concerned with specific locations such as those working in business or government show a keen interest in learning about population dynamics in cities, suburbs and smaller subareas (Myers, 1990). The emergence of Demographic Information Systems is a clear expression of this concern for a detailed monitoring of these dynamics.

The spatial distribution of the population is the central element in the recursive relation between household development and the housing market. New neighbourhoods arise as a result of the growing number of households, the composition of the new stock being determined by shifts in aggregate housing demand. The uneven spatial distribution of dwelling types and living environment in turn, causes a spatial sorting of the households within a region, because it directs the residential mobility process. Most of the research in this field has been done by geographers and has been descriptive by nature. Understanding dynamics however calls for more explanatory research, which is a prerequisite for modelling small-area population change.

Many descriptive studies are based on a simple life cycle model of neighbourhood change. Recently this has been replaced by a more integrated framework, relating the residential mobility behaviour of households to the characteristics of dwellings and neighbourhoods (e.g. Musterd, 1985). Building on this experience it has been suggested to combine a vintage analysis of neighbourhoods with a cohort analysis of the population (Hoogvliet and Hooimeijer, 1989). The idea behind this is relatively straightforward: at the time of construction, most of the dwelling characteristics and the location of the neighbourhood are being fixed. Over time the relative appreciation and relative location changes as a result of new additions to the stock. As a result the neighbourhood will attract households in various phases of their housing career in subsequent periods. The present household composition of a neighbourhood is an intersection of cohorts which have settled in various periods from a differing housing career perspective. In an older neighbourhood one might find elderly households which moved in at middle age, planning to stay there for a long time, young households which moved in recently, moving out again as soon as better housing opportunities become available and middle-aged households of low socio-economic status to whom better opportunities are not accessible. In this way changes in turnover in this neighbourhood can be related to the changing distribution of the population over these household groups. Household specific intra-urban migration flows can be explained from the combination of stock-characteristics of neighbourhoods and the household composition of the population.

These ideas still have to be put to more empirical testing and probably could be extended to include the effects of new construction on the dynamic system. The matching of population accounts and the housing inventory at the level of the individual dwelling which has been achieved in a number of Dutch cities could provide an excellent data set, offering ample opportunities to control for household, dwelling and neighbourhood characteristics in an explanatory study of intra-urban mobility. This could be described as the bottom-up approach in the study of the spatial redistribution of households.

The most promising modelling attempts on household relocation within a region show a clear resemblance to the models described in the previous paragraph. In a number of European city-regions attempts have been made to model this proces, e.g. Stockholm (Harsman and Snickers, 1983), Dortmund (Wegener, 1983), Vienna (Aufhauser and Fisher, 1987) and Amsterdam (Rima and Van Wissen, 1987). The last model is fully operational and has an important advantage over the models described before. It has been set up for a regional housing market and also includes a spatial distribution component within this region. The start is an occupancy matrix of six household types distributed over eleven dwelling submarkets and twenty zones. Input and output are very detailed. The modelling itself however is, compared to the national models rather crude. This is (partly) caused by the fact that the number of observations for one region is comparatively small. Due to the lack of any substitution mechanism the model produces contra-intuitive results.

However the model structure does have a very sound accounting and could be extended to yield better results. The parameters for the household model could be estimated in a more reliable fashion by studying the divergence from the national model, rather than directly on a small subset of data. Inclusion of income in the state space of the model could be reached in the same way. Substitution behaviour should be modelled explicitly. First with respect to sectoral substitution (between dwelling types). Second with respect to spatial substitution (between zones). An interesting aspect of the spatial substitution is that it appeared from the research by Rima and Van Wissen that 85%-90% of the household wanted to move within the same zone. The preference for other zones could be explained completely by the supply of preferred dwelling in these zones. This evidence is supported by the analysis of Deurloo, Dieleman and Clark (forthcoming) of actual moves between municipalities within the Randstad. This probably means that to most households spatial substitution is no options, while to others the location of the dwelling is largely irrelevant, as long as it is within the region. However, to little is known about substitution behaviour in general and of spatial substitution in particular.

This type of modelling can be described as the top-down approach in the study of household relocation. It is based on a general parameterization of household development and residential mobility, which is used to simulate housing market behaviour in space. Although the behavioural basis is the same as in the study of neighbourhood change, the approach is completely different. Eventually however, the results should be identical.

5 Conclusion

The programming studies of the middle-eighties concentrated on the effects of demographic change on the housing market. In this contribution a slightly different approach has been adopted. The recursive relation between household development and housing is the central issue. At the national level the demography is predominantly causal, leading to changing patterns of aggregate demand and therefore indicative of the type of new construction. At the local level however the relation is vice versa. The composition of the local housing stock directs the spatial disaggregation of households. The residential mobility process was identified as the key element in linking demography and housing, therefore no attention has been paid to interregional migration which is known to be work related and not housing related. Economic influences have been largely ignored. They form the explicit subject of other contributions.

With respect to a number of topics recommendations for further research have been made. These will be summed up briefly:

A. Household development
1. Comparative research on micro- and macrosimulation models of household development, evaluating model structures with respect to their applicability in a housing context.
2. Explanatory research on the heterogeneity in households transitions, linking them to events in other careers (education, health, labour and housing) in particular with respect to cohabitation and separation.
3. Study of the effects of regional differences and changes in housing provision on household transitions, particularly with respect to household formation.

B. Housing demand and residential mobility
1. Exploratory analysis of the sectoral substitution behaviour of households, by means of simulation of household decision behaviour.
2. Extension of the housing market models with income, modelling the dynamic interaction of household development, income change and housing market behaviour.
3. Disaggregating dynamic housing market models to the regional level.

C. Household relocation and spatial redistribution
1. Explanatory research on small-area population (households) change, in which dwelling and neighbourhood characteristics of areas from subsequent vintages are related to the housing career of subsequent cohorts of their population.

2. Extending regional dynamic housing market models with a spatial redistribution module, based on the analysis of spatial substitution of dwelling preferences.

The order is not coincidental. The exploratory and explanatory research can be done simultaneously, but has to proceed the modelling research. Models are ordered in increasing complexity. The development of the models should be carried out consecutively.

References

Aufhauser, E. and M.M. Fisher (1987), *An empirical test of a nested multinomial logit model of housing choice*, Bardoneccia: 5th European Colloquium on Quantitative and Theoretical Geography.

Baanders, A.N., L.Th. van Leeuwen and M.J.H. Ploegmakers (1989), *Uit huis gaan van jongeren*, Den Haag: Ministerie van VROM.

BSM (1984), *Trendrapport Volkshuisvesting 1982*, Delft: Bureau voor Strategisch Marktonderzoek.

Buijs, C.C.M. and H.I.E. Dijkhuis-Potgieser (1988), *Ontwikkelingen op de woningmarkt 1987*, Den Haag: Ministerie van VROM.

Deurloo, M.C. (1987), *A multivariate analysis of residential mobility*, Utrecht, Ph.D.

Deurloo, M.C., F.M. Dieleman and W.A.V. Clark (forthcoming), *The spatial element in housing choice*.

Dieleman, F.M. (1984), *Demografische ontwikkelingen en bouwen en wonen*, Utrecht: Geografisch Instituut.

Giessen, G.J. van (1987), Geboorteregeling 1982-1985, *Maandstatistiek van de bevolking*, Vol. 35, no. 3, pp. 10-11.

Harsman, B. and F. Snickars (1983), A method for disaggregate household forecasts, *TESG*, nr. 74, pp. 282-291.

Harts, J.J. and L. Hingstman (1986), *Verhuizingen op een rij*, Utrecht, Ph.D.

Heida, H.R. and H.J. den Otter (1988), *QUATRO*, Delft: INRO/TNO.

Heida, H.R. and H.E. Gordijn (1985), *PRIMOS-Huishoudenmodel*, Den Haag: Ministerie van VROM.

Heida, H.R., P. Hooimeijer and M.A.J. Linde, *Evaluatie van het PRIMOS model* (forthcoming).

Hoogvliet, A. and P. Hooimeijer (1989), Population change in early-twentieth-century neighbourhoods, *The Netherlands Journal of Housing and Environmental Research*, Vol. 3, no. 2, pp. 133-149.

Hooimeijer, P. and M.A.J. Linde (1988), *Vergrijzing, individualisering en de woning-markt*, Utrecht, Ph.D.

Keilman, N.W. and J. van Dam (1987), *A dynamic household model*, Den Haag: NIDI.

Keilman, N.W. and N. Keyfitz (1988), Recurrent issues in dynamic household modelling, in: N.W. Keilman, A.C. Kuijsten and A.P. Vossen, eds., *Modelling Household Formation and Dissolution*, Oxford: Clarendon Press.

Kuijsten, A.C. and A.P. Vossen (1988), Introduction, in: N.W. Keilman, A.C. Kuijsten and A.P. Vossen, eds., *Modelling Household Formation and Dissolution*, Oxford: Clarendon Press.

Leslie, G.R. and A.M. Richardson (1961), Life cycle, career pattern and the decision to move, *American Sociological Review*, no. 26, pp. 894-902.

Lierop, W. van (1985), *Spatial interaction modelling and residential choice analysis*, Amsterdam, Ph.D.

Linde, M.A.J., F.M. Dieleman and W.A.V. Clark (1986), Starters in the Dutch housing market, *TESG*, no. 77, pp. 243-250.

Musterd, S. (1985), *Verschillende structuren en ontwikkelingen van woongebieden in Tilburg*, Amsterdam, Ph.D.

Myers, D., ed. (1990), *Housing demography*, Madison Wisconsin: University of Wisconsin Press.

Nelissen, J.H.M. (1989), Microsimulatiemodel NEDYMAS, *Planning*, no. 35, pp. 27-35.

PCDO (1986), *Demografisch onderzoek: advies en balans*, Den Haag: NIDI.

Ploegmakers, M.J.M. and L.Th. van Leeuwen (1985), *Huishoudens in Nederland: twee decennia verandering*, Den Haag: Ministerie van VROM.

Rima, A. and L.J.G. van Wissen (1987), *A dynamic model of household relocation*, Amsterdam, Ph.D.

Rooij, G. de and J.W. van der Marel (1988), *Het Woningbehoefte Onderzoek*, Den Haag: Ministerie van VROM.

Rossi, P. (1955), *Why families move*, Glencoe: The Free Press.

SCP (1988), *Sociaal en Cultureel Rapport 1988*, Den Haag: Sociaal en Cultureel Planbureau.

Timmermans, H.J.P. and A. Borgers (1985), *Spatial choice models*, Eindhoven: University of Technology.

VRA-OGO (1985), *Onderzoeksprogramma bouwen en wonen*, Zoetermeer: Ministerie van Onderwijs en Wetenschappen.

Wegener, M. (1983), A simulation study of the Dortmund housing market, *TESG*, 74, pp. 267-282.

Emerging Issues in Demographic Research
C.A. Hazeu and G.A.B. Frinking (Editors)
© Elsevier Science Publishers B.V. , 1990

Chapter 18

TOWARDS A SPATIAL DEMOGRAPHY OF HOUSING; A COMMENT

William A.V. Clark

1   Introductory comments

I am pleased to have been invited to this organisational meeting for a programme on Population Studies in the Netherlands and to offer whatever insights I can on the programme and the themes that in my opinion will be the important themes of the next two decades especially with respect to the intersection of housing and population. I should be clear at the outset that I have my own set of biases and I want to express these directly so that my comments will not be misinterpreted. There are three preliminary points I wish to make:

a. First, although there has been a great deal of important work in demography in general the work has been for the most part a-theoretical. Empiricism has triumphed at the expense of theoretical work on demographic processes and demographic change. To some extent I am reflecting the comments in the paper by Willekens and the review by Keyfitz.

b. Second, the strongest parts of demography have been those areas which have used mathematical modelling strategies to solve problems and answer questions. There is a great deal of what I will call demographic commentary which has been useful in producing new ideas but certainly not productive of new theory. At the same time there is a serious trade off between mathematical sophistication, technical tinkering and substantive results. The parallel with economic forecasting and mathematical models of the economy is not irrelevant here. Elsewhere I have argued for robust models of housing/demographic relationships (Clark, Deurloo and Dieleman, 1988).

c. Third, there is insufficient attention to important social problems which have demographic underpinnings. In particular this shows up in the present papers none of which address such issues as the spread of AIDS and the impact of political destabilisation on developed western countries.

2 The notion of spatial demography

The recognition that many demographic processes have an important spatial component or at the very least take place in space and that location is an important part of understanding both processes and outcomes has led to the development of the notions of spatial demography. Certainly geographers have been amongst those who have emphasized the role of space in population studies. While this was initially little more than studying populations within regions now the work in multi-state demography by a wide ranging group of geographers and demographers has firmly placed spatial demography at the center of population studies. An obvious extension is to the issue of housing demography or the spatial demography of housing because quite simply the most notable characteristic of housing so often reiterated by housing experts is the spatial fixity of the housing stock and the importance of its relative location within the urban mozaic.

As Myers (1990) has noted elsewhere the notion of housing demography and the focus on links between housing and population is quite recent and for most of the recent decades studies of housing and demographic studies were quite fragmented. Indeed, and I will say more about this later, Hooimeijer is particularly sensitive to the need to bring the two foci together. Why the separation persisted for so long is not a topic for my comments but it is worth noting that in part the separation was one of a misdirected focus on race and inequality rather than seeing these topics as subsidiary to the issues of housing affordability, access and homelessness. At its essence the focus on housing demography is the focus on the attempt to link population and housing formally. What are the central elements which underly these changes? They include household formation and composition, housing choices (and here residential mobility and tenure choice are central elements of any conceptual framework) and housing construction and housing stock change (see Moore and Clark, 1990, for discussion of linking housing and household). The first of these topics is related to the field of family formation and dissolution. How are households formed and how do these formations affect housing choices? Because housing units increasingly provide both shelter and status, the complexity of choice behaviour can no longer be expressed as simple economic determinants. Still the basic dimensions of choice are tenure, type and size of unit. The understanding of the construction of the housing stock is a third element of housing demography and has to a large extent been the province of economic analysis. Here the question of whether demand or supply has the major influence on the production of the stock is relevant.

3 The thesis of Hooimeijer

In the paper Towards a Spatial Demography of Housing the thesis is advanced that:

> "purely demographic trends and societal changes together produce changes in the number and composition of households, and household development is at the heart of the functioning of the housing market".

Hooimeijer emphasizes the recursiveness of the relationship to the extent that

"changes in household composition in aggregate will lead to specific additions to the housing stock while ... relocation decisions of households will be influenced by the composition of the stock".

He further develops this recursive relationship to note that the recursive relationship is such that at the national level, demography is causal (leading to changed patterns of demand) while at the local level housing is casual in creating the spatial outcomes of location. We will evaluate this specifically. Another way of thinking about this is to suggest that national is downloaded to the local.

4   Evaluating the thesis

In evaluating the usefulness of this thesis and how it might be used as a central element of a population research project it is useful to recall that in the thesis reflects a view of demographic processes at two scales. On the one hand there is the scale of national population change and the necessity to develop adequate models to forecast population change at an aggregate level. In turn these forecasts can include expectations about family change and ageing, two of the important components of demographic change. At the second and local scale, there is the issue of small area population change. It is the national issue brought down to the local arena. Just as at the national level, the topics of importance at the local level are the effects of ageing, ethnic changes, and family and household composition changes.

It is hard to argue with the thesis at the most general level but it is certainly appropriate to examine the recursive relationships between housing and population. In fact, is it always recursive, or is it a case of primacy to population at some times and to housing at other times and how are we to assign primacy in the recursive relationship? These are not clear and the thesis requires elaboration if it is to be the center of a major research effort.

The second element of examining the thesis is related to the always present issue of fundamental versus applied research objectives. Indeed it could be argued that although the thesis is plausible it has no theory to underpin it. And, the emphasis in the paper on the applied models further emphasizes the limited theory which underlies the thesis.

5   Research needs and specific commentary

The commentary in the Hooimeijer paper is focused on topics which are mentioned as central in the study of links between housing and population. These topics, household development, housing demand and household relocation/redistribution each have a number of important elements related to understanding the links between housing and population. But the clear message from the Hooimeijer paper is his interest and belief in the models which are currently (in the main) nationally focused on household change and demand. Beginning with the PRIMOS model there has been a major concern in the Netherlands to provide estimates on the number of households in relation to the construction of new dwellings. The development of this model at Utrecht as the WODYN model, which has as a major component a micro simulation approach, is a real advance on other models which link housing and population. Of course there are a number of elements of the model which are still to be spelled out and perhaps even more important for the future of centers of population and housing research in the Netherlands is the need to 'export' these models to other regions both in Europe and the United States. As an aside I would strongly suggest that when the center or centers are established that they link with the major demographic centers in the United States and the Population Association of America to disseminate these models to a wider audience than within Europe only.

Specifically with respect to the WODYN model I would like to see it run in several scenarios and results compared with other models. Although the author notes one comparison that is forthcoming I believe that greater operationalization is an essential part of further research on these models. Yes, the limitations of income in simulation housing distributions are important and I am unclear about the discussion of substitutions between housing sectors.

Even more important the model must be developed for the small scale analysis which is the critical dimension of the housing-population link. We are not given any details on how this might be accomplished but it is necessarily a priority. There is no discussion of the WODYN model in the section on household relocation and redistribution but this must be a major research priority. To this point a major criticism of other research on small area population change is that it is excessively descriptive. An important point which is raised in passing is the role of spatial substitution in the creation of particular housing patterns.

6 Summary and suggestions

There is a long list of possible topics for research but even to address this list requires a moment devoted to the larger picture within a research programme on housing and population. While the aim is basic research the interest in demographic processes is likely to focus government attention on centers of population study and it is not unreasonable to keep accountability in mind in the research programmes that are developed. Indeed as I have argued elsewhere, if we are to continue to receive large sums for our research activities there is necessarily a by-product of our research which will be useful at the national and local levels.

The above comments suggest a limited number of well focused research themes (perhaps the following topics can be used to organise a number of the papers which are being presented here):

a. forecasting and population change
b. family organisation and family change
c. housing demography

These very broad topics allow a variety of specific endeavours but they also organise the possible research agenda.

Within the last of these topics (and I did not promise an unbiased consideration) there are three strands which are of concern on both sides of the Atlantic. First, can we develop a theory which will enrich the understanding of relationships between population and housing and what role do economic and societal factors play in that theory? Certainly a simple utility framework which has been the guide of most economic analyses is insufficient as a base for this theory. Second, can we develop a small area component to the models of housing and population which are (to some extent) operational at the national level? And third, can we link the small area research with models of neighbourhood change and the role of racial and ethnic change in these arenas?

I have chosen to emphasize broad but central themes and allow the specifics to emerge from the working research groups which might emulate the physical science model of laboratories and their staffs.

To return to the opening comments, the central issue for housing demography revolves around the question of access and consumption. Who is getting what and where are they getting it? Hooimeijer has emphasized that the answers to this question involve a study of the interrelationship of housing and population and it is hard to disagree with this conclusion.

References

Clark, W.A.V., M.C. Deurloo and F.M. Dieleman (1988), Modeling strategies for categorical data: examples from housing and tenure choice, *Geographical Analysis*, 20, pp. 198-219.

Moore, E.G. and W.A.V. Clark (1990), Housing and households in American cities. Structure and change in population mobility, in: D. Myers, ed., *Housing Demography*, Madison, Wisconsin: University of Wisconsin Press.

Myers, D. (1990), The emerging concept of housing demography, in: D. Myers, ed., *Housing demography*, Madison, Wisconsin: University of Wisconsin Press.

Emerging Issues in Demographic Research
C.A. Hazeu and G.A.B. Frinking (Editors)
© Elsevier Science Publishers B.V. , 1990

Chapter 19

ON HISTORICAL ROOTS OF CONTEMPORARY DEMOGRAPHIC PROBLEMS

Theo L.M. Engelen

The reason for this workshop is to discuss the 'Research Programme on Population Issues' prepared by a committee of 'The Netherlands Organization for Scientific Research'. In this programme the importance of historical demographic research is stressed on several places. When studying the papers for this meeting, however, one must conclude that this historical aspect of the programme is neglected. There is nothing new in that. At the European Population Conference 1987 for instance the same remark could be made. The threat of sustained subreplacement in Europe was a major item at that conference too and the historical scope limited. In this paper I hope to demonstrate how meaningfull knowledge of demographic developments in the past can be for the understanding of current issues.[1]

I firmly believe social scientists, including demographers, underestimate the historical dimension of their objects of study. Sometimes they legalize this attitude by coining new concepts, in this way placing historical developments in a separate category to be dealt with in one page of the introduction, and go on with their research of contemporary material as though these phenomena are not partly determined by the past.

This general remark, of course, is rather bluntly phrased and general in character. Now to be more precise, I would like to use the example of the concept of the socalled 'Second demographic transition'.[2]

Personally I wonder whether there is reason to subdivide the demographic transition in two parts, one historical – the period 1880-1930 –, and one beginning around 1965.

The point I wish to make here is that there is only one demographic transition originating somewhere around 1800-1850 and still going on nowadays. In this statement I will mainly focus on the decline in fertility, as this is the major reason for the population

---

[1] Although there is an enormous amount of literature on the subject, I will refrain from references, unless a very specific monograph or article is mentioned.

[2] D.J. Van de Kaa, Europe's second demographic transition, *Population Bulletin*, Vol. 42, No. 1, March 1987.

problems we are facing today in Western countries. The decline in fertility levels has been structural since 1880 and has only been interrupted by a relatively short upswing in the postwar period. From the early fifties on the structural decline became apparent again and gradually but inevitably reached the point of subreplacement. In Figure 1 the marital fertility rate of the Netherlands is shown, clearly demonstrating the above mentioned development. There is no reason to take 1965 as a turning point.

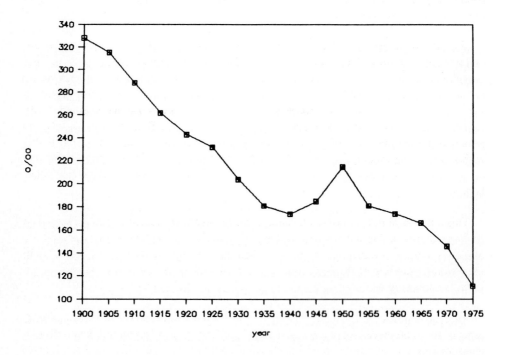

Figure 1   Marital fertility (15-45), the Netherlands, 1900-1975

Van de Kaa characterises the two demographic transitions by the keywords 'altruistic' for the first and 'individualistic' for the second. On the other hand he mentions the disappearance of the Malthusian pattern of family formation at the beginning of the 'first' demographic transition. Again the historian might be critical. The marriage pattern in the Malthusian period has denied individuals for centuries to do as they wished. Late or completely deferred marriage and therefore abstinence in sexual matters was a means to reach the societal goal of more or less stable populations to avoid positive checks. Neo-Malthusian practices therefore constitute a dramatic change in attitudes. Young people increasingly neglected marriage restriction and married at an earlier age. The proportion ever-married in the population at the same time increased rapidly. Birth-control within marriage now became the necessary alternative for marriage-control. So, if there is a change in attitudes from altruistic to individualistic, this change probably occured in the nineteenth century rather then around 1965. In the sixties we only witnessed the widening of the variety of individualistic reasons for having less children, not the beginning. Statistically the downward trend in fertility passed the replacement level of 2.1 births per woman. But then again, this was to be expected when keeping in mind the secular movement.

Should this, in my view, have consequences for the research programme? There are two lines of reasoning. On the one hand, the refined models and statistical methods used in contemporary demography are only applicable for the recent years as they do entail the use of data not available for earlier periods. Therefore an artificial dividing point in 1965 for pragmatic reasons is understandable. On the other hand however, the fertility decline is a process which originates a century ago and it would be wise to learn, if possible, the lessons from the past. Lesthaeghe and Wilson, for instance, provided us with a promising model, containing economic motivation for birth-control on the one hand, mental acceptation on the other and the varying relative importance of both factors.[1]

This rather straightforward model deserves to be taken into account by social scientists studying demographic behaviour of the eighties. Although the factors must and can be refined, the general outline is interesting, the more so because it proved of great value for the understanding of the beginning of the transition process. And this process, in my view, is still going on.

Even an historian has to admit that from the sixties onward some new demographic aspects are to be discerned. I refer to increasing divorce rates, cohabitation and illigitimate fertility on the one hand and decreasing nuptiality on the other hand. Still, even these phenomena, all of them changes in nuptiality, can be seen in historical perspective. After the Malthusian period of late and deferred marriage and the Neo-Malthusian period of almost universal and young marriage, now we have entered an era in which marriage once again seems to have lost his attraction. I am tempted to call this the third phase of the nuptiality transition. At first nuptiality acted as a regulator of population, oppressing sexual needs of individuals. At the end of the nineteenth century society did not have the power anymore to dictate this rather rigid behaviour on her members, who had become more individualistic. But even then, sexuality could only be legalized by marriage. Thus

---

[1] R. Lesthaeghe and C. Wilson, Les modes de production, la laïcisation et le rythme de la baisse de la fécondité en Europe de l'Ouest de 1870 à 1930, *Population* 37 (1982), pp. 623-645.

the explosive growth of nuptiality in the twentieth century can be explained. Seculariz-
ation, individualization and economic independence however gained strength in such a
way that in our time, once again, society has lost its grip on the sexual moral. The sexual
life of individuals does not have to be legalized by marriage anymore. In this way even
the demographic phenomena which seem new at first sight, are the result of a process of
centuries.

    There is still another historical matter that draws our attention and is worthwile
studying. With the benefit of hindsight we can not but wonder why it took scientists as
well as politicians so long before they realized the consequences of demographic
processes occuring under their very eyes. As late as 1972 a socalled 'State Committee
Population Problems' was established in the Netherlands to study the prospects and
possible consequences of overpopulation in the country. In that very year the fertility
decline had already a history of almost a century, but the government, myopic by a short
term view, evidently could not read the signs of the time. And yet the net replacement
index was already diminishing since 1963 and crossed the 1.0 barrier in the same year
1972![1]

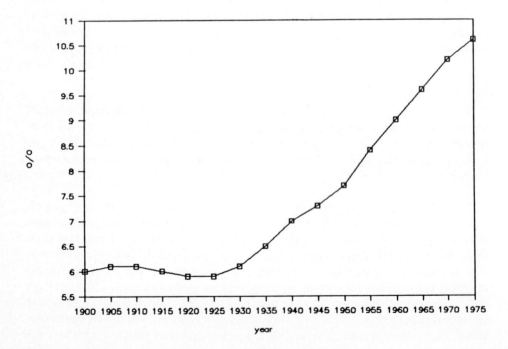

Figure 2   Population over 65 (in %), the Netherlands 1900-1975

---

[1]   C.B.S., *Statistisch Zakboek 1976*, Voorburg 1976, pp. 27-28.

As for the greying of society, the same goes. Figure 2 shows the percentage of persons over 65 in Dutch society since 1900. The rise of this percentage since 1930 is overwhelmingly clear. This fact, in combination with the fertility decline, as shown in Figure 1, logically leads to the greying of society. Why then is it that this topic has only recently been 'discovered'? Some of the future research therefore, could focus on the problem of what mechanisms inhibited the scientific and governmental world to forsee at an earlier stage the movement of the population. By this the problems of forecasting future developments will not be solved, but the amount of possible errors might be reduced.

My conclusion is obvious. Fertility decline, the greying of population and the various digressions from traditional marriage are no surprising new items of the last two decades, but the preliminary end of a process which started more than a century ago. So why not take the long view if we study contemporary demographic problems? The contribution of historical demography is only one of many, but certainly of importance. Last but not least, the historical study of demography itself might reveal why this workshop did not take place in 1965!

Emerging Issues in Demographic Research
C.A. Hazeu and G.A.B. Frinking (Editors)
Elsevier Science Publishers B.V. , 1990

Chapter 20

EPILOGUE; THE RESEARCH PROGRAMME ON POPULATION STUDIES

Gerard A.B. Frinking

1 The conclusions of the workshop

In the two-day discussion on Emerging Issues in Demographic Research held during the NWO workshop, a number of important conclusions were reached. Firstly, it became clear that the interest in the study of determinants of demographic processes at micro-level is an international phenomenon. Consequently we can benefit greatly from experiences with and results of studies of this kind which have meanwhile been carried out abroad. In connection with this direction in demographic research, a number of new developments can be detected. Because the decision-making processes that influence demographic behaviour (fertility, the forming of relationships, death and migration) have a temporal and a spatial dimension, the study of demographic phenomena takes on a wider perspective. The application of behavioural theories developed in the field of social sciences will considerably broaden the existing theoretical framework. At the same time this will strengthen the interdisciplinary character of demographic practice. Furthermore, it can be noted that, in order to process the multiplicity of interactions between the moments of choice in question adequately, the tool of micro-simulation is being used increasingly. In the long term, some progress will only be possible if theory and practice are conjoined and properly coordinated. The programme needs to take both aspects into account. A second conclusion reached in the workshop concerns the quality of the Dutch research in the field of household formation. Thanks to the efforts of, in particular, demographers and geographers, a great deal of information has been acquired in the Netherlands on the formation and disintegration of households and on the implications of household trends with regard to processes of supply and demand on the property market. Naturally, this area of research occupies a prominent place in the proposed priority programme. Finally, the participants in the workshop emphasized the social importance of the demographic trends. This applies particularly for Dutch society, in which the idea and practice of planning and control (continue to) play an important role, as evidenced, for instance, by the great influence of the various national planning agencies (RPD, CPB, SCP) on government policy. Since the drop in the number of young people and the proportional rise in the ageing population will progressively alter the size and composition of the population in the coming decades, insight into the social significance of these developments is of great importance. It will not suffice to carry out status quo calculations which merely take into account the demographic consequences in separate sectors (such as housing, health care and social security). Research in this field should take at least two new directions. Firstly, the autonomous impact of demographic processes on each of the relevant sectors must be considered. In addition, the impact of demographic changes on a number of relevant areas will have to be studied by considering the different areas in relationship to each other. Thus, a growing need for official welfare provisions as a result of the rise in the ageing population can only be avoided by deploying unofficial care, which, among other things, requires a knowledge of the size and composition of future family networks. This is a good example of how the economic question of collective expenditure is very closely bound up with that of the social dimension of the modern welfare state. The way in which these conclusions have been fleshed out in selected research fields and research themes is shown in the last section.

2   Selected fields of research

The committee responsible for structuring the research programme on population problems finally decided to concentrate the research on the following fields:

1. decision-making processes that influence demographic behaviour at micro-level;
2. the development of (forecast) models of families, family relationships and households;
3. social consequences of demographic developments in a number of important areas.

In choosing these fields of research, the committee applied the following criteria:

a. Demographic behaviour is characterised by an increasing diversity and multiformity in the choice of the relationships entered into and ended, the number of children wanted, the place of residence and the type of housing sought. The potentially greater freedom of choice of individuals in these areas spells an increasing need for studying the decision-making processes at micro-level.
b. In terms of planning and policy, the importance of information regarding the future size and composition of the population is so obvious that the choice of this field hardly requires an explanation. The reason for concentrating on the aforementioned sections of the population is in part the bridging role which the research in this field fulfils in relation to the research in the other fields. We should also point out that the quality of the Dutch research in this field has by now been internationally recognised, a point which also emerged during this workshop.
c. In a number of areas, the effect of individual decisions pertaining to demographic behaviour will trigger off social consequences that will present society with new challenges. In selecting the subjects where further research is urged, the degree of demographic influence is a determining factor. Because of the effect of demographic processes, resulting in a drop in the number of young people and a rise in

the ageing population, the social problems that arise will require research into questions of distribution. In connection with this, the forthcoming increase of various types of household will also render it necessary to consider the growing need for certain provisions. Of the many subjects which may be researched, the committee therefore deems it relevant - from a social point of view - to opt for research into housing, employment, health in relation to care, and economic questions.

The description of these fields of research shows that the research programme consists of three related parts. By choosing the themes referred to below, which in the last instance will have to be worked into concrete project proposals, the internal structure of the programme will be clearly revealed. For each of the three fields of research the following themes can be distinguished.

A   Decision-making processes that influence demographic behaviour

Two clustered themes are of importance here:

a. research into the way in which individuals or couples opt for the relevant behaviour alternatives open to them with regard to forming and ending relationships, and forming a family or household;
b. research into the way in which individuals independently or in the context of a household choose a place of residence or home.

Although the two themes are mentioned separately, it should not be forgotten that new methodological insights in the field of course-of-life analysis and micro-simulation (inter alia dynamic process models), as well as a number of general theories (such as rational choice) have proved the need for studying the growing diversity of lives in these fields as an interconnected whole.

B   Development and (forecast) models

Research in this field should focus on two interrelated subjects, namely:

a. model development with reference to families and family relationships.
   This means research into changes in the nature, duration and stability of relationships, and into changes that occur in the distribution of the population amongst the different life styles.

b. model development with reference to households.
   This implies research in the field of dynamic modelling and advance assessment of the formation and disbanding of households, and particularly, insight into the degree in which key demographic processes such as the forming of relationships, fertility, migration and death are determined by characteristics of primary living context, besides individual characteristics.

In making advance assessments of the population for the longer term, the emphasis should be more on an exploratory function. The application of the scenario method can be deemed useful in this context. The exploratory function of the longer-term advance calculation will prove valuable when, in addition to the more usual scenarios, 'surprising' and normative demographic scenarios are designed which vary greatly in structure.

C   Social consequences

For the study of the social consequences, four areas have been selected: housing, employment, health(care) and economic issues.

a. housing

Particularly as a result of the continued growth and changing composition of the number of households, and also as a result of a continued mobility of the population, often due to housing requirements, there is still (in terms of quality) a shortage on the housing market. There are serious regional discrepancies, moreover, between the supply and the demand for homes. Research into the functioning of the housing market, partly in conjunction with research into relevant themes in the first two fields of research, deserves high priority.

b. employment

The relatively limited participation of women in the labour process in the Netherlands is inextricably linked with the role she has been assigned of caring for and bringing up children. In this respect the Netherlands still takes up a special position in Europe. The recent rise in the percentage of working women leads one to suspect, however, that today the presence of (young) children forms less of an impediment to (a return to) paid employment than in the seventies. This development requires further research into the correlation between forming relationships, forming a family and employment opportunities for women. In view of the emancipation and population policy advocated by the government, the social importance of this theme is also considerable.

c. health(care)

Mortality is shifting towards ever higher age groups, and death is often preceded by a lengthy period of chronic morbidity and handicaps. Research into the relationship between these two phenomena means studying the size, structure and dynamics of healthy, chronically ill and handicapped groups of the population. Knowledge regarding the state of health of the population is an important factor in the health care issue. In this context, unofficial care in particular should be taken into account. Owing to the prospective rise in the number of older people and an expected thinning out of family networks, research into the supply of and demand for this form of unofficial care is of great social importance.

d. economic issues

Under this heading we give a summary of problems, the 'economic aspect' being the primary issue. In particular, we are concerned here with questions of optimal growth politics and adaptation politics in the case of a non-stationary rise or fall in the population. Special attention is given to aspects of investment in capital and know-how. Particular consideration will also have to be given to social security problems and to optimal ways of combining financing methods for pension provisions (for instance the pay-as-you-go method and the funding method).

LIST OF CONTRIBUTORS

Becker, Henk A. (the Netherlands, 1933) is professor in sociology at the Department of Planning, Organization and Policy Studies, University of Utrecht, the Netherlands

Clark, William A.V. (USA, 1938) is professor in geography at the Department of Geography of the University of California, Los Angeles, USA

Dalen, Hendrik P. van (the Netherlands, 1961) is assistant professor in economics of the public sector at the Faculty of Economic Sciences of the Erasmus University Rotterdam, the Netherlands

Engelen, Theo L.M. (the Netherlands, 1950) is associate professor at the department of economic and social history of the Catholic University of Nijmegen, the Netherlands

Ermisch, John F. (UK, 1947) is an economist at the National Institute of Economic and Social Research in London, United Kingdom

Frinking, Gerard A.B. (the Netherlands, 1939) is professor in demography at the Faculty of Social Sciences, Catholic University of Brabant, Tilburg, the Netherlands

Hazeu, Cornelius A. (the Netherlands, 1955) is an economist at the Netherlands Organization for Scientific Research (NWO), The Hague, the Netherlands

Hooimeijer, Pieter (the Netherlands, 1955) is associate professor at the Faculty of Geographical Science of the University of Utrecht, the Netherlands

Imhoff, Evert van (the Netherlands, 1959) is an economist at the Netherlands Interdisciplinary Demographic Institute, The Hague, the Netherlands

Keyfitz, Nathan (USA, 1913) is head of the Population Program of the International Institute for Applied Systems Analysis, Laxenburg, Austria

Knipscheer, Kees C.P.M. (the Netherlands, 1940) is professor in sociology/social gerontology at the Faculty of Social Sciences of the Free University of Amsterdam, the Netherlands

Lindenberg, Siegwart M. (Germany, 1941) is professor in theoretical sociology at the Faculty of Social Sciences of the University of Groningen, the Netherlands

Masuy-Stroobant, Godelieve (Belgium, 1948) is chercheur qualifié on behalf of the Belgium National Research Council (FNRS) at the Catholic University of Louvain, Louvain-la-Neuve, Belgium

Nelissen, Jan H.M. (the Netherlands, 1955) is associate professor in economy at the Faculty of Social Sciences of the Catholic University of Brabant, Tilburg, the Netherlands and at the Faculty of Economic Sciences of the Erasmus University Rotterdam, the Netherlands

Pestieau, Pierre (Belgium, 1943) is professor in population economics and public economics at the Department of Economics of the University of Liège, Liège, Belgium

Poppel, Frans W.A. (the Netherlands, 1947) is a demographer at the Netherlands Interdisciplinary Demographic Institute, The Hague, the Netherlands

Ritzen, Jozef M.M. (the Netherlands, 1945) is (since November 1989) Minister of Education and Science in the Netherlands and is former professor in the economics of the public sector at the Faculty of Economic Sciences of the Erasmus University Rotterdam, the Netherlands

Siegers, Jacques J. (the Netherlands, 1948) is associate professor at the Economic Institute/Centre for Interdisciplinary Research on Labour Market and Distribution Issues of the University of Utrecht, the Netherlands and is associated with the Netherlands Interdisciplinary Demographic Institute, The Hague, the Netherlands

Willekens, Frans, J. (the Netherlands, 1946) is staff member of the Netherlands Interdisciplinary Demographic Institute, The Hague, the Netherlands and is professor in demography at the University of Groningen, the Netherlands and at the University of Utrecht, the Netherlands

Wissen, Leo J.G. van (the Netherlands, 1956) is associate professor in spatial economics at the Faculty of Economic Sciences of the Free University of Amsterdam, the Netherlands